FUN WITH THE FAMILY

Southern California

Praise for the *Fun with the Family* series

"Enables parents to turn family travel into an exploration."
—Alexandra Kennedy, Editor, *Family Fun*

"Bound to lead you and your kids to fun-filled days,
those times that help compose the
memories of childhood."
—Dorothy Jordon, *Family Travel Times*

Help Us Keep This Guide Up to Date

Every effort has been made by the authors and editors to make this guide as accurate and useful as possible. However, many changes can occur after a guide is published— establishments close, phone numbers change, hiking trails are rerouted, facilities come under new management, etc.

We would love to hear from you concerning your experiences with this guide and how you feel it could be improved and be kept up to date. While we may not be able to respond to all comments and suggestions, we'll take them to heart, and we'll make certain to share them with the authors. Please send your comments and suggestions to the following address:

The Globe Pequot Press
Reader Response/Editorial Department
P.O. Box 480
Guilford, CT 06437

Or you may e-mail us at: editorial@GlobePequot.com

Thanks for your input, and happy travels!

Barnes & Noble Booksellers #2751
160 S. Westlake Blvd.
Thousand Oaks, CA 91362
805-446-2820

STR:2751 REG:004 TRN:7975 CSHR:David B

Fun with the Family sout
9780762748884
(1 @ 13.95)   13.95
Spectrum Test Prep Grade
9780769686240
(1 @ 9.95)   9.95

Subtotal   23.90
Sales Tax (8.250%)   1.97
TOTAL   25.87
AMEX   25.87
Card#: XXXXXXXXXXXXX06
Expdate: XX/XX
Auth: 533327
Entry Method: Swiped

A MEMBER WOULD HAVE SAVED   2.40

Thanks for shopping at
Barnes & Noble

V101.16   04/04/2009 09:28PM

Return Policy

With a sales receipt, a full refund in the original form of payment will be issued from any Barnes & Noble store for returns of new and unread books (except textbooks) and unopened music/DVDs/audio made within (i) 14 days of purchase from a Barnes & Noble retail store (except for purchases made by check less than 7 days prior to the date of return) or (ii) 14 days of delivery date for Barnes & Noble.com purchases (except for purchases made via PayPal). A store credit for the purchase price will be issued for (i) purchases made by check less than 7 days prior to the date of return, (ii) when a gift receipt is presented within 60 days of purchase, (iii) textbooks returned with a receipt within 14 days of purchase, or (iv) original purchase was made through Barnes & Noble.com via PayPal. Opened music/DVDs/audio may not be returned, but can be exchanged only for the same title if defective.

After 14 days or without a sales receipt, returns or exchanges will not be permitted.

Magazines, newspapers, and used books are not returnable. *Product not carried by Barnes & Noble or Barnes & Noble.com will not be accepted for return.*

Policy on receipt may appear in two sections.

Return Policy

With a sales receipt, a full refund in the original form of payment will be issued from any Barnes & Noble store for returns of new and unread books (except textbooks) and unopened music/DVDs/audio made within (i) 14 days of purchase from a Barnes & Noble retail store (except for purchases made by check less than 7 days prior to the date of return) or (ii) 14 days of delivery date for Barnes & Noble.com purchases (except for purchases made via PayPal). A store credit for the purchase price will be issued for (i) purchases made by check less than 7 days prior to the date of return, (ii) when a gift receipt is presented within 60 days of purchase, (iii) textbooks returned with a receipt within 14 days of purchase, or (iv) original purchase was made through Barnes & Noble.com via PayPal. Opened music/DVDs/audio may not be returned, but can be exchanged only for the same title if defective.

After 14 days or without a sales receipt, returns or exchanges will

FUN WITH THE FAMILY SERIES

FUN WITH THE FAMILY

Southern California

Hundreds OF Ideas FOR Day Trips WITH THE Kids

SEVENTH EDITION

Laura Kath and Pamela Price

travel

Guilford, Connecticut

The prices, rates, and hours listed in this guidebook were confirmed at press time. We recommend, however, that you call establishments to obtain current information before traveling.

To buy books in quantity for corporate use
or incentives, call **(800) 962-0973**
or e-mail **premiums@GlobePequot.com**.

Text design by Nancy Freeborn and Linda Loiewski
Maps by Rusty Nelson © Morris Book Publishing, LLC
Spot photography throughout © Photodisc and © RubberBall Productions

ISSN 1541-8952
ISBN 978-0-7627-4888-4

Printed in the United States of America

10 9 8 7 6 5 4 3 2 1

To Anna Hubble Kath, my inspirational mom
—Laura Kath

To Harris Jacob Lechtman, my darling grandson
—Pamela Price

Contents

Acknowledgments viii

Introduction ix

The Central Coast 1

Greater Los Angeles 44

Orange County 85

The Inland Empire and Beyond 113

The Deserts 149

San Diego County 187

Annual Events 222

Index 241

About the Authors 251

Acknowledgments

Researching the best family fun throughout Southern California could not have been accomplished without the invaluable assistance of so many generous individuals, organizations, and attractions. From the tips of our achy fingers to our swollen feet, we gratefully acknowledge just a few of the many (and hereby apologize if we've neglected to mention anyone).

Anaheim/Orange County Visitor and Convention Bureau; Barnstorming Adventures; California Office of Tourism; Disneyland Resort; Hilton Anaheim; Janis Flippen Public Relations; Joshua Tree National Park; Vern Lanegrasse, the Hollywood Chef; Los Angeles Convention and Visitors Bureau; Long Beach Area Visitors and Convention Bureau; Oxnard Convention and Visitors Bureau; Palm Springs Bureau of Tourism; Palm Springs Desert Resorts Convention and Visitors Bureau; Riverside Convention and Visitors Bureau; San Diego Convention and Visitors Bureau; San Diego North Visitors and Convention Bureau; San Luis Obispo Conference and Visitors Bureau; Santa Barbara Conference and Visitors Bureau; SeaWorld; Santa Ynez Valley Visitors Association; Solvang Visitors Bureau; Susan Bejeckian Public Relations; Universal Studios; Ventura Visitors and Convention Bureau.

Pamela thanks her son Tony for his continued outspoken opinions on what families will find festive in Southern California and her son Artie and grandson Harris for their unflagging enthusiasm in exploring dozens of attractions on and off the road map. Pamela values Doris Mechanick, child-development authority, for her lifelong friendship and support. Laura especially appreciates her supportive family members and friends who are always eager to explore the wonders of SoCal attractions with her. "Ant Laura" thanks nieces and nephews John, Lisa, Emi, Eli, Jen, Bill, Alexandra, Amanda, and Cameron for their special insights. Laura gratefully acknowledges the caring "author encouragement" provided by Amrit Joy, Jane Baxter, Rev. Dr. Sandra Cook, Mary Harris, Fred Klein, William Morton, Peggy Wentz, and Lee Wilkerson. Ultimately, Laura will always treasure "the Kath Party" for providing her very first "fun with the family" car trips!

Last but never least, we acknowledge the supportive staff at The Globe Pequot Press for giving us the opportunity to write about all this Southern California fun starting back in 1994!

Introduction

Southern California is a kaleidoscope—no matter which way you turn, something amazing appears! There is just no way we can include every fun-worthy thing and place for your family in a volume this size. However, we do believe that this guide will give you and your family a very practical, yet comprehensive way to experience the Golden State, starting from the Central Coast and heading south all the way to the Mexican border.

Both of us, along with our families, have traveled thousands of miles by trains, planes, automobiles, horses, mules, and aching feet to discover the best in Southern California family fun. We are very proud of our adopted home state—Pamela originally hails from Minnesota and Laura from Michigan—and have spent more than fifty combined years as journalists researching and describing life on the "left coast" of the United States. We are thrilled to share the adventure with you!

We believe the most important element to family fun in Southern California is time. Be sure you allow yourself and the kids plenty of it. Concentrated in this golden nugget of real estate are enough activities, sights, sounds, and sensations to fill a dozen or more visits. Be sure to carefully select the elements that satisfy your family's unique tastes. Don't kid yourself; Southern California is not as laid-back as you might think. Just ask any parent who has been done in by a day at an amusement park or managed to hit one of our famous freeway rush hours near dinnertime. Distance between activities can be deceptive. Five miles does not necessarily mean five minutes away. Be sure you plan "kick back" time—to relax on a beach or bench and to soak up some of Southern California's 300-plus days of sunshine. Don't worry, we will be sure to save more for your next visit—promise!

If you and your family seek natural beauty, Southern California offers you the Pacific Ocean and its awesome beaches—some favorites include Moonstone Beach near Cambria, Butterfly Beach in Santa Barbara, Venice Beach near Santa Monica, and the pristine sands of Coronado. The mountain ranges, inland valleys, rivers, and freshwater lakes such as Nacimiento, Cachuma, Big Bear, and Arrowhead are wonderful total recreation zones. Deserts such as Anza-Borrego, Palm Springs, Mojave, and Death Valley provide amazing contrasts to the palm-lined shores.

How about recreation? Participant or spectator, you can experience it all here. Teams such as basketball's Los Angeles Lakers, hockey's Mighty Ducks of Anaheim, baseball's L.A. Dodgers and Los Angeles Angels of Anaheim, and football's San Diego Chargers offer the thrill of professional action. Needless to say, waterfront activity should rate high on your list when visiting Southern California—boating, fishing, sailing, sunbathing, surfing, and swimming are what "California dreams" are made of. If you visit between December and April, whale watching along the Pacific is an absolute must-see thrill. You and the kids can get into the swing of golf and tennis at hundreds of public facilities. Of course, biking and hiking trails abound to explore, yet they preserve all the area's natural beauty. Don't forget to pack a picnic basket and take time to smell the perennially blooming flowers.

You can visit natural parks full of wildlife and sea life or human-made amusement parks stocked with thrills. Southern California museums are filled with hands-on displays of fun things from archives to outer space. Be certain to include the magnificent J. Paul Getty Museum as well as the California Science Center in Los Angeles. California's history, rich with Native American, Spanish, and Mexican influences, provides your family with plenty of cultural diversity education, not to mention the thrill of deciphering foreign names—such as San Luis Obispo, Port Hueneme, Ojai, and Temecula.

We have also included just a few of our preferred accommodations, family-friendly dining, and shopping places to make your stay more enjoyable. We hope you will take the time to try some one-of-a-kind places to eat and stay that are not part of national chains. But let's be honest here—your kids would never forgive you if you didn't make a stop at a Carl's Jr., Hard Rock Café, or In-N-Out Burger, all headquartered here.

Southern California is blessed with hundreds of annual special events—starting with January's immensely popular Rose Parade in Pasadena, right through holiday lighted boat parades all along the coast. There is always Carpinteria's Avocado Festival or the numerous Oktoberfests held in many towns. Since festivals have varying dates from year to year, we have included phone numbers you can call for specifics.

Southern California is like an endless summer vacation. Where else can you travel from the desert to a futuristic metropolis to some mountain snow skiing and, finally, take in the sunset at the beach—all in one day, all year-round? Would you expect anything less from the birthplace of Hollywood and Disneyland?

In this edition we have provided special sections under many area listings entitled "Where to Stay" and "Where to Eat"—describing just a few of the many outstanding establishments available for your family's enjoyment. Dollar signs provide a very general sense of the price range for each property. For meals, the prices are per individual dinner entrees, without tax or gratuity. For lodging, the rates are for a double-occupancy room, European plan (no meals unless indicated), exclusive of hotel "bed tax" or service charges.

Please keep in mind that meal prices generally stay the same throughout the year, but lodging rates fluctuate seasonally and by day of the week. Higher rates generally prevail in the summer season and holidays (when more families are on the go). Always be sure to inquire about special packages and promotional discounts.

Rates for Lodging

$	up to $50
$$	$51 to $75
$$$	$76 to $99
$$$$	$100 and up

Rates for Restaurants

$	most entrees less than $10
$$	most entrees $10 to $15
$$$	most entrees $16 to $20
$$$$	most entrees more than $20

Admission prices for attractions are in dollar signs, which indicate the following price ranges:

Rates for Attractions (for Adults and Children)

$	up to $5 per person
$$	$6 to $10 per person
$$$	$11 to $20 per person
$$$$	more than $20 per person

Please let us know what you like about our *Fun with the Family Southern California* guidebook. What other activities or attractions do we need to include in future editions? We really value your impressions. Write us today in care of The Globe Pequot Press, P.O. Box 480, Guilford, CT 06437.

Imagination, recreation, relaxation, nature, geography, cultural diversity, and history—complemented by a warm, sunny year-round climate—are waiting here for you. We know this guidebook will map out memorable family fun you will treasure and want to repeat, because Southern California makes every visitor feel young at heart. Enjoy!

Attractions Key

The following is a key to the icons found throughout the text.

SWIMMING		**FOOD**	
BOATING / BOAT TOUR		**LODGING**	
HISTORIC SITE		**CAMPING**	
HIKING / WALKING		**MUSEUMS**	
FISHING		**PERFORMING ARTS**	
BIKING		**SPORTS/ATHLETIC**	
AMUSEMENT PARK		**PICNICKING**	
HORSEBACK RIDING		**PLAYGROUND**	
SKIING/WINTER SPORTS		**SHOPPING**	
PARK		**PLANTS/GARDENS/NATURE TRAILS**	
ANIMAL VIEWING		**FARMS**	

the Central Coast

The Central Coast has always been considered the northern edge of Southern California. However, there is really a Midwestern feeling of friendliness and hospitality in the three geographically close yet quite diverse counties of San Luis Obispo, Santa Barbara, and Ventura. You have all the quintessential Southern California trademarks here—great year-round weather, fun-filled recreation, attractions, and, of course, sandy beaches woven between wide-open fields planted with veggies and fruit, soaring foothills, mountains, streams, and the glittering Pacific—all presented by locals with warm graciousness. With fewer people than the megalopolises to the south, the Central Coast is much more laid-back and casual.

So much about the Central Coast says "welcome" to your family. Hearst Castle in San Simeon, spring hikes through the wildflowers of Montana de Oro State Park, the trendy beaches and shopping of Santa Barbara, kids' hands-on museums and zoos, boat cruises out to the Channel Islands, and surfing on the Rincon—or how about the simple pleasures of just hanging out in the 320-plus days of annual sunshine and basking in the waves and smiles from fellow Golden State dwellers and visitors? The Central Coast's two main arteries, the magnificent Pacific Coast Highway 1 and the inland U.S. Highway 101, can be your twin pathways to some of the best, and surprisingly most affordable, tastes of your Southern California dream vacation.

San Luis Obispo County

San Luis Obispo County's 3,316 square miles contain the Central Coast's most varied terrain—from windswept beaches to interior lakes, from grass-covered rolling hills to meticulously tended farmlands, plus recurring topographical evidence of seismic shifts along California's main earthquake zone, the San Andreas Fault. There are 85 miles of coastline for exploring.

The climate of San Luis Obispo (San Lewis Oh-bis-poe) features mild summers and winters, with patches of dense seasonal fog along the coast. Temperatures range from coastal lows in the thirties in the winter to inland valley highs in the nineties-plus in the

THE CENTRAL COAST

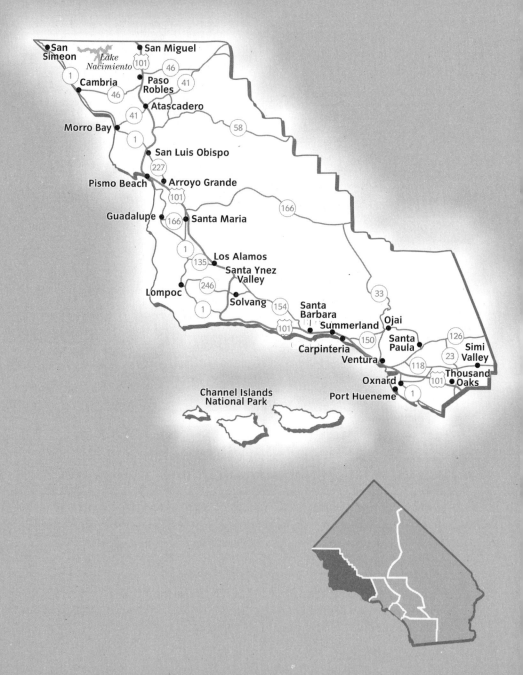

summer. Year-round temperatures average sixty to seventy degrees, with around 22 inches of rain, mostly in the winter.

Native Americans occupied the land for thousands of years before its discovery by Spanish explorers in the sixteenth century. Two of California's famous chain of twenty-one missions are here in San Luis Obispo County, preserving the area's Spanish and Mexican heritage. The railroad arrived in the late 1890s, bringing more families and increasing the dominance of agriculture and tourism in the area. Outdoor recreation and historic attractions top the must-see list of county adventures.

For More Information

San Luis Obispo Chamber of Commerce. 1039 Chorro Street, 93401; (805) 781-2777; www.visitslo.com.

San Luis Obispo County Visitors and Conference Bureau. 811 El Capitan Way, Suite 200, 93401; (805) 541-8000 or (800) 634-1414; www.sanluisobispocounty.com.

San Simeon

Founded in the 1850s by fishermen and whalers, the little seaside village of San Simeon really came into its own in the late 1800s, when most of the area's land was purchased and developed by senator George Hearst. His son, William Randolph Hearst, began construction on his fantasy "ranch" in 1919. This incredible estate, and the opportunity to visit it, has put San Simeon on the map. Most of the original village has faded, but Sebastian's General Store and Post Office is fun for kids to explore. The newer tourist town of San Simeon Acres is 4 miles south of Hearst Castle on Pacific Coast Highway 1 and plays host to various motels, restaurants, and a miniature golf course/arcade—facilities to snap you back into modern-day realities.

Hearst San Simeon State Historical Monument (ages 6 and up)

Forty-one miles north of San Luis Obispo on Pacific Coast Highway 1; (805) 927-2020 or (800) 444-4445 (have your credit card ready to purchase tour tickets in advance); www .hearstcastle.org. Open daily, except New Year's Day, Thanksgiving, and Christmas. $$$$

Don't miss a chance to go on a fascinating tour of publishing baron William Randolph Hearst's real-life fantasy home built between 1928 and 1951, officially called Hearst San Simeon State Historical Monument and unofficially called Hearst Castle. See for yourself the lifestyle of someone rich and famous. Advance ticket reservations are strongly recommended.

This is the most popular attraction on the Central Coast, and there are a limited number of tickets and tour times available. If you arrive without reservations, you most likely will have to wait and might find a sold-out/standby situation (especially in the busy summer, weekend, and holiday times).

There are four different guided tours to choose from. Each is seventy-five minutes long, plus a thirty-minute bus ride to and from the castle. For first-timers, **Tour Number 1,** also called the Experience Tour, is the best bet. It includes the National Geographic movie *Hearst Castle: Building the Dream.* When you arrive at the "castle," park free at the modern visitor center just off the highway. This family-friendly center has a snack bar, gift shop, restrooms, lockers, and a fascinating **free** exhibition on Hearst himself, which you can visit as you wait for your tour number to be called. You'll then board school buses for the 5-mile, fifteen-minute drive up the hill to see highlights of the 165-room "La Casa Grande"—the main house—plus three separate guest houses on the 127-acre grounds overlooking the Pacific and the surrounding Santa Lucia Mountains.

There is something for every member of your family to ogle in Hearst Castle, including enormous swimming pools; the lavish dining room (complete with Hearst's favorite Heinz ketchup bottle among the silver and china); the playroom with billiards and trophy animal heads; incredible art, antiques, tapestries, and collectibles from around the world; plus Hearst's private movie theater with his vintage home movies for your viewing pleasure.

If you want more of a Hearst fantasy fix, take **Tour Number 2** for upper levels of the main house, the libraries, and the kitchen or **Tour Number 3** for the North Wing, gardens, and a special video on the construction of the castle. **Tour Number 4,** for more gardens, the wine cellar, and another private guesthouse, is offered April through October. **Tour 5** is a very special lighted evening tour on Friday and Saturday from March through May and September through December. The tour lasts one hundred minutes, plus a thirty-minute bus ride. Tour 5 combines the best elements of the above tours at a higher fee, but it really is appropriate only for older children, teens, and adults.

For More Information

San Simeon Chamber of Commerce. 250 San Simeon Avenue, 93452; (805) 927-3500; www.sansimeonchamber.org.

Cambria

Nine miles south of San Simeon and 33 miles northwest of San Luis Obispo on Highway 1 is the quaint, small-town artist's haven of Cambria. This village is a welcome respite from the excesses of Hearst Castle and is a family-friendly place to stay for this part of your coastal explorations. The West Village is adjacent to Highway 1; the East Village, or Old Town, is about a mile inland. Moonstone Beach Drive is right on the Pacific and has many inns and beachcombing spots. Both parts of town are connected by Main Street. Cruise down Main Street and check out the art galleries, antiques emporiums, children's book-stores, and toy shops. There is a farmers' market every Friday afternoon at the Vet's Hall on Main Street.

Moonstone **Beach**

Just north of Cambria, Moonstone Beach is the place to find smooth, milky-white stones and gnarled pieces of driftwood. Don't think about swimming here, because the water is really too cold, but beachcombing is the best! You can often see migrating whales passing by in January and February and hear the cries of sea otters and sea lions year-round. There are several bed-and-breakfast inns, motels, and restaurants along Moonstone Beach Drive if you want to savor the crashing surf.

Where to Eat

Linn's Easy as Pie Café and Linn's Gourmet Goods, 4241 Bridge Street; (805) 924-3050; Linn's Main Bin Restaurant, 2277 Main; (805) 927-0371; www.linnsfruitbin.com. Famous for Olallieberry Pie, preserves, and bakery delights. Serving breakfast, lunch, dinner classics since 1985. Not to be missed. $

Mustache Pete's, 4090 Burton Drive; (805) 927-8589; www.mustachepetes.com. Lunch, dinner of hand-made pizzas, Italian specialties, and delish prime rib for eat-in, take-out, or delivery. Fun outdoor patio dining. Family favorite since 1986. $$

Where to Stay

Best Western Fireside Inn, 6700 Moonstone Beach Drive; (805) 927-8661 or (888) 910-7100; www.bestwesternfiresideinn.com. You'll find spacious rooms, many with fireplaces and oceanview patios. Other highlights include refrigerators, coffeemakers, complimentary continental breakfast, a heated pool, and a whirlpool. Excellent value along the beach. $$$

Cambria Pines Lodge, 2905 Burton Drive; (805) 927-4200 or (800) 445-6868; www.cambriapineslodge.com. A wonderful place for families to stay. Located on a hilltop overlooking the village, the lodge has 125 units, including nice two-room family suites with connecting baths, fireplaces, microwaves, fridges, and coffeemakers. You'll also enjoy an indoor heated pool, whirlpool, game room, lawn sports, and a restaurant serving California cuisine for breakfast, lunch, and dinner. $$

For More Information

Cambria Chamber of Commerce. 767 Main Street, 93428; (805) 927-3624; www.cambriachamber.org.

Lake Nacimiento

Just over the mountains from Hearst Castle lies Nacimiento, arguably the Central Coast's most beautiful human-made lake. Damming the Nacimiento River created 165 miles of gorgeous shoreline. Fishing, boating, water sports galore, and outstanding hiking make this one of the most popular family recreation destinations in San Luis Obispo County.

Lake Nacimiento Resort
From US 101 take County Road G-14 out of Paso Robles, drive 16 miles northwest;10625 Nacimiento Lake Drive, Paso Robles, 93466; (805) 238-3256 or (800) 323-3839; www .nacimientoresort.com. $$$

Owned and operated by the Heath family since 1962, there is a full-service marina and dock where you can rent Jet Skis, Wave Runners, canoes, boats (power, paddle, and pontoon), sport fishing tackle, and equipment for diving and windsurfing.

The lake is famous for its plentiful white bass, waterskiing, and salt-free swimming. The fully stocked general store has everything, including provisions for a barbecue or picnic; plus a summer cafe.

Facilities include the boat launch, picnic grounds, playground, volleyball and basketball courts, swimming pool, and hiking trails around the meandering 165-mile shoreline. Overnight accommodations include nineteen lodge units; one-, two-, and three-bedroom town houses (complete with mini-kitchens and decks) right on the lakeshore; plus forty RV hookups and 270 campsites. Extremely popular April to October, but winter season has mild weather, fewer crowds, and, of course, the same gorgeous scenery.

Paso Robles and Atascadero

Paso Robles (Spanish for "pass of the oaks") is located at the junction of US 101 and Highway 46. Atascadero (Spanish for "place of much water") is just south of Paso Robles at the crossroads of US 101 and Highway 41. To enjoy the local waters, consider boating, fishing, picnicking, and camping at nearby **Lake San Antonio Recreation Area** (info: 805-472-2313) or **Santa Margarita Lake Regional Park** (info: 805-788-2357). This area is famous for its stately trees, agriculture, and award-winning 170-plus wineries and vineyards. Perhaps a taste of the grape for Mom and Dad before hitting the dusty trail again? (Phone the **Paso Robles Wine Country Alliance** at 805-239-8463 for current maps and tasting rooms or visit www.pasowine.com.) Meanwhile, be sure to explore these area attractions with the entire family.

Paso Robles Event Center/California Mid-State Fair
Riverside Avenue between Twenty-first and Twenty-fourth Streets, just off US 101, Paso Robles; (805) 239-0655; www.midstatefair.com.

Top draws at the Center include the Central Coast Roller Derby, Mid-State Fall Home Show, Central Coast Boat Show, and the Great Western Bike Rally. Call for annual lineup of musical and rodeo events. For two weeks in late July/early August, the annual fair turns Paso Robles into a rockin' and thumpin' western town. Kids will enjoy the 4-H animal exhibits, crafts, art, food booths, carnival rides, plus world-class live entertainment (in years past, Aerosmith, Kenny Rogers, Diana Ross, Julio Iglesias, and the Beach Boys have appeared).

Pioneer Museum

2010 Riverside Avenue between Nineteenth and Twentieth Streets, Paso Robles; (805) 239-4556; www.prpioneermuseum.org. Open year-round Thursday through Sunday from 1:00 to 4:00 p.m. Free admission; donations welcome.

Young cowpokes can amble over to see the farm equipment from the turn of the last century, while their folks check out home furnishings.

Lake Atascadero Park and Charles Paddock Zoo

South of Paso Robles, Morro Bay/Highway 41, exit off US 101, west 1.5 miles, Atascadero; (805) 461-5080; www.charlespaddockzoo.org. Open 10:00 a.m. to 4:00 p.m.; hours extended in summer and vary by season. $

Thirty-five acres of water and wonder. This very intimate site allows close proximity to some one hundred rare and wonderful species. Among the selection: gleaming black brother-and-sister jaguars from Brazil, a pair of Bengal tigers, furry lemurs, sinewy pythons and boas, strutting pink flamingos, and crested porcupines (can you make them strut their stuff?). Lake Atascadero is next to the zoo. Walk around the 2-mile perimeter of the lake and picnic on benches or dockside at the Lakeside Pavilion's snack bar. Strollers, a gift shop, refreshments, and restrooms all make a visit easier for families.

The Ravine Waterpark

2301 Airport Road, Paso Robles, 93446; (805) 237-8500; www.ravinewaterpark.com. $$$

Open seasonally May through September. Call for hours, special events. Opened in 2007, wet and wild water adventure with slippery slides and interactive fun for all ages. Hop on a tube and race down the 325-foot-long flume slides; drift along Kickback Kreek; surf the 175,000-gallon wave pool, or head to 9,000-square-foot Kiddie Cove for little ones.

Children's Museum at the Paso Robles Volunteer Firehouse

623 Thirteenth Street, P.O. Box 2526, Paso Robles, 93447; (805) 238-7432; www.pasokids .org. Ages 2 to 13. Open Thursday through Monday. Call for times and special events. $

Opened in November 2007, the historic former volunteer firehouse has been transformed into an interactive, educational, play-filled environment. Exhibits include a fire truck and gear, naturally, plus an oak tree for exploration, a toddler farm and goofy grape stomp, Newton's playhouse, a physical science corner, pizza kitchen, El Mercado, puppet theater, and arts and crafts stations.

Where to Eat and Stay

Big Bubba's Bad BBQ, 8050 El Camino Real, Atascadero, 93422; (805) 466-9866; 1125 Twenty-fourth Street, Paso Robles, 93466; www.bigbubbasbadbbq.com. Since opening the first restaurant in Paso in 2002, Bubba's has become a fave family place for its generous portions of smokey ribs, chicken, pulled pork, turkey legs, and yummy sides.

Ag **Adventures**

The Central Coast Agritourism Council is a nonprofit organization dedicated to supporting small farmers and ranchers by promoting their homes and farms as visitor destinations. Members love showing you and the kids where food starts on its journey to your table and answering questions about their livelihood. You can experience life on a family farm, explore the open trail on horseback, ride in a stagecoach, learn about fiber and wine grape production, sample olive oil, or pick your own lavender and olallieberries out in the field. For events, classes, open houses, and more, call (805) 238-3799 or visit www.agadventures.org.

Ride the mechanical bull, enjoy the country-western music, and have some fun at lunch and dinner daily. $$$

Holiday Inn Express Hotel & Suites,
2455 Riverside Avenue, Paso Robles, 93446; (866) 224-6196 or (805) 238-6500; www.hix paso.com. Right across from Events Center/Mid-State Fair. Family suites, free Smart breakfast daily. Smart Collection beds, Smart Bathroom amenities, high-speed Internet, fridge, microwave, 27-inch TV with HBO, coffee/tea maker. Heated indoor pool. Special family packages available year-round. $$$

For More Information

Atascadero Chamber of Commerce.
6550 El Camino Real, 93422; (805) 466-2044; www.atascaderochamber.org.

Paso Robles Chamber of Commerce and Visitors and Conference Bureau.
1225 Park Street, 93446; (805) 238-0506 or (800) 406-4040; www.pasorobleschamber .com.

Morro Bay

Noted for two landmarks—nature's awesome Morro Rock and the human-made trio of smokestacks at the waterfront power plant—bustling Morro Bay has a busy commercial fishing fleet and is a prized recreational and tourist town. You can't miss the magnificent 578-foot, dome-shaped Morro Rock, a long-extinct volcano, which marks the oceanfront end of the Embarcadero—several miles of waterfront filled with shops, restaurants, motels, and dozens of companies with boats, barges, kayaks, canoes, and sailing vessels for charter or guided excursions.

Sub/Sea Tours and Kayaks

699 Embarcadero #9; (805) 772-9463; www.subseatours.com. Call for reservations and current rates. $$$

The company offers forty-five-minute trips in a semi-submersible vessel daily, generally on the hour depending on the tides. Got to love "diving" and seeing kelp forests and marine life. All trips narrated by a naturalist.

Morro Bay State Park

At the south end of town, off State Park Road; (805) 772-2560 or (800) 444-7275; www
.parks.ca.gov/?page_id=594. Open daily year-round.

Nearly 2,000 acres along the Pacific shore contain many picnic and camping areas, an
eighteen-hole golf course, a marina, a cafe, a primitive natural area, an estuary (great for
bird-watching), and boat rentals.

Museum of Natural History

Perched on White Point, overlooking the bay and Morro Rock inside the Morro Bay State
Park; (805) 772-2694; www.morrobaymuseum.org. Open daily 10:00 a.m. to 5:00 p.m.
except New Year's Day, Thanksgiving, and Christmas. $

Traditional and educational interpretive displays of local marine life, geology, and the his-
tory and culture of Native peoples predominate. Video presentations in the auditorium.
This is the last remaining blue heron rookery reserve between San Francisco and Mexico.
These rare birds can be observed from hiking trails on the museum grounds.

Montana de Oro State Park

US 101 at Los Osos Valley Road, just south of Morro Bay in the tiny town of Los Osos; (805)
528-0513; www.parks.ca.gov/?page_id=592. Open year-round. Free day use; camping
fees vary.

It is considered the Central Coast's premier park for hiking, nature walks, tide-pooling,
horseback riding, camping, and shore fishing. The Spanish name means "mountain of
gold," referring to the golden fields of poppies, mustard grass, and wildflowers envel-
oping the hillsides every spring. You can easily spend a day at this incredibly beautiful,
8,000-acre paradise.

Where to Eat and Stay

**Harbor Hut Restaurant and Lil Hut
(take-away),** 1205 Embarcadero; (805) 772-
2255. It's right in the heart of the waterfront
action. The seafood is fresh from the trawlers
docked in front, making the Hut popular with
locals and visitors alike. Meals served daily
from 11:00 a.m. $$

The Inn at Morro Bay, 1 mile south on
Main Street, right before the entrance to
Morro Bay State Park, 60 State Park Road,
93442; (805) 772-5651 or (800) 321-9566;
www.innatmorrobay.com. Located on the
bay, this comfortable ninety-eight-room,
full-service hotel has both water- and garden-

view rooms. Be sure to ask for a bay view
with a balcony or patio. Enjoy the Wellness
Center & Spa as well as complimentary beach
cruiser bikes. Two dining rooms offer unob-
structed views of the estuary and bay front-
age while you are enjoying California cuisine
for breakfast, lunch (The Bay Club), and din-
ner (The Orchid). $$$

For More Information

**Morro Bay Visitors Center and Cham-
ber of Commerce.** 845 Embarcadero Road,
Suite D, 93442; (805) 772-4467 or (800) 231-
0592; www.morrobay.org.

City of San Luis Obispo

This county seat sits in an inland valley ringed by pretty hills. A remarkably friendly municipality of 45,000 that is also home to California Polytechnic State University (known as Cal Poly), San Luis Obispo has a vibrant downtown area filled with historic sites, shopping, and restaurants. The 25-cent downtown trolley runs a circuit that will give you and the kids a chance to take in the sights and sounds.

Mission San Luis Obispo de Tolosa

Chorro and Monterey Streets, in the heart of Mission Plaza; (805) 543-6850; www.mission sanluisobispo.org. Open daily 9:00 a.m. to 5:00 p.m. except major holidays. Free admission; donations welcome.

Founded in 1772 and still in operation, the mission is the fifth in the twenty-one-mission chain of parishes founded by Father Junipero Serra. Take a self-guided tour through the Life at the Mission history exhibits and pause in the adobe-brick chapel constructed by the native Chumash people. The mission is named for a thirteenth-century saint, the bishop of Toulouse, often called "Prince of the Missions."

County History Center and Museum

696 Monterey Street, opposite the mission; (805) 543-0638. Open Wednesday through Sunday 10:00 a.m. to 4:00 p.m. Closed holidays. Free admission; donations appreciated.

Another trip down memory lane with old photographs and artifacts, all housed in a Romanesque granite, sandstone, and brick building that used to be the city library.

San Luis Obispo Children's Museum

1010 Nipomo Street, corner of Monterey Street, downtown (same side of the creek as the mission); (805) 545-5874; www.slocm.org. Open Tuesday through Sunday. Call for hours. $$

Since 1990, the museum has provided a safe, educational environment for ages two through twelve; the original building closed in September 2004 and reopened in Fall 2008 with a brand-new 8,400-square-foot facility and twenty-one amazing indoor and outdoor activities.

Gum Alley

Higuera Street, between Garden and Broad Streets.

Before leaving downtown, you must seek out a relic you'll probably hate and your kids will undoubtedly love. Since the late 1950s, locals (mostly collegians) and visitors alike have been depositing their used gum on the narrow alley walls. Folk art or disgusting nuisance, who's to say, for this representation (it's the one and only) has been featured in *Smithsonian* magazine and on the *Ripley's Believe It or Not TV* show. Care to leave your sticky imprint? Let your taste decide.

Farmers' Market

Downtown, Higuera Street. Every Thursday evening from 6:00 to 9:00 year-round.

Not to be missed is this world-famous farmers' market (a 7-block-long street fair). Kids will love the excitement of musicians, puppeteers, face painters, skate dancers, fire eaters, and, obviously, loads of fresh fruit, veggies, and mouthwatering barbecue. Don't be shy—join thousands of curbside dining families downing tasty ribs, chicken, or beef tri-tip sandwiches. Fantastic people-watching, too!

California Polytechnic State University (Cal Poly)

About 2 miles north of downtown via Santa Rosa Street and Highland Drive; (805) 756-1111 or (805) 756-5734; www.calpoly.edu. Call for general information and to ask about guided inner-campus tours.

Located on more than 6,000 acres at the base of the Santa Lucia Mountain range, Cal Poly is renowned for its agribusiness department and the West's largest schools of engineering and architecture. Visitors and families are always welcome. Hike into Poly Canyon to see experimental architecture and construction or visit the Leaning Pine Arboretum. Kids of all ages will want to check out the Dairy Creamery, where you can buy fresh-made cheese and other dairy products from Cal Poly cows. Info: (805) 756-6644 or www.calpoly cheese.com.

Where to Eat and Stay

Apple Farm Mill House, Restaurant and Inn, 2015 Monterey Street at US 101, just outside downtown San Luis Obispo; (805) 544-2040 or (800) 255-2040 for reservations and free video tour; www.applefarm.com. An authentic working gristmill is set among gardens and waterfalls. The kids will love watching, and then eating, the results of an intricate series of pulleys, shafts, gears, and water producing fresh apple cider; andeven ice cream is available for purchase at the Market at the Mill, which also features gourmet sandwiches, salads, candies, and gifts. The family restaurant here serves American favorites for breakfast, lunch, and dinner daily. The Inn has sixty-five deluxe accommodations and thirty-five Trellis Court motel rooms, plus two deluxe Millhouse suites and two Family suites; all 104 units have gas fireplaces and Country-Victorian decor. Prices here will not "grind" you! $$$

Madonna Inn, roadside just south of downtown at US 101 and Madonna Road; (805) 543-3000 or (800) 543-9666; www.madonna inn.com. Not named after the provocative entertainer, this nonetheless hard-to-miss pink-and-white inn was built in 1958 by Alex and Phyllis Madonna. Each of the 109 guest rooms is wackily different. The Caveman Room was carved out of solid rock, for heaven's sake. The men's restroom is world famous for its imaginative waterfalls. The kids will definitely want to check this out! Enjoy freshly baked treats from the Pastry Shop adjoining the Copper Café. The Gold Rush Steak House is over the top in its pink decor (and its prices, too) for basic American fare. Stay if you dare, but eat elsewhere. $$$

Pismo Beach Area

The Pismo Beach coastal resort area actually comprises the neighboring communities of Oceano, Grover Beach, Pismo Beach, Shell Beach, Avila Beach, and Port San Luis. The area stretches along US 101 and is only ten minutes south of the city of San Luis Obispo. Don't miss the **Pismo Monarch Butterfly Grove,** where these beautiful creatures congregate each winter (www.monarchbutterfly.org). Tide-pooling is a great family activity at low tide; you never know what marine life or artifact you may find. Outdoor recreation is prime here, including such exciting activities as kite surfing, horseback riding, paragliding, airplane and helicopter rides, and Hummer and ATV dune tours. The 1,200-foot Pismo Pier downtown is prime for fishing and strolling.

Oceano Dunes State Vehicular Recreation Area

Call (805) 473-7223 (recorded) or (805) 473-7220 or (800) 444-7275 or visit www.ohv.parks .ca.gov for complete details and entrance fees. Open daily.

This is a geologically unique sand-dune complex that is an impressive off-highway vehicular (OHV) playground that also offers activities such as swimming, surfing, fishing, camping, and hiking. Children younger than eighteen must be accompanied by an adult over 21 years old and take a two-hour state certification safety test to pilot their own dune buggy here.

B.J.'s ATV Rentals

197 Grand Avenue, Grover Beach; (805) 481-5411 or (888) 418-5411; www.bjsatvrentals .com. Cost per ATV starting at $45 for two hours. Children's machines also available.

Since 1982, the best place to rent your dream machine, with more than 200 to choose from. The staff is really helpful and concerned with your safety.

Port San Luis

At the very end of Avila Beach Road; (805) 595-5400.

This is a bustling fishing pier and commercial marina. Don't miss the chance to stroll down Harford Pier to find the **free** marine touch tank and look into a fish-processing plant. You'll be amazed how fast sea creatures are transformed into seafood. Tons of salmon, crab, albacore, halibut, cod, shark, and swordfish are brought in here every year by approximately seventy commercial fishing vessels.

Great American Melodrama and Vaudeville Theatre

1863 Front Street (Highway 1), Oceano; (805) 489-2499 for schedule and ticket prices; www .americanmelodrama.com.

Enjoy side-splitting comedy and family entertainment. Don't be put off by the industrial surroundings. Once inside this 260-seat old-fashioned cabaret-style hall, complete with sawdust on the floor, you'll feel completely at home. The theater is owned and operated by Lynn Schlenker and her family. The actors and actresses do triple duty—they serve you food and drinks before they perform, then act onstage, and finally they fraternize with you and other audience members after the show. The best time to attend is definitely during December for the Holiday Extravaganza.

Where to Eat

F. McLintock's Saloon & Dining House, 750 Mattie Road, off US 101 between Spyglass Drive and Price Street exits, Pismo Beach; (805) 773-1892; www.mclintocks.com. No visit to this area would be complete without enjoying dinner at this joint. It's easy to avoid the saloon and slip right into the dining rooms (voted as having the best kids' menu in SLO County), where servers will amaze you with their fun attitudes and ability to pour water. (Don't ask, just go and experience this!) The onion rings are a personal favorite, especially dipped in homemade salsa. Open for dinner daily. $$$

Splash Café, 197 Pomeroy, Pismo Beach; (805) 773-4653; www.splashcafe.com (also a sister bakery in downtown San Luis Obispo). Since 1989, famous for award-winning clam chowder in fresh-baked sourdough bread bowls (more than 15,000 gallons served annually), plus other fish dishes, burgers, and salads in a totally casual, friendly, beachy plastic-chair joint. Open daily at 10:00 a.m. with most menu items under $5. $

Where to Stay

Spyglass Inn & Restaurant, 2705 Spyglass Drive, Pismo Beach, adjacent to US 101–Pacific Coast Highway 1, between Spyglass and Price Street exits; (805) 773-4855; www.spyglassinn.com. Located on the cliffs overlooking the Pacific Ocean, this nautical themed eighty-two-room property is a super family value. Be sure to inquire about seasonal packages and specials. Guest rooms are spacious, and many have ocean views. The heated pool and whirlpool make a relaxing destination after a day of "doing the coast." The Spyglass Restaurant, with its outdoor terraced decks, provides stunning ocean views and serves traditional American breakfast, lunch, and dinner daily—at prices that won't shock your wallet. Highly recommended. $$

Sycamore Mineral Springs Resort, 1215 Avila Beach Drive, Avila Beach; (805) 595-7302 or (800) 234-5831; www.smsr.com. Built around a natural spring in 1897 on one hundred wooded acres only 1 mile from the beach, this facility has magically evolved to become a luxurious, seventy-four-unit full-service resort featuring standard rooms, two-room suites, and an ideal family three-bedroom/three-bath guest house (all with private spas, and many fed by the natural mineral springs). Amenities include the Treatment Center, with massage and skin care; the Healing Arts Institute; pools, gardens, labyrinth walk, and hiking trails; a gift shop; and Gardens of Avila Restaurant (which serves healthy California cuisine for breakfast, lunch, dinner, and Sunday brunch). Ask about special packages that are extra values. A definite favorite with our family. $$$$

For More Information

Pismo Beach Chamber of Commerce and Conference & Visitors Bureau. 581 Dolliver Street, 93449; (805) 773-4382 or (800) 443-7778; www.pismochamber.com and www.ClassicCalifornia.com.

California Welcome Center Pismo Beach. 333 Five Cities Drive at US 101 exit, in the Prime Outlets Mall, Pismo Beach, 93449; (805) 773-7924; www.visitcwc.com/destinations/pismo/index.php. Free statewide information and local area specifics.

Arroyo Grande

"Wide gulch or streambed" is an English translation of this village's Spanish moniker. Founded in 1862, "A-roy-oh Grahn-day" was settled in a wide, fertile valley on either side of a creek that flows from the Santa Lucia Mountains to the Pacific Ocean. Branch Street is the main thoroughfare, a quarter mile east off US 101. Many of the nineteenth-century buildings, like the Methodist church, have been restored, and several have been turned into bed-and-breakfast inns, shops, and restaurants. Access www.arroyograndecc.com for information on the annual Strawberry Festival (Memorial Day weekend) and events at the Clark Center for Performing Arts.

Doc Burnstein's Ice Cream Lab

114 West Branch Street, downtown; (805) 474-4068; www.docburnsteins.com. Open daily at noon. $

Features hand-crafted, super-premium (16 percent butterfat) ice cream presented in glass dishware in the only nostalgic ice cream parlor on the Central Coast. You can also watch through the Lab viewing window as the Doc (proprietor Greg Steinberger) and his Lab Assistants turn fresh hormone-free dairy cream into 140-plus flavors of award-winning treats including malts, floats, sundaes, mud pies, and banana splits. Delish, not to be missed!

Mustang Water Slides and Lopez Lake
Recreational Area

Outside Arroyo Grande, only fifteen minutes off US 101 via Branch Street; (805) 489-8898 or (805) 788-2381 for directions and operating hours; www.mustangwaterslides.com and www.slocountyparks.org/activities/lopez.htm.

There is camping, fishing, picnicking, waterskiing, and windsurfing year-round at Lopez Lake, with 22 miles of man-made shoreline. The water slide is open from May through August and features two 600-foot curving waterslides, a "Stampede" inner tube ride down a 38-foot drop, tot pool with mini-slides, waterfall trees, and relaxing picnic areas. A refreshing good time!

Santa Barbara County

What do space rocket launchers, wine, olives, lemons, avocados, strawberries, Danish pastries, and tri-tip barbecue have in common? They all are produced in the richly varied domain known as Santa Barbara County, named after the patron saint of mariners and travelers. With such a blessing, no wonder people from around the world are drawn here to visit and experience the joys of life. Santa Barbara County's Pacific sea breezes mean warm days and cooler nights both along the coast and in the interior valleys. The average annual temperature in Santa Barbara County is a mild sixty-two degrees. Very seldom do temperatures drop below forty in the winter or climb above ninety in the summer. Such great weather makes visitors as well as plants happy.

The region's colonial history began when Portuguese explorer Juan Rodriguez Cabrillo sailed along the California coast in 1542 and claimed everything he saw for the Spanish crown. Sixty years later, another Portuguese seafarer, Sebastian Viscaino, dropped anchor in the bay. The day was December 4, the feast day of Saint Barbara, which explains the name given to the area. Both explorers were greeted warmly by the native Chumash Indians, who for 10,000 years or so had thrived in the area's gorgeous climate and year-round growing season. Viscaino's diary records the first evidence of the vaunted and legendary Santa Barbara hospitality. Today you can still experience the same warm welcome here with your family. Start at the northern boundary of the county's Santa Maria River. Here's what you will discover.

Santa Maria

Heading south from San Luis Obispo County on US 101, you will cross into the Santa Maria Valley and find gentle foothills that descend toward the city of Santa Maria. It is surrounded by well-tended farms, where yummy you-can-pick-them strawberries and lots of produce are cultivated. Many award-winning vineyards and wineries are also located here; growers have discovered a microclimate very similar to that in France. The town's roots are very deep in agriculture and ranching. The twenty-first century has seen dramatic growth in housing and retail shopping.

The History of Santa Maria–Style Barbecue

The region's ranching heritage is most evident in the continuing tradition of Santa Maria–style barbecue. This cooking style dates from the Spanish vaquero (cowboy) days, when a special cut of beef was butchered, marinated, and slow-cooked over red-hot oak wood. This triangular cut of sirloin, the "tri-tip," is served with special Santa Maria Valley–grown pinquito beans, garden fresh tossed salad, toasted French bread, and spicy salsa. You can find tri-tips sizzling most every weekend in barbecue pits on downtown street corners or marketplaces, presided over by cooks who are generally raising money for local service clubs.

Santa Maria Valley Discovery Museum

705 South McClelland Street; (805) 928-8414; www.smvdiscoverymuseum.org. Open Monday through Saturday. Call for seasonal times and fees. $

More than thirty-five activities with eleven permanent exhibits and many rotating displays means you'll always find something fun for kids of all ages. Favorites include Shark Tank, Shipwreck, Fish Market, First 5 Garden Infant Playground, Creation Station, and plush "cowches" to rest and relax upon.

MotionZ Laser Tag

218 Town Center East, second level; (805) 922-6922; www.motionz.net. Height restriction of at least 42 inches. Open daily; times and special promotions change. Call for schedule and fees. $$

State-of-the-art family-entertainment center features a 7,000-square-foot multilevel laser-tag arena with radio-controlled real-time system for up to thirty players. Observation deck; video, virtual reality, and table games and concessions.

Santa Maria Museum of Flight

3015 Airpark Drive; (805) 922-8758; www.smmof.org. Open Friday through Sunday 10:00 a.m. to 4:00 p.m. $

Guadalupe Dunes

Head 9 miles west out of Santa Maria to the end of State Route 166, and your kids will think you've landed in the Sahara Desert by the Sea—officially known as the **Guadalupe-Nipomo Dunes Preserve.** Sand dunes up to 500 feet tall stretch for 18 miles along the Pacific Ocean here. More than 1,400 species of animals, including 200 kinds of birds, and 244 species of plants migrate or live in this undisturbed, windswept landscape. To fully appreciate this magnificent work of nature, make your first stop at the **Dunes Visitor Center,** located in a restored Victorian house in downtown Guadalupe at 1055 Guadalupe Street (805-343-2455; www.dunescenter.org). This wonderful, family-oriented facility provides entertaining interactive exhibits on dune mammals, birds, plants, and history. (Did you know that Cecile B. DeMille's 1923 film set of *The Ten Commandments* is buried underneath these dunes?) Free maps and tour programs are provided. If hunger strikes, mosey into the **Far Western,** a family-owned and -operated dining hall serving families lunch and dinner daily since 1958 at 899 Guadalupe Street (805-343-2211; www.farwesterntavern.com). Your kids will get a kick out of the rawhide booths and ranching artifacts while you savor the excellent steaks (as featured on BBQ with Bobby Flay's Food Network TV show.)

Aviators and wannabe pilots need to gear up for a visit to this exhibit, located next to the (SMX) city airport within two historic hangars. You can see the Fleet Model 2 and Stinson V77-Reliant airplanes, an extensive collection of model planes, and the once-secret Norden bombsight and its accessories.

Santa Maria Speedway
One-third mile north of US 101/Highway 166, Bakersfield exit to Hutton Road; Infoline (805) 922-2233 or Office (805) 202-1492; www.santamariaspeedway.com. $$

Take your family to the stock-car races in a natural amphitheater surrounded by eucalyptus trees. Every Saturday night mid-April through October. Dedicated family section with no smoking or alcohol allowed is our best suggestion for a good time.

Waller County Park

300 Goodwin Road, Orcutt Expressway and Waller Lane; (805) 934-6123; www.sbparks .com/2007/Parks/waller.html. Open daily 8:00 a.m. to sunset. Free admission for day use; group fees apply.

A 153-acre park with lake, fountains, a waterfall, fishing, playgrounds, baseball diamonds, and, most important for kids, pony rides (fee).

YMCA Skateboard Park

3400 Skyway Drive; (805) 937-8521; www.smvymca.org/skate.html. Call for fees and operating hours.

Located adjacent to the YMCA facility, this 15,000-square-foot park contains numerous ramps, including quarter pipes, half pipes, boxes, rails, jumps, hills, and a vertical ramp. A special area for beginners is available.

Where to Eat and Stay

Klondike Pizza, 2059 South Broadway; (805) 348-3667. Open daily from 11:00 a.m. Total family-fun food—pizza, burgers, salads—and free roasted peanuts in shells that you're encouraged to throw on the floor. We sure do! $

Historic Santa Maria Inn, 801 South Broadway, exit Main Street west off US 101, then south on Broadway; (805) 928-7777; www.santamariainn.com. Near Santa Maria Town Center Mall shopping and area attractions, this English-style country inn was built in 1917 and has expanded over the years to include a restaurant serving lunch and dinner, a wine cellar, a gift shop, and newer tower suites for a total of 164 units. Be sure to inquire for current family package plans and special deals. A good choice for value in the area. $$$

For More Information

Santa Maria Valley Chamber of Commerce and Visitor & Convention Bureau. 614 South Broadway, 93454; (805) 925-2403 or (800) 331-3779; www.santamaria .com.

Lompoc Valley

Say Lompoc (Lahm-poke) with me now, and then your entire family can start saying "oooh" and "aahhh" if you visit during the late spring and summer, when awesome fields of flowers bloom practically everywhere you gaze. Lompoc is a Chumash Indian word meaning "little lake" or "lagoon." More than 67,000 people call this beautiful valley home now, including the military personnel at Vandenberg Air Force Base. Don't miss the more than sixty murals throughout the city. (Contact the chamber of commerce for a map.)

Lompoc Flower Fields
Downtown Lompoc at the corner of Ocean Avenue and C Street; as well as along Highway 246, Highway 1, and Sweeney Road.

This valley produces a good part of the world's flower seeds. More than 1,000 acres are covered with more than 200 varieties of flowers, including marigolds, asters, larkspur, calendula, lavender, and cornflowers. To help "blooming idiots" identify these gems, there is a helpful, fully labeled display garden. The Lompoc Flower Festival is held every June to celebrate this incredible presentation of nature (www.flowerfestival.org).

La Purisima Mission State Historic Park
Three miles northeast of Highway 246 at 2295 Purisima Road; (805) 773-3713; www.lapurisimamission.org. $

See the Americanos' complete and authentic restoration of this important mission back to the way it was in the 1800s. La Purisima Mission was the eleventh mission of the twenty-one Spanish missions established on December 8, 1787. There are gardens, hiking trails, and picnic facilities. Living History Days are not to be missed—call for scheduled activities and reenactments.

Vandenberg Air Force Base (ages 10 and up)
Public Affairs Office, 747 Nebraska Avenue, Room #A103, VAFB; (805) 606-3595; www.vandenberg.af.mil.

This base, begun in 1941, is located on the outskirts of Lompoc on 99,000 acres of incredibly beautiful Pacific oceanfront property that also includes an ecological preserve. Vandenberg Air Force Base is headquarters for the 30th Space Wing—which manages Department of Defense space and missile testing, and placing satellites into polar orbit from the West Coast using expendable boosters. Two-hour public base tours are offered through the Public Affairs office the second Wednesday of each month. Reservations are required at least two weeks in advance. No walk-ons are accepted the day of the tour. Tours may be cancelled when mission requirements dictate.

Lasso-ed into **Los Alamos**

As you travel US 101, midway between San Luis Obispo and Santa Barbara, you'll discover a genuine western town worth your family's visit. Now inhabited by about 1,500 friendly folks, Los Alamos (Spanish for "the cottonwoods") was founded by ranchers in 1876 and became a popular stagecoach and railroad stop—its appearance hasn't changed much since. For accommodations, check into the hillside **Skyview Motel,** with stunning 360-degree valley views at value rates (805-344-3770). The historic 1880 Union Hotel is currently being restored. For foodstuffs, check out the Quakenbush Cafe and Art Brut Gallery, Full of Life Flatbread Pizza, Charlie's Drive-in, Twin Oaks Restaurant, or Javy's Mexican Cafe, all on the main drag, Bell Street (Highway 135). Don't miss the Depot Mall Antique Center in the old railroad station. The town honors its heritage during the last weekend of September with an annual Old Days Celebration. See www .LosAlamosInfo.com.

For More Information

Lompoc Valley Chamber of Commerce and Visitors Bureau. 111 South I ("Eye") Street, 93436; (805) 736-4567 or (800) 240-0999; www.lompoc.com.

The Santa Ynez Valley

South of Santa Maria on US 101, bordered by the Santa Ynez and San Rafael Mountains, lies the Santa Ynez Valley. Some families bypass this magnificent triangle bisected by Highways 154 and 246, home of more than seventy award-winning wineries and vineyards—some of which were seen in the 2005 Academy Award–winning movie *Sideways*. Don't you dare miss these five towns that are only forty-five minutes inland from the coastal city of Santa Barbara yet feel like a world away: Buellton—home of the original Pea Soup Andersen's Restaurant, and the commercial gateway to the valley; Ballard—with its continuously operating one-room school; Los Olivos—where the movie *Return to Mayberry* was filmed and many artists and galleries reside; Santa Ynez itself—a thoroughly western burg; and the largest town, Solvang—truly another world, it is Southern California's little bit of Denmark. As the locals say, "Velkommen!"

Solvang means "sunny fields" in Danish. You and your family will find plenty of sunny hospitality in this beautiful village, where the spirit of the founding Danes lives on. Visualize

Wining and Picnicking

The Santa Ynez Valley is the premier, award-winning wine region of Southern California and home to more than seventy wineries, vineyards, and tasting rooms. Older children may be fascinated by the rituals of grape growing, harvesting, and winemaking, but they will have to wait until they are twenty-one to do more than sniff the bouquet. Many vineyards and wineries have lovely picnic areas that make delightful lunch spots for the entire family year-round. Contact the Santa Barbara County Vintners Association at (800) 218-0881 or www.sbcountywines.com for a free map and more information.

windmills, thatched-roof cottages with dormers and gables, fresh Danish pastries, groaning smorgasbords, 150 unique shops (no chain stores), friendly folks, comfortable lodging, and lots of sunshine. You may become laden with goodies, including porcelain figurines, handmade lace, music boxes, jewelry, sweaters, candies, and western wear.

Hans Christian Andersen Museum
1680 Mission Drive in the Book Loft building; (805) 688-2052. Open daily. Free.

Andersen was the Danish father of the modern fairy tale. See his books, sketches, paper cutouts, and collages.

Elverhoj Museum of History and Art
1624 Elverhoj Way; (805) 686-1211; www.elverhoj.org. Open Wednesday through Sunday. Free, donations welcomed.

Located on a residential street, this attraction lets you discover the origins of Solvang's fascinating history and Danish legacy with rotating exhibits of Danish and modern art, free events, workshops, and craft classes.

Mission Santa Ines
1760 Mission Drive, right near the village center; (805) 688-4815; www.missionsanta ines .org. $

Number nineteen in the chain of twenty-one missions along the coast. Dedicated in 1804, Mission Santa Ines continues to hold services as well as to provide a museum for original Chumash Indian paintings, seventeenth-century European artworks, and religious

vestments. The mission also houses a serene meditation garden in a quadrangle inside the walls. A perfect escape if your family is overdosing on Danish.

Pacific Conservatory of the Performing Arts (PCPA)

In Solvang's outdoor Festival Theater at 420 Second Street; (805) 922-8313 or (800) 549-7272 for tickets and schedules; www.pcpa.org. Open June through September.

Stages world-class professional Theater Under the Stars, a Santa Barbara County family tradition. Don't miss out on the experience during your visit! The 2009 season will feature *Les Miserables, The Music Man,* and *The 25th Annual Putnam County Spelling Bee.*

Windhaven Glider Rides

Santa Ynez Valley Airport, off Highway 246, near intersection of Highway 154; (805) 688-2517; www.gliderrides.com. Open Wednesday through Sunday for glider plane flights, weather permitting. Reservations highly recommended. Call for fares.

Two-seater planes flown by FAA-certified commercial pilots at approximately 2,500 feet and, pardon the pun, up from there! An incredible experience for older children to share with the folks.

Nojoqui Falls County Park

Seven miles southwest of Solvang on Alisal Road; (805) 934-6123; www.sbparks.com/2007/Parks/nojoqui.html. Open daily 8:00 a.m. to sunset. Free.

This 182-acre site is worth a visit to see the 164-foot waterfall (after a rainy season, of course). Head for the waterfall on the well-marked trail. Plenty of picnic spots, barbecue grills, a playground, and places to savor your Danish treats from nearby Solvang.

Quicksilver Miniature Horse Ranch

1555 Alamo Pintado Road, just east of Solvang; (805) 686-4002. www.syv.com/qsminis. Open daily except Thanksgiving and Christmas from 10:00 a.m. to 3:00 p.m. Free.

Has everything from 18-inch-high newborns to 34-inch "tall" mature animals that will be sure to amaze and delight everyone. Breeding and caring for "minis" since 1983.

Danish **Food**

No visit to Solvang would be complete without tasting *aebleskivers*—the raspberry-jam-draped, powdered-sugar-coated Danish pancake balls sold throughout the village. This Danish version of the donut is made with a special flour in a unique round cast-iron pan and is definitely delicious. Be on the lookout for *frikadeller* (meatballs), *medisterpolse* (sausages), and *rodkaal* (red cabbage), as well as pastries, tarts, and breads at four Danish-owned bakeries as well as numerous family-friendly restaurants such as the Bit O'Denmark, Red Viking, and Solvang Restaurant.

Horsing around the Valley

The Valley is well known throughout the equestrian world for its thorough-bred, Arabian, and Icelandic horse ranches and training and breeding facilities. For periodic shows and events, contact the Santa Ynez Valley Equestrian Association (www.syvea.org) or the Santa Ynez Valley Arabian Horse Association (www.syvaha.com).

If your family is hankering to ride, check out **Rancho Oso Guest Ranch & Stables,** off Highway 154 and Paradise Road; (805) 683-5110; www.rancho-oso.com. Offering guided trail rides to children ages eight and older, camping in covered wagons, cabins, and backcountry grub. Another option is **Circle Bar B Stables and Guest Ranch,** off US 101 at Refugio Road; (805) 968-3901; www.circlebarb.com. Trail rides near President Reagan's former ranch over-looking the Pacific, plus lodge, cabins, and dinner theater.

Ostrich Land

610 East Highway 246 between Buellton and Solvang; (805) 686-9696; www.ostrichland .com. Generally open every day. Tours and feeding opportunities for all ages. $

This ranch is home to hundreds of the biggest birds in the world, reaching 8.5 feet in height and weighing up to 350 pounds when mature. Impress your children with the fun fact that ostriches run faster than any two-legged animal. How fast? Up to 45 miles per hour! Gift shop and farm stand as well where you can buy ostrich eggs in season.

Santa Ynez Valley Historical Museum and Parks-Janeway Carriage House

3596 Sagunto Street, downtown Santa Ynez; (805) 688-7889; www.syvm.org. Open Wednesday through Sunday, closed most major holidays. **Free.** Donations welcome.

You can relive the valley's Old West origins with vehicles, including a full-size, outfitted covered wagon, phaetons, donkey carts, and a stagecoach. Don't miss the farm machinery, implements, saddle collection, and works by famed silversmith Edward Borein.

Cachuma Lake Recreation Area

Twenty minutes outside Solvang, 18 miles northwest along Scenic Highway 154 over the San Marcos Pass from Santa Barbara; (805) 686-5054; www.cachumalake.com. $$

This human-made lake (pronounced Ka-choo-ma) takes its name from a nearby ancient Chumash village. The reservoir has a dual purpose as Santa Barbara's water supply, but it is more famous as the winter home of hundreds of bald eagles. The eagle cruises, aboard comfortable pontoon (patio) boats, bring you and your "eagle-eyed" children within 200 yards of the birds' roosting sites. More than 275 other species of birds have been identified on the lake, plus plenty of fish, other wildlife, trees, and plants. Call for schedule and fees. The nature center offers **free** hikes, docent-led programs, and family activities year-round.

Forty-two miles of shoreline offer 550 regular campsites, rental cabins, and 90 EWS hookups on a first-come, first-served basis. There are hiking, fishing, boating, and other facilities galore, including a general store, Laundromat, snack bar, marina, picnic areas, and barbecues for daytime use year-round. Check out the yurt camping option. A cross between a tepee and a tent, yurts are on platforms, sleep five to six people, and have gorgeous lake views.

Where to Eat

Cold Spring Tavern, 5995 Stagecoach Road, 0.5 mile off Highway 154, approximately thirty minutes from Solvang and twenty minutes from Santa Barbara; (805) 967-0066; www.coldspringtavern.com. Make a detour as you go over the San Marcos Pass upon leaving the Santa Ynez Valley and wet your whistle like horse-drawn passengers on the stagecoaches of yesteryear did. Since the 1880s, this historic spot has been serving lunch and dinner and libations daily. Hearty country breakfast on Saturday and Sunday. Kids will love the rustic walls, stone floors, and chance to eat buffalo burgers and venison stew. $$$

Pea Soup Andersen's Restaurant and Motor Inn, 1 block west of junction of US 101 and Highway 246 in Buellton; (805) 688-5581. Open from 6:30 a.m. to 10:30 p.m. every day. Home of the original (1924) restaurant serving hearty, bottomless bowls of split pea soup and other family favorites. This is one of our family's traditional stopovers, no matter what the occasion. The inn has ninety-seven rooms around an attractive central courtyard with a pool, spa, and putting green. Good value for a roadside respite. $$

Where to Stay

Alisal Guest Ranch and Resort, two minutes south of the village of Solvang at 1054 Alisal Road; (805) 688-6411 or (800) 4A-ALISAL; www.alisal.com. Rates include dinner and full American breakfast served in the comfortable Ranch Room. This is a truly one-of-a-kind family-owned and family-operated haven. The resort boasts seventy-three family bungalows with wood-burning fireplaces and no television or telephones in your room. (There is Wi-Fi in the business center if you must stay connected.) The peace of this 10,000-acre working ranch envelops you immediately upon driving up the tree-lined lane.

Organized family activities and supervised play are featured all summer long. Year-round, you and yours can swim, spa, take in a movie, read in the library, play on one of the Alisal's two championship golf courses, try your hand at tennis, go horseback riding, or spend a day at Alisal's private ninety-acre spring-fed lake for fishing, swimming, canoeing, and sailing.

A two-night minimum stay is required—and worth every moment! Be sure to call for special seasonal packages. Since 1946, the Alisal has been welcoming generations of families with its western hospitality and charm. We recommend you consider starting a family tradition of your own here. $$$$

For More Information

Buellton Visitors Bureau & Chamber of Commerce. 376 Avenue of Flags, 93427; (805) 688-STAY or (800) 324-3800; www .buellton.org.

Los Olivos Business Organization. Box 280, Los Olivos 93441; (805) 688-1222; www .losolivosca.com.

Santa Ynez Valley Visitors Association.
Box 1918, Santa Ynez 93460; (800) 742-2843;
www.syvva.com.

Solvang Conference & Visitors Bureau.
1511 Mission Drive, 93464; (805) 688-6144 or
(800) 468-6765; www.solvangusa.com.

Solvang Chamber of Commerce. Box
465, 93464; (805) 688-0701; www.solvangcc
.com.

Santa Barbara

If you and the kids want outdoor recreation, nature, scenery, stars, shopping, history lessons, museums, art, culture, great restaurants, and trendy places to hang out, just make
your plans for the destination resort of Santa Barbara, the "American Riviera." The city of
Santa Barbara was first hailed as a prime tourist stop in 1872 by East Coast travel writer
Charles Nordhoff, who said, "Santa Barbara certainly is the most pleasant place throughout the state." The blend of Chumash, Spanish, Mexican, and American cultures has given
Santa Barbara an extremely rich heritage—which is visible in the city's lovely buildings
with red-tiled roofs and whitewashed adobe walls. Devastated by an earthquake in 1925,
downtown Santa Barbara was rebuilt in a Spanish-Moorish colonial motif that is strictly
regulated by law.

Along with architecture, locals are proud of their area's well-preserved natural beauty,
bounded by the Santa Ynez Mountains to the north and Pacific Ocean to the south. Yes,
that's right. All the beaches face south along the Pacific (the only place in the United
States where this happens), so when you want to check out the magnificent sunsets, you
face the beach and look to the right!

Mission Santa Barbara

**2201 Laguna Street, at the corner of Laguna and East Los Olivos Streets, approximately
five minutes from downtown; (805) 682-4149; www.sbmission.org. Open daily from 9:00
a.m. to 5:00 p.m. except Easter, Thanksgiving, and Christmas. $**

You will definitely want to tour "the Queen of the Missions" and still the longest continuously operating parish among California's renowned chain of twenty-one missions.
Founded on December 4, 1786, the feast day of Saint Barbara, and finally completed in
1820, it is one of the best-preserved missions. A fascinating self-guided walking tour that
includes artworks, fountains, a courtyard, and a cemetery is recommended.

Santa Barbara Museum of Natural History and Planetarium

**2559 Puesta del Sol Road (just around the corner from the Mission Santa Barbara); (805)
682-4711; www.sbnature.org. Open daily (except major holidays). $$, free to all on the
third Sunday of every month.**

The museum has exhibits on early Native American tribes as well as animals, birds,
insects, plants, minerals, marine science, and geology. The planetarium hosts impressive
star shows. Call (805) 682-3224 for a schedule.

Special Santa Barbara **Festivals**

Festivals and celebrations abound in the city of Santa Barbara year-round. Oak Park, on the city's north side, hosts ethnic and cultural festivals in the spring and summer. However, the following two events are worth a special visit for your entire family, from toddler to grandparent.

- **Summer Solstice Celebration.** This is a fantasy fun romp celebrating the arrival of summer on the Saturday closest to the first day of summer. The parade features no motorized floats or amplified music, but almost one hundred "non-floats," including bands, clowns, dancers, and perhaps a rubber sea of sharks, rolling bubble machines, or even a briefcase brigade of lawyers. A different theme is carried out each year. The theme for 2008 was "Solar Flair." After the parade up State Street from the waterfront, the participants and spectators all congregate at Alameda Park at the corner of Sola and Anacapa Streets. You will love the energy, color, food booths, and vendors at this post-parade party until early evening. The free Children's Area features a stage with storytellers, musicians, drama, mimes, and more. For more information and a detailed schedule of events, call (805) 965-3396 or visit www.solsticeparade.com.

- **Old Spanish Days (Fiesta).** If you visit during the first weekend of August, experience the sights, sounds, and foods of California's early settlers during Old Spanish Days. Commonly known as Fiesta, the celebrations begin with the padre's blessing on the steps of the historic mission on Wednesday evening, followed by performances by the junior (younger than age twelve) and senior (younger than age eighteen) Spirit of Fiesta Dancers. Your family will shout "Viva la Fiesta!" along with the natives during Friday's Annual El Desfile Historico—one of the world's most colorful parades, attracting the most horses and riders in America, along with 100,000 enthusiastic spectators.

Your kids can participate in El Desfile de Los Ninos (the Children's Parade) on Saturday morning. During the five-day festival, the entire family can enjoy the *mercados* (marketplaces with traditional foods), carnival rides at the beach, and the family entertainment spectacular, Noches de Ronda, each evening under the stars in the gardens of the courthouse. Call (805) 962-8101 year-round for free brochures and schedules or visit www.oldspanishdays-fiesta.org.

Santa Barbara Botanic Garden

1212 Mission Canyon Road, just above the natural history museum, about 2 miles into Mission Canyon; (805) 682-4726; www.sbbg.org. Open daily except for major holidays; call for seasonal hours and special exhibits. $

Kids will love exploring the miles of trails through forests and plant life on seventy-eight exquisite acres devoted only to California species. Self-guided and guided tours available.

Santa Barbara Historical Museum and Covarrubias Adobe

136 East de la Guerra Street, downtown; (805) 966-1601; www.santabarbaramuseum.com. Open Tuesday through Saturday 10:00 a.m. to 5:00 p.m. Free. Donations appreciated.

The museum's permanent exhibits include documents, furniture, decorative and fine arts, and costumes that tell the region's story from the age of the Chumash Indians to the Space Age. Casa Covarrubias Adobe, circa 1817, may have served briefly as the headquarters of Pio Pico, the last Mexican governor of California, and represents an easier, slower lifestyle.

El Presidio de Santa Barbara State Historic Park

100–200 blocks of East Canon Perdido Street, downtown; (805) 965-0093; www.sbthp.org/presidio.htm. Open daily 10:30 a.m. to 4:30 p.m. except for major holidays. $

This was the last military outpost built by Spain in the New World, dedicated in 1782. A continuous project restores the actual structures, including El Cuartel, the padre's quarters; the chapel; and the commandant's office. A slide show and guided tours are offered upon request. This is a piece of living history you just can't ignore. Our kids really liked the story of the lost cannon. Ask a docent for the details.

Santa Barbara Museum of Art

1130 State Street; (805) 963-4364; www.sbmuseart.org. Open Tuesday through Saturday 11:00 a.m. to 5:00 p.m., Friday to 9:00 p.m., and Sunday noon to 5:00 p.m. $. Free admission every Sunday.

The museum has important works by American and European artists, including Monet and other impressionists. Displays include American, Asian, and nineteenth-century French art, plus Greek and Roman antiquities and major photographic works. Special exhibits rotate throughout the year. Narrated tours available, usually at 1:00 p.m. The Children's Gallery is outstanding. And don't miss the lovely Museum Store.

Karpeles Manuscript Library Museum

21 West Anapamu Street (one-half block off State); (805) 962-5322; www.rain.org/~karpeles/. Open daily 10:00 a.m. to 4:00 p.m. Closed Christmas and New Year's Day. Free.

Book Zone

Located along Anapamu Street on opposite sides of State Street, this area is affectionately called "book row." It is anchored by the impressive 250,000-volume Santa Barbara Public Library at 40 East Anapamu (805-962-7653). You and your family will discover the joy of finding every type of literature imaginable in the following unique, independent Santa Barbara bookstores. Special events with authors and storytellers abound, so be sure to contact each shop for schedules and hours of operation.

- **Pacific Travellers Supply,** 12 West Anapamu; (805) 963-4438. Guidebooks, maps, and luggage.

- **Metro Comics & Entertainment,** 6 West Anapamu; (805) 963-2168; www.metro-entertainment.com/.

- **The Book Den,** 15 East Anapamu; (805) 962-3321; www.bookden.com. Used, rare, and out-of-print books.

- **Paradise Found,** 17 East Anapamu; (805) 564-3573; www.paradise-found.net. Metaphysical books.

Each fall, the **Santa Barbara Book and Author Festival** (805-962-9500; www.sbbookfestival.org) celebrates reading and writing with an inspiring two-day event downtown featuring famous authors, book signings, panels, and awards.

Houses original manuscripts of great authors, scientists, and leaders from all periods of history, including an original copy of the Declaration of Independence. Rotating exhibits show fascinating glimpses into antiquity.

Kids World
In Alameda Park, at the corner of Micheltorena and Garden Streets, downtown. Free.

Designed by city children and built by them, as well as community volunteers, this two-story wooden playland is truly a kid's dream come to life. A tot lot and sandbox are available for the very young, while older sibs can cruise through tunnels and stride over bridges or clamber up the tree house.

Santa Barbara County Courthouse
1100 Anacapa Street, downtown; (805) 962-6464; www.sbcourts.org/general_info/cthouse_info.htm. Open Monday through Friday 8:00 a.m. to 5:00 p.m., Saturday and Sunday 10:00 a.m. to 5:00 p.m. Free.

Most kids would not want to tour a courthouse, except in Santa Barbara, where you can climb the 80-foot clock tower stairs (or take the elevator, for us fogeys) for a stunning panoramic view over the city, all the way to the ocean. The courthouse was built in 1929.

"Take a Vacation from Your Car!"

It's easy to do by accessing www.santabarbaracarfree.org, calling (805) 696-1100, or writing Santa Barbara Car Free Project, Box 60436, Santa Barbara 93160. Discover **free** walking tours, bike maps, bus routes, AMTRAK schedules, maps, and vacation packages/hotel discounts. State Street, Santa Barbara's most famous thoroughfare, begins at the beach and leads into the heart of downtown. It is extremely pedestrian- and family-friendly, with benches, outdoor dining, and plenty of greenery. When you get tired of walking, hop aboard the nifty electric shuttle buses (operated by the Metropolitan Transit District [MTD]; www.sbmtd.gov). Santa Barbara Car Free Project is an award-winning ecotourism partnership sponsored by the County Air Pollution Control District, committed to alternative transportation for cleaner air and a healthier planet.

You cannot miss the award-winning Spanish-Moorish design from anywhere in the city. Its sunken gardens are perfect for picnicking and are the site of many events during the year, such as Earth Day Festival and Fiesta.

Santa Barbara Zoological Gardens

500 Ninos Drive, 2 blocks from East Beach off Cabrillo Boulevard; (805) 962-5339; www.santabarbarazoo.org. Open daily 10:00 a.m. to 5:00 p.m. except Thanksgiving and Christmas. $$

This is as wild as Santa Barbara gets! The 30-acre zoo is renowned for its easy accessibility and more than eighty exhibits with 500 child-friendly animals, including big cats, roaring elephants, and gangly giraffes. The huge aviary is a favorite. The zoo, on a former estate overlooking the glittering Pacific, is a must-see. Take a picnic lunch to eat after your morning visit or savor a tasty snack in the Ridley-Tree House Cafe. The miniature train that circumnavigates the zoo's beautiful garden setting is a big plus, and so are the dedicated playground and all the services (easy-access bathrooms, strollers, guided tours, and zoo-camp programs for children, just to name a few).

Chase Palm Park & Carousel

Stretching east from Stearns Wharf along the waterfront on both sides of beachfront Cabrillo Boulevard.

The ten-acre north side of the park has a totally festive antique carousel (enclosed in its own pavilion, nominal fee, open daily); a kids-only (toddler through age twelve) Shipwreck Playground with a rubberized deck; grassy knolls and picnic tables; restrooms; a snack bar; and an entertainment zone. Adjacent is Skaters Point, a popular beachfront 12,000-square-foot concrete mecca for skateboarders open dawn to dusk. **Free.**

On the **Waterfront**

Stearns Wharf. At the foot of State Street on the waterfront; (805) 564-5518; www.stearnswharf.org. Parking is $2 per hour or **free** with a wharf merchant purchase validation. Built in 1872 to serve cargo and passenger ships, this Santa Barbara historic landmark is now the site of specialty shops, family-friendly restaurants, the Ty Warner Sea Center, a boat charter dock, and fishing spots. You can actually drive as well as walk onto the wharf. The kids think it sounds like rumbling thunder when you drive across the wooden planks. Don't worry, it really is quite safe.

Ty Warner Sea Center. 211 Stearns Wharf; (805) 962-2526; www.sbnature .org/seacenter. Open daily 10:00 a.m. to 5:00 p.m.; closed major holidays. $$; children under 2 **free.** Owned and operated by the Santa Barbara Museum of Natural History. Enter the two-story glass foyer and be greeted by a 39-foot, life-size model of a California gray whale and her calf. Crawl through a tunnel inside a 1,500-gallon surge tank to see ocean life such as sea stars, urchins, limpets, and more up close and personal. Many interactive exhibits are perfect for kids of all ages to experience the wonders of oceanography, including live tide pool animal encounters.

Santa Barbara Maritime Museum. In the marina, 113 Harbor Way; (805) 962-8404; www.sbmm.org. Open daily except Wednesday, 10:00 a.m. to 4:00 p.m. Call for hours and admission fees. **Free** on the third Thursday of the month. Located in the former Naval Reserve Building in the heart of the harbor, the museum illustrates the evolution of nautical technology, starting with local origins in the Chumash culture up to modern-day boats and submarines. Highly interactive exhibits are kid friendly.

Santa Barbara Yacht Harbor, Marina, and Breakwater. West of Stearns Wharf, motor entrance along Cabrillo Boulevard just past Castillo Street intersection. Harbor Master's office phone, (805) 564-5520. More than 1,000 work and pleasure craft rest here, home to the city's commercial fishing fleet. Where else can you get so close to a spiny sea urchin heading off to market or purchase shrimp, rock cod, and crab fresh from the fisherfolk themselves?

Sea Landing. 301 West Cabrillo Boulevard; (805) 963-3564; www.sealanding .net. Hook your own seafood on a fishing expedition charter boat that docks here, or sign up for a dive trip or whale-watching excursion. A full-service tackle shop, dive shop, and rental department are also available.

Condor Cruises. (805) 882-0088; www.condorcruises.com. Call (888) 77-WHALE for current schedules and fares. Sea Landing is the home dock of the award-winning Condor *Express*, a 75-foot, 149-passenger high-speed jet-powered catamaran, custom designed specifically for naturalist-led whale-watching trips, sunset cruises, and group charters.

Truth Aquatics. In the marina; (805) 962-1127; www.truthaquatics.com. Call for seasonal times, schedules, and fares. Arranges popular sea kayaking, scuba, and diving charters and also acts as official concessionaire for boat trips to the **Channel Islands National Park,** some 20 miles offshore. (See listing in Ventura County section for more details on the park.)

Santa Barbara Sailing Center. In the marina; (805) 962-2826 or (800) 350-9090; www.sbsail.com. Rent a sailboat—there are more than forty to choose from (with or without a skipper). This is the home dock of the *Double Dolphin* catamaran, a forty-nine-passenger sailboat that runs whale-watching trips, sunset cruises, and private charters. The ASA-certified sailing school here offers beginning through advanced instruction.

The University of California at Santa Barbara (UCSB)
In the neighboring town of Isla Vista, 2 miles south of US 101 via Ward Memorial Boulevard (Highway 217); (805) 893-2485; www.ucsb.edu. Free campus tours.

The gorgeous 989-acre, oceanfront campus features the landmark Storke Tower, University Center, and renowned Marine Sciences Institute, home of 18,000 students and 900 faculty, including five Nobel Prize winners. During July and August, the UCSB Alumni Association offers the Family Vacation Center, with eight weeklong sessions, providing a fully programmed family resort. Rates include three meals daily, residential-hall living, recreational and social activities, all-day child care, and theme programs. This incredible Santa Barbara family vacation bargain sells out each summer. Visit www.familyvacationcenter .com or call (805) 893-3123.

South Coast Railroad Museum
300 North Los Carneros Road in adjacent town of Goleta; (805) 964-3540 for track times for the miniature train; www.goletadepot.org. Generally open Wednesday through Sunday. Free. Donations requested.

Budding conductors and engineers will want to explore the wooden Goleta depot. Built in 1901, the depot was in use until 1973, when it was dismantled and moved to its current site. Restoration began in 1981, and the collection of railroad memorabilia continues to grow.

Where to Eat

Beachside Cafe, 5905 Sandspit Road, on the sand at Goleta Beach County Park, Goleta; (805) 964-7881. Open daily 10:30 a.m. to 11:30 p.m. Seafood is queen here, as well as popular American dishes and killer desserts matched only by the oceanfront location. Try to snag a table on the outdoor heated patio with fireplace to fully enjoy the view and crashing surf. Families of all ages return again and again (we do!). Close to UCSB and Santa Barbara Airport as well. $$

Sambo's on the Beach, 216 West Cabrillo Boulevard, 2 blocks from Stearns Wharf; (805) 965-3269. This is the original and only remaining Sambo's restaurant, founded here in 1957 by two Santa Barbara friends (Sam Battistone and Newall "Bo" Bohnett). Owned and operated by Sam's grandson Chad Stevens, Sambo's dishes up hearty breakfasts, featuring its famous pancakes and syrup, and all-American lunches, served seven days a week. $$

McConnell's Ice Cream & Yogurt Shop, 201 West Mission; (805) 569-2323; www .mcconnells.com. Open daily at 11:00 a.m. Since 1949, serving Super Premium (17 percent butterfat) ice cream with no articificial ingredients or stabilizers, ever. Incredibly delicious if not nutritious, don't leave Santa Barbara without having some (also available in pints in grocery stores as well as served in area restaurants). Chocolate Burnt Almond and Island Coconut (our faves) even attract celebs like Barbara Streisand and Kelsey Grammer. $

Santa Barbara County Certified Farmers Market, (805) 962-5354 for seasonal times; www.sbfarmersmarket.org. The freshest fruits and veggies available for a super-fresh family picnic. The most popular site is in downtown Santa Barbara every Saturday, at the corner of Cota and Santa Barbara Streets (2 blocks off State) from 8:30 a.m. to 12:30 p.m. Kids will love the musicians, jugglers, and clowns, plus the free samples available from generous vendors. Also in Goleta, Carpinteria, and Montecito. $

Where to Stay

El Capitan Canyon, 11560 Calle Real, Goleta; (805) 685-3887 or (866) 352-2729; www.elcapitancanyon.com. An oceanside retreat only 17 miles from downtown Santa Barbara, this property on 300 acres features cozy cabins and safari-canvas tents. A kids' camp, botanical hikes, massages, swimming pool, campfires, and outdoor summer

Whale-**Watching**

The Santa Barbara Channel is becoming well-known not only for the traditional California gray whale migration that occurs annually here between late January and mid-April but also as a year-round whale-viewing and research destination. More than twenty-seven different types of whales inhabit the waters offshore. Blue whales, the largest animals ever to live on earth, have been seen here for the past few summers, apparently feeding on the abundant krill. Humpback whales, minke whales, and orcas, or killer whales, are also often sighted on channel excursions, not to mention porpoises, dolphins, sea lions, and harbor seals. Contact any of the charter boat operators at the harbor or marina for current whale-watching schedules and fees.

concerts are highlights, along with bicycling. It's only a half mile from the State Beach for water sports. A grocery store, gift shop, and deli are here, too. Absolutely ideal for families. $$$

Fess Parker's Doubletree Resort, 633 East Cabrillo Boulevard; (805) 564-4333 or (800) 879-2929; www.fpdtr.com. Owned in part by local resident Fess Parker (famous for his Davy Crockett acting role), this Spanish Mission–style property has all the requirements of a headquarters for your family oceanfront vacation. Located on twenty-three acres across from East Beach, this 360-room resort (Santa Barbara County's largest) has a heated outdoor swimming pool, whirlpool, fitness center, new spa, beauty salon, gift shop, putting green, tennis and basketball courts, bicycle and skate rental shop, game room, and full concierge services. Try the California cuisine of Cafe Los Arcos for breakfast, lunch, and dinner (best for kids); Rodney's Steakhouse for dinner; and Barra Los Arcos, hosting happy hours and live entertainment. Roomy accommodations feature ocean, mountain, or courtyard views—many with patios or decks—great for enjoying the fresh sea breezes. Call for seasonal specials and package plans. $$$$

Upham Hotel & Garden Cottages, 1404 De La Vina Street, just 2 blocks off State Street, downtown; (805) 962-0058 or (800) 727-0876; www.uphamhotel.com. Built in 1871, the Upham is Santa Barbara County's oldest continuously operating hotel. It is located on an acre of eye-catching gardens. You can choose from fifty different Victorian-style rooms or cottages, filled with comfortable, not stuffy, antiques. Kids like to play in the garden courtyard, while the older folks enjoy complimentary afternoon wine and cheese. All rates include a deluxe continental all-you-can-eat breakfast buffet, plus Oreo cookies and milk in the evening. The hotel has always been independently owned and operated and feels like a family home. Call and inquire for special rates and packages. Louie's Restaurant on premises serves delicious California-cuisine lunch weekdays and dinner every night on the historic veranda. $$$

For More Information

Goleta Valley Chamber of Commerce. 271 North Fairview, Suite 104, Box 781, 93116; (805) 967-2500 or (800) 646-5382; www.goletavalley.com.

Santa Barbara Region Chamber of Commerce Visitor Center. 1 Garden Street at Cabrillo Boulevard, 93101; (805) 965-3021; www.sbchamber.org. Walk-up info on the beachfront. Open 364 days a year.

Santa Barbara Conference & Visitors Bureau and Film Commission. 1601 Anacapa Street, 93101; (805) 966-9222, (800) 927-4688, or (800) 676-1266; www.Santa BarbaraCa.com.

Outdoor Santa Barbara Visitor Center. 113 Harbor Way, fourth floor, 93109; (805) 884-1475; http://outdoorsb.noaa.gov/.

Summerland

About 5 miles southeast of Santa Barbara is this historic antiques and artists' haven just off US 101. Exit and head toward the oceanfront Lookout Park, with restrooms, volleyball courts, playground, and easy access to an uncrowded 2-mile stretch of beach.

Where to Eat

Summerland Beach Cafe, 2294 Lillie Avenue; (805) 969-1019; www.summerlandbeach cafe.com/. Located in a rambling white clapboard house with a big veranda, this is the place for the best omelets and breakfast fare, as well as lunch, served daily from 7:00 a.m. to 3:00 p.m. The decor is eclectic and sure to hold the family's interest, including some old booths with their own phones. $

Carpinteria

The small seaside community of Carpinteria, about 12 miles southeast of Santa Barbara, down the coast along US 101, was originally a Chumash fishing village and canoe-building spot. It boasts the Carpinteria State Beach, aka the "world's safest beach"—a claim justified, perhaps, by a natural reef breakwater that prevents nasty riptides. There are outstanding recreational opportunities and a variety of camping facilities around and inland from the beach. Many flower firms are based here, growing roses, orchids, and mums. Another of Carpinteria's blossoms, a hardy perennial fruit if you will, is celebrated with the popular California Avocado Festival, held the first weekend of October downtown on Linden Avenue (www.avofest.com). From April through October, thrill to the sport of kings at the Santa Barbara Polo Club (www.sbpolo.com), located in the Carpinteria foothills.

Carpinteria Valley Historical Society and Museum

956 Maple Avenue; (805) 684-3112; www.carpinteriahistoricalmuseum.org. Open Tuesday through Saturday from 1:00 to 4:00 p.m.; closed holidays. Free. Donations welcome.

Check out the valley's heritage from Chumash Indian settlement to today with charming exhibits and knowledgeable docents.

Where to Stay

Holiday Inn Express & Suites, 5606 Carpinteria Avenue; (805) 566-9499. This 108-unit property has easy access to US 101, beaches, and local attractions. A nice outdoor pool, a spa, and complimentary continental breakfast buffet are other highlights. Ask about special package rates. $$$

For More Information

Carpinteria Valley Chamber of Commerce. 1056-B Eugenia Place, Box 956, 93014; (805) 684-5479 or (800) 563-6900; www.carpchamber.org.

Ventura County

The mighty US 101, known hereabouts as the Ventura Highway (and popularized in the '70s hit song by America), winds south from Santa Barbara County. It is the major artery through such rapidly growing communities as San Buenaventura (Ventura for short), Oxnard, Port Hueneme, Camarillo, Westlake Village, and Thousand Oaks. Exiting this concrete thoroughfare into the interior of Ventura County will reveal such treasures as the artistic and spiritual town of Ojai, rugged Santa Paula, and burgeoning Simi Valley. Embracing its cultural and geographic diversity is a key to enjoying Ventura County. With its mild climate and proximity to Los Angeles, the county offers an affordable getaway less than an hour from the big city. If you have limited time to show your family some California beach living, you can quickly and easily do it in the place Los Angelinos call "up the coast."

Ventura

Wrapped around the east-west ribbons of US 101, the city of Ventura has a historic downtown area that includes the restored Mission San Buenaventura; the Ventura Pier and State Beach, approximately 6 blocks from downtown; and the Ventura Harbor Village, some 2 miles away. Ventura has a population of about 100,000 and is a major agricultural center for citrus and other fruits. Its warm, sunny climate and value-priced accommodations and restaurants make this a very affordable family vacation spot as well as a jumping-off point for visiting the Channel Islands National Park.

Ventura Harbor Village

1583 Spinnaker Drive, about 1 mile west of the Harbor Boulevard/Seaward exit from US 101; (877) 89-HARBOR or (805) 642-8538; www.venturaharborvillage.com.

Sailing, fishing, scuba diving, and sightseeing trips can all be arranged at this thirty-three-acre village. Dozens of shops and restaurants too along the scenic Promenade. Home of the Channel Islands National Park Visitor Center. (See sidebar in this chapter for more information.)

Island Packers Company

1691 Spinnaker Drive, Suite 105 B, adjacent to Channel Islands National Park Visitor Center; (805) 642-1393; www.islandpackers.com.

A tour operator based here since 1968 and offering scheduled charters to all the islands, as well as whale-watching trips and cruises—home dock for the *Islander* and the *Island Adventure*. Call for special packages and itineraries. Nearby satellite office and the home dock for the *Vanguard* is located in The Channel Islands Harbor, 3600 South Harbor Boulevard, Oxnard 93035.

Our Fortieth National Park

The Channel Islands National Park Robert J. Lagomarsino Visitor Center is located at 1901 Spinnaker Drive in Ventura Harbor Village (805-658-5730; www.nps.gov/chis/). It is open daily, except Thanksgiving and Christmas. Less than 20 miles off the coast of Ventura and Santa Barbara Counties, the **Channel Islands National Park** comprises five of the eight offshore Channel Islands: Santa Barbara, Anacapa, Santa Cruz, Santa Rosa, and San Miguel. These islands provide an unparalleled introduction for your family to the flora and fauna of the local marine environment. Nature, unspoiled and unsullied by humans, is the main attraction here; quite frankly, it's the only attraction! Because the balance of nature on these islands and their surrounding waters is so fragile, visitors' activities are strictly regulated. For instance, there are no snack bars or RV campgrounds, and when you tour the area, you must bring (and take back what remains of) your own food, water, and other supplies. Rangers conduct guided hikes on San Miguel and Santa Rosa. Private concessionaires' boats or charter craft provide transportation across the channel to specific embarkation points.

The waterfront visitor center houses quality exhibits that graphically describe the entire park, including its ecosystem, mammals, and birds. Plus, the center has an indoor tide pool, great for learning about the sea creatures your kids will see en route. There is also a movie and video about the islands shown here. A stairway and elevator lead up to the observation tower that will give you a 360-degree view of the harbor and, on most clear days, all the way to the islands themselves. Taking a day to visit our fortieth national park is well worth the effort and will be a sea journey to another dimension your family won't forget.

Where to Stay

Pierpont Inn & Restaurant, 550 Sanjon Road, adjacent to US 101, northbound exit Sanjon Road, southbound exit Seaward Avenue; (805) 643-6144 or (800) 285-4667; www.pierpontinn.com. Children ages twelve and younger stay **free** at this attractive, seventy-seven-unit property, established in 1928. Check out the two cottages! Some rooms have fireplaces, and most rooms have ocean views with balconies. Even though you are across the highway from the beach, this property has two heated pools (one indoor).

It also has twelve lighted tennis courts and a very friendly, helpful staff. The ocean-view restaurant, Austen's, serves breakfast, lunch, and dinner daily as well as Sunday brunch. $$$$

For More Information

Ventura Convention and Visitors Bureau. 101 South California Street, 93001; (805) 648-2075 or (800) 333-2989; www.ventura-usa.com.

Digging into History

These three nearby attractions all make for refreshing steps back into early California history. Each is located in downtown Ventura, within easy walking distance, and can be accomplished in a long morning. While you're in the downtown shopping and dining zone, catch some vintage stores and antiques emporiums.

Ventura County Museum of History and Art. 89 South California Street (temporary); (805) 653-0323; www.venturamuseum.org. Open Tuesday through Sunday 11:00 a.m. to 6:00 p.m. $. Major expansion/construction began in April 2008 of the original 100 East Main Street location (scheduled to return there in 2009–10). Features attractive displays blending local chronicles and illustrations along with the popular George Stuart historical figures, changing exhibits, and a good research library.

Albinger Archaeological Museum. 113 East Main Street; (805) 648-5823. Open Wednesday through Sunday 10:00 a.m. to 4:00 p.m. Free. Museum contains artifacts spanning 3,500 years, all excavated from a single dig site next to the Mission San Buenaventura. Available on request: audiovisual programs describing the labor-intensive process of excavation.

Mission San Buenaventura. 211 East Main Street; (805) 648-4496; www.san buenaventuramission.org. Open Monday through Friday 10:00 a.m. to 5:00 p.m., Saturday 9:00 a.m. to 5:00 p.m., and Sunday 10:00 a.m. to 4:00 p.m. $. Founded in 1782 and completed in 1809, ninth in the chain of twenty-one California missions. The current mission includes a small museum and a restored church that continues to be an active parish. It's the only mission in the United States with bells made of wood. The reason is still a mystery.

Ojai

From Ventura, you can take either Highway 150 or Highway 33 inland to reach Ojai, a warm, dry, spiritually inclined artists' colony nestled in a peaceful valley. Say "Oh-high," and you will have mastered the most difficult part of the area. The drive here alone is worth the trip because of the scenic mountains and lakes. The quaint downtown features **Libbey Park**—home of the annual Bowl Full of Blues concert series and the Ojai Music Festival. The **Ojai Center for the Arts** has displays by California artists and a changing calendar of events. Call (805) 646-1107 or visit www.ojaiartcenter.org for current happenings.

Ojai Valley Museum

130 West Ojai Avenue, located downtown in the historic chapel; (805) 640-1390; www
.ojaivalleymuseum.org. Open Wednesday through Friday 1:00 to 4:00 p.m. and Saturday
and Sunday 10:00 a.m. to 4:00 p.m. $ (under 6 free).

Changing exhibits of art, natural history, and local lore. Chumash garden and gift shop
provide interesting diversions.

Lake Casitas Recreation Area

Off Highway 150, approximately 3 miles west of junction of Highway 33, about fifteen minutes from downtown Ojai; 11311 Santa Ana Road, Ventura, 93001; reservations: (805) 649-
1122 or info: (805) 649-2233; www.lakecasitas.info. Open year-round for day use during
daylight hours. Four hundred overnight campsites subject to availability; fees vary.

Set in a valley of its own, this 35-mile-long, irregularly shaped lake is actually a human-
made reservoir that provides drinking water for Ventura County. Consequently, there is
no swimming in the lake, but the fishing for trout, bass, crappie, and catfish is excellent.
Powerboats, canoeing, and sailing are fun here, too, year-round. There is a basic snack
bar, small grocery store, boat rental, bait shop, and a large kids' playground. The Water
Adventure Area offers two distinctly wet playgrounds—an 18-inch-deep pool or the Lazy
River tube float pool, both open only in summer. Our advice is to pack a picnic lunch and
come kick back here for the day.

Where to Eat

Boccali's, 3277 Ojai-Santa Paula Road, at the
corner of Reeves Road; (805) 646-6116; www
.boccalis.com. Casual, fun dining inside or
outside on the patio. Great pizzas and loads
of pastas. Family owned and operated since
1986; friendly atmosphere; takeout available.
Serving dinner seven nights a week and lunch
Wednesday through Sunday. $

Where to Stay

Ojai Valley Inn & Spa, 905 Country Club
Road, just west of town off Highway 150;
(805) 646-5511 or (800) 422-6524; www
.ojairesort.com. Named one of the Top 10
Best Family-Friendly Resorts in the USA by
Child magazine (2006); this magnificent AAA
five-diamond rated resort nestled in the foothills is a one-stop family fun destination since
1923. If you and yours can't find something
to keep you happy here, go home! Situated
on 220 landscaped acres, the resort offers
308 first-class rooms and suites overlooking
gardens, pools, a golf course, and woods.
This is the home of the Senior PGA Tour, and
the eighteen-hole golf course is very challenging, yet forgiving. Warm up on the putting
green, or perhaps try tennis (four courts),
horseback riding, a jogging course, hiking,
and biking (rentals available). Better yet, let
the kids enjoy the petting zoo and incredible
supervised Camp Ojai children's programs
(ages five to twelve) that change with the season and feature a small-animal farm tour and
pony rides available 365 days/year. Mean-
while, you can experience the 31,000-square-
foot spa facility—featuring a full complement
of deluxe services such as hydrotherapy,
massage, facials, manicures, beauty, toning,
aromatherapies, and more. Maravilla Dining
Room (dinner guests over age thirteen only)

and Oak Café (all ages, breakfast, lunch, and dinner) and Spa Café (lunch) are open daily, but feasting poolside is our favorite. Be sure to call for special family packages and rates. A destination resort not to be missed! $$$$

For More Information

Ojai Valley Chamber of Commerce. 201 South Signal Street, 93023; (805) 646-8126; www.ojaichamber.org.

Santa Paula and Fillmore

Exiting US 101 onto Highway 126 leads you through Heritage Valley citrus groves and ranches to the pretty villages of Santa Paula and Fillmore. The **Santa Paula Airport** at Santa Maria and Eighth Streets has an extensive collection of privately owned antique, classic, and homebuilt aircraft. Call the chamber of commerce for a current schedule of tours and air shows or visit www.discoversantapaula.com.

California Oil Museum of Santa Paula

1001 East Main Street; (805) 933-0076; www.oilmuseum.net. Open Wednesday through Sunday; closed holidays. $

Thinking about a career in oil or gas? The museum depicts the history of oil exploration in California through relics, photos, computer games, and videos.

Fillmore & Western Railway

Central Park Plaza, downtown Fillmore. Will Call/Ticket Office is the Red Ticket Caboose, located next to Fillmore City Hall, 250 Central Ave; (805) 524-2546 or (800) 773-TRAIN; www .fwry.com. Runs Saturday and Sunday, but not all major holidays. Times change seasonally. $$$

This antique train offers one-hour scenic sightseeing trips between Fillmore and Santa Paula. Vintage cars include a 1920s Pullman and restored dining, sleeper, and parlor carriages. Train workers dress in period costume. Theme parties and dinners are popular, especially the Pumpkinliner and Christmas tree trains. Call for a current schedule and fares.

For More Information

Santa Paula Chamber of Commerce. Santa Barbara at Tenth Street, 93060; (805) 525-5561; www.santapaulachamber.com.

Fillmore Chamber of Commerce. 275 Central Avenue, 93015; (805) 524-0351; www .fillmorechamber.com.

Heritage Valley Tourism Bureau. 270 Central Avenue, Fillmore, 93015; (805) 524-7500; www.heritagevalley.net.

Oxnard

What could you possibly find to do, see, or enjoy in a place with the funny name of Oxnard? Plenty of affordable family fun! The town got its name from entrepreneur Henry T. Oxnard, a visionary who foresaw that the fertile plains just north of the Conejo Hills would be an excellent place to raise sugar beets. When the day came in 1903 to register the town's name with the clerk in the state capital of Sacramento, Henry had a bad phone connection and settled for his surname. Sweet history aside, Oxnard has grown into a culturally and economically diverse community, with business parks, 7 miles of sandy beaches, and a fine marina, just 60 miles north of Los Angeles. Hailed as "California's Strawberry Coast," Oxnard boasts fields of fresh fruit, roadside farm stands you should not avoid, and the nationally recognized California Strawberry Festival held the third weekend in May. In late July, strawberries make way for spicy foods and sizzling entertainment at the Oxnard Salsa Festival celebrating the area's Latino culture.

Heritage Square

Downtown at 715 South A Street; (805) 483-7960. **Free.** Open daily; guided tours Saturday, 10:00 a.m. to 2:00 p.m.

The square reflects the area's past century, with its faithful restorations of a late-1800s church, water tower, pump house, and eleven vintage homes. The buildings were moved from various parts of Oxnard to this single block combined with fresh twenty-first century energy. Summer Friday Night Concerts delight audiences of all ages. It's also home to the Petit Playhouse and Oxnard's award-winning Elite Theatre Company as well as the nearby historic Woolworth Building, recently restored with a small museum, cafes, retail shops, and offices.

Gull Wings Children's Museum (ages 2 to 12)

418 West Fourth Street, downtown, a bit off the beaten path in the old USO Hall; (805) 483-3005; www.gullwings.org. Open Tuesday through Saturday from 10:00 a.m. to 5:00 p.m. $

Indoor sports abound at this innovative museum, from a variety of hands-on exhibits to a medical room with cutaway models to a simulated campground and farmers' market.

Carnegie Cultural Arts Center

424 South C Street; (805) 385-8157; www.vcnet.com/carnart. Open Thursday through Saturday 10:00 a.m. to 5:00 p.m. and Sunday 1:00 to 5:00 p.m. $

A dozen art galleries are scattered about like candy waiting to be unwrapped for the arty family unit. **Carnegie Art Museum** is housed in an imposing, two-story structure built in 1906 as a library. The museum's permanent collection focuses on twentieth-century California painters. Ever-changing exhibits highlight photography, sculpture, oils, watercolors, and some humorous displays. Across the street is **Centennial Plaza,** with a fourteen-screen first-run movie theater, specialty restaurants, and shops, plus, nearby for the adults, Herzog Wine Cellars (the nation's largest kosher winery/restaurant/gift shop; 3201 Camino Del Sol; 805-983-1560; www.herzogwinecellars.com).

Channel Islands Harbor & Visitor Center

2741 South Victoria Avenue, Suite F; (805) 985-4852; www.channelislandsharbor.org.

Fisherman's Wharf, Harbor Landing, and the Marine Emporium Landing (www.marine emporiumlanding.com) have shopping, fine dining, and plenty of sailing and fishing options as well. Twenty-six hundred working and pleasure craft call this bustling port home. There are plenty of parks, a swimming beach, and the Maritime Museum. Throughout the year various events are held including the Celebration of the Whales, visits by the Tall Ships, Fireworks by the Sea on July Fourth, the Ventura County Boat Show, Ventura Vintage Rods Harbor Run Classic Car Show, and the annual Holiday Parade of Lights. Fresh fruits and vegetables plus arts and crafts are at the Harbor's Farmer's Market held at the Marine Emporium Landing from 10:00 a.m. to 2:00 p.m. every Sunday to create your perfect harborside picnic. The Channel Islands Water Taxi, with its painted-on smiling face, is the best way to see the seafront. Call (805) 985-4677 for current schedule and fares.

Ventura County Maritime Museum

2731 South Victoria Avenue, just past Channel Islands Boulevard; (805) 984-6260. Open daily 11:00 a.m. to 5:00 p.m. Closed major holidays. Free.

You and your mates will find a collection of ship models, made with materials ranging from bone to wood to metals, that reflect maritime history from ancient to modern times. Changing exhibits deal with maritime commerce, art, Channel Islands history, whaling, and shipwrecks.

Murphy Classic Auto Musuem

2230 Statham Boulevard; (805) 487-4333; www.murphyautomuseum.com. Open Saturday and Sunday 10:00 a.m. to 4:00 p.m.

This museum's 45,000 square-feet contains a wide variety of vintage, milestone, and special interest vehicles, including a large collection of Packards from 1927–1958. Have fun, fun, fun until daddy takes your T-bird away!

Where to Eat and Stay

Embassy Suites Mandalay Beach Resort & Capistrano's Restaurant, 2101 Mandalay Beach Road on the beach, just off Channel Islands Boulevard; (805) 984-2500; www.mandalaybeach.embsuites.com. All 250 units here are two-room, two-bath suites, just perfect for family accommodations. You will love the deluxe amenities in every suite—fridge, microwave, coffeemaker, two TVs, plus a free cooked-to-order hot breakfast every morning and free beverages and refreshments every evening in the garden courtyard. This resort is right on the sand, with its own beach, and you can rent boogie boards, bicycles, beach chairs, snorkeling gear, or just kick back in the spacious serpentine pool. Dine at ocean-view Capistrano's on fresh seafood and pasta for lunch and dinner or stop by for the award-winning Sunday brunch. $$$$

For More Information

Oxnard Convention & Visitors Bureau. 1000 Town Center Drive, Suite 130, 93036; (805) 385-7545 or (800) 2-OXNARD; www.visitoxnard.com.

California Welcome Center. 1000 Town Center Drive, Suite 120, 93036; (805) 385-7545; www.visitcwc.com/destinations/oxnard/index.php. The newest of dozens of statewide free information centers, make this one your "Central Coast Concierge."

Port Hueneme

In 1941 the U.S. Navy took advantage of the only natural deepwater harbor between Los Angeles and San Francisco to build its Construction Battalion (known as CB or Seabee) in Port Hueneme (pronounced Why-nee-me). Named after a Chumash settlement, Weneme, that occupied the site, this town of 22,000 actually was plotted in 1869, but its prominence today is its military importance as the home base of the U.S. Navy Civil Engineer Corps (CEC). These skilled construction experts have actively fought in military engagements around the world. Plus, it is also the only commercial port for international shipping between Los Angeles and San Francisco, employing more than 4,000 and boasting niche markets of cars and fruit cargoes. Public educational port tours are offered. For schedules, call (805) 488-3677 or visit www.portofhueneme.org.

CEC/Seabee Museum

U.S. Naval Construction Battalion at Ventura Road and Sunkist Avenue, within the gates of the Naval Base Ventura County; www.seabeehf.org. Call ahead to confirm hours and current accessibility to civilians at (805) 982-5165. Children younger than age 16 must be accompanied by an adult. Free.

You can see models of equipment, actual weapons, and uniforms of the Civil Engineer Corps (CEC) and U.S. Navy Seabees.

Simi Valley

The Simi Valley lies on a plateau at around 800 feet above sea level, about twenty minutes inland from Oxnard. Highway 118 (also known as the Ronald Reagan Freeway) bisects the valley, connecting it to Highway 23 with access to US 101 along the coast. With a population of more than 100,000, this area is a popular bedroom community for adjacent Los Angeles County. For more information call the Simi Valley Chamber of Commerce & Visitors Center at (805) 526-3900 or visit www.simichamber.org.

Ronald Reagan Presidential Library & Museum and Air Force One Pavilion

40 Presidential Drive. Five miles inland from US 101 at Simi Valley off Highway 118 (follow the signs); (805) 522-2977 or (800) 410-8354; www.reaganfoundation.org. Open daily 10:00 a.m. to 5:00 p.m.; closed New Year's Day, Thanksgiving, and Christmas. $$$

Located in a Spanish Mission–style building constructed around a courtyard and set on a hilltop, this site provides you with an incredible view of the rolling hills leading down to the Pacific Ocean, including the late president's memorial site and final resting place. Within the library's museum are photographs and memorabilia of President Reagan's entire life (1911–2004), gifts of state he received during his administration, and a replica of the Oval Office. Perhaps most impressive to the younger generation is a piece of the crumbled Berlin Wall. This facility provides all generations with a compelling look at "The Great Communicator" and his legacy as the fortieth U.S. president. The Air Force One Pavilion houses the former president's Boeing 707 airplane, available for boarding and tours, along with exhibits about presidential travel.

Where to Eat and Stay

Grand Vista Hotel, 999 Enchanted Way, exit First Street off Highway 118, only 2 miles from Reagan Library, Simi Valley; (805) 583-2000 or (800) 455-7464; www.grandvistasimi .com. Very spacious 195-room, full-service hotel with two swimming pools (one heated) and the Vistas Restaurant ($$$). Complimentary full breakfast buffet (Monday through Saturday) will get your family off to a good start. $$$$

Thousand Oaks and Westlake Village

The adjoining cities of Thousand Oaks and Westlake Village (joint population estimated 125,000) are located just off US 101 in the southernmost section of Ventura County; halfway between Santa Barbara and Los Angeles and 12 miles inland from the Pacific Ocean. Originally part of a Spanish land grant called Rancho El Conejo (co-nay-ho), today this lovely residential area still has plenty of open rangeland, parks, and things for your family to savor. The Santa Monica Mountains National Recreation Area Visitors Center at 401 West Hillcrest provides guided walks, trail maps, and special events calendars (805-370-2301). For more information contact Thousand Oaks-Westlake Village Regional Chamber of Commerce at (805) 370-0035 or visit www.towlvchamber.org. Conejo Valley Days (www.conejovalleydays.com) is an annual spring festival with parades, a rodeo, and a carnival.

Stagecoach Inn Museum

51 South Ventu Park Road, off US 101, Newberry Park; (805) 498-9441; www.stagecoach museum.org. Open Wednesday through Sunday 1:00 to 4:00 p.m.; closed holidays. $

First opened in 1876, this Monterey-style structure, now faithfully restored, was a major stopover on the stage route between Los Angeles and Santa Barbara. The carriage house, pioneer house, adobe, and ever-changing exhibits will give the kids a great taste of western life in the 1800s.

Thousand Oaks Civic Arts Plaza

2100 East Thousand Oaks Boulevard, Thousand Oaks; (805) 449-2787; www.toaks.org/ theatre/.

Performance art in every shape and form takes place here year-round. This complex has beautiful sculpture, fountains, an 1,800-seat auditorium, a 400-seat theater, and a seven-acre park. Be sure to call for a current schedule of events. There is always something happening here for families.

Where to Eat and Stay

Westlake Village Inn, 31943 Agoura Road, Westlake Village, exit Westlake Boulevard South off US 101; (818) 889-0230 or (800) 535-9978; www.westlakevillageinn.com. This beautifully landscaped, seventeen-acre full-service property has 140 rooms and 18 suites to house your family in luxury. Relax from your travels in the pool/whirlpool spa area or play golf (eighteen holes), practice on the putting green, play tennis (ten courts), or merely stroll around the pretty lake. Package plans and special rates for families abound at this deluxe oasis in the tony community of Westlake. Mediterraneo (818-889-9105; $$$$), overlooking the lake and gardens, serves breakfast, lunch, and dinner daily in an elegant atmosphere, best suited for older children and teens. $$$$

Greater Los Angeles

S ay it like a native—El Aye—and you're already on the road (or freeway, as it were) to unlocking the mystique of one of the most fascinating places on earth. For L.A. is many different things to many millions of ethnically diverse people. For some the city is synonymous with Hollywood and the legends of glamour that go along with it. For others it is the leading metropolis of the Pacific Rim, a cutting-edge capital of culture and industry where culture happens to be a thriving industry unto itself.

For just about everyone L.A. means paradise. Palm trees, beaches, and the best-darned weather in the world. L.A. is the birthplace of the Internet, Barbie, DC-3 planes, the Mazda Miata, and BMX (bicycle motocross). The vaunted laid-back mind-set of Los Angelinos belies their determination to make L.A. as livable as it can possibly be. Creativity, hard work, and frequent trips to the beach help make civic aspirations come alive.

The size of the city provokes inspiration or consternation, depending on your point of view. On a clear day—of which, contrary to popular belief, there are many—one gets a sense of its general proportions. The core of Los Angeles, city and county, is a vast, level basin studded with palm trees and laced with freeways. (By the way, always remember the name and the number of the freeway you are on or looking for, as both locals and road signs use them interchangeably. Thus "the 5" is also the Golden State, "the 101" is also the Hollywood, which turns into the Ventura, etc. Radio traffic reports generally refer to freeways by their names.) The L.A. basin is flanked on all sides by foothills and the San Gabriel Mountains, many of which are snowcapped in winter. In the city itself, the higher up in the hills you go, the bigger the mansions get. These are actually the Santa Monica Mountains, an enchanting urban oasis with miles of hiking trails, scenic drives, and, after a good rain, even a waterfall or two. Of course, L.A. is prime beach country: In the land where *Beach Blanket Bingo* was born, there are 81 miles of county coastline, from Malibu in the north to Long Beach in the south. Oldies radio stations have an unabashed bias for Beach Boys hits. But despite its reputation for sunshine and stars, L.A. County also boasts a vast array of stellar cultural attractions.

Over the years, a patchwork of quite separate cities and towns in the L.A. basin was incorporated into the City of Los Angeles, creating a sprawling urban tapestry of contrasting colors and textures. Even if you're superparents, you won't be able to explore

GREATER LOS ANGELES

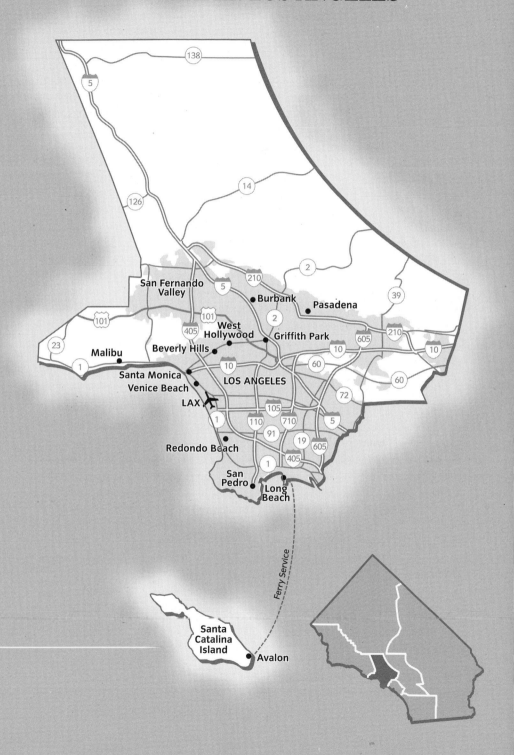

all 4,083 square miles of Los Angeles County, or even the City of Los Angeles's 467 square miles. No matter, because the most interesting things to see and do are relatively concentrated in five major areas: downtown; Hollywood; Westside and Beverly Hills; the valleys—San Fernando (including Burbank), San Gabriel (including Pasadena), and Santa Clarita; and coastal Los Angeles County–from northernmost Malibu heading south through Santa Monica, Venice Beach, Marina del Rey, LAX, Redondo Beach, the port of L.A./San Pedro, and Long Beach. By East Coast standards, things are still very spread out, but that merely adds to the adventure, even for natives. Equipped with a reliable car—an absolute necessity—a full tank of gas, and the stamina to tackle the world's most extensive network of freeways, you and your family are prepared for experiencing a great deal of the excitement this pocket of the world has to offer.

Downtown Los Angeles

Start at the center. That's as good a rule as any for those unfamiliar with the greater L.A. area. Downtown Los Angeles has been the commercial and cultural core of this sprawling city since it was merely a pueblo. Downtown gives the city a focus, and many central district attractions are perennial favorites. You will instantly recognize downtown by its cluster of skyscrapers. There are seven major districts in downtown L.A.: the **Fashion District,** between Broadway and Wall Street, Seventh Street and Pico Boulevard, designer wear at a discount anchored by the historic California Mart and Cooper Building at Ninth and Los Angeles Streets; the **Jewelry District,** on Hill Street between Sixth and Seventh Streets, where you'll find discount diamonds, gold, and bangles galore; the **Toy District,** bordered by Third, Fifth, Los Angeles, and San Pedro Streets, and a mecca for wholesale toys and children's clothing; **Little Tokyo,** between Central Avenue, First, Fourth, and San Pedro Streets; **Chinatown,** between North Broadway and North Hill Streets, for Chinese shopping, dining, galleries, and cultural festivals; the **Theatre District,** on Broadway between Third and Ninth Streets, where you'll find architecturally amazing theaters such as the Orpheum; and **Bunker Hill,** bordered by First, Fifth, Flower, and Olive Streets, and featuring the Music Center, Disney Hall, and performing-arts venues.

The *Los Angeles Times* (ages 10 and older for tours)

202 West First Street, right across the street from City Hall; (213) 237-5757 (tour info); www .latimes.com.

The *Los Angeles Times* is the nation's biggest metro daily newspaper. Kids love to see the newsroom and printing facility, with its mesmerizing, rapid-fire machinery that churns out more than a million newspapers each day. Three **free** tours (Monday through Friday at 9:30 a.m., 11:00 a.m., and 1:30 p.m.) are offered by advance reservation only. The first option is the "editorial" tour of the newsroom, and the second is of the printing plant on Olympic Boulevard. Tour hours vary. Tour participants must be at least ten years old.

Music Center

135 North Grand Avenue; (213) 972-7211; www.musiccenter.org.

Tours are **free** at this world-class performing-arts complex that includes the Dorothy Chandler Pavilion (LA Opera; www.losangelesopera.com), the Mark Taper Forum (Center Theatre Group, www.taperahmason.com), the Ahmanson Theatre, and the Walt Disney Concert Hall. The striking, stainless-steel $247-million Disney Hall (www.disneyhall.com), designed by Frank O. Gehry, premiered in October 2003 as the new home of the LA Philharmonic (www.laphil.com) and LA Master Chorale (www.lamc.org). Get your kids interested in arts and architecture with a self-guided audio tour, available daily for **free.** Call (213) 972-4399 for schedule and times. The hall also features REDCAT (Roy & Edna Disney CalArts Theatre—www.redcatweb.org for an eclectic performance) as well as gardens; a dedicated children's outdoor amphitheater; five restaurants of the Patina Group, under the direction of uber chef/founder Joachim Splichal; Library of Congress/Ira Gershwin Gallery; and an underground parking garage.

Grand Central Market

317 South Broadway; (213) 624-2378; www.grandcentralsquare.com. Open Monday through Sunday 9:00 a.m. to 6:00 p.m.

Opened in 1917, Grand Central Market is L.A.'s oldest and largest food market. Here you can sample not just a cross section of L.A.'s ethnic diversity but also some of the

L.A. LIVE Emerges

A twenty-seven-acre, one-of-a-kind sports, entertainment, hotel, restaurant, and residential complex is emerging adjacent to the Staples Center and the Los Angeles Convention Center downtown at the corner of Olympic Boulevard and Figueroa Street. The 7,100-seat Nokia Theatre Los Angeles and Nokia Plaza opened in October 2007 as the first phase of this new district. The Nokia is now the home of the Primetime Emmy® Awards; as well as live music concerts, comedy shows, family programs, short-run Broadway and community theater productions—2008 saw performances from Willie Nelson, Aretha Franklin, Larry the Cable Guy, Juanes, and The Moody Blues. For current schedules, visit www.nokiatheatrelalive.com. The second phase, scheduled for late 2008–09 emergence, includes Fleming's Prime Steakhouse, Katsuya, the Yard House, Rosa Mexicano, ESPN Zone Sports Bar, and a new Wolfgang Puck eatery, plus a Starbucks and a New Zealand Natural Ice Cream shop as well as Club NOKIA, the legendary Conga Room nightclub, and the Lucky Strike Bowling Center. Currently under construction and slated for 2010 openings are two new luxury hotels: a 124-room boutique Ritz-Carlton with 220 condos and an 876-room JW Marriott. For complete details, go to www.lalive.com.

country's best Mexican and Asian food. Locals come here to bargain for bananas, try authentic burritos, or indulge in raspberry guava smoothies at the all-natural exotic juice bar. You may hear more Spanish than English, but that's half the fun, and *gracias* is really all the Spanish you need to know anywhere in Los Angeles.

Museum of Contemporary Art (MOCA)

250 South Grand Avenue, in California Plaza; (213) 626-6222; www.moca.org. Open Thursday through Monday. 11:00 a.m. to 5:00 p.m.; may vary seasonally. Children under 12 free. $$

Kids will find the often outrageous and totally unexplainable artwork here to be, well, mysterious. Many people do! The eclectic, always changing, never boring collections range from the cute to the controversial. Kids can roam at will through the museum to see an artistic show, including enormous multimedia sculptures, unpredictable creations of various shapes and sizes, and monochromatic paintings of nothing much at all. **Free** on-site children's workshops are offered. And stop by the museum's cafe, Patinette, for an imaginative California-style salad or pasta. After placing your order, you can sit inside or on the patio.

Cathedral of Our Lady of the Angels

555 West Temple Street; (213) 680-5200; www.olacathedral.org.

Whether you're Catholic or not, you can't miss this twenty-first-century architectural wonder that opened in September 2002. Its concrete angularity and lighting is awe-inspiring inside and out. Open daily to the public for self-guided tours. **Free** guided tours Monday through Friday at 1:00 p.m. Gardens, artwork, sculpture, fountains, a cafe, and a gift shop on the plaza surround this home of the Roman Catholic Archdiocese of Los Angeles. Daily masses in English and Spanish as well as other liturgies, special events, concerts, and exhibitions. Call for current schedule and times.

The Museum of Neon Art

136 West Fourth Street; (213) 489-9918; www.neonmona.org. Open Thursday through Saturday noon to 8:00 p.m., Sunday noon to 5:00 p.m. $$, children age and younger free.

Here's the place to gaze upon a glowing collection of electronic-media neon signs. Nostalgia lovers will enjoy the exhibits of the neon signs their grandparents grew up with as well as hundreds of contemporary forms and uses.

Wells Fargo History Center

333 South Grand Avenue, 2 blocks south of the Music Center; (213) 253-7166; www.wells fargohistory.com/museums/museums_la.htm. Open Monday through Friday 9:00 a.m. to 5:00 p.m. Closed on bank holidays. Free.

Chronicles more than a century of western history. Step into an original Concord stagecoach; view a gold nugget, and see a re-created ticket agent's office.

Exposition Park Area

Just south of downtown Los Angeles, bounded by Figueroa Street, Vermont Avenue, Exposition Boulevard, and Martin Luther King Jr. Boulevard; www.nhm.org/expo/expopark.htm.

This has been a civic, cultural, and recreation area since the turn of the twentieth century. Here you'll find the Coliseum, Sports Arena, Natural History Museum, the California Science Center and IMAX Theater, Swimming Stadium, and the California African American Museum, as well as a seven-acre Rose Garden containing 16,000-plus specimens of 190-plus varieties. **Free** and open daily until sunset. Adjacent to the park is the world-famous urban campus of the University of Southern California (USC; www.usc.edu). Across the Harbor Freeway (Highway 110) is the ethnic restaurant, retail, and entertainment complex Mercado La Paloma (The Dove Marketplace), 3655 South Grand Avenue; (213) 748-1963; www.mercadolapaloma.com.

Natural History Museum of L.A. County

900 Exposition Boulevard, Exposition Park; (213) 763-DINO (3466); www.nhm.org. Open Monday through Friday 9:30 a.m. to 5:00 p.m., Saturday and Sunday 10:00 a.m. to 5:00 p.m. Closed major holidays. $$, children younger than 5 **free.**

Kids love the museum because of its lifelike dinosaur replicas, animal habitat dioramas, insect zoo, Native American Cultures exhibit, plus the Halls of Birds, Gems & Minerals, and Marine Life. The Discovery Center is awesomely interactive. Grab a bite at the newly reopened Café. Well worth your time!

The California Science Center & IMAX Theater

700 State Drive, west of the 110 freeway; (213) 744-2019; www.californiasciencecenter.org. Open 10:00 a.m. to 5:00 p.m. daily. Closed Thanksgiving, New Year's Day, and Christmas. **Free.**

Popular for its fun, innovative, and interactive exhibits, including the Air and Space Gallery with NASA capsules and a real jet fighter plane. The Explore Store is enlightening shopping. For current IMAX production schedule and admission fees, call (213) 744-2019. Attractions include Creative World, World of Life, and Science Court, or take a ride on the high-wire bicycle. Visit often to explore changing exhibits like FADE: the dark side of light.

California African American Museum

600 State Drive; (213) 744-7432; www.caamuseum.org. Open Tuesday through Saturday from 10:00 a.m. to 5:00 p.m. and Sunday from 11:00 a.m. to 5:00 p.m. **Free.**

This 44,000-square-foot facility includes three full-size exhibition galleries, a theater gallery, Sculpture Court, a conference center/special events room, and an archive and research library. History, culture, and art are featured in ongoing and special exhibits.

Los Angeles Memorial Coliseum and Sports Arena

3911 South Figueroa Street; (213) 748-6136 or (213) 747-7111; www.lacoliseum.com.

First opened in 1923 and refurbished extensively in the 1990s, this 92,516-seat stadium hosted the 1932 and 1984 Olympics, two Super Bowls, and NFL football teams, and it is currently home to the USC Trojan football team. On March 29, 2008, the Los Angeles Dodgers drew 115,300 people here for an historic exhibition game versus the Boston Red Sox (Dodgers lost 7–4). The total eclipsed the long-standing Guinness World Record for the largest crowd ever to attend a baseball game. The adjacent indoor Sports Arena opened in 1959 and hosts an incredible variety of events and concerts. Call for schedules.

Little Tokyo

Between Central Avenue, First, Fourth, and San Pedro Streets.

This is the social, cultural, and economic center of Southern California's Japanese-American community. The Kyoto Grand Hotel and Gardens, the Japanese American Cultural and Community Center, and the Japanese American National Museum (www.janm.org) are here, along with great ethnic restaurants and shops for your family to explore—Village Plaza, Little Tokyo Plaza, and Weller Court Shopping Center—with no passport required.

Chinatown

Generally bordered by North Broadway and North Hill Streets and Cesar Chavez Avenue (near Union Station).

Chinese shops and restaurants line the "Street of the Golden Treasures" or Gin Ling Way. The Chinese Chamber of Commerce coordinates parades, festivals, and other events. Call (213) 617-0396 for information or visit www.lachinesechamber.org.

El Pueblo de Los Angeles Historic Monument/Olvera Street

At the heart of El Pueblo de Los Angeles Historic Park, 125 Paseo de la Plaza; (213) 628-1274; www.olvera-street.com. Open Monday through Saturday 10:00 a.m. to 3:00 p.m. (to 8:00 p.m. in the summer). Shops open 10:00 a.m. to 7:00 p.m.

This is an authentic L.A. experience that is ideal for the family. Kids will love the wide variety of brightly colored piñatas—splendid, reasonably priced souvenirs. Don't ask us how you'll get one on the plane or in your trunk. This forty-four-acre cluster of shops and landmark buildings is the birthplace of Los Angeles. Every day seems to be Cinco de Mayo at El Pueblo, located at the site of a Spanish farming village founded in 1781. Kids and adults alike may be surprised to learn Los Angeles was actually a Mexican city from 1835 (when Spain ceded it to Mexico) until 1847, when it became American. Nowhere in the city is the proud Spanish heritage kept alive to the extent it is here.

The effect is like making a detour to Mexico without a passport. More than twenty historic buildings line the colorful streets of El Pueblo. One is the Avila Adobe, built in 1818, today the oldest house still standing in Los Angeles. At the center of El Pueblo is La Placita (the Plaza), where the rich Spanish influence is visible in art and architecture. Kids love the

Spectator **Sports**

There is a sport for all seasons in greater L.A., so if your family likes to watch professional sports action, here's where to go.

Auto Racing. NHRA drag racing takes place at Pomona Raceway (www .pomonaraceway.com) at the L.A. County Fairplex (800-884-6472). NASCAR, CART, Grand American Road Racing Association, IRL, and US Superbike races run at Auto Club Speedway (www.californiaspeedway.com) in Fontana (800-944-7223). Stock cars, midgets legends, and trucks hit the track at Toyota Speedway at Irwindale (626-358-1100; www.toyotaspeedwayatirwindale.com).

Baseball. Head downtown for Chavez Ravine and Dodger Stadium, 1000 Elysian Park Avenue (866-DODGERS; www.dodgers.com), home of the MLB National League Los Angeles Dodgers.

Basketball. The NBA Los Angeles Lakers (www.lakers.com), the NBA Los Angeles Clippers (213-742-7555; www.clippers.com), and the WNBA Los Angeles Sparks (www.wnba.com/sparks) all play round ball at the sparkling Staples Center, 1111 South Figueroa Street (www.staplescenter.com). For ticket information call (213) 742-7340.

Football. The Arena Football League (AFL; 310-788-7744; www.laavengers .com) Los Angeles Avengers take to the turf at Staples Center.

Hockey. The Staples Center ices down and plays host to the NHL's Los Angeles Kings (888-KINGS-LA; www.lakings.com).

Soccer. The MLS Los Angeles Galaxy and Club Deportivo Chivas USA (877-244-8271) take to the field at The Home Depot Center, 18400 Avalon Boulevard, Carson, 90746 (on the campus of Cal State University-Dominguez Hills). For tickets call (877) 342-5299. The Home Depot Center (www .homedepotcenter.com) has a 27,000-seat soccer stadium, 8,000-seat tennis stadium, 10,000-seat track–and-field facility, and a 2,450-seat indoor velodrome. The Center is also home to Major League Lacrosse's (MLL) Los Angeles Riptide; U.S. Soccer Federation (USSF); United States Tennis Association (USTA); an official training site for USA Cycling and USA Track & Field; The David Beckham Academy for youth soccer; Andre Agassi's Safe Passage tennis All Stars; and the nationally recognized Athletes' Performance training center.

Experience L.A. **without a Car!**

Start at historic Union Station, 800 North Alameda Street (213-683-6875). First opened in 1939, it's an architectural gumbo of Spanish Mission, art deco, and Streamline Moderne styles that somehow fit together. The waiting room has marble floors, wood-beamed ceilings more than 50 feet high, and stunning art deco chandeliers. Huge archways lead to patio areas laced with flowering trees—and have been featured in many films, including *The Way We Were*, *Bugsy*, and *Blade Runner*. It has all been scrubbed, polished, and reupholstered, and is once again a pleasure to visit. Union Station welcomes long-distance Amtrak trains (Coast Starlight, Southwest Chief, Sunset Limited, Texas Eagle; 800-USA-RAIL or www.amtrak.com); Pacific Surfliner trains running north to San Luis Obispo and south to San Diego; and Metrolink trains to Ventura, San Bernardino, Orange County, Riverside, and other destinations (www.metrolinktrains.com); plus Los Angeles' Metro subway and light-rail systems (Metro Rail Red, Gold, Blue, Orange, and Green lines; 800-COMMUTE or www.metro.net).The new Metro Day Pass makes it easier than ever—you can ride any Metro bus or rail line all day long for just $5. Buy your Day Pass onboard any Metro Bus or at any Metro Rail station. You'll get all of L.A. for five bucks a day.

Twenty-five-cent DASH shuttle buses (children age four and younger ride for free and seniors 65-plus are 10 cents) are ideal for navigating all the great sites and scenes car-free. DASH Customer Service: (213) 808-2273; www.ladottransit.com/dash/index.html.

old-fashioned candy shops and the sound of mariachi music in the Mexican marketplace. Everyone loves the aroma of Mexican food and the unparalleled sombrero-buying opportunities. Not even Disneyland has atmosphere like this.

Where to Eat

Ciudad, 445 South Figueroa Street, Suite 100; (213) 486-5171; www.ciudad-la.com. As long as you are downtown, make it a point to visit this colorful (yellow!), noisy, and always busy restaurant. It has an exciting Latin-inspired menu for adults and a good one for the kids created by Mary Sue Milliken and Susan Feniger, known around these parts as the Two Hot Tamales. Among the choices para los ninos are el Cubanao Wedges with roasted pork, ham, Swiss cheese, and pickles, served with fries. $$$

The Original Pantry Cafe, 877 South Figueroa Street, downtown Los Angeles; (213) 972-9279; www.pantrycafe.com. This historic institution (since 1924) in Los Angeles is owned by a former mayor of Los Angeles, Richard Riordan. His slogan is "Never closed. Never without a customer!" The restaurant has an incredibly diverse menu of traditional American favorites at exceptional values for L.A.—for example: two hotcakes, one egg, and potatoes with fresh orange juice for $4.75. Cash only—no credit cards. $–$$

Philippe The Original, 1001 North Alameda Street; (213) 628-3781; www .philippes.com. If the kids' taste buds don't blossom over the prospect of a platter of sushi or sopapillas, you might stroll over to Philippe's, the city's best-known place for classic sandwiches since 1908. Arrive early (before noon) to secure one of the roomy booths and dig into a classic Philippe's French Dip sandwich (beef, pork, ham, lamb, or turkey), a heaping portion of coleslaw or potato salad, and a fresh slice of pie for under $10. Remember that there are no hamburgers served here. An added perk: free parking adjacent to the restaurant and across the street from Union Station. Open every day from 6:00 a.m. to 10:00 p.m. $–$$

Where to Stay

Millennium Biltmore Hotel, 506 South Grand Avenue; (213) 624-1011 or (800) 245-8673; www.thebiltmore.com. Host to presidents, kings, and Hollywood celebrities since it opened in 1923, the Biltmore's central location puts you and the kids in easy walking/shuttle distance of all the great downtown attractions. This landmark property has 683 luxurious rooms and suites, a full array of concierge services (super babysitting), health club facilities (love the gilded indoor pool), and five restaurants (including Smeraldi's, which serves breakfast/lunch/dinner daily and has an excellent children's menu). For a real treat, check out the traditional afternoon tea served daily from 2:00 p.m. to 5:00 p.m. in the famed Rendezvous Court. $$$$

For More Information

City of Los Angeles. For civic information and assistance, dial 3-1-1 inside city limits or (866) 4-LACITY in Southern California, and visit this special City Web site for kids' activities: http://kids.lacity.org.

L.A. Inc.—The Los Angeles Convention and Visitors Bureau/Visitor Center. 685 Figueroa Street, 90071; (213) 689-8822; www .discoverLosAngeles.com.

Flyaway Bus Service

So you're flying into LAX (Los Angeles International Airport)—and don't want to rent a car (now or ever)—or just need to get into downtown, the Westside, or the San Fernando Valley cheaply and without a hassle? Check out the Flyaway Bus—comfortable, large motor coaches running 24/7 (usually every thirty minutes) to/from LAX to downtown's Union Station, Van Nuys in the San Fernando Valley, and Westwood/UCLA. In 2008 adult fares one way were $4, children two to twelve were $2, children under age two are free. It's a super value, especially coming into Union Station—where you can connect to so many other alternative transportation options. For LAX Flyaway locations, schedules, service hours, parking, passenger drop-off/pick-up, and driving directions, dial (866) 435-9529 or visit www.lawa.org/lax/LAXflyAway.cfm.

Hollywood

Movie stars, glamour, palm tree–lined streets, and excitement in the air—hooray for Hollywood! If downtown is the city's historic center, Hollywood is its heart. For millions around the world, Hollywood is Los Angeles, an illusion promoted by movie studios that remains very much alive in these quarters. Although the "Golden Age" of Hollywood is long gone, the 50-foot-high HOLLYWOOD sign still proclaims it to be the entertainment capital of the world. With the exception of the beaches, Hollywood is probably where your kids will have the most fun in Los Angeles. For that reason we suggest you spend at least two full days here.

Hollywood & Highland Entertainment Complex

6801 Hollywood Boulevard, corner of Hollywood Boulevard and Highland Avenue; (323) 817-8220 or visitor's center: (323) 467-6412; www.hollywoodandhighland.com.

Located in the thumping heart of Hollywood, this enormous complex is a must-see that's sure to please everyone in your family somehow! Opened in 2001 and hosting more than fifteen million visitors annually, the center features over sixty top retailers, nine of L.A.'s finest restaurants, two popular nightclubs, and Lucky Strike Lanes—and the world-famous Kodak Theatre, home of the Academy Awards® ceremonies as well as other notable awards shows, concerts, and events. The on-site Renaissance Hollywood Hotel features 640 sumptuously appointed rooms, including thirty-three luxury suites and an elegant, Mid-Century Modern decor.

Kodak Theatre

6801 Hollywood Boulevard, anchor of the Hollywood & Highland Entertainment Complex; (323) 308-6300 or (323) 308-6363 (box office and guided-tour information); www.kodak theatre.com. Daily thirty-minute guided tours from 10:30 a.m. to 2:30 p.m. (subject to change depending on events scheduled). $$$. Be sure to call for tickets in advance since tours fill quickly, with only twenty people allowed per group. Children under 12 must be accompanied by an adult/guardian.

Since opening in November 2001, the theater has hosted a range of prestigious artists and events, including the Academy Awards Ceremonies, Celine Dion, Prince, Elvis

Save Big Bucks with Hollywood CityPass

CityPass is the best way to enjoy Hollywood at one low price (up to 50 percent savings off tickets purchased separately). With CityPass, you get to choose four admission tickets to famous attractions, including Hollywood Wax Museum, Starline Tours of Hollywood, Red Line tours, and your choice of Kodak Theatre Guided Tour or the Hollywood Museum in the Historic Max Factor Building. CityPass is good for nine days from first day of use. Visit www.citypass.com or call (888) 330-5008.

Costello, Barry Manilow, American Ballet Theatre, ESPY Awards, and even the *American Idol* finals. Be sure you don't miss this chance to step behind the velvet rope and personally experience the glamour of the permanent home of the Oscar ceremonies. During your tour, you'll see an Oscar statuette, visit the exclusive George Eastman VIP Room (where stars party), view twenty-six Academy Awards images, learn where this year's Oscar nominees sat (and maybe sit there, too), and gain an insider's view of behind-the-scenes production from friendly, knowledgeable actor/tour guides.

Walk of Fame

Hollywood Boulevard from Gower Street to La Brea Avenue and along Vine Street from Yucca to Sunset Boulevard.

In Hollywood even the sidewalks have stories to tell. This is most visibly apparent on the Walk of Fame. There is no admission charge to stroll along sidewalks with more than 2,000 terrazzo-and-brass stars etched into them. Some stars' famous sidewalk addresses are: 1644 Hollywood Boulevard (Marilyn Monroe), 1719 Vine Street (James Dean), 1750 Vine Street (John Lennon), and 6777 Hollywood Boulevard (Elvis Presley).

El Capitan Theatre

6838 Hollywood Boulevard; (323) 468-8262; www.elcapitantickets.com.

Disney and Pacific Theaters restored this historic theater in 1989, now on the National Register of Historic Places. Originally opened in 1926, it is now an exclusive first-run theater for Walt Disney Pictures and hosts live stage shows, world premieres, and other special events that have helped restore showmanship to Hollywood Boulevard. The restored 4/37 Wurlitzer pipe organ—known as the "Mightiest of the Mighty Wurlitzers"—is just one of the jewels of this architectural masterpiece. It is across the street from Mann's Chinese Theatre.

Mann's Chinese Theatre

6925 Hollywood Boulevard; (323) 461-3331; www.manntheatres.com/chinese. $$

Hollywood doesn't get any more Hollywood than at the unofficial emperor of Hollywood Boulevard. Both the young and young-at-heart revel at the sight of what looks like the entrance to a Chinese imperial palace. But the main attractions here are in the theater's forecourt, where the handprints, footprints, and signatures of Hollywood celebrities dating from 1927 are quite literally cast in stone. "Gee, Mom, did Rita Hayworth really have such tiny feet?" The proof is in the pavement. VIP Backstage Tours are offered by reservation only seven days a week (323-463-9576).

On busy street corners along Hollywood Boulevard and particularly in front of Mann's Chinese Theatre, you might spot tanned young men and women wearing sun visors and holding clipboards. If they don't approach you, make a point of approaching them: They have passes for movie previews at area studios, and sometimes you are paid to see them: It's a way the studios get audience feedback before films are released and a way for you to learn about an important, if little known, aspect of the entertainment industry.

Hollywood Celeb Homes

If you want a guided tour past Hollywood celeb homes, here are some choices:

- **Hollywood Tours,** 7095 Hollywood Boulevard #705; (800) 789-9575; www .hollywoodtours.us. Air-conditioned minivans, open-air trolley, or double-decker buses. Dozens of itineraries including options to see the Hollywood sign up close.

- **Starline Tours,** (323) 463-3333 or (800) 959-3131; www.starlinetours.com. Has two-hour tours in Beverly Hills and Bel Air. The company promises forty celebrity homes and offers excellent value on more than twenty other Hollywood/L.A. itineraries—in business with their infamous double-decker red buses since 1935 (other buses and vans and limos, too!).

Hollywood Guinness World Records Museum

6764 Hollywood Boulevard; (323) 463-6433; www.guinnessattractions.com. Open daily 10:00 a.m. to midnight. $$

The museum showcases offbeat testimonials to a wide variety of facts, feats, and incredible achievements. It is located in Hollywood's first movie house, the Hollywood, which is now a National Historic Landmark. Hands-on exhibits include technology, space adventures, and natural phenomena.

Hollywood Wax Museum

6767 Hollywood Boulevard; (323) 462-8860; www.hollywoodwax.com. Open daily from 10:00 a.m. to midnight. $$

The wax museum has 220 life-size renditions of celebrated film stars, political leaders, and sports greats. Park at the rear of the building and visit all the museums at one stop. For a discount, purchase one ticket for both the wax museum and the Guinness museum.

Ripley's Believe It or Not! Odditorium (ages 5 and up)

6780 Hollywood Boulevard; (323) 466-6335; www.ripleys.com. Open 10:00 a.m. to 10:00 p.m. daily, later on weekends, summer. $$

No problem finding the place; there's a giant Tyrannosaurus rex poking his mighty head and substantial torso out of the rooftop. The Odditorium claims to have the world's most outstanding collection of the bizarre and unusual, and it probably does. Kids love the innovative special effects, which actually help them learn some quirky facts of history they'd really have to dig for in schoolbooks.

Capitol Records

1750 North Vine Street; http://capitolrecords.com.

This landmark building is one of Hollywood's most recognized icons. The light on its rooftop spire flashes "Hollywood" in Morse code. In the lobby gold albums of many Capitol recording artists, such as John Lennon and Garth Brooks, are displayed.

Hollywood Toys and Costumes

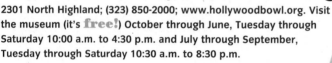

6600 Hollywood Boulevard; (323) 464-4444; www.hollywoodtoys.com. Open daily.

Here's where kids can find that monster mask they won't find back home or that conversation-starter costume perfect for next Halloween. There are tiaras in all shapes and sizes and novelties too numerous to describe. In town since 1950, this has to be the biggest supermarket of Hollywood-inspired memorabilia and trinkets.

Hollywood Bowl and Hollywood Bowl Museum

2301 North Highland; (323) 850-2000; www.hollywoodbowl.org. Visit the museum (it's **free!**) October through June, Tuesday through Saturday 10:00 a.m. to 4:30 p.m. and July through September, Tuesday through Saturday 10:30 a.m. to 8:30 p.m.

The summer home of the Los Angeles Philharmonic Orchestra, the bowl is a terrific place to take in a concert. *Pollstar* magazine's Best Major Outdoor Venue (three years in a row), the Hollywood Bowl is the largest natural outdoor amphitheater in the United States. Pack a picnic to get the most out of an outdoor performance at this gleaming Los Angeles landmark.

Samuel French Inc. Bookstore

7623 Sunset Boulevard; (323) 876-0570; www.samuelfrench.com. Open Monday through Friday 10:00 a.m. to 6:00 p.m., Saturday 10:00 a.m. to 5:00 p.m.

This is the ultimate bookstore for entertainment-industry-related publications. It has a wide selection of books for kids—along with an extensive selection of works on the theater, movies, television, and the other performing arts. This is your chance to add a serious and educational dimension to the pomp and puffery purveyed by Hollywood's ubiquitous PR spin doctors.

Hollywood's Rock Walk of Fame

7425 West Sunset Boulevard, in the outer lobby of Hollywood's Guitar Center; (323) 874-1060; www.rockwalk.com. Open Monday through Friday 10:00 a.m. to 9:00 p.m., Saturday 10:00 a.m. to 6:00 p.m., and Sunday 11:00 a.m. to 6:00 p.m. **Free.**

Inductees include Black Sabbath, Elvis Presley, Johnny Cash, Bo Diddley, the Doobie Brothers, Jimi Hendrix, and Eddie Van Halen, just to name a few.

Where to Eat

Musso & Frank Grill, 6667 Hollywood Boulevard; (323) 467-5123. Open 11:00 a.m. to 11:00 p.m.; closed Sunday and Monday. A Hollywood institution where movers and shakers have "done deals" over classic flannel cakes, steaks, and Thursday-only chicken potpies since 1919. Whether you go for the atmosphere or the food, you simply must go to say you've been! For kicks, request table number 1 in the west room, which was Charlie Chaplin's regular place. $$

Pink's, 709 North La Brea Avenue (corner of Melrose and La Brea); (323) 931-4223; www.pinkshollywood.com. Open daily 9:30 a.m. to 2:00 a.m. (sometimes later).You can't miss the line that has wrapped around this pink building since it opened in 1939, where they serve probably the best chilidog in L.A. Chilidogs, chili fries, chiliburgers, turkey dogs, burrito dogs—every imaginable presentation of the wiener can be found here. No matter what time of day or night, you will find yourself standing in line with tourists, corporate climbers, and celebrities. Cash only. $

For More Information

Hollywood Chamber of Commerce. 7018 Hollywood Boulevard, 90028; (213) 469-8311; www.hollywoodchamber.net.

The Hollywood Visitor Information Center. 6801 Hollywood Boulevard, 90028; (323) 467-6412; www.discoverlosangeles.com. Open Monday through Friday 8:30 a.m. to 5:00 p.m. Pick up the free handy pocket guides on dining, shopping, and entertainment in Los Angeles County.

Griffith Park

Located just west of the Golden State Freeway (Interstate 5), roughly between Los Feliz Boulevard on the south and the Ventura Freeway (Highway 134) on the north; Open to the public from 6:00 a.m. to 10:00 p.m. daily. Bridle trails, hiking paths, and mountain roads are closed at sunset. Attractions/activities include Autry National Center, bicycle rentals, Greek Theatre, merry-go-round, Griffith Observatory, L.A. Equestrian Center, L.A. Live Steamers Railroad Museum, L.A. Zoo, pony rides, and Travel Town. www.lacity.org/rap/dos/parks/griffithPK.

Los Angeles Zoo

Griffith Park, Golden State Freeway at Ventura Freeway, downtown; (323) 644-6400; www.lazoo.org. Open daily from 10:00 a.m. to 5:00 p.m. $$

Let your kids run wild in this 120-acre parklike setting where 1,200-plus mammals, birds, and reptiles from around the world now reside. Don't miss the Children's Discovery Center and Winnick Family Children's Zoo, Chimpanzees of Mahale Mountain, and World of Birds, all accessible via a tram around the perimeter. In 2008 the new $19 million habitat for six African lowland gorillas, Campo Gorilla Reserve, provides the gorillas with an environment that closely resembles their native West African homeland. There are seven cafes located throughout the zoo that feature a wide variety of meals suitable for almost everyone, so nobody can get too hungry when you see the animals being fed!

Autry National Center

4700 Western Heritage Way; (323) 667-2000; www.autry-museum.org. Open Tuesday through Sunday 10:00 a.m. to 5:00 p.m. $$.

The Autry National Center celebrates the American West through three important institutions: the Museum of the American West, the Southwest Museum of the American Indian, and the Institute for the Study of the American West. The Autry was established in 2003 following the merger of the Southwest Museum, the Women of the West Museum, and the Museum of the American West (formerly the Autry Museum of Western Heritage that opened in 1988). Thousands of Old West artifacts and hands-on exhibits are here, including many designed with children in mind. Special exhibits explore America's western heritage, including Native American culture, early tourism, and weaving. Check out the Golden Spur Café for great grub.

Travel Town

Griffith Park, 5200 Zoo Drive; (323) 662-5874. Open weekdays 10:00 a.m. to 4:00 p.m., weekends 10:00 a.m. to 5:00 p.m. Free admission. Rides $; donations appreciated.

Since 1952, kids have loved this outdoor transportation museum with steam locomotives to scramble over and Live Steamers, a large collection of miniature trains.

Universal City/North Hollywood

North of downtown Los Angeles, and known as "Gateway to the San Fernando Valley," this dynamic area has a population of more than 210,000 and is headquarters to entertainment industry giants such as NBC Universal Studios Hollywood, The Walt Disney Company, Warner Brothers, DreamWorks SKG, Academy of Television Arts & Sciences, Nickelodeon Animation Studios, and CBS Studio Center. For more info, contact the Universal City/North Hollywood Chamber of Commerce at (818) 508-5155 or www.noho.org. For our families, it's home to a not-to-be-missed movie-based theme park and incredible entertainment.

Universal Studios Hollywood

100 Universal City Plaza (Universal Center Drive or Lankershim Boulevard from the 101 Hollywood Freeway); (818) 622-3801 or (800) UNIVERSAL; www.UniversalStudiosHollywood .com. Open daily 9:00 a.m. to 6:00 p.m.; expanded hours for summer and holidays. $$$$

Ask about special values and packages including the new "All You Can Eat Pass." Universal Studios is an integral part of L.A.'s history. And while another version is now in Florida, for Southern Californians there is but one Universal Studios. Three recent additions include the first-ever mega-attraction based on the blockbuster TV series, The Simpsons Ride; Universal's World of Entertainment, never-before-seen props, costumes, wardrobe, and artifacts with special effects displays from the latest to the earliest films amassed from Universal Pictures film library; and the Adventures of Curious George, a 30,000-square-foot interactive play zone featuring "Curious George Flies to Space," (where you can get drenched as

Filmed before a **Live Studio Audience**

Hollywood is the place to see the television industry in action. Live studio audiences are always needed, and tickets are free. Don't ever pay for TV taping tickets. They are given out free, always by production companies and studio representatives. Remember: little taping is done during the summer months because shows are on hiatus. There are age requirements for attending most TV show tapings. Most sitcom tapings require audience members to be at least age eighteen, but game shows and children's variety shows sometimes set the age requirement at age twelve. This rule is strictly enforced, so be sure to check in advance. Not all shows use audiences (e.g., most soaps). The more popular the show, the harder it is to get tickets. Comedies shoot a few times a month, usually from September to March. Besides having to show up early to get through security, most tapings last three to six hours, so allow yourself plenty of extra time. Soundstages generally have bleacher-type seating, and it's sometimes hard to see the action even though you're right in front of the stage, so most stages have video monitors that show what's going on. Most scenes are shot several times, and this can get boring for kids (and adults, too). To help pass the down times between shooting, a comic often entertains the audience. Soundstages are notoriously cold, so bring a sweater—the lights only heat up the actors. Here are some of the best sources for tickets.

Audiences Unlimited, Inc. (www.tvtickets.com). More than forty sitcom, pilot, and talk-show tickets available. Tickets are offered online starting approximately thirty days prior to show date. This is an excellent Web site and a good source of information about what to expect, along with maps on how to reach the studios.

www.tvtix.com. This easy-to-navigate Web site offers tickets to a wide variety of game shows, talk shows, specials, and sitcoms. You can search by date and/or the show you want to see—and print out your ticket selection right away.

Paramount Pictures (5555 Melrose Avenue, Hollywood, 90038; 323-956-1777; www.paramountstudios.com). This is the only remaining "big name" studio lot still located and operating in Hollywood. If you're up for a non–theme park and want an inside, historic look at a real working studio, Paramount is THE place for a very special experience. Two-hour guided backlot tours are given Monday through Friday for ages twelve and up by advance reservations only. $$$$. To arrange tickets for TV shows taping at Paramount, contact Audiences Unlimited (see above listing).

you wait in the blast-off zone but thankfully, there is a dry zone), "Curious George Goes to the Jungle," and "Curious George Visits the Zoo." Also be sure to check out the cutting-edge roller-coaster Revenge of the Mummy—the Ride, Shrek 4-D, House of Horrors, Backdraft, and Jurassic Park®—The Ride (you will get soaked!).

But it's the classics that make Universal a genuine blast for both kids and adults. The staple is the forty-five-minute tram ride (catch one every five to ten minutes), during which Hollywood history and special effects cast their magical spell. You're whisked past the set from Steven Spielberg's *War of the Worlds, Jurassic Park,* and the Norman Bates House (from the movie *Psycho*), over a collapsing bridge, into a Mexican village that falls prey to a flash flood, and through a Red Sea that parts just for you. Then there's a landslide and a simulated fishing village where the naughty shark from the movie *Jaws* surfaces with a vengeance. The tram ride also takes visitors past enormous studio backlots , reminding you that this is the world's biggest film and television studio. Something is almost always in production, and chances are you'll catch a bit of the action—scenes from shows such as *CSI* and Jennifer Love Hewitt's *Ghost Whisperer* are being filmed here regularly.

Universal CityWalk Hollywood

1000 Universal Center Drive, Universal City; (818) 622-4455; www.citywalkhollywood.com. Open Sunday through Thursday 11:00 a.m. to 9:00 p.m., Friday and Saturday 11:00 a.m. to midnight. Free admission.

An eclectic, electric outdoor pedestrian promenade with an atmosphere made to resemble a studio backlot. There are actually two streets lined with palms and joined by a central courtyard area with fountains. But all is not so sedate: A mammoth King Kong clings to the facade of one building. Get the picture? There are more than thirty retail shops and dozens of restaurants here, including B.B. King's Blues Club and a Hard Rock Cafe. Plus, CityWalk Hollywood boasts nineteen movie theaters all with surround-sound, plush stadium-style seating, and IMAX. For show times, visit www.CityWalkHollywood.com/cinemas or call (818) 508-0711. CityWalk also connects to the **Gibson Amphitheatre,** an outstanding concert and performance venue with no seat more than 150 feet from the stage. Visit www.citywalkhollywood.com/concerts.php or call (818) 622-4440 for event schedules. The newest adventure located at CityWalk is **iFLY Hollywood** (818-985-4359; www.iFLYHollywood.com), where you can actually experience human flight with this unique indoor skydiving adventure in a vertical wind tunnel. No experience is necessary, but you must be age three or older to ride. Open daily, call for times, flight instructions and complete details on this adrenaline-charged adventure. $$$$

Where to Stay

Sheraton Universal, 333 Universal Hollywood Drive, Universal City; (818) 980-1212 or reservations (800) 325-3535; www.sheraton .com/Universal. A high-rise landmark since 1969 (with a $30 million renovation in 2008). Enjoy 436 rooms and suites with tremendous views. Excellent packages for families. You'll appreciate the free shuttle service to Universal Studios. $$$$

Universal Studios Hollywood
VIP Experience Tour

For the ultimate insider's perspective on the world's largest movie and television studio as well as genuine hospitality and personal special treatment, treat yourself and your family to the "VIP Experience" tour. You will have your own private tour escort (with encyclopedic knowledge) for the entire day (only fifteen people per group) and enjoy front-of-the-line admission and the best views and seating at all attractions and rides. Plus your tour escort will take you deep into the "Back Lot," where you'll have special access to soundstages—many in use by your favorite stars. Best of all, instead of the huge tram you'll have a private trolley bus that can stop and let you out to take pictures. Feel like a movie star yourself. It's expensive but worth the truly VIP experience! For more information call (800) UNIVERSAL, option 3.

Sportsmen's Lodge Hotel, 12825 Ventura Boulevard, Studio City; (818) 769-4700 or (800) 821-8511; www.slhotel.com. A Valley classic since 1962, the "Lodge" has 200 recently renovated country-style rooms, Olympic-size heated outdoor pool with large lounge deck, Patio Café for reasonably priced breakfast, lunch, and dinner daily; plus **free** Universal Studios shuttle and discount tickets for guests. $$$

West Hollywood

Pop-culture types regard West Hollywood (incorporated in 1984), while small by Los Angeles standards (just 1.9 square miles), as the creative center of L.A. This enclave, bordered by Beverly Hills on the west, is a trendy one that will appeal to older, more "cool-conscious" kids. Unpredictable and irreverent, West Hollywood-ites work and play by their own rules (of which there aren't many). Situated at the base of the Hollywood Hills, "WeHo" is known as the place where the stars come out to play. Few drives in Los Angeles are as exhilarating as **Sunset Boulevard.** Originating downtown, Sunset winds up at the Pacific Ocean. Zipping along its famous curves in Beverly Hills, you'll see stunning mansions and gorgeous gardens at every turn. But the most famous stretch, hands down, is the **Sunset Strip,** directly after Beverly Hills in West Hollywood. The heart of the action, the 1.2-mile portion between numbers 8221 and 9255 is the mecca of L.A. nightlife. Celebrities are sighted so often here that they hardly raise eyebrows. After cruising Sunset (preferably in a convertible), park your car **free** at number 8600, **Sunset Plaza,** an open-air mall. From here you can see the entire city of L.A. teeming and (if it's nighttime) twinkling below.

Where to Eat

House of Blues, 8430 Sunset Boulevard; (323) 848-5100; www.hob.com/venues/club venues/sunsetstrip/. Take the kids to dinner at the ultimate Sunset hot spot. Great Southern cooking, a wild decor, and daily live blues performances will make for an unforgettable evening. Try the popular Sunday Gospel Brunch. The menu features "eclectic Southern fare" such as barbecue chicken and ribs.

The House of Blues Restaurant is the best compromise if you wish to steer the kids clear of the area's irresponsibly loud and obscenely crowded evening concerts. To enjoy the decor (recycled bottle caps, auto license tags, etc.), take your time. Don't leave without pigging out on a warm apple tart with vanilla ice cream and caramel sauce. Afterwards, work off those calories by simply strolling along the boulevard's trendy boutiques, sidewalk cafes, and record stores—all aglow under a sea of neon lights. $$

Mel's Drive-In, 8585 Sunset Boulevard; (310) 854-7201; www.melsdrive-in.com. Formerly Ben Frank's diner, this location opened in 1997 but still looks like a classic 1950s kitsch-and-neon joint made famous by the movie American Graffiti. Open twenty-four hours, it cannot be beat for burgers, fries, and shakes. A bonus is the fifty-seat outdoor patio, perfect for people-watching and soaking up the sunshine. $

For More Information

West Hollywood Marketing and Visitors Bureau. 8687 Melrose Avenue, Suite M-38, 90069; (310) 289-2525 or (800) 368-6020; www.visitwesthollywood.com.

Westside

In this immense, loosely defined swath of the city, punctuated by estates and eateries, museums and boutiques, trendiness reigns supreme. Here you may quite acceptably judge your neighbors according to where they "do lunch." You're more apt to bump into a celebrity in the Westside than in Hollywood, and if you spend only five minutes driving around tony Beverly Hills, you'll find out why. There is one (perhaps only one) rule in these parts: If you've got it, flaunt it—and preferably in style. And the sheer amount of wealth people have here simply must be seen to be believed.

But not all of the Westside is given over to ostentation and glitz. Here it must be said that, to an Angelino, certain areas of L.A. defy easy geographical classification. One of these is **Melrose Avenue,** which is neither part of the Westside nor quite part of anything else, either.

Melrose Avenue, immortalized by the hit TV series *Melrose Place,* actually begins (or ends, depending on your point of view) in Hollywood. The hippest sections begin at La Brea and branch out toward the west. But the street is as much a state of mind as it is a chunk of asphalt. This is a place with a carnival-like atmosphere, where anything goes. Find a parking spot (keep looking, you'll find one) and simply drift. Whatever boutique, gallery, or cafe you settle into is not as important, though, as the simple act of "doing" Melrose, which affords a close-up look at what makes Los Angeles tick. An hour or two or three here, and you'll begin to understand the triple L.A. creed: creativity, individuality, and sunshine.

Getty Center

1200 Getty Center Drive; (310) 440-7300; www.getty.edu. Open Tuesday through Thursday and Sunday 10:00 a.m. to 6:00 p.m. and Friday and Saturday 10:00 a.m. to 9:00 p.m. Closed Monday and major holidays. Admission is free. Parking is $8. This landmark complex on a dramatic hilltop location commands breathtaking views of Los Angeles, the Santa Monica Mountains, and the Pacific. Its vast collection of art defies imagination. The 110-acre complex, designed by Richard Meier, is designed as a nexus for families and neighbors, as well as scholars and students. It all begins with a tram ride to the summit, where your family will be awed by panoramic views of the L.A. area. The center will fascinate every family member, even the two-year-olds in strollers with microscopic attention spans. At the central plaza, you'll find gardens, terraces, and dramatic architecture and a wonderful cafe.

Start your exploration by viewing the orientation film so you can best decide how to spend the next few hours. There are five two-story pavilions around an open courtyard. Each gallery pavilion has an information room: Stop here to watch an artist carve a block of marble or have your kids handle a piece of wood. These hands-on experiences are accentuated by ongoing films, concerts, and demonstrations. Try to visit on the weekends when family festivals give you and your kids "new ideas about the cultures and people behind the art."

Just to give you a hint of the magnitude of the collection, there are fourteen galleries of French furniture and decorative arts, including four eighteenth-century paneled rooms.

For more Getty art, check out the **Getty Villa** in Malibu, approximately 25 miles west of downtown L.A. (See the Malibu section for more information.)

No tour of the Westside would be complete without visiting Westwood Village, a vibrant neighborhood just west of Beverly Hills bounded by Wilshire Boulevard, the 405 (San Diego Freeway), and the UCLA (University of California, Los Angeles; www.ucla.edu) campus, where you can enjoy visiting the Botanical Garden, the Sculpture Garden, the Hammer Museum—a cutting-edge arts institution—and the Fowler Museum of Cultural History. UCLA's presence imbues Westwood with a youthful air. It is an ideal area for walking around, browsing in record stores, or simply "hanging out" at a cafe or ice-cream parlor. College students aside, it's movies that really make Westwood tick. Movie theaters are everywhere, and these are not your ordinary theaters. Screens are enormous. Seats are plush and tilt back. Popcorn is fresh and usually made with real butter. We're talking cinematic heaven here.

Museum Row

Stretching along the "Miracle Mile" of busy Wilshire Boulevard, "Museum Row" is the home of a singularly fun and educational selection of family-worthy museums.

Page Museum at the La Brea Tar Pits

5801 Wilshire Boulevard; (323) 934-7243; www.tarpits.org. Open Monday through Friday 9:30 a.m. to 5:00 p.m. and Saturday, Sunday, and holidays 10:00 a.m. to 5:00 p.m. $$. Free admission on the first Tuesday of the month.

The La Brea Tar Pits are a black and slightly malodorous lake of ancient goo that trapped thousands of Ice Age creatures. More than 100 tons' worth of their fossilized remains have been extracted from the pits, and new discoveries are always being made. Dozens of saber-toothed tiger and wolf skulls, woolly mammoth skeletons, and other specimens are on display in the 57,000-square-foot museum. This is educational, unadulterated magic for adults and the under-twelve crowd. You might recall the pits erupting in the film *Volcano*. Don't worry, the site is perfectly benign.

Los Angeles County Museum of Art

5905 Wilshire Boulevard; (323) 857-6000; www.lacma.org. Open Monday, Tuesday, and Thursday noon to 8:00 p.m., Friday noon to 9:00 p.m., Saturday and Sunday 11:00 a.m. to 8:00 p.m.; closed Wednesday. $$

The anchor museum for Museum Row, explore a collection with more than 100,000 works of art at LACMA, the largest encyclopedic museum west of Chicago. Experience European masterpieces, cutting-edge contemporary art, an extensive collection of American art from the United States and Latin America, a major Islamic art collection, one of the most comprehensive Korean art collections outside of Korea, and the stunning Pavilion for Japanese art. In February 2008, the Broad Contemporary Art Museum (BCAM) opened here, a $56-million, three-story museum that you start visiting from the top down. Music, film, and educational events happen year-round, and there's a good chance something is happening during your stay. LACMA's "transformation" project is just that, and you don't want to miss it.

Petersen Automotive Museum

6060 Wilshire Boulevard; (323) 930-2277; www.petersen.org. Open Tuesday through Sunday 10:00 a.m. to 6:00 p.m. $$, children five and younger free.

This museum, opened in 1997 and already a landmark by virtue of its striking, futuristic design, celebrates L.A.'s icon, the automobile—its history and role in the development of Southern California. In its 300,000 square feet of exhibition space, you'll find more than 200 cars and motorcycles, plus loads of fascinating automotive memorabilia.

Farmers Market

6333 West Third Street, a few footsteps north of Museum Row; (323) 933-9211; www.farmers marketla.com. Open Monday through Friday 9:00 a.m. to 9:00 p.m., Saturday 9:00 a.m. to 8:00 p.m., and Sunday 10:00 a.m. to 7:00 p.m. Some merchant hours may vary. Free entrance.

This is the Westside's answer to downtown's Grand Central Market, with seventy leased stalls of grocers, restaurants, produce stands, and retail stores thriving since 1934 (still owned and operated by the Gilmore family). Be sure to check out Kip's Toyland, Bennett's Ice Cream (where you can watch them make it), Thee's Continental Pastries (decorates cakes in the window), and more.

The Grove

189 The Grove Drive, adjacent to the Farmers Market at Third and Fairfax, 90036; (888) 315-8883 or (323) 900-8080; www.thegrovela.com. Open Monday through Thursday 10:00 a.m. to 9:00 p.m., Friday and Saturday 10:00 a.m. to 10:00 p.m., and Sunday 11:00 a.m. to 8:00 p.m.

Featuring more than 100 of the finest retail emporiums, cafes, fourteen luxury movie theaters, and anchored by Nordstrom, The Grove is one of L.A.'s most "happening" places to see and be seen. Don't miss the "Dancing Fountain" that shoots thirty-two pulsing water jets to heights of 60 feet every thirty minutes accompanied by hip music in the center courtyard.

American Girl Place Los Angeles

189 The Grove Drive, 90036; (877) 247-5223; www.americangirl.com/stores/location_la.php. Open Monday through Friday 10:00 a.m. to 9:00 p.m., Saturday 9:00 a.m. to 9:00 p.m., and Sunday 9:00 a.m. to 7:00 p.m.

Everything anyone would want, need, or even dream about purchasing or experiencing involving the popular American Girl dolls that first debuted in 1986. The Cafe on the second floor is the place for lunch, afternoon tea, dinner, and parties. Check out the Photo Studio where you can pose for a picture with your fave Girl; but first, head into the Doll Hair Salon or Doll Hospital for personal attention, attend a special show or event in the theater, and of course, shop—for dolls, books, clothing, furniture, and accessories.

Museum of Tolerance

At the Simon Wiesenthal Center. Simon Wiesenthal Plaza, 9786 West Pico Boulevard, between Century City and Beverly Hills; (310) 553-8403; www.wiesenthal.com or www .museumoftolerance.com. Open Monday through Friday 10:00 a.m. to 5:00 p.m., and Sunday 11:00 a.m. to 5:00 p.m. Closed every Saturday, Jewish holidays, January 1, July Fourth, Thanksgiving, and December 25. Some exhibits recommended for kids age twelve and older. Tickets are available for specific times and for specific exhibits. Pre-paid advance reservations are recommended to ensure admittance to the museum. $$

Founded in 1993, and hosting an estimated 350,000 visitors annually, MOT is a one-of-a-kind facility that offers a series of high-tech exhibits dedicated to the promotion of understanding among people from all backgrounds and walks of life. Interactive exhibits chronicle the history of racism in American history and the events and consequences of the Holocaust. The presentations have been crafted with historical precision and much sensitivity. Both children and adults will leave the museum enlightened and moved by history and the dangers of forgetting it.

The Skirball Cultural Center and Museum

2701 North Sepulveda Boulevard; (310) 440-4500; www.skirball.org. Open Tuesday through Friday noon to 5:00 p.m. and Saturday and Sunday 10:00 a.m. to 5:00 p.m. Closed Monday. $$, children younger than two admitted free.

This museum highlights the experiences of American Jews as they transitioned from the Old World to the New World. Do not miss the new Noah's Ark experience—inspired by the ancient flood story, which has parallels in diverse cultures around the world. This one-of-a-kind floor-to-ceiling wooden ark, filled to the rafters with whimsical animals, is where you and your family will play, build, climb, explore, collaborate, and connect more with one another. While visiting the galleries, meet a puppet, create a take-home art project, or hear a story. For lunch, Zeidlers, at the museum entrance, can't be beat, and the gift shop here has an impressive range of books covering the Jewish experience, with an excellent selection of books for children.

Where to Eat

Apple Pan, 10801 West Pico Boulevard; (310) 475-3585. Closed Monday. Here's a diner of sorts that has been feeding hungry Angelinos since the 1940s. The layout is simple: a long, three-sided countertop with a kitchen in the center. Wait for a vacant stool (there are no tables), then move in for the kill: The burgers served here are so divine they have been known to reconvert vegetarians. Many visit for the apple pie (it's the Apple Pan, after all), but the banana cream is also really luscious. $

Eiger Ice Cream, 124 East Barrington Place, off Sunset Boulevard and North Barrington Avenue; (310) 471-6955. Hours vary daily. The decor is minimalist; the ice cream is not. With an18 percent butterfat content, we're talking ice crème de la crème here. Most flavors, including the ever-popular dark chocolate and raspberry combo, taste surprisingly light because of the purity of the ingredients. No wonder Eiger is a favorite snack spot for quality-conscious Westside families. Cash only. $

Beverly Hills

If you continue west on Wilshire Boulevard, you will enter the heart of Beverly Hills. The chief appeal of this city (population 34,000) for many families will be strolling up and down **Rodeo** (row-DAY-oh) **Drive,** a scaled-down version of New York's Fifth Avenue—with palm trees. It's fun to do a little window shopping at the most exclusive boutiques in Los Angeles. This is the center of the Golden Triangle district, framed by Crescent Drive and Wilshire and Little Santa Monica Boulevards, which represents the crème de la crème of Beverly Hills shopping. **Two Rodeo** (www.2rodeo.com), adjacent to Rodeo Drive, is a cobblestoned cache of shops and eateries at the Wilshire Boulevard end that resembles a charming European village.

After the price tags make you wonder who in the world can afford all of this stuff, hop in your car and find out. The gracefully curving palm- and jacaranda-lined streets between

Santa Monica and Sunset Boulevards are home to affluent Mediterranean-style villas and many an elegant English Tudor–style manse. North of Sunset, however, especially in the exclusive **Bel Air** neighborhood farther west on the boulevard, is where the real estate truly boggles the mind.

Beverly Center

8500 Beverly Boulevard; (310) 854-0071; www.beverlycenter.com. Call for hours.

A megamall with 160-plus shops and restaurants (anchored by Macy's and Bloomingdale's) and a thirteen-screen cineplex, where Beverly Boulevard meets La Cienega.

Paley Center for Media

465 North Beverly Drive; (310) 786-1000; www.paleycenter.org. Open Wednesday through Sunday noon to 5:00 p.m.; closed on January 1, July Fourth, Thanksgiving, and Christmas. Free admission. Donations are welcome and suggested.

Previously known as the Museum of Television & Radio, the Paley Center was founded in 1975 by William S. Paley, a pioneering innovator in the industry. More than 140,000 archived broadcasts (duplicating the first museum founded in New York City) reside in this museum, which opened in 1996. Everything you and your family want to know about eighty-plus years of broadcasting is here. Special exhibits and screenings year-round. Call for schedules and times.

Where to Eat and Stay

Nate 'n Al Delicatessen Restaurant, 414 North Beverly Drive; (310) 274-0101; www .natenal.com. Open daily 7:00 a.m. to 9:00 p.m. Since 1945, serving top-notch smoked fish, cured meats, and matzo ball soup to hungry locals, visitors, celebrities, and families in a bustling, joyous atmosphere. Don't miss the matza brei, potato latkes, corned beef brisket, and anything made with pastrami. $$

Beverly Wilshire, A Four Seasons Hotel, 9500 Wilshire Boulevard; (310) 275-5200, www.fourseasons.com/beverlywilshire/. This 386-room and -suite world-class hotel is an oasis of elegance and impeccable service located at one of the world's most famous intersections—Wilshire Boulevard and Rodeo Drive (this place was featured in the movie *Pretty Woman,* starring Julia Roberts, remember?). When making your reservation,

tell the agent the ages of your kids and they will receive complimentary welcome gifts like toys and cute robes. Family packages are also available. $$$$

For More Information

Beverly Hills Chamber of Commerce. 239 South Beverly Drive, 90212; (310) 248-1000; www.beverlyhillschamber.com.

Beverly Hills Conference and Visitors Bureau. 239 South Beverly Drive, 90212; (800) 345-2210; www.beverlyhillsbehere.com.

The Valleys

Did you think a trip to L.A. would be, like, complete without a visit to the valleys? Think again, dude! The valleys are worlds unto themselves.

When you hear people talk about "the Valley," they are referring to the **San Fernando Valley,** home of more than a million people and bigger than metropolitan Chicago. You can get an overview of the valley from serpentine **Mulholland Drive,** which bisects the Santa Monica Mountains, the natural topographical separator of the Los Angeles Basin from the vast valley floor.

If you have time for an outdoor interlude, by all means explore the **Santa Monica Mountains National Recreation Area.** These chaparral-covered slopes, which stretch 55 miles from Griffith Park all the way to Point Mugu in Ventura County, have provided the backdrop for many a Hollywood movie. For instance, *M*A*S*H* (movie and TV show) was filmed at **Malibu Creek State Park** (alongside Las Virgenes Road/Malibu Canyon) and at **Paramount Ranch,** Agoura Hills, 1813 Cornell Road (805-370-2301). The latter, once owned by Paramount Studios, still has the fabricated western town used in dozens of films and TV shows. Horseback riding and nature walks through the canyons covering 2,400 acres also make for refreshing mini-escapes from the city's bustle.

If you have more time, explore the stretch of miles-long **Ventura Boulevard,** which bisects Encino and Sherman Oaks. Together with U.S. Highway 101 (the Ventura

The **Canyons**

Coldwater Canyon (which connects Beverly Hills to Studio City) and, about 10 miles to the west, **Topanga Canyon** (connecting Malibu to Woodland Hills) are sights to see. Topanga is a Chumash Indian word meaning "mountains that crash down to the sea." You'll see what the Chumash meant if you drive the length of the canyon. If you park your car along any of the turnouts along the road and look closely at the exposed mountain sides, you may well see fossils of ancient sea creatures—proof positive the whole area was once under water.

The intersection of Topanga and Old Topanga Canyon Roads is marked by the village of—no surprise here—Topanga, with its health-food stores, hippie feel, and more. One place you'll want to visit is the **Will Geer Theatricum Botanicum,** 1419 North Topanga Canyon Boulevard, 5 miles from US 101 (310-455-2322 or 310-455-3723; www.theatricum.com), an open-air ancient Greek-style amphitheater that features first-rate performances of Shakespearean works and other classics and a children's concert series. Open in June, this outdoor theater offers more than culture. It occupies a natural setting with a youth drama camp, youth classes, and a variety of plays. Call ahead for schedule.

Freeway), "the Boulevard" is the valley's main artery. Of the two, Encino has the more upmarket sections, whereas Sherman Oaks (along Ventura Boulevard) has a myriad of Melrose-like establishments.

Burbank

Among the largest cities in California (population 100,000-plus) is Burbank, known as the home of major film and television studios, a bustling airport, and shopping malls. Many jokes have been made by television shows that emanate from here about "beautiful downtown Burbank," but you and your family will want to visit those studios.

Warner Bros. Studio VIP Tour (ages 8 and over)

3400 Riverside Drive, Gate 6, VIP Tour Center; (818) 972-8687; www.wbstudiotour.com. Tours generally Monday through Friday 9:00 a.m. to 3:00 p.m., with expanded hours in summer. Call for schedule. Reservations are required. $$$

This is an insider's look at a very busy and famous motion picture and television studio—past and present. The tour begins with a short film highlighting the movies and television shows created by Warner Bros. talent. Then, via electric tour carts to the Warner Bros. Museum and from the museum, you visit back-lot sets, soundstages, and craft/production shops. Routes change from day to day to accommodate production on the lot, so no two tours are exactly alike. Tours last approximately two and a half hours.

Five-hour Deluxe Tours including lunch in the Studio Commissary ($$$$) are also available.

NBC TV Studios (ages 5 and over)

3000 West Alameda Avenue; (818) 840-3537 or (818) 840-4444. $$

Escorted seventy-minute walking tours are generally available on a first-come, first-served basis Monday through Friday, every hour on the hour between 9:00 a.m. and 3:00 p.m. If you're lucky, you might see Jay Leno or his famous Studio 3. Call for current tour schedules and fees.

Where to Stay

Marriott Burbank Airport Hotel & Convention Center, 2500 Hollywood Way; (818) 843-6000; www.marriottburbankairport.com. Located across the street from the Burbank Bob Hope Airport (the airport closest to Hollywood, Universal Studios, NBC, and ABC). Free airport shuttle service. An excellent "home base" for exploring greater L.A., it has 488 comfortable rooms and 77s suite, two large heated pools, The Daily Grill restaurant, Starbucks in the lobby, and friendly staff to assist with your travel plans. $$$

For More Information

Burbank Chamber of Commerce. 200 West Magnolia Boulevard, 91502; (818) 846-3111; www.burbankchamber.org.

Santa Clarita Valley

Just twenty-five minutes north of Hollywood, discover Valencia—home to the Six Flags California Entertainment Complex, a not-to-be-missed area for your thrill-seeking family!

Six Flags Magic Mountain—The Xtreme Park

26101 Magic Mountain Parkway; (661) 255-4111; www.sixflags.com. The complex is located off I-5, from the Magic Mountain Parkway exit, thirty minutes north of downtown Los Angeles. Open daily from March through September; weekends and holidays rest of year. Call for exact schedule and opening and closing hours. $$$$

Known worldwide as a thrill-ride haven, the 260-acre theme park features sixteen roller coasters—the most on the planet—and more than one hundred rides, games, and attractions for the entire family. Enjoy such exciting thrill rides as SCREAM; X, the world's first and only four-dimensional roller coaster; Deja Vu, the world's fastest and tallest suspended, looping boomerang coaster; Goliath, the coaster giant among giants; the Riddler's Revenge, the world's tallest and fastest stand-up roller coaster; Superman the Escape, towering 415 feet in the air; Colossus; Batman the Ride; Viper; and many more. For younger guests there is Bugs Bunny World, featuring rides and attractions that provide real thrills for kids and adults alike; Goliath Junior coaster; and Thomas the Tank Engine, Merrie Melodies Carousel, and Canyon Blaster Coaster for kids and parents together. In addition, meet your favorite Looney Tunes characters—Bugs Bunny, Daffy Duck, Yosemite Sam, and Sylvester. All this in one day!

Six Flags Hurricane Harbor

Located next door to Six Flags Magic Mountain; (661) 255-4100. Open weekends May through August and daily Memorial Day through Labor Day. Call for exact schedule and times. $$$$

This tropical-themed water-park attraction features more than twenty-two slides and attractions, including Tornado, a six-story, 75-foot funnel, with two of the tallest enclosed speed slides in Southern California; Lizard Lagoon, a 7,000-square-foot pool for teen and adult activities; Bamboo Racer, an exciting 45-foot-tall, six-lane racing attraction; Castaway Cove, an exclusive children's water-play kingdom; Shipwreck Shores, with water-play activities for the entire family; the Forgotten Sea wave pool; and the River Cruise lazy river. Way cool fun!

For More Information

Santa Clarita Valley Tourism Office.
23920 Valencia Boulevard, Suite 235, Santa Clarita, 91355; (661) 255-4318 or (800) 868-7398; www.visitsantaclarita.com.

Pasadena

Pasadena is the shining star of the San Gabriel Valley, just northeast of downtown L.A. While the annual **Tournament of Roses Parade** (626-449-4100; www.tournamentof roses.com), held every January 1 since 1890, and **Rose Bowl Stadium** (626-577-3100; www.rosebowlstadium.com) have made the city famous, the charm is in Old Pasadena with its Spanish Mission–style buildings, many of which are listed on the National Register of Historic Places.

Huntington Library, Art Collections and Botanical Gardens

1151 Oxford Road, San Marino (2 miles from Pasadena); (626) 405-2100; www.huntington .org. Open Monday, Wednesday, Thursday, and Friday noon to 4:30 p.m. and weekends 10:30 a.m. to 4:30 p.m.; closed Tuesday. $$

Three art galleries and a library showcase magnificent collections of paintings, sculptures, rare books, manuscripts, and decorative arts. The botanical collection features over 14,000 different species of plants. A private, nonprofit institution, The Huntington was founded in 1919 by railroad and real estate developer Henry Edwards Huntington and opened to the public in 1928. At the 207-acre Huntington, you can walk through perfectly manicured gardens on your way to view a precious scrap of Emily Dickinson poetry or other historical documents and manuscripts. The library is home to many first-edition books, including a Gutenberg Bible. The wonderful exhibits bring history into perspective, reminding us how people managed to communicate before computers. The oil paintings, furniture, and decorative accessories are elegantly displayed. There's a restaurant, the Rose Garden Cafe (enjoy an English tea; 626-683-8131), and an excellent bookshop. The Helen and Peter Bing Children's Garden offers one acre of kinetic sculptures and activities for children ages two through seven.

Kidspace Children's Musuem (ages 1 to 10)

480 North Arroyo Boulevard, Pasadena, across from the Rose Bowl; (626) 449-9144; www .kidspacemuseum.org. Open Tuesday through Sunday from 9:30 a.m. to 5:00 p.m.; daily June through August. $$

Features twenty world-class interactive exhibits and 2.2 acres of outdoor learning environments designed to encourage your kids to discover the excitement of learning while engaging in the creativity of play—such as unleashing an earthquake, feeding giant bugs, crafting art through nature, and climbing raindrops 40 feet into the air.

Santa Anita Park (Seabiscuit's Home Stable)

285 West Huntington Drive, Arcadia; (626) 574-7223 or (626) 574-6677; www.santaanita .com. Open December through April.

Located just a few miles east of Pasadena, Santa Anita Park is more than just a racetrack. The architecture is art deco, and the cuisine is outstanding. Thoroughbred racing is the main event at the track, but this 320-acre park is relaxing, exquisitely landscaped, and worth the trip. The Seabiscuit tram tour includes riding by Seabiscuit's barn, looking at the locations where the movie *Seabiscuit* was filmed in 2003, observing the daily activities of the stable area and more. Tours depart from the tram boarding area across from the receiving barn at 8:30 a.m. and 9:45 a.m. every Saturday and Sunday during racing season only. **Free.** Family Fun Days (noon to 4:00 p.m.) include **free** activities in the infield. Call for weekend schedule.

Raging Waters

111 Raging Waters Drive (take the Raging Waters Drive exit off Interstate 210), San Dimas (east of Pasadena), where the 10, 210, and 57 freeways meet; (909) 592-1457, twenty-four-hour information line (909) 802-2200; www.ragingwaters.com. Open daily June 1 through late September; weekends in May. It is essential you call in advance as hours and days of operation constantly change. $$$$

The fifty-acre park, California's largest waterpark and ranked number three nationally by the Travel Channel in its top 10 ranking of U.S. water parks, houses fifty million gallons of water and more than thirty-six water attractions for aquatic thrill seekers, including the Vortex, a four-story tower with two enclosed, 270-foot-long, spiral body flumes, and the world's highest head-first water ride, the High EXtreme. For those not inclined to plunge from such heights or velocities, there are tamer options, including a children's activity pool and play area.

Where to Stay

The Langham Huntington Hotel and Spa, 1401 South Oak Knoll Avenue; (626) 568-3900; http://pasadena.langhamhotels .com. Located in Pasadena, fifteen minutes from downtown Los Angeles (formerly The Ritz-Carlton), this lovingly restored historic landmark first opened in 1907 and recalls the grace and elegance of a past era with all the twenty-first-century amenities your family needs. The hotel has 380 newly renovated guest rooms, two restaurants, a full-service spa, twenty-three acres of gardens and grounds, and eight guest cottages with working fireplaces. Special packages are available. $$$$

For More Information

Pasadena Convention and Visitors Bureau. 171 South Los Robles Avenue, 91101; (626) 795-9311 or (800) 307-7977; www.PasadenaCal.com.

Coastal Los Angeles

After a few days spent driving, museum hopping, driving, stargazing, driving, shopping, and driving some more, you and the kids may begin to feel a little antsy. If you're starting to think "L.A.'s great, but . . ." then it's high time you hit the beach. Whereas in cities like Boston or New York there are only gradations of stress—it never totally dissipates—in

L.A., stress can be lowered to tolerable levels thanks to the proximity of a long and stunning coastline and the beach. And when it comes to beaches, you're truly spoiled with choices in Southern California. Three areas are absolute must-sees for families on vacation: Venice Beach, Santa Monica, and Malibu. While there are other beaches, none bear the singular L.A. signature as indelibly as these. (The Long Beach area is discussed separately.)

Venice Beach and Marina del Rey

Venice Beach lies due south of Santa Monica. Venice is sort of like Melrose Avenue (see Westside, earlier) meeting the sea: Anything goes, but with copious amounts of suntan oil.

While L.A. beaches are endowed with more than 22 miles of bicycle paths, the most colorful swath is **Oceanfront Walk** in Venice, where bikers, roller skaters, and zany in-line skaters all compete with pedestrians for maximum mobility. Add street performers—from jugglers and mimes to musicians and comedians—and you'll get an idea of the carnival-like atmosphere permeating the place. People come to Venice Beach not so much for the beach, which is actually quite nice, but to watch other people. A serious amount of body spotting goes on at **Muscle Beach,** a section of the sand where bodybuilders work out in the sun and flex their Schwarzenegger deltoids, pectorals, and biceps. If your kids are needling you for souvenirs, this is the place (and remember that when buying trinkets on the beach, tackiness is a virtue). For more information visit www.venicebeach.com.

Marina del Rey lies adjacent to Venice Beach, on the shore of the Pacific Ocean, 4 miles north of Los Angeles International Airport (LAX) and 3 miles south of Santa Monica. It boasts the world's largest human-made marina (more than 5,000 vessels), and every conceivable type of water sport is offered here, from boats and watercraft you pedal, paddle, sail, or drive to windsurfing, sunbathing, swimming, and surfing. Other water-based options include boat charters, harbor cruises, whale watching, and ocean fishing. From "the Marina," bike, skate, walk, or run along a 22-mile coastal path that stretches from Malibu at the northern end through the marina and south to Torrance. Kid-friendly **Mother's Beach,** as the name implies, is a must for families; as is **Fisherman's Village,** a quaint area of shops, restaurants, and charter/cruise boat docks.

Where to Eat and Stay

Tony P's Dockside Grill, 4445 Admiralty Way, Marina del Rey; (310) 823-4534; www.tonyps.com. Totally family-friendly waterfront casual dining. Open daily for lunch and dinner and on Saturday and Sunday for an all-American breakfast. Generous portions of steak, fresh seafood, pasta, and burgers at reasonable prices. The "Dinghy Club" kids' menu is one of the best we've seen for ages ten and younger. Every kid gets a gift bag of little toys. What kid can resist a nonalcoholic "FooFoo drink" such as a piña colada or strawberry margarita? If kids clean their plate, they get a free dessert. $$

Best Western Jamaica Bay Inn, 4175 Admiralty Way, Marina del Rey; (310) 823-5333; www.bestwestern-jamaicabay.com. Forty-two spacious guest rooms right on the sand (private beach) with stunning views of the bustling marina. Casual, laid-back atmosphere; great for relaxing but close to so many attractions you want to visit. The Beachside Café serves breakfast and lunch daily around the pool. Great values; ask for family packages. $$$

For More Information

Marina del Rey Convention and Visitors Bureau. 4701 Admiralty Way, 90292; visitor information line: (310) 305-9545; www .VisitMarina.com.

Santa Monica

Santa Monica has been a favorite family hideaway since the early 1930s when wealthy Easterners came for winter respites and never left. Just 8.3 square miles and surrounded on three sides by Los Angeles (and the fourth side by the Pacific Ocean), the city's safe, eco-friendly environment is easy to navigate. Most of the major hotels, attractions, shopping, and dining outlets are conveniently located within a 14-block radius. Be sure to check out **Palisades Park,** a cliff-top twenty-six-acre greenbelt overlooking the Pacific with miles of lush greenery and shady palms for walking, resting, jogging, picnicking, and bicycling. Three miles of coastline, two excellent beaches, historic Santa Monica Pier, hike-friendly mountains, and year-round warm weather in which to enjoy it all!

Santa Monica Pier and Pacific Park

The oldest pleasure pier on the West Coast, Santa Monica opened in 1909. The pier also features Heal the Bay's Santa Monica Pier Aquarium, the historic Hippodrome, and a handcrafted carousel (circa 1922) with forty-four handpainted wooden horses. Here you'll discover dining, amusement games, shops, and a fresh fish market. Year-round live entertainment is offered.

Pacific Park (310-260-8744; www.pacpark.com) is a traditional, small family amusement park. Hours vary by season, so be sure to call in advance. Admission to the park is **free,** with all twelve rides and dozens of games on a "pay-as-you-go" basis, or you can buy an all-day wristband for unlimited rides. The world's first solar-powered Ferris wheel offers stunning views from its nine-story height. A special Kiddy Zone has pint-size rides for kids less than 42 inches tall. Of course, there are bumper cars, a roller coaster, minigolf, a nine story plunge tower, and a flying swing for the big kids. $

Bergamot Station Arts Center

2525 Michigan Avenue; www.bergamotstation.com. Take Olympic Boulevard to Cloverfield and a right to Michigan Avenue, where you will find the gated entrance. Open Tuesday through Friday, 10:00 a.m. to 6:00 p.m.; Saturday, 11:00 a.m. to 5:30 p.m.; closed Sunday and Monday. **Free** admission and parking.

Check your street map because this enclave of forty eclectic art galleries exhibits a range of art. This is a light industrial area, so galleries have metallic roofs, high ceilings, and lots of wall space. From sculpture and wearable art to paintings, photography, and prints, this is a wonderland of creativity. There is a schedule listing each gallery, openings, and current exhibits. The Gallery Cafe is a good place to stop first and take a moment to plan your gallery stops. The **Santa Monica Museum of Art** has changing exhibits as well, and kids will find it a friendly place to start their art exploration. Plan to spend about an hour. Parking is free. For information call (310) 586-6488 or visit www.smmoa.org. Hours are Tuesday through Saturday 11:00 a.m. to 6:00 p.m.

Third Street Promenade
(310) 393-8355 or www.thirdstreetpromenade.com.

In Santa Monica, some of the best times await families just a few blocks from the sand. Here you can shop in the sunshine or at night until midnight at this ultra-lively spot that begins at Broadway (actually at the Santa Monica Place mall) and stretches north to Wilshire Boulevard along Third Street. Now one of the hippest areas in L.A., the promenade overflows with shops, restaurants, entertainment centers, and street performers. The Farmer's Market on Wednesday and Saturday mornings is a great scene and tasty, too (310-458-8712)! Wander and enjoy.

Magicopolis
1418 Fourth Street; (310) 451-2241; www.magicopolis.com. $$$

This 350-person, two-theater club welcomes all ages to ninety-minute magic shows on Saturday and Sunday. World-class magicians entertain at 2:00 and 8:00 p.m.

Where to Eat

Typhoon, 3221 Donald Douglas Loop South, at the edge of the Santa Monica Airport; (310) 390-6565; www.typhoon-restaurant.com. Kids can watch the airplanes land between bites of Pan-Asian cuisine, such as Vietnamese spring rolls, fried rice, and puffy bao buns. Also on the menu are insects! Yes, there are crunchy crickets, stir-fry crickets, giant mountain ants, and Thai-style crispy scorpions. Now that's a mouthful! Celebrities such as John Travolta have been known to fly their private planes to Typhoon, so be prepared for a stellar dining experience. $$$

Where to Stay

The Georgian Hotel, 1415 Ocean Avenue; (310) 395-9945 or (800) 538-8147 (toll-free reservations); www.georgianhotel.com. This distinctive turquoise and gold art deco gem, built in 1933 as a seaside getaway for the exclusive Hollywood set, has been beautifully restored and refurbished. Choose from fifty-six spacious rooms and twenty-eight suites overlooking the city and Santa Monica Bay. A real historic treat for your family. $$$$

Loews Santa Monica Beach Hotel, 1700 Ocean Avenue; (310) 458-6700; www.santamonicaloewshotel.com. Operating since 1989 in an unbeatable location adjacent to Santa Monica Pier overlooking the Pacific, with excellent beach access out the back ground-floor doors. This casually elegant 342-room luxury property has an outstanding children's program that includes lending game libraries, special menus, tours, welcome gifts for children younger than age ten, and supervised recreational programs. Children younger than age eighteen stay free in same room as parents. The spa, fitness suite, ocean-view pool, and whirlpool are perfect for relaxing after a hard day's touring. $$$$

For More Information

Santa Monica Convention and Visitors Bureau. 1920 Main Street, Suite B, 90405; (310) 319-6263 or (800) 544-5319; www.santamonica.com.

Malibu

Malibu is Beach Boys country, where a dozen or so beaches beckon alongside the Pacific Coast Highway (PCH) at the foot of the Santa Monica Mountains. Although part of Los Angeles County, Malibu is actually a separate city—and a funny-shaped one at that. Because of the area's geography, Malibu is barely 1.5 miles wide but some 27 miles long. PCH is the lifeline of this seaside community and the commuting route to Hollywood for the hundreds of celebrities who live in seaside villas and estates here. You might even bump into one or two on the beach—it happens all the time.

One of the finest stretches of sand is **Malibu Beach,** on either side of the **Malibu Pier** (you can't miss it). White sand, pounding surf, sun-bronzed lifeguards with fluorescent-colored zinc oxide on their noses—yes, this is Malibu. Even in summer, the beach is not as crowded as those in Santa Monica and Venice, and there is less emphasis on people-watching. Malibu-ites know what's really important in life: surfing at Zuma Beach.

It's not all sand and surf here, with the 2006 reopening of the Getty Villa, a lavish art museum and outdoor theater complex owned by J. Paul Getty Trust.

Getty Villa

17985 Pacific Coast Highway, 1 mile north of Sunset Boulevard; (310) 440-7300; www .getty.edu. Open Thursday through Monday 10:00 a.m. to 5:00 p.m. Closed major holidays. Free admission. Advance, timed tickets are required for each individual older than five. On-site parking is available for all ticket holders and is $8 per car (cash only).

Reopened in 2006 after a nine-year closure for extensive remodeling, the Villa presides on a hill overlooking the Pacific. There is 48,000 square feet of gallery space on two floors designed as a palatial country home in the time of the Caesars, with elaborate ponds, gardens, and fountains, and twenty-three rooms exhibiting 1,200 carefully collected and curated pieces depicting life at the beginning of civilization. A must-do, one-of-a-kind cultural attraction.

Where to Eat

Dukes at Malibu, 21150 Pacific Coast Highway; (310) 317-0777; www.dukesmailbu.com. Lunch and dinner daily. Named after Duke Kahanamoku, the "father of surfing," this is the ideal place for your family to get the feeling of the Malibu lifestyle, thanks to the magnificent stretch of windows overlooking the beach. The prices are reasonable, and the

kids will like the exhibit of surfing memorabilia. You might remind them about the Beach
Boys and all of those surfing movies from the
1960s. $$

For More Information

Malibu Chamber of Commerce. 23805
Stuart Ranch Road, Suite 100, 90265; (310)
456-9025; www.malibu.org.

Long Beach

As its name indicates, life in Long Beach centers around things of a coastal nature, with
more than 50 miles of sandy beaches and shorelines. Settled by the Spaniards in 1784,
Long Beach has been a visitor-friendly place ever since. Real live guides are at visitors'
disposal in the animated downtown area. Though close to downtown Los Angeles, Long
Beach has a distinctly different, somewhat lower-key feel. If you have the time, give your-
self two full days here.

In Long Beach, you will find an array of peaceful beaches that invite sunbathing and
sand-castle building. Thanks to a human-made breakwater, the beaches of Long Beach do
not experience high surf and are therefore ideal for families with small children.

Long Beach offers countless ways to spend a pleasant morning or afternoon. The
15-block stretch of Second Street in the **Belmont Shore** area has swimming, lots of bou-
tiques, and restaurants that range from Indian to Chinese to New York–style bagel shops.
A mile and a half away, down Ocean Boulevard, downtown activity hustles and bustles
along revitalized Pine Avenue.

Museum of Latin American Art

**628 Alamitos Avenue; (562) 437-1689; www.molaa.com. Open Tuesday through Friday
11:30 a.m. to 7:00 p.m., Saturday 11:00 a.m. to 7:00 p.m., and Sunday 11:00 a.m. to 6:00
p.m. Call ahead for calendar of events. Children younger than age tweve admitted** free.
Friday is free **to everyone.**

The 20,000-square-foot building was built in 1920 and houses the Robert Gumbiner Foun-
dation collection of Latin American art (since the 1940s), galleries for rotating showings,
Viva Cafe and Museum Store, a research library, and a performance area. It is the only
museum in the western United States that exclusively features contemporary Latin Ameri-
can art.

Long Beach Aquarium of the Pacific

**100 Aquarium Way; (562) 590-3100; www.aquariumofpacific.org. Open daily 9:00 a.m. to
6:00 p.m. except Christmas. $$$**

When you see the full-scale model of a blue whale, you'll know you're at the Long Beach
Aquarium, a 156,000-square-foot facility that covers five acres and includes 550 species
and 12,500 specimens. After you've checked out the wonderful exhibits, including Sea
Lion/Seal Tunnel, Baja Gallery, Wetlands Discovery Lab, Pacific Gallery, Coastal Corner,
Live Coral Discovery, Lorikeet Aviary, and the Shark Lagoon, head for Kid's Cove. A

Queen *Mary*

There are many fun family attractions in Long Beach, but none so famous as the majestic *Queen Mary*. The world's largest luxury liner is permanently docked in the fifty-five-acre **Queen Mary Seaport,** located at the end of the 710 Freeway. There are many hotels in Long Beach, but if this is your first visit, try the **Hotel Queen Mary,** 1126 Queens Highway; (562) 435-3511 or (800) 437-2934; www.queenmary.com. The ship has been converted into the 307-stateroom hotel. While aboard, you can take a Behind-the-Scenes guided tour or dine in one of the ship's restaurants. The **Chelsea** serves lunch and dinner. Here you'll also find the **Piccadilly Circus,** the boat's original shopping center. If you can't stay on the ship for a night or two, be sure to indulge in a tour. Add a tour of the Soviet Foxtrot Submarine *Scorpion* anchored adjacent or do the Ghosts and Legends Show onboard for some paranormal fun. $$$

playground of the Pacific Ocean, Kid's Cove is a hands-on interactive aquarium experience for kids of all ages. The focus is on feeding habits, family structures, and the lives of the exhibit specimens. Dine at the Bamboo Bistro or Cafe Scuba. Behind-the-scenes tours and ninety-minute ocean educational cruises aboard *The Conqueror* are real winners, too.

Where to Eat

King's Fish House, 100 West Broadway at Pine Avenue; (562) 432-7463; www.kingsfish house.com. Here are the ingredients for a popular family restaurant: friendly service, comfortable wood booths, and fair, never fishy, prices. It all adds up to our favorite seafood restaurant in Long Beach. $$

Parker's Lighthouse, 435 Shoreline Village Drive; (562) 432-6500; www.parkers-lighthouse.com. Serves lunch and dinner daily. Just look for the lighthouse to find this family-friendly restaurant. The view is terrific from the patio: the *Queen Mary* and harbor. The down-to-earth menu includes fresh fish, mesquite-grilled with a choice of side sauces or blackened, seared, poached, or Cajun seasoned as well as sushi, and an Angus burger to satisfy any carnivores. $$$

Where to Stay

Dockside Boat & Bed, Rainbow Harbor; (562) 436-3111; www.boatandbed.com/longbeach.html. Four private moored yachts to stay aboard overnight. All boats fully furnished; continental breakfast basket provided. Next to Aquarium of the Pacific and Shoreline Village. A highly recommended unique family-lodging experience with an extraordinary view you'll never have in a hotel. $$$$

For More Information

Long Beach Area Convention and Visitor's Bureau. 1 World Trade Center, third floor, 90831; (562) 436-3645 or (800) 452-7829; www.visitlongbeach.com.

On the Water

Gondola Getaway. 5437 East Ocean Boulevard, Long Beach; (562) 433-9595; www.gondolagetawayinc.com. The Getaway features Venetian-style gondolas that cruise through narrow canals in the "backyards" of affluent home owners. Cruises last fifty minutes.

Alfredo's Beach Rentals. Long Beach and locations throughout L.A. and Orange Counties; (562) 434-6121; www.alfredosbeachclub.com/south_bay .htm. Boogie boards? Skates? Bikes? All of the equipment you couldn't get on the plane and in your car can be rented from Alfredo!

Harbor Breeze Cruises. Rainbow Harbor Dock #2; (562) 432-4900; http://2see whales.com/. Double-deck 6- foot, 149-passenger sightseeing vessels.

Rainbow Rocket. (562) 43-ROCKET; www.rocketboat.net. 124-passenger 200 hp speedboat. Fast fun for everyone!

Long Beach Sport Fishing. (562) 432-8993; www.longbeachsportfishing.com.

Offshore Water Sports. (562) 436-1996; www.owsrentals.com.

Pacific Sailing. (562) 590-0323; www.pacificsailing.net. Charters or learn to sail.

Spirit Cruises at Shoreline Village. (562) 495-5884; www.spiritdinnercruises .com. Sail aboard a 90-foot motor yacht. All tours include narration, and Shoreline guarantees whale sightings or a second trip is free.

San Pedro—Port of Los Angeles

Originally settled as a commercial fishing village in the 1800s, today San Pedro is home to the Port of Los Angeles, one of the world's largest deepwater commercial seaports. Here you also will find the **World Cruise Center** (located at Berths 91, 92, and 93A/B), point of embarkation for more than a million passengers annually sailing on vacations to Mexico, Alaska, Hawaii, and beyond onboard ships from Celebrity Cruises, Costa Cruise Lines, Crystal Cruises, Cunard, Disney Cruise Line, Holland America, Norwegian, Oceania, Princess Cruises, Radisson Seven Seas, Royal Caribbean, and others. Located at the end of the 110-Harbor Freeway, San Pedro offers value-priced lodging, restaurants, and shopping options. It is easy to explore the attractions via the San Pedro Red Car Electric Trolley route currently stretching 1.5 miles along Harbor Boulevard with terminals at Swinford Street, Sixth Street, Ports O' Call Village, and Miner Street. From Friday through Monday, Red Cars leave from Swinford Street every twenty minutes, beginning at 10:00 a.m. Another Red Car leaves from Miner Street every twenty minutes, beginning at 10:00 a.m. All Red Cars run until 5:30 p.m. Fares are $1 per person (children six and under **free**) for unlimited rides (310-732-3473 or www.railwaypreservation.com/page8.html).

Los Angeles Maritime Museum

Berth 84, at the foot of Sixth Street in John S. Gibson Park; (310) 548-7618; www.lamaritime museum.org. Open Tuesday through Sunday 10:00 a.m. to 5:00 p.m. $

Built in 1941, this "Streamlined Moderne" building was the base for an auto ferry. Saved and beautifully restored, it now houses the largest maritime museum in California. This 75,000-square-foot facility features more than 700 ship and boat models, a variety of navigational equipment, and an operating amateur radio station. Try your hand at tying any of the sixty-four types of seaman's knots on display.

Cabrillo Marine Aquarium

3720 Steven White Drive; (310) 548-7562; www.cabrilloaq.org. Open Tuesday through Friday noon to 5:00 p.m., Saturday and Sunday 10:00 a.m. to 5:00 p.m. Free, but a suggested donation of $5 for adults and $1 for children is appreciated.

Featuring thirty-eight aquaria, these innovative exhibits will teach kids about the plant and animal life of Southern California. The simulated "tide pool touch tank" is a good place to start this aquatic journey. In addition, there are whale trips organized from December through March focusing on the Pacific gray whale. This museum predated the Aquarium of the Pacific in neighboring Long Beach by sixty-five years. Here's where it all started, and that's no fish story.

SS *Lane Victory*

Berth 94 off Harbor Boulevard; (310) 519-9545; www.lanevictory.org. Open for tours daily 9:00 a.m. to 4:00 p.m. except for six Saturday daylong cruises each summer. $

This operational World War II cargo ship with wartime armament was built in 1945 and saw service in World War II, Korea, and Vietnam. Decommissioned and fully restored, her 455-foot length and 10,000 tons are a marvel to behold. If your family is visiting the Los Angeles area in the summer, make every attempt to secure reservations on one of the day cruises, where the seamen's lives will come alive as you sail. You will even be buzzed by attacking biplanes. This ship is a living memorial to all Merchant Marines.

For More Information

Port of Los Angeles. 425 South Palos Verdes Street, 90731; (310) SEA-PORT; www.portoflosangeles.org.

San Pedro Peninsula Chamber of Commerce. 390 West Seventh Street, 90731; (310) 832-7272 or (888) 447-3376; www.sanpedrochamber.com or www.sanpedro.com.

Leave the Driving to Someone Else

Riding the rails—it's the "green" alternative to driving on your trip through Southern California. AMTRAK has excellent routes in the West, and it's the best way to circumvent the traffic. The train that does it best in Southern California is called the Pacific Surfliner, with daily service between San Diego, Los Angeles, Santa Barbara, and San Luis Obispo. Among the attractions along the route are Disneyland, the missions at San Juan Capistrano, Sea World in San Diego, the beaches of Santa Barbara, and bustling Los Angeles, with connections to the Metrolink buses and light rail and DASH shuttles.

Children's discounts offer great savings for families. Kids ages two to fifteen are entitled to a 50 percent discount every day, any day when traveling with an adult paying full fare. Call AMTRAK at (800) USA-RAIL or visit www.amtrak.com.

Santa Catalina Island

Part of the chain of eight Channel Islands off the coast of southern California, Santa Catalina Island was first discovered by the European explorer Juan Rodriguez Cabrillo and claimed for Spain in 1542. Sixty years later, explorer Sebastian Viscaino reclaimed the island and gave it its current name in honor of Saint Catherine. You can easily sail away to the Mediterranean-like island, a relaxing 22-mile (one-hour) boat trip from Long Beach or San Pedro Harbor. You might want to spend a couple of days on this enchanted isle, where you won't need a car for a change (since they are restricted to residents). In our opinion, the best way to get to Santa Catalina is aboard *Catalina Express* high-speed vessels (with ports in Long Beach, San Pedro, and Dana Point; 310-519-1212 or 800-481-3470; www.catalinaexpress.com). You'll arrive at the green "Pleasure Pier" in the sun-splashed city of Avalon. With its restaurant- and boutique-filled streets and a population of around 3,000, it's Catalina's biggest town and your headquarters for fun.

Catalina Casino

You can't miss this red-roofed Avalon landmark as you approach Avalon harbor. Never actually used for gambling, the casino is famed for its ballroom and the Avalon Theatre, the first designed for sound movies. Art deco murals of stylized underwater scenes grace the theater, which also has a full-scale pipe organ with 250 miles of wire. On the ground floor, visit the Catalina Island Museum, (310) 510-2414 or www.catalinamuseum.com, for tours and information.

Santa Catalina Island Company's Discovery Tours

(310) 510-2500 or (800) 626-1496; www.visitcatalinaisland.com. $$$

Operating since 1894 and departing from Avalon and Two Harbors, Discovery Tours by Land include the Avalon Scenic Tour, Casino Tour, Skyline Drive Tour, and Inland Motor Tour (the most comprehensive at four hours). Discovery Tours by Sea include Undersea Tour, Glass Bottom Boat Trip, Seal Rocks Cruise, Sundown Isthmus Cruise, and the Flying Fish Boat Trip. Money-saving combinations are the best way to tailor the tours to your family at a 25 percent discount off regular pricing. Reservations are recommended, especially during the busy times of weekends, holidays, and the summer season.

Catalina Adventure Tours
On the green Pleasure Pier; (310) 510-2888; www.catalinaadventuretours.com.

Tours via modern air-conditioned buses include the Avalon Explorer, City Passport, City Botanical, and Inside Adventure (the most popular). On the water, tours include the SS *Nautilus* (a semi-submersible sub), *Sea View* (glass-bottom boat), Seal Rock Explorer Cruise, and a Scenic Harbor cruise. Village walking tours are also offered.

Where to Eat and Stay

Catalina Coffee & Cookie Company, 205 Crescent Avenue, Avalon; (310) 510-2447; www.metropolemarketplace.com/html/body_catalina_cookie_company.html. Need a pick-me-up? Come here for an Eclipse, a fudge cookie dipped in white chocolate. Open daily at 5:00 a.m. year-round. $

The Cottage, 615 Crescent Avenue, Avalon; (310) 510-0726. Totally traditional family breakfast and lunch favorites served daily. The "Chef's Mess" omelet contains everything but the kitchen sink and, like every breakfast item, is available all day. $

Pavilion Lodge, 513 Crescent Avenue, Avalon; (310) 510-2500 or (800) 626-1496; www.visitcatalinaisland.com/avalon/hote_pavilionLodge.php. Seventy-three rooms in a central location perfect for families. Excellent values and packages; **free** continental breakfast, and kids under twelve stay **free.** It's just "fourteen steps from the beach." $$

For More Information

Catalina Island Visitors Bureau and Chamber of Commerce. On the green Pleasure Pier in the center of town, P.O. Box

On the **Wild Side**

Catalina now has a four-hour off-road tour that is ideal for families. Visiting the "wild side" of the island on the **Cape Canyon Tour,** passengers ride in a four-wheel-drive vehicle driven by a Catalina Island Conservancy–trained guide. The tour features a scenic drive along a ridgeline overlooking coves of west Avalon, a guided tour of the American Bald Eagle Habitat at Middle Ranch, and a ride in Cape Canyon for stunning views of the Catalina outback. Lunch is included at the famous Catalina Airport-in-the-Sky. Reservations required; call (310) 510-2000 or visit www.visitcatalinaisland.com.

217, Avalon 90704; (310) 510-1520; www.visit
catalina.org or www.catalinachamber.com.

Santa Catalina Island Company. P.O.
Box 737, Avalon 90704; (310) 510-2000 or

(800) 626-1496; www.visitcatalinaisland.com.
Owners of Discovery Tours, Pavilion Lodge,
Hotel Atwater, Banning House Lodge, Catalina Country Club, Descanso Beach Club, and
other services.

Redondo Beach

Known as the South Bay (because the area is south of Long Beach), Redondo Beach is
within a forty-five-minute range of Disneyland, Knott's Berry Farm, Universal Studios,
Six Flags Magic Mountain, the La Brea Tar Pits, Catalina Island terminals, and the *Queen
Mary*. Redondo has the Galleria at South Bay (with 150 stores), superb sportfishing, and
charters at the Redondo Beach King Harbor Marina. If you should base the family here,
you'll have the best of both worlds—the atmosphere of a small, seaside village and the
accessibility of most of Greater L.A.'s attractions. The oceanfront location places you
but 6 miles from LAX and within walking distance of King Harbor, Seaside Lagoon, and a
27-mile-long coastal walking and biking path passing through Venice, Santa Monica, and
Malibu. For more information, call (310) 318-0631 or visit www.redondopier.com.

Where to Eat and Stay

Captain Kidd's, 209 Harbor Drive; (310)
372-7703; www.CaptainKidds.com. Open for
breakfast, lunch, and dinner daily. Fresh-from-
the-market fish and crab are prepared grilled,
Cajun-style, charbroiled, or deep fried and
come with two generous side dishes. Check
the Captain Kidd's Meal for choices all under
$5. $$

**The Fun Fish Market & Restaurant/
Fun Factory Amusement Center,** 121
International Boardwalk; (310) 374-4277 or
(310) 374-9982; http://redondo.com/rff/. The
Redondo Pier has a big amusement center,
which is good, but even more appealing
around mealtime is Fun Fish, where fresh
fish is served any way you like it. Kids will like
selecting their fish from a tank. And don't for-
get the chowder! $$

Portofino Hotel and Yacht Club, 260 Por-
tofino Way; (310) 379-8481 or (800) 468-4292;
www.hotelportofino.com. The Portofino's 163
rooms include 90 with views of the Pacific.
Fifty-six rooms are smoke-free. An assort-
ment of complimentary family amenities is
provided, from "baby joggers" and snugglies
to high chairs and diapers. Breakfast, lunch,
and dinner are served waterside at the Break-
water Restaurant. $$$$

For More Information

**Redondo Beach Chamber of Commerce
and Visitors Bureau.** 200 North Pacific
Coast Highway, 90277; (310) 376-6911 or
(800) 282-0333; www.redondochamber.org.
Ask for a Visitors Passport, which features
good discounts all over town.

Orange County

The land on which the visionary Walt Disney built his Magic Kingdom in 1955 was discovered more than 150 years earlier by a Spanish explorer. Gaspar de Portolá gazed upon the magic river bringing life to the fertile valleys and fields leading to the Pacific Ocean and named it Santa Ana. In 1857 German immigrants bought portions of the area, at the time a Spanish land grant, for a mere $2 an acre. They called their new settlement Anaheim, which means "home of the Ana." With cuttings from their native Rhineland, the settlers began growing California's first grapes and making wine. In the late 1880s, the vineyards of California's wine capital in Anaheim were devastated by blight. So the settlers decided to plant oranges instead, and the current name Orange County was created, now immortalized by television's popular teen drama *The O.C.,* and the TV reality-show *The Real Housewives of Orange County.*

Today's fastest-growing crops in the area are neither grapes nor oranges but amusement parks, sports attractions, and a galaxy of animated stars from Disney—all ready and waiting for the picking by you and your fun-starved entourage. If oranges thrive in this climate, so will you! Wintertime highs of 65 degrees rise to but 79 degrees in summer, and overnight lows—even in winter's darkest hours—rarely dip below 45 degrees. December through February is what passes for the area's "rainy season," although total annual rainfall is only 13 inches. Days are sunny and mild, nights clear and cool—that's the forecast for your Orange County visit.

Casual clothing is the way to go for 90 percent of your family fun here. Be sure to pack shorts, T-shirts, cotton pants, skirts, and really comfortable walking shoes or sandals. Bring a sweater or light jacket for evenings—along the waterfront it may get nippy. Don't forget your bathing suit and shades (but never fear, you can always buy the latest beachwear and gear at one of the numerous malls or gift shops).

Your family can still visit the city of Orange itself, with its historic district featuring a nineteenth-century soda fountain; relax on the beaches of Newport and Laguna; check out the world-class surfing at Huntington Beach; shop 'til you drop in Costa Mesa; and see the swallows in Capistrano and the marine life in Dana Point. By popular kid demand, however, you will doubtless make your first Orange County stop in Anaheim at "Uncle Walt's place"—the unparalleled Disneyland Resort, which includes the original

ORANGE COUNTY

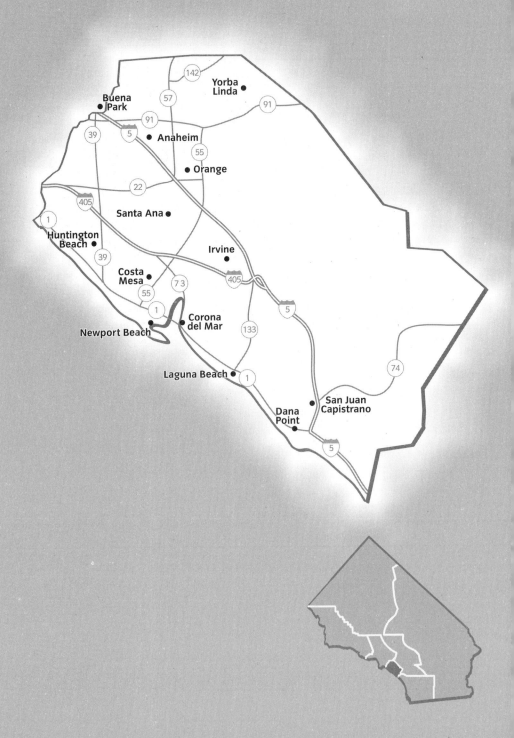

Disneyland and the new Disney's California Adventure parks, plus the Downtown Disney District.

Anaheim Resort Area

From Los Angeles drive south on Interstate 5 to the city of Anaheim and vicinity, the family fun center of Orange County. Using Disneyland Resort as your Orange County starting point makes much sense geographically and economically. Family-style lodging and restaurants are plentiful and very affordable in Anaheim and neighboring Buena Park. Make room reservations as far in advance as you can, especially for summertime and holiday periods, since Anaheim attracts twenty-million-plus visitors every year, including many who visit at the West Coast's largest exhibition center, the Anaheim Convention Center. Many hotels and motels provide package plans that include Disneyland Resort tickets (passports) as well as **free** breakfasts and transportation services.

Disneyland Park

1313 Harbor Boulevard, at the intersection of I-5; (714) 781-4565; www.disneyland.com. $$$$

Hours: During the fall, winter, and spring, hours are generally Monday through Friday 10:00 a.m. to 8:00 p.m., Saturday 9:00 a.m. to midnight, and Sunday 9:00 a.m. to 10:00 p.m. Summertime hours are usually 8:00 a.m. to midnight every day. Extended hours are in effect during holiday periods. Very important note: Hours are subject to change, so call ahead for exact opening and closing times on your preferred days to avoid disappointment.

Directions: Follow the signs to designated parking areas. Trams are provided to the Transit Plaza/Main Entrance for both Disney parks and Downtown Disney. (Parking is $11 per car per day).

Since 1955, the magic of Disneyland has existed in eight "themed lands." Begin with your entrance on Main Street USA, a composite of America in the 1900s. Move along to Adventureland, housing Tarzan's Treehouse; the Indiana Jones Adventure (one of our favorites); the Jungle Cruise; and the Enchanted Tiki Room (a good place we found to sit in a cool room for twenty minutes for the animated show). New Orleans Square features the classic Pirates of the Caribbean and Haunted Mansion. Critter Country has the wettest ride—Splash Mountain—and Many Adventures of Winnie-the-Pooh. Fantasyland is highlighted by the new Disney Princess Fantasy Faire (complete with dress-up and meet royalty options), Sleeping Beauty's Castle, King Arthur's Carousel, Mr. Toad's Wild Ride, Peter Pan's Flight, and the breathtaking Matterhorn Bobsleds. Next comes Frontierland, with the Big Thunder Mountain mine ride and the chances to cruise on the Mark Twain riverboat or Sailing Ship Columbia around Tom Sawyer's Island. The Fantasmic! special-effects show is presented nightly each summer and on weekends. Mickey's Toontown is base camp for all your young ones' favorite Disney characters. See Mickey's and Minnie's residences and Goofy's Bounce House, and ride Roger Rabbit's Car Toon Spin and the new kiddie ride—Gadget's Go Coaster. Tomorrowland is the launching pad for space-age attractions. Here you will thrill to classics such as Star Tours and Space Mountain, plus the Astro Orbitor, 3-D "Honey I Shrunk the Audience," "Buzz Lightyear Astro Blasters," and the "Finding Nemo Submarine Voyage." The Disneyland Monorail, once the coolest ride in Tomorrowland, now just runs back and forth from Downtown Disney instead of around the park. The steam-engined Disneyland Railroad still circumnavigates the park with stops at various lands. We recommend you take the full twenty-minute circuit for a calming respite from all the excitement!

Disney's California Adventure Park

1313 Harbor Boulevard, at the intersection of I-5 (you can also exit at Disneyland Drive); (714) 781-4565; www.disneyland.com. Open year-round, generally Monday through Friday 10:00 a.m. to 8:00 p.m., Saturday 9:00 a.m. to 10:00 p.m., and Sunday 9:00 a.m. to 10:00 p.m. Extended hours during the summer and holiday periods. NOTE: Hours are very subject to change; call ahead for exact opening and closing times on your preferred days to visit. Admission fees are also subject to change. Many special packages and promotions are offered throughout the year. $$$$

Opened in February 2001 and continually adding new rides and shows, this fifty-five-acre theme park celebrates the great state of California—from Disney's imaginative perspective. You'll enter the park, affectionately known as DCA for short, from the promenade

Doing Disneyland

With three attractions—the original Disneyland (opened 1955), Disney's California Adventure, and the Downtown Disney District (both opened in 2001)—this trip can be a visual and physical overload for you and your family. We strongly advise a minimum two-night stay and three days to really enjoy all the fun available. (It's practically impossible to do both parks in one day; even one overnight and two full days can be very tricky, depending on your stamina.) For first-timers, begin with the original Disneyland early in the day. Take a short break midday for lunch and naps, then return for the afternoon and evening shows (such as the fireworks over the Magic Castle). You'll need a second full day to really explore DCA (Disney's California Adventure) because many of the activities are live stage shows and movies presented at specific times. On the third day, revisit favorite attractions at either park and get in some shopping and dining or a movie at Downtown Disney. Always check park operating hours and plan your visit around your kids' eat-sleep schedule. The best time-saving option is the FASTPASS, a computerized ticketing system that allows you to reserve a time slot for the most popular rides. When you arrive at your designated time period with your computer-generated pass, you'll go to a special line and get on within minutes. Highly recommended!

area under a replica of San Francisco's Golden Gate Bridge into the **Sunshine Plaza** fountain area to explore four distinct lands. Paradise Pier re-creates a beachfront amusement zone reminiscent of Santa Monica Pier or the Santa Cruz boardwalk. Check out California Scream-in'—a superfast steel roller coaster that loops you upside down around a Mickey Mouse head icon. The 150-foot Sun Wheel Ferris wheel, Orange Stinger, Maliboomer, Mulholland Madness mini-coaster, and King Triton's Carousel get family fun points here, along with plenty of concessions and food vendors along the midway.

The second land, dubbed the Hollywood Pictures Backlot, has huge soundstages that hold attractions such as Jim Henson's *Muppet Vision* 3-D movie; Hyperion Theater's live hip musical/dance perfor-mances; and the Animation Center, featuring "Turtle Talk with Crush" from the movie *Finding Nemo*. The Twilight Zone Tower of Terror drops you thirteen stories faster than the speed of gravity (do not eat before this one, really!). *Monsters, Inc.: Mike and Sully to the Rescue* is a another 3-D attraction that re-creates the streets of Monstropolis from the animated film. New in 2008 is the live show "Playhouse Dis-ney," where your kids can sing and dance along with these fun charac-ters onstage (floor seating for 550 guests, so be ready to participate).

The Golden State land features the must-do Soarin' Over California experience, where you will hang with feet dangling as you fly like an eagle—visually—around an 80-foot dome-shaped motion-picture screen filled with an amazing view of the best California scenery. Don't miss Grizzly River Run, a white-water-rafting ride that swirls you down two waterfalls (you will get wet); Bountiful Valley Farm with its demonstration veggie and fruit gardens; Robert Mondavi's Golden Vine Winery, with wine tasting for us adults; Pacific Wharf, where you can watch Boudin's Bakery make sourdough bread and Mission brand tortillas pop out; and a movie starring Whoopi Goldberg in the Golden Dreams Theatre.

"A Bug's Land" is a fourth area including five attractions inside Flik's Fun Fair. Plenty of food and beverage options inhabit DCA, and be prepared to spend some gold nuggets to enjoy the diverse range of fare, ranging from traditional burgers, dogs, and fries to sushi, chowder, pizza, and Chinese and Mexican cuisine. Scheduled for 2008–09—"Toy Story Mania" will be an interactive feature plus an indoor attraction based on *The Little Mermaid*. Disney's California Adventure certainly embraces Walt's original promise: "Dis-neyland will never be complete as long as there is imagination left in the world."

Angel Stadium of Anaheim

2000 Gene Autry Way. Baseball season runs April through September; call (714) 940-2000 for a schedule and ticket prices; www.angelsbaseball.com. $

The 45,000-seat stadium is home to Major League Baseball's Los Angeles Angels of Ana-heim. During the Angels off-season, "behind the scenes" tours take place every Tuesday

Anaheim **GardenWalk**

Located at 321 West Katella Avenue at Clementine, just east of Harbor Boulevard and within walking distance of the Disneyland Resort, GardenWalk is a unique 440,000-square-foot outdoor shopping and dining experience set among beautifully manicured walkways and gardens that is opening in phases during 2007–09. GardenWalk includes "300," an upscale bowling lounge, a fourteen-plex theater, and various establishments including Aveda, Banana Republic, Bar Louie, Chico's, Harley Davidson, Heat Ultra Lounge, White House/Black Market, and XP Sports. Its first phase of restaurants debuted in late 2007/early 2008 including national favorites California Pizza Kitchen, The Cheesecake Factory, McCormick & Schmick's Grille, P.F. Chang's China Bistro, and Roy's (Hawaiian Fusion Cuisine), plus the super-family friendly **Bubba Gump Shrimp Company**—modeled after the 1994 hit movie *Forrest Gump*—the restaurant combines a casual, playful atmosphere with high quality and quantities of seafood, especially shrimp prepared myriad ways, tasty appetizers, humongous desserts and a reasonably-priced kids menu featuring "Bus Bench Burger," Hubba Bubba Popcorn Shrimp, and Yummy Smoothies (714-635-GUMP or www.bubba gump.com).

(with the exception of holidays) at 9:30 a.m, 11:00 a.m., and 1:00 p.m. During the season, tours are held on Tuesday and Wednesday at 9:30 a.m., 11:00 a.m., and 1:00 p.m. when the team is out of town. Tours are not offered on dates when the Angels have a home game. Advanced reservations are required for tours by calling (714) 940-2070.

Honda Center (formerly Arrowhead Pond)

2695 East Katella Avenue; (714) 704-2400; www.hondacenter.com.

This 18,900-seat enclosed arena—ranked number three entertainment venue in the world by *Billboard* magazine—hosts many events and concerts and is home to the National Hockey League's Stanley Cup Champion Mighty Ducks, who skate from October through March (714-704-2000; http://ducks.nhl.com). Call for ticket prices and schedules.

Glacial Gardens Skating Arena

3975 Pixie Street,Lakewood; (562) 429-1805; www.glacialgardens.com. Open daily, with varying times and fees for open figure skating, instruction, and hockey matches. $$

This is the place to go if your family would rather participate than watch ice sports. Head over to this triple-rink facility (Olympic size NHL size, and a slightly smaller training rink), complete with a pro shop, snack bar, locker rooms, and skate rentals.

Adventure City (ages 2 to 12)

1238 Beach Boulevard between Cerritos Avenue and Ball Road, on the outskirts of Anaheim; (714) 236-9300 for current operating hours or visit www.adventurecity.com. Generally open daily in summer from 10:00 a.m. to 5:00 p.m. and in winter Friday through Sunday, but hours are subject to change without notice. $$$

Adventure City, "the Little Theme Park Just for Kids," resembles a storybook village designed and proportioned for children ages two to twelve. For a wonderfully relaxing experience, consider visiting this two-acre park with its ten kid-size rides that are quiet yet still zoom and thrill, as well as hourly puppet shows, a 25-foot climbing wall, live theater, storytelling, and face painting. Parent-child interaction is made easy here because the atmosphere is very casual and low-hype. There are plenty of park benches for parental units to sit and relax on while the kids go brave the Kid Coaster or the carousel.

Children's Museum at La Habra (ages 2 to 10)

301 South Euclid Avenue, La Habra, approximately thirty minutes from Disneyland; (562) 905-9793; www.lhcm.org. Open Tuesday through Friday 10:00 a.m. to 4:00 p.m.; Saturday 10:00 a.m. to 5:00 p.m., and Sunday 1:00 to 5:00 p.m.; closed major holidays. $$

Opened in 1977 as California's first children's museum, this facility is located in a renovated 1923 Union Pacific train depot. It features seven galleries and fourteen different hands-on exhibits, an outdoor dinosaur topiary and historic 1942 caboose, and a seasonal feature exhibit that changes four times per year. In Summer 2008, you could go on a "Backyard Safari" and learn about ants, earthworms, butterflies, and all the cool things that live in your backyard

MUZEO

241 South Anaheim Boulevard; (714) 956-8936; www.muzeo.org. Open 10:00 a.m. to 5:00 p.m. daily except holidays. $$$

MUZEO means "museum" in the international Esperanto language. It opened in October 2007 as part of a complex that includes Anaheim's original 1908 Carnegie Library surrounded by two courtyards that connect to apartments and stores to create a very user-friendly urban setting. MUZEO is a revolutionary 25,000 square-foot facility that combines high-tech innovations of today (state-of-the-art self guided audio podcasts, Wi-Fi access, interactive displays) with incredible interchangeable exhibits of history, art, architecture and natural science from yesterday and the future. There are three traveling exhibitions per year—such as "Jane Goodall Presents: Discovering Chimpanzees" in Summer 2008. Each special exhibit has programs, events and activities attached to it—which make it fascinating to visit no matter when your family is nearby.

Crystal Cathedral of the Reformed Church in America

13280 Chapman Avenue, Garden Grove. Call the visitor center at (714) 971-4000 to check tour times or (714) 544-5679 to reserve tickets for the extremely cherished holiday pageants; www.crystalcathedral.org. Free tours are generally available Monday through

Saturday, but times are subject to change due to church services and events. Donations appreciated.

For some religious and architectural history, visit the dramatic, all-glass sanctuary designed by Philip Johnson, considered a dean of American architects. This incredible place features 10,000 glass panes covering a weblike steel frame resembling a four-point star. The 2,890-seat cathedral hosts the annual Glory of Christmas and Glory of Easter pageants, with live animals, flying angels, and incredible special lighting reflected from the twelve-story glass walls and ceilings.

Nixon Presidential Library and Museum

18001 Yorba Linda Boulevard, Yorba Linda. From Anaheim take the Riverside Freeway Route 57 northbound and exit Yorba Linda Boulevard, then travel about 5 miles east to the library, on the left-hand side (watch carefully for signs); (714) 993-5075 or (800) 872-8865; http://nixon.archives.gov and www.nixonlibraryfoundation.org. Open Monday through Saturday 10:00 a.m. to 5:00 p.m. and Sunday 11:00 a.m. to 5:00 p.m. $$

The facility was first opened and dedicated on July 19, 1990, and inherited by the Federal government in 2007 from the private foundation that had previously controlled the library. Be sure to schedule at least half a day to let your family experience the political and world history depicted at this nine-acre site. You'll begin your tour in the auditorium, which shows vintage campaign films, news footage, and historically significant television appearances by President Nixon; then proceed to the permanent galleries displaying images, video, and artifacts related to President Nixon's career, family life, and volunteer

Anaheim Resort Transit—the car-free and care-free way to get around!

The newest, hassle-free way to navigate the Anaheim Resort Area and avoid parking fees and traffic (and reduce air pollution) is via ART (714-563-5287 or www.rideART.org), a fixed fifteen-route transportation system using zero-emission electric buses and clean fuel propane trolleys. Be sure to purchase an ART Pass before you get on the bus (or you'll be charged the $3 one-way cash fee). There are convenient ticketing kiosks at all the stops that accept major credit cards and you can also purchase online. The routes run to/from Disneyland Resort Transit Plaza/Main Entrance about every fifteen to twenty minutes from all major hotels, the Honda Center, Angel Stadium, and the Amtrak/Metrolink Railway station—giving you a complete car-free option to arriving at the Magic Kingdom (http://rideart.org/amtrak.html). In 2008 a one-day unlimited ART Pass was $3 for adults, $1 for children ages three to nine, and free for children two and under. Multiple-day ART Passes are also readily available. We found ART extremely convenient in getting us back and forth between our Anaheim hotel and the Disneyland Resort. Highly recommended!

Downtown Disney District

Opened in January 2001, this twenty-acre dining, shopping, and entertainment area is located between Disneyland and Disney's California Adventure and encircles three Disneyland Resort hotels. The district is free and open to the public year-round. It features lovely landscaped gardens and promenades interspersed with 300,000 square feet of retail shops, restaurants, and twelve AMC movie theaters. Some highlights: excellent pastries and espresso at La Brea Bakery; wood-fired pizza at Naples Ristorante; tapas at Catal Restaurant; Ralph Brennen's Jazz Kitchen for Cajun food; the House of Blues for live entertainment (the Sunday gospel brunch is inspiring!); Rainforest Cafe for tropical treats; and the ESPN Zone for a fantastic sports fix (live sports broadcasts, interactive games, and food). Shopping includes the ubiquitous World of Disney store and Build-A-Bear, plus plenty of other gift, souvenir, music, jewelry, and fashion emporiums. For more information call (714) 300-7800 or visit www.disneyland.com.

service. One of our favorites details the space program during the Nixon presidency, featuring an astronaut's space suit, the telephone President Nixon used to call Neil Armstrong and Buzz Aldrin on the moon, and an actual moon rock. There's an interactive presidential forum, where you can ask a "virtual" President Nixon a whopping 279 questions about his life and presidency. Check out the 1967 Lincoln Continental limousine he used (also utilized by Presidents Johnson, and Ford); and see a replica of the East Room of the White House as well as President Nixon's helicopter and birthplace. The exhibits portray America's thirty-seventh commander in chief right up until his death on April 22, 1994. Both President and Mrs. Nixon are buried here in the tranquil First Lady's Garden. You may visit the gravesite, the reflecting pool, and the white clapboard farmhouse where Nixon was born on January 9, 1913. It remains precisely as it was when Nixon and his family lived there, right down to the bed where he was born. The intimate museum store on the premises contains commemorative souvenirs, postcards, and a selection of Nixon's books.

Where to Eat and Stay

Disney's PCH Grill at Disney's Paradise Pier Hotel, 1717 Disneyland Drive; (714) 999-0990. Open daily for breakfast, lunch, and dinner. Hours vary seasonally. PCH stands for Pacific Coast Highway, California's prime and celebrated coastal route. Dining in the PCH Grill for lunch and dinner celebrates all the foods and beverages that make up California cuisine. Menu maps plot your meal course by course and feature fresh seafood, pastas, oak-fired pizzas, burgers, and desserts. If you're looking for traditional American fare, this is probably not the best spot for you, but you know what they say: "When

Getting in **the Swing**

The ever-popular **Golf N'Stuff** is conveniently located across the street from Disneyland at 1656 South Harbor Boulevard (714-778-4100) and has two beautifully landscaped eighteen-hole miniature golf courses and an arcade center open seven days a week. Real golf enthusiasts can swing out under the instruction of PGA pros at the **Islands Golf Center**, 14893 Ball Road (714-630-7888; www.theislandsgolfcenter.com), on eighteen acres of practice tees, greens, and a fairway on a ten-acre lake. There are more than twenty other Orange County golf options.

If your family wants to swing out with a racket, you can choose from twelve championship hard-surface tennis courts at the **Anaheim Tennis Center Inc.,** located at 975 South State College Boulevard (714-991-9090; www.anaheimtenniscenter.com). The center is open year-round and offers computerized, self-loading ball machines as well as professional instruction. More than fifty tennis courts can be found at hotels and in Orange County's public parks. Call (714) 771-6731, ext. 220 or visit www.ocparks.com or call (866) OCPARKS for information on the county's 37,000 acres of parkland and open space including regional and wilderness parks, nature preserves and recreational trails, historic sites, harbors, and beaches.

in California, eat like the Californians do," or something like that. Your best bet for the family at the PCH Grill is breakfast, because Lilo and Stitch characters make this a fun-filled Disney dining experience that also features a magic act onstage with Mr. Wizard. (Kids get to help perform tricks between bites.) You can order off the menu or cruise the buffet for your favorite breakfast items. $$$

Goofy's Kitchen at the Disneyland Hotel, 1150 Magic Way; (714) 778-6600. Your kids will not want to miss Goofy's, one of the nine restaurants on-site. Open every day—breakfast, lunch, and dinner. Call for specific hours as they vary seasonally. You can dine with Disney characters (and get your picture taken!), eat Disney Character Meals, try out the all-you-can-eat buffet, and receive a free souvenir button. Our kids insist on this "dining experience" every time! $$$

Hilton Anaheim, 777 Convention Way; (714) 750-4321; www.hilton.com. Only 2 blocks from Disneyland, this full-service hotel adjacent to the Anaheim Convention Center opened in 1984; during 2008, it was undergoing an extensive $60 million renovation of the 1,572 guest rooms and suites as well as other facilities. The hotel boasts a large heated outdoor pool on the fifth floor, four whirlpools, three rooftop garden sundecks, a Spa & Fitness Center with an indoor pool, basketball gym, sauna, steam room, private tanning salon, and massage services, beauty salon, and retail shops, plus in-lobby Starbucks, the Avenue Bar, and the Sushi Bar and Café Oasis for breakfast, lunch, and dinner—where kids ages ten and under dine **free** on the extensive breakfast buffet with an adult buffet purchase (a filling way to start your family's day). Kidz Korner Playroom and activities are offered seasonally. $$$$

Disneyland Hotel, 1150 Magic Way; (714) 778-6600 or direct to reservations at (714) 956-6400. Just west of Disneyland and connected by the futuristic monorail, this hotel opened at the same time as the park in 1955 and has continued to evolve. It features 990 guest rooms and suites in three high-rise towers surrounding the magical Peter Pan–themed Neverland pool complex (with water slides, bridges, and shallow play areas); a kids' playground; and a sandy beach with rental pedal boats, remote-control tugboats, and dune buggies. There are nine restaurants and lounges to choose from, plus four swimming pools, a hot tub, the Team Mickey Fitness Center, gift shops, and an eighty-game video arcade. New for 2008—nineteen guest rooms that are highly themed to either Mickey Mouse or the regal Disney Princesses. These "Character Quarters" each feature two twin beds and are available adjoining a standard room. They are perfect for a family of five or more. (Of course, advance reservations are required for these high-in-demand lodgings.) This hotel is a destination within itself, and you should plan some time to enjoy all the amenities. Family-friendly features include no charge for children younger than age seventeen staying in same room as parents; free roll-aways and porta-cribs, and babysitting referrals to licensed "grandmother types." Value-priced hotel and park package plans are prevalent and include early admission into both parks one and a half hours before the regular opening. Be sure to ask what's available when making reservations. Another great service is the Package Express, which delivers all your park purchases to your hotel room for **free.** $$$$

Disney's Grand Californian Hotel & Spa, 1600 South Disneyland Drive; (714) 635-2300. Opened in February 2001, this AAA-4-diamond rated luxurious 745-room hotel with its striking California Craftsman architectural design is located on the northwest corner of Disney's California Adventure. This hotel is the only one to offer direct access straight into the park, a wonderful time-saving feature for your family. Guest rooms come equipped with a choice of king, two queens, or a queen and a set of bunk beds—a real family-fun plus for us! The concierge level offers extra amenities including complimentary continental breakfast and evening wine and cheese and an array of recreational activities for the entire family. We adults savor the Mandara Spa with some precious pampering and personal service. We all enjoyed the Fountain Pool and the Redwood Pool with waterslide; and for ages five to twelve, there is nothing better than Pinocchio's Workshop—an

All-Suite Hotels near Disneyland

Like California wildflowers, an amazing variety of all-suite hotels have sprung up near the park in recent years. This trend really is a boon for traveling families like us, who like to have a private bedroom for the adults and a multifunction living room/dining area with hide-a-bed arrangements for the kids. Each suite hotel has varying amenities such as **free** breakfasts, kitchenettes, pools, and spas. You might want to investigate the **Castle Inn & Suites** (714-774-8111), the **Peacock Suite Resort** (714-535-8255), **Carousel Inn & Suites** (newly renovated with a rooftop pool and fitness center; 714-758-0444), or **Anaheim Portofino Inn and Suites** (714-782-7600), as well as all the national chains.

evening of arts and crafts, computer games, Disney movies, dinner, and snacks with a licensed supervisor. The storytelling hour in front of the massive lobby fireplace with kids in pint-size wooden rockers is a perfect example of the Disney detail you can enjoy for your family here.

From the moment you arrive (and are offered valet parking), you are treated with outstanding hospitality and service. Hotel dining options include twenty-four-hour room service and the excellent Storyteller's Cafe with its tasty breakfast buffet and American cuisine for lunch and dinner daily (and visits from Disney characters such as Chip 'n Dale), plus the stunning Napa Rose Restaurant (with an open exhibition kitchen), Hearthstone Lounge, and White Water Snacks Poolside. We really like this property and feel the higher room rates are justified given the ease of park accessibility combined with the outstanding amenities and service. $$$$

Disney's Paradise Pier Hotel, 1717 Disneyland Drive; (714) 999-0990 or direct to reservations at (714) 956-6400. This fifteen-story, full-service hotel overlooks the festive Paradise Pier area at Disney's California Adventure. Choose from 489 nicely furnished guest rooms and suites. There are four restaurants and lounges, an outdoor pool and spa deck, a game arcade, convenient indoor/outdoor parking, and gift shops. There is no charge for children younger than age eighteen staying in the same room as parents. $$$$

For More Information

Anaheim/Orange County Visitor and Convention Bureau. 800 West Katella Avenue, 92802; (714) 765-8888 or (888) 598-3200; www.anaheimoc.org.

Buena Park

Now it's time to gear up for another round of great family adventure in nearby Buena Park—only fifteen minutes from Anaheim and Disneyland. This area's development began in 1920, when Walter and Cordelia Knott and their three young children arrived and started farming on twenty acres of leased land. The Knotts set up a roadside produce stand on Beach Boulevard to sell their crops, and in 1932 Walter Knott started propagating a cross blend of raspberry, blackberry, and loganberry plants that he named boysenberry. In 1934, to help make ends meet during the Great Depression, Cordelia Knott began serving chicken dinners for 65 cents on her wedding china to passing motorists. Soon Knott's Berry Farm boysenberry fruits, jams, jellies, and pies, along with the Chicken Dinner Restaurant, became so popular that the family decided to build an attraction to keep waiting patrons amused. In 1940 Walter Knott began moving old buildings to the site from various ghost towns. The Calico Mine Ride followed in 1960, and a re-creation of Philadelphia's Independence Hall was constructed in 1966. In 1968 the amusement park area was enclosed, and for the first time a general admission fee was charged. Knott's Berry Farm forms the nucleus for many attractions in this commercial section of Orange County. Plan on spending at least two days here in order to do it all "berry good."

Knott's Berry Farm

8039 Beach Boulevard at the corner of La Palma Avenue; (714) 220-5200; www.knotts.com. Open daily except Christmas. Summer hours 9:00 a.m. to midnight. In winter the park operates weekdays 10:00 a.m. to 6:00 p.m., Saturday 10:00 a.m. to 10:00 p.m., and Sunday 10:00 a.m. to 7:00 p.m. Extended hours are offered during holiday periods. All admissions after 4:00 p.m. are reduced year-round. Parking across the street and accessed by a special walkway or tram is $7 per car. Be absolutely sure to call in advance for current ticket prices and schedules since all are subject to change without notice. $$$$

Knott's Berry Farm was family-owned and -operated until its 1997 purchase by Cedar Fair, L.P. It attracts more than five million guests each year to its entertainment park and marketplace, featuring 165 attractions, rides, live shows, restaurants, and shops. The lushly landscaped 160 acres have plenty of flowers, trees, waterfalls, and shady spots.

Five theme areas include the original Ghost Town, where you can pan for gold and go for a great log ride and take the Ghost Rider, the longest wooden coaster in the West; Camp Snoopy, the official home of the Peanuts gang, including Woodstock's air mail ride; and Fiesta Village, prowling ground for the Jaguar!, a 2,700-foot-long steel roller coaster that winds its way above the park and loops through Montezooma's Revenge (another thrilling coaster with its own 76-foot-high loop). The Boardwalk has Xcelerator, Perilous Plunge, Riptide, the Boomerang (ever been on a roller coaster that rolls backward? Definite queasy alert!), and Supreme Scream (312 feet of vertical excitement), as well as Sky Cabin and Wipeout. The Mystery Lodge is a magical multisensory show focusing on native North American culture located in the Wild Water Wilderness. Come here at the end of your day if you plan on riding Bigfoot Rapids. Speaking from personal experience, heed the warning signs: You will get wet on this ride—most likely drenched! It may feel great on a hot summer day, but squishy shoes and clothing can get mighty uncomfortable mighty fast. "Indian Trails" gives you a chance to dry off and watch Native American arts, crafts, and music. New for 2008 is the Pony Express coaster, a horseback relay launching at a speed of 0 to 38 mph in less than three seconds—speeds never imagined in the Old West!

Knott's Soak City U.S.A.—Orange County

Across the street from Knott's Berry Farm, 8039 Beach Boulevard at La Palma Avenue, adjacent to Knott's Independence Hall; (714) 220-5200; www.knotts.com/soakcity/oc/index .shtml. Open daily Memorial Day through Labor Day; open Saturday and Sunday in May, September, and October. $$$$

This California-beach-theme water park features twenty-three separate water rides and attractions, including tube and body water slides, a wave pool, a lazy river, a family fun house, restaurants, snack bars, a sand beach, a pier, and gift shops.

Ripley's Believe It or Not! Museum

7850 Beach Boulevard, 1 block north of Knott's Berry Farm along the Buena Park entertainment corridor; (714) 522-7045; www.ripleys.com. Open Monday through Friday 11:00 a.m. to 5:00 p.m., Saturday and Sunday 10:00 a.m. to 6:00 p.m. year-round. $$

Use your parental discretion on the age appropriateness of this attraction. In our opinion, mouse fetus wine, edible maggot jewelry, and a four-eyed man might be a little disconcerting to the very young.

One of the many Ripley's around the country, this 10,000-square-foot structure opened in 1990 with an "Odditorium" featuring a unique collection of the bizarre, the strange, and the beautiful found during the worldwide travels of adventurer Robert Ripley, born on Christmas Day 1893. Some of the exhibits are educational, like the 200 B.C. Venus de Milo statue, Chinese art, and primitive currency.

Medieval Times Dinner and Tournament

7662 Beach Boulevard; (714) 521-4740 or (888) WE-JOUST; www.medievaltimes.com. Open nightly year-round with special Sunday matinees. $$$$

You'll eat in an arena filled with more than 1,100 people, divided into six sections, wearing colored hats, waving streamers, and cheering their favorite knight on to victory over the course of a two-hour eleventh-century show. Included is a four-course meal of twenty-first-century food (appetizer, vegetable soup, chicken, ribs, baked potato slice, and apple turnover) in medieval style (no modern knife, fork, or spoon to assist you). Make sure you bring plenty of extra cash to buy banners to wave, souvenir programs, and photos taken during dinner. Beer, wine, sodas, and coffee are included in the admission price; however, these prices are subject to change and do not include gratuity for your hardworking serving wenches and serfs. Call the colorful castle for daily showtimes—advance reservations are required. Make sure you arrive at least one hour before your scheduled showtime to navigate the parking lot with your chariot and negotiate the check-in line.

This is outstanding family fun that is not to be missed—you and the kids can release all kinds of pent-up vocal energy as you yell for "your" knight in armor during a pageant of excellent horsemanship and tournament games of skill and accuracy. A pricey outing, but we think you definitely will agree that "your day's not over until you've seen those knights!"

Pirate's Dinner Adventure

7600 Beach Boulevard, immediately off the 91 freeway; (714) 690-1497 or (866) 439-2469; www.piratesdinneradventure.com. Open daily; call for showtimes and specials. Doors open ninety minutes prior to the show for appetizers in the ship's "lounge." Showroom doors open fifteen minutes prior to performance, and seating begins in an authentically replicated eighteenth-century Spanish galleon anchored in a 250,000-gallon indoor lagoon with six "audience ships" around the perimeter—each equipped with color-coded character pirate you are encouraged to cheer and interact with throughout the evening. Show is ninety minutes. $$$$

Formerly the site of Wild Bill's Wild West Show, at Pirate's Dinner Adventure up to 750 guests can enjoy this new extravaganza, featuring an astonishing display of special-effects wizardry, aerial trapeze artistry, swashbuckling swordplay, pirate fights, and dynamic duels. While all this action is going on, you can eat your "Port of Call Feast" including, garden salad, choice of beef with seafood (shrimp and scallops) or marinated chicken with seafood, West Indies yellow rice with Caribbean seasonings, and steamed vegetables with warm apple cobbler a la mode for dessert washed down with a choice of soda, beer, or wine. Our recommendation: The show is geared for ages ten and up, but there certainly are plenty of younger guests in attendance and participating in the pirates' activities during the show—just seemed a bit too much excitement, noise, lights, and fights for a kiddie activity. Ahoy!

Where to Eat

Knott's California Marketplace, just outside the main entrance of Knott's Berry Farm, 8039 Beach Boulevard at the corner of La Palma Avenue; (714) 220-5200. This area is filled with shops and restaurants for your family's pleasure, but the best is Mrs. Knott's original Chicken Dinner Restaurant. Hearty American fare is served for breakfast, lunch, and dinner at very reasonable prices. The kids' menu comes complete with crayons and a coloring book. We recommend eating here for lunch (go early or late to avoid crowds). Don't plan on taking any rides anytime·near your consumption of that delicious chicken, mashed potatoes, and boysenberry pie. (We speak from experience here. Trust us!) $$

Where to Stay

Knott's Berry Farm Resort Hotel, 7675 Crescent Avenue, adjacent to Knott's Berry Farm; (714) 995-1111; www.knottshotel.com. Its 320 units include a limited number of "Peanuts" theme rooms with nightly Snoopy character turndown service. Free Snoopy gift for kids at check-in. Outdoor kiddy pool, adult pool, whirlpool, fitness center, sauna, and steam room. Festive Italian family food at Amber Waves Restaurant with kids' menus and daily visits from Snoopy to add to the fun. Gift shops. **Free** parking. $$$

For More Information

Buena Park Convention and Visitors Office. 6601 Beach Boulevard, Suite 200, 90261-2904; (714) 562-3560 or (800) 541-3953; www.visitbuenapark.com.

Orange

How would you like to find a slice of the midwestern United States buried in the heart of Orange County? Look no further than the historic city of Orange, sandwiched between Santa Ana and Anaheim, the two largest cities in all of Orange County. Approach the city of Orange by way of eastbound Chapman Avenue, off I-5 or from Highway 57. As you enter downtown, cobblestone, tree lined thoroughfares take you into the intersection of Chapman and Glassell Streets, where you will discover a circular central plaza. The "Plaza City" boasts a 1-square-mile historic district, where nineteenth-century architecture is preserved and cherished, and the appeal is decidedly homespun and friendly. Check out the living-history lessons presented in the myriad antiques shops scattered around the plaza.

Watson's Drugs and Soda Fountain

116 East Chapman; (714) 633-1050. Open Monday through Saturday 6:30 a.m. to 9:00 p.m. and Sunday 8:00 a.m. to 6:00 p.m. $

The best place to soak up the flavor of Orange is on a stool at a joint that has been continuously serving heaping scoops of ice cream, traditional American meals, and remedies at its Plaza Square location since 1899. The root beer floats are so frothy you will wonder how you lived this long without one, and the malts are the real deal—hand-dipped ice cream with a scoop of malt and real milk. Sweet! Breakfast, lunch, and dinner daily, featuring a kids' menu for those age twelve and younger. Go in anytime to see an authentic soda fountain in action and watch the servers in their period outfits and hairdos play soda jerks. The interior and exterior have been used to film many movies and commercials, including Tom Hanks's film *That Thing You Do!*

Dromo 1

1431 North Main Street; (714) 744-4779; www.dromo1.com. Open daily. Call for schedules, times, and special promotions. $$$

This indoor facility is home to some of the most competitive go-kart racing in Southern California. No training or previous experience is necessary. The only requirement for drivers is a minimum height of 5 feet (60 inches)—making this suitable for older kids. All racers must sign a liability release form; an accompanying parent or legal guardian will need to sign for those under eighteen years of age. For speed-racing enthusiasts, this is the place.

For More Information

City of Orange Chamber of Commerce. 439 East Chapman Avenue, Suite A, 92866; (714) 538-3581 or (800) 938-0073; www.orangechamber.org.

Santa Ana

Orange County's largest city is also the county seat of government and home to the **John Wayne/Orange County Airport (SNA)** (949-252-5200; www.ocair.com/). Downtown Santa Ana combines Fiesta Marketplace, a bustling Latino-style pedestrian mall, with a contemporary $50 million civic center and about a hundred historic buildings that would make the Spanish explorer Portolá proud of the city he christened in 1796.

Bowers Museum of Cultural Art and Kidseum

2002 North Main Street; (714) 567-3600; www.bowers.org. Open Tuesday through Friday 10:00 a.m. to 4:00 p.m., Saturday and Sunday 10:00 a.m. to 6:00 p.m. Open holidays except Christmas, Thanksgiving, and New Year's Day. Closed Monday. $$

A significant part of Santa Ana's past is found in its first museum, created in 1936 through a bequest from Charles and Ada Bowers to preserve the local history of Orange County.

Through gifts and acquisitions, the Bowerses' collections have grown over the years, and the museum has enlarged its space three times. It is now considered one of the finest cultural arts repositories in the West. The museum specializes in the arts of the Americas, the Pacific Rim, and Africa, along with its ongoing commitment to chronicle the story of Orange County. From May through October 2008, Bowers hosted an exclusive exhibition of China's famed Terra Cotta Warriors—the largest loan of terra-cotta figures and significant artifacts to ever travel to the United States from the First Emperor's enormous mausoleum. The museum store has unique art treasures, cards, and gifts not readily available in traditional museum gift shops.

In 1994 the 11,000-square-foot Bowers Kidseum opened 2 blocks away at 1802 North Main Street. This amazing center has been competently designed for youth ages six to twelve as a place where children can learn about other cultures, music, art, and history through interactive, hands-on exhibits. Hours of operation for the general public run Tuesday through Friday from 1:00 to 4:00 p.m. and Saturday and Sunday from 10:00 a.m. to 4:00 p.m. Admission fees are identical and reciprocal with the Bowers Museum. Thematic "explorers' backpacks" covering various cultural differences are just one example of this outstanding opportunity for your kids to actually learn something valuable while vacationing. The Kidseum perfectly bridges the gap between amusement and education.

Centennial Heritage Museum

3101 West Harvard Street; (714) 540-0404; www.centennialmuseum.org. Open Wednesday through Friday 1:00 to 5:00 p.m. and Saturday and Sunday 11:00 a.m. to 3:00 p.m. Closed major holidays. $

This historic museum, located in the fully restored, 1898 Victorian Kellogg House, is your family's chance to step back in time to the 1800s. Kids can try on Victorian costumes, wash clothes on a scrub board, play a pump organ, or talk on a hand-cranked telephone. This is a very fun yet informative way to learn early California history. The eight-acre Nature Center has interpretive trails.

The Santa Ana Zoo at Prentice Park

1801 East Chestnut Avenue; (714) 835-7484; www.santaanazoo.org. Open daily 10:00 a.m. to 4:00 p.m., extended hours in summer. Closed holidays. $$

This charming zoo will calm your kids' animal urges with its 250 species of primates, other mammals, and birds. Refreshments are available in the food court, and vendors around the grounds sell snacks and ice cream. A playground, the Crean Family Farm (interactive feeding), and Zoofari Express miniature train rides are offered. Call for current programs and times.

Discovery Science Center

2500 North Main Street (at the corner of I-5 and the Santa Ana Freeway); (714) 542-CUBE; www.discoverycube.org. Open daily 10:00 a.m. to 5:00 p.m. except major holidays. $$$

"The Amusement Park for Your Mind" opened in 1998 in a 59,000-square-foot multi-story facility devoted to sparking children's natural curiosity and increasing everyone's understanding of science, math, and technology. More than 120 highly interactive exhibits make you think, search for answers, and participate in the learning process. Themed areas include Perception, Dynamic Earth, Quake Zone, Showcase Gallery, Boeing Delta III Rocket, Air & Space, Techno Arts, and Digital Lab. Our personal favorites include the Shake Shack to experience an earthquake, lying down on a bed of nails, and dancing on the musical floor. This is a marvelous family activity that you should not miss! Highly recommended.

For More Information

Santa Ana Chamber of Commerce. 2020 North Broadway, second floor, 92702; (714) 541-5353; www.santaanachamber.com.

California Welcome Center–Santa Ana. Westfield MainPlace, 2800 N. Main Street, Suite 112, 92705; (714) 667-0400; www.visit cwc.com.

Irvine and Costa Mesa

The city of Irvine is the largest master-planned community in the United States. It was first developed in 1959 as a site for the University of California-Irvine on an old Spanish land grant. Billboards, overhead power lines, and TV antennas are banned here in an area divided into thirty-eight urban villages featuring a plethora of parks, all connected by greenbelts and bike paths. Shopping centers and services are all conveniently located nearby. The central corridor of high-rise buildings, such as the Irvine Spectrum and Koll Center, provide headquarters for plenty of Fortune 500 firms as well as some family fun.

The adjacent city of Costa Mesa, also home to many corporations as well as a popular residential community, became a player on the Orange County shopping and entertainment scene in 1967 with the opening of South Coast Plaza: the Ultimate Shopping Resort, a great place for your family to satisfy those shopping urges.

Irvine Spectrum Center

At the intersection of Interstate 405 (exit Irvine Center Drive) and I-5 (exit Alton), Irvine. Open daily 10:00 a.m. to 9:00 p.m.; hours can vary for restaurants and during holiday periods and special events. Call (949) 753-5180 for more information or visit www.shopirvine spectrumcenter.com.

This premier entertainment plaza offers twenty-one IMAX movie cinemas, world-class restaurants, nightlife, specialty shops from around the globe, a 108-foot-tall Giant Wheel (Ferris wheel), and a carousel.

Wild Rivers Waterpark (age 3 and older)

8770 Irvine Center Drive, Irvine; (949) 768-WILD; www.wildrivers.com. Open daily from Memorial Day weekend throughout the summer season from 10:00 a.m. to 8:00 p.m.; call for winter hours. $$$$

Your high-tech children will definitely want to take advantage of this twenty-acre park with more than forty water rides, including the Edge, the Ledge, and the Abyss; two wave pools; kiddie wading pools; sunbathing areas; a water slide; log flumes; picnic areas; and a video arcade to complete the family-fun mix.

South Coast Plaza: The Ultimate Shopping Resort

3333 Bristol Street, at the intersection of I-405 and Bristol Street, Costa Mesa; (800) 782-8888 or call the concierge at (949) 435-2034 for a current special-event and promotion schedule; www.southcoastplaza.com.

More than one hundred world-renowned stores call this internationally recognized address home, as do restaurants, art galleries, and even a day spa. The kids will clamor to check out the fabulous Disney Store.

Trinity Christian City International

3150 Bear Street (across I-405 from the South Coast Plaza Mall); (714) 832-2950 or (714) 708-5405; www.tbn.org. Free

This striking, classically inspirational building houses broadcast studios and the popular gift and bookshop of this Christian television network. The Virtual Reality Theater presents free motion pictures daily. Call for current titles and showtimes. All ages are welcome.

Orange County Performing Arts Center

600 Town Center Drive, South Coast Plaza, Costa Mesa; (714) 556-2121 or www.ocpac.org for current events and admission charges. $$$$

Opened in 1986, the 3,000-seat Segerstrom Hall is where major symphony concerts, operas, ballets, and Broadway musicals are presented year-round; joined in 2006 by the new 1,700-seat Renée and Henry Segerstrom Concert Hall and the intimate Samueli Theater. It is the home of four Resident Companies: Pacific Symphony, the Philharmonic Society of Orange County, Opera Pacific, and Pacific Chorale. Children's programs dominate around the Christmas holidays. Call (714) 556-2122, ext. 4259, for a schedule of free backstage tours.

Orange County Fair and Event Center

88 Fair Drive, Costa Mesa; (714) 708-1567 or www.ocfair.com/ocf/ for current activities.

Discover a variety of fun family events, including swap meets, automobile and motorcycle speedway races, and concerts. In July the Orange County Fair takes over, featuring top-name entertainment, livestock, carnival rides, rodeo, foodstuffs, arts, crafts, contests, and demonstrations.

For More Information

Costa Mesa Conference and Visitor Bureau. P.O. Box 5071, Costa Mesa, 92628-5071.For more information call (866) 918-4749 or (714) 435-8530; www.travel costamesa.com.

Irvine Chamber of Commerce Visitors Bureau. 2485 McCabe Way, Suite 150, Irvine, 92614; (949) 660-9112 or (877) IRVINE-7; www.irvinecvb.org.

Huntington Beach

Waterfront action or just plain relaxation will provide a respite from all your inland encounters. Orange County's beaches are part of the defining Southern California experience. Traveling along the Pacific Coast Highway, commonly known as PCH or just the Coast Highway, begin your waterside explorations at Huntington Beach, Orange County's third-largest city (after Santa Ana and Anaheim). It is growing into a thriving resort area with more than 8 miles of uninterrupted shoreline. Between Goldenwest Street and Brookhurst Street along PCH, the Bolsa Chica and Huntington Beaches provide plenty of area for safe swimming, picnicking, and surfing. Beach parking fees are charged and vary according to time and season.

Huntington is one of the surf capitals of Southern California, and it thus has been named "Surf City USA." Your kids will probably know this because of the mega-television coverage afforded the surfing championships and international competitions held here every summer. You can easily spend a day on the beaches of Huntington, just enjoying the beautiful surf, sand, and sea. (Do remember to use your sunscreen liberally. Ask any Huntington Beach surfer dude—sunburn is not cool!) The town's ambitious redevelopment efforts along Main Street, just off PCH, contain postmodern shopping plazas and condos alongside the original turn-of-the-last-century waterfront clapboards, which now house trendy clothing stores, beach shops, and bistros. Strolling the 1,856-foot municipal pier is a favorite pastime. Pier Plaza, on PCH at Main, hosts a farmers' market on Friday and live entertainment.

International Surfing Museum

411 Olive Avenue; (714) 960-3483; www.surfingmuseum.org. Displays, admission fees, and opening and closing hours change like the tides (well, not really that frequently!), so call for the current schedule and low admission donations, dudes. Free, but donations welcome.

An art deco–ish building downtown, home of radical exhibits, artifacts, and memorabilia ranging from vintage surfboards to surf wear and surf films, all preserving the heritage of "Surf City USA." Dedicated in May 1994, the **Huntington Beach Surfing Walk of Fame** marked an historic addition to "Surf City." Each inductee receives a granite stone placed in the sidewalk extending from the corners of Pacific Coast Highway and Main Street. Categories include Surf Pioneer, Surf Champion, Surfing Culture, Local Hero, Woman of the Year, and the Honor Roll.

Bolsa Chica Ecological Reserve and Interpretive Center

Between Warner Avenue and Goldenwest Street on the Pacific Coast Highway, just opposite the entrance to Bolsa Chica State Beach; (714) 846-1114; www.bolsachica.org. Open daily, dawn to dusk. Free.

It is both relaxing and educational to walk through this 300-acre reserve, one of the largest salt marsh preserves in Southern California. The reserve supports such rare migratory waterfowl as avocets, egrets, plovers, and terns. A 1.5-mile walkway with explanatory signs leads the way throughout the ecosystem. Ask about guided public tour schedule.

Shipley Nature Center at Huntington Central Park

17829 Goldenwest Street (south of Slater Avenue); (714) 960-8847; www.shipleynature.org. Center is generally open Monday through Saturday 9:00 a.m. to 1:00 p.m.; park is open 5:00 a.m. to 10:00 p.m. Free admission.

For another view of plants and animals, check out this park, home to hundreds of bird species. For human guests there are picnic areas and playgrounds, plus walking and bicycling trails that wind past ponds, waterways, and woodlands.

Where to Eat and Stay

Dwight's at the Beach, on the Boardwalk, 1 block south of the pier; (714) 536-8083. Open daily; call for seasonal times. Since 1932, serving juicy burgers, hot dogs, ice cream, and famous cheese strips—tortilla strips and cheddar cheese topped with secret hot sauce. $

Lazy Dog Café, 16310 Beach Boulevard, at MacDonald Avenue, just south of the 405 freeway near Huntington Beach in Westminster; (714) 500-1140; www.thelazydogcafe .com. Open daily for lunch and dinner. They're serious about food here, but they don't take themselves too seriously since they offer build-your-own pizzas for kids, a plate of delicious mini chili-cheese dogs, and even a dessert served in a dog bowl. The extensive children's menu, which is broken down into "Puppy Dogs" (ages zero to seven) and "Big Dogs" (ages eight to twelve) also features a special dessert—a cup of string licorice with fruit loops for making your own edible necklace or bracelet. $$

Hyatt Regency Huntington Beach Resort & Spa, 21500 Pacific Coast Highway; (714) 698-1234; www.huntingtonbeach.hyatt .com. Garden and ocean views from 517 guest rooms and 57 suites in Andalusian-inspired style. This luxurious hotel directly across from the beach via a pedestrian walkway features three restaurants (the Californian for fine dining, Pete Mallory's Surf City Sunset Grille, and Mankota's Grill poolside), the Village shopping plaza, and the 20,000-square-foot Pacific Waters Spa. Two Camp Hyatt children's programs are offered daily from 9:00 a.m. to 9:00 p.m. Campers receive a welcome gift upon arrival and a packet describing on-site activities. Kids ages three through seven can become Camp Hyatt Beach Clubbers and make shell necklaces, do beach sand art, and roast s'mores by the fire. The SophistiKids program for youth ages eight through twelve includes cool pool and beach play, koi fish feeding, or surfboard making. Other options include parents and kids shared spa treatments as well as Adventure Hyatt programs such as kayaking, learning to surf, and sportfishing tours. $$$$

For More Information

Huntington Beach Conference and Visitors Bureau. 301 Main Street, Suite 208, 92648; (714) 969-3492 or (800) 729-6232; www.surfcityusa.com.

Newport Beach Area

Just south of Huntington Beach along the glittering Pacific lies a city of villages, islands, and private enclaves first incorporated in 1906. The Newport Beach area comprises Balboa, Balboa Island, Lido Isle, Newport Heights, Harbor Island, Bay Shore, Linda Isle, and Corona del Mar. It includes one of the West Coast's most famous yacht harbors, containing approximately 9,000 pleasure craft. In addition, a 6-mile "inland" beach lies along the peninsula between Newport Bay and the ocean. You and your family will discover what many believe to be the trendiest Southern California beach life here.

Balboa Pavilion

400 Main Street, located at the Newport Bay end of Main Street, on the Balboa Peninsula; (800) 830-7744; www.balboapavilion.com. Open daily 10:00 a.m. to 10:00 p.m. Free.

Begin your exploration of the waterfront action at this classic building constructed in 1905 and now listed on the National Register of Historic Places. Here you will discover a marine recreation center offering ferries to quaint Balboa Island and Catalina Island and charter boats for sailing, whale watching, sightseeing, and sportfishing. The Fun Zone has a carousel, Ferris wheel, and arcade.

Davey's Locker Sportfishing

400 Main Street, Balboa Pavilion, Balboa; (949) 673-1434; www.daveyslocker.com. Open daily; hours vary according to season. $$$$

Your headquarters in Newport Beach for harbor excursions, whale watching, and half-, three-quarter, and full-day fishing excursions for catching yellowfin tuna, bonito, sand bass, and rockfish. Twilight fishing trips are offered in the summer, too. These folks are pros, and they will make you feel very comfortable and safe on the water.

Pavilion Paddy Cruises

400 Main Street in the Balboa Pavilion, Balboa; (949) 673-5245; www.catalinainfo.com/HarborCruise.htm. Call for cruise times. $$$$

At the end of the Balboa Peninsula and Pier, do not miss taking a forty-five- or ninety-minute sightseeing cruise aboard the old-fashioned riverboat Pavilion Paddy. You will wind your way through the meandering channels of Newport Harbor and see some imposing homes and dazzling yachts of the rich and famous (such as the late John Wayne and Shirley Temple Black). Tours run mostly year-round. Sunday brunch cruises are also available in season.

Cruising to Catalina from Orange County

The Catalina Passenger Service operates the *Catalina Flyer*, its 500-passenger catamaran vessel, from Balboa Pavilion in Newport Beach. It offers one round-trip seventy-five-minute cruise daily to neighboring Santa Catalina Island, a pristine, unspoiled isle only 26 miles out to sea yet a world away. (See the Greater Los Angeles chapter for other Long Beach/San Pedro embarkation choices.) Fares and departure times are subject to change seasonally. Reservations are required. Phone (949) 673-5245 or (800) 830-7744 for current schedules or visit www.catalinainfo.com. $$$$

The Newport Harbor Nautical Museum

In the heart of Balboa Peninsula's Fun Zone, 600 East Bay Avenue, Newport Beach; (949) 673-3377; www.nhnm.org. Open Wednesday through Monday 10:00 a.m. to 6:00 p.m. Closed Tuesday. $

This interesting museum gives a photographic history of the harbor, a fascinating ships-in-a-bottle exhibit, and a display of navigational instruments and model ships, including one made of bone and human hair, and one made of 22 karat gold and silver.

Hornblower Cruises and Events

2431 West Pacific Coast Highway, Suite 101, Newport Beach; (949) 646-0155; www.hornblower .com. Cruises on climate-controlled large yachts offered year-round. Evening and Sunday brunch cruise schedules vary according to season and demand for private charters. Brunch cruises sail for two hours and include an all-you-can-eat buffet with champagne for adults; children ages four to twelve half price. Gratuity and cocktails additional. $$$$

Excellent service from nautically attired crew and California cuisine prepared fresh onboard make this an upscale cruising, dining, and sightseeing experience to remember. Recommended for older children; for our families, we like the Sunday brunch cruises best.

Newport Sports Museum

100 Newport Center Drive, Suite 100; (949) 721-9333; www.newportsportsmuseum.org. Open Tuesday through Sunday from 10:00 a.m. to 5:00 p.m. Free admission; donations welcome.

This 6,000-square-foot museum features one of the world's largest collections of sports memorabilia, assembled in fifteen themed rooms containing 10,000 items. Highlights include jerseys from Michael Jordan, Larry Bird, Dr. J, and Wilt Chamberlain and auto-graphed baseballs from every Cy Young winner. There's even a baseball park with actual seats from places such as Yankee Stadium and Wrigley Field! The collection started in 1953 when John W. Hamilton, at the age of twelve, was given a "Look All-American Football" by a family friend. Hamilton has been collecting sports memorabilia ever since, with the majority of the items being personally given to him by athletes.

Shopping and More **with an Ocean View**

Luring you away from the Newport Beach and harbor area, but with the ocean firmly in sight, the 600-acre **Newport Center,** just above the Pacific Coast Highway between MacArthur Boulevard and Jamboree Road, is an office, luxury hotel, and entertainment complex built in 1967. It hosts a must-stop shopping center—the trendy **Fashion Island.** Call (949) 721-2000, the concierge contact number, or visit www.shopfashionisland.com for schedules of children's activities, fashion shows, and great promotions. Containing more than 200 major chain stores and regional specialty shops, Newport Center is also home to the luxurious AAA-rated five-diamond **Island Hotel** (949-759-0808; www.islandhotel.com), as well as forty restaurants in the Atrium Court. This is where you and the kids can chill out after a hard day at the beach!

Sherman Library and Gardens

2647 East Pacific Coast Highway, south of Newport Beach in Corona del Mar; (949) 673-2261; www.slgardens.org. Gardens are open daily from 10:30 a.m. to 4:00 p.m. $

This two-acre cultural center has botanical gardens displaying tropical and subtropical flora in addition to its research library of southwestern U.S. history. The touch-and-smell garden is a major wow for your kids; you will enjoy the respite in the tea garden for lunch served Monday through Friday (949-673-0033).

Where to Eat

Back Bay Cafe, 1131 Back Bay Drive, Newport Beach; (949) 729-1144. Call for hours (seasonal). In the Newport Dunes Resort, Back Bay overlooks the calm inland waters of Upper Newport Bay as well as all the action at the adjacent boat launch/marina. Totally family friendly, casual, nautical atmosphere both indoors and out on the patio. California/American traditional foods for breakfast/lunch/dinner/Sunday brunch buffet. $$

Where to Stay

Hyatt Regency Newport Beach, 1107 Jamboree Road, .5 miles from Pacific Coast Highway, Newport Beach; (949) 729-1234 or (800) 233-1234; www.newportbeach.hyatt.com. This 410-room California-casual property has 26 spacious acres of beautifully landscaped grounds. The value is here for your family, with package plans and special rates. There are three heated pools; a wading pool for the kids; a nine-hole, par-three golf course; plus Fitness Center if you're feeling flabby from lying on the beach. Two restaurants serve daily meals. You'll appreciate the shuttle service to nearby shopping and attractions. $$$

The Newport Dunes Waterfront Resort, 1131 Back Bay Drive, just off PCH and Jamboree Boulevard; (949) 729-3863 or (800) 765-7661; www.newportdunes.com. Overnight camping site and a seven-lane boat-launch ramp are open twenty-four hours. This hundred-acre "Ritz of RV Parks" waterfront resort provides more than 400 hookups for recreational vehicles and campers, each separated by tropical vine-covered fences. A dozen basic studio cottages inland plus twenty-four beachfront cottages that sleep from two to eight people and are equipped with kitchens and full baths make ideal family headquarters (the Kath family had a wonderful reunion here in 2007!). You can rent bikes, kayaks, windsurfers, paddleboats, and sailboats here for hours of fun. Lots of family activities planned for guests year-round, such as "movies on the beach" in summer. Call for current rates. $$

For More Information

Newport Beach Conference and Visitors Bureau. 110 Newport Center Drive, Suite 120, 92660; (949) 722-1611 or (800) 94-COAST; www.visitnewportbeach.com.

Laguna Beach

Unspoiled by time or tide, the dazzling white sands of Laguna Beach, combined with its artist-colony heritage and year-round mild climate, add up to a unique Orange County destination resort worth exploring. All the major beach action along the Pacific Coast Highway can be found here—your kids will "dig" the sand and the playground at Main Beach downtown, while you stroll the art galleries, boutiques, and bistros that line the Pacific Coast Highway.

Festival of Arts and Pageant of the Masters

In Irvine Bowl Park, 650 Laguna Canyon Road, near the ocean. The annual festival is staged in July and August. For a complete program and brochures, call (949) 494-1145 or (800) 487-3378; www.lagunafestivalofarts.com. $$$$

The Festival of Arts features 150 of the area's most accomplished artists in a rigorously juried show requiring that all pieces on display or for sale be original, including paintings, sculpture, pastels, drawings, serigraphs, photographs, ceramics, jewelry, etched and stained glass, weaving, handcrafted furniture, musical instruments, model ships, and scrimshaw.

Each summer evening the park's natural amphitheater is the site of the Pageant of the Masters, a world-famous event, where amazingly faithful re-creations of famous artwork are presented on stage by live models. Narrators and a full orchestra make these tableaux vivants (living pictures) an extraordinary dramatic experience, particularly the finale—a stunning live portrayal of Leonardo da Vinci's *Last Supper*. There is so much for your kids to see and do, including participating in hands-on workshops, watching performing artists, listening to music, even viewing the junior art displays of local schoolchildren.

The Sawdust Art Festival Winter Fantasy

935 Laguna Canyon Road; (949) 494-3030 for this year's Winter Fantasy dates and nominal admission fees; www.sawdustartfestival.com. $

This favorite Laguna Beach event is held on four consecutive weekends in November and December in a fragrant eucalyptus grove. Wander three acres of paths containing 150 booths filled with holiday arts and crafts while your kids play in the snow (trucked in daily!). A children's art workshop, food, and entertainment make this a wonderful addition to your wintertime vacation experience in Southern California.

Where to Eat and Stay

Hotel Laguna and Claes Restaurant, 425 South Pacific Coast Highway; (949) 494-1151 or (800) 524-2927; www.hotellaguna .com. This historic, sixty-five-room property right on the sand in the absolute center of town was built in 1930. The three-story old girl has undergone several face-lifts over the years but remains a favorite. Don't expect ultramodern furnishings but revel in the California-beach quirky atmosphere. Be sure to request a room on the ocean side because the street side is way too noisy. Private beach access, complete with your own beach chairs and food/drinks/towel attendant, make this the ultimate place to people-watch while the kids create sand castles. **Free** continental breakfast included. We really enjoy Claes Restaurant and the Terrace for lunch or early dinner (the bar gets a little hectic later on). You can dine overlooking the beach and all the action. $$$

For More Information

Laguna Beach Visitors and Conference Bureau. 252 Broadway (Highway 133), 92651; (949) 497-9229 or (800) 877-1115; www.lagunabeachinfo.org.

Dana Point

At the turn of the nineteenth century, Dana Point (named after Richard Henry Dana, author and mariner) was the only major port between Santa Barbara and San Diego. Now this natural cove has picturesque and modern marinas hosting 2,500 craft. It is famous for its whale-watching cruises from late December through March. The town celebrates its annual Harbor Whale Festival in March with street fairs and plenty of outdoor activities.

Ocean Institute

24200 Dana Point Harbor Drive; (949) 496-2274; www.ocean-institute.com. Open daily; hours vary by season. Closed major holidays. Ship tours are Sunday from 10:00 a.m. to 2:30 p.m. Admission fee is voluntary; donations are gladly accepted.

Be sure to investigate this fun place that has outstanding sea-life exhibits, tide-pool tours, and a hands-on aquarium touch tank. While you're there, take a tour of the tall ship *Pilgrim,* a replica of the vessel on which Richard Henry Dana, author of the book *Two Years Before the Mast,* sailed to Southern California in the 1830s. In July and August, musical and dramatic productions with a nautical theme are presented on the *Pilgrim*'s deck. Your kids will love the chance to really see sea life in action!

Dana Point Harbor Information Service

P.O. Box 701, Dana Point 92629; (949) 496-1094; www.danapointharbor.com.

Your best point of contact for waterfront activities and special events, including whale watching; rentals of Jet Skis, kayaks, canoes, and sailboats; parasailing; and windsurfing.

Southern California **CityPass**

The Southern California CityPass debuted in 2003 and continues to be an outstanding money saver for you and your family. It includes a three-day Disneyland Resort Park Hopper Ticket, valid for unlimited admission to both Disneyland park and Disney's California Adventure park for three days; a one-day visit to Universal Studios Hollywood; and ample time to motor down the coast to stunning San Diego and two world-class parks, SeaWorld and your choice between the San Diego Zoo or San Diego Zoo's Wild Animal Park. CityPass delivers the best of Southern California fun at a savings of almost $100 off regular admission fees. Plus, you have four-teen days to take it all in from the first day you use it! Purchase the Southern California CityPass at any of the participating attractions or online at www.citypass.com.

Where to Stay

Doubletree Guest Suites Doheny Beach, 34402 Pacific Coast Highway, across from Doheny State Beach, next to the Yacht Harbor; (949) 661-1100. This full-service, 196-suite hotel is located along a 10-mile stretch of beautiful white-sand beach. All suites have a bedroom and a sitting room (our fave floor plan) with a wet bar, microwave, fridge, two remote control TVs, a VCR, and panoramic views to boot. If you get bored with the beach (heresy), you can always take a dip in the pool or work out in the fitness center. The casual restaurant Tresca has a California-beach fusion menu, open daily for all three meals and Sunday brunch. $$$

For More Information

Dana Point Chamber of Commerce and Visitors Center. 24681 La Plaza #115, Box 12, 92629; (949) 496-1555; www.danapoint chamber.com or www.danapointvisitorcenter .com.

San Juan Capistrano

The village of San Juan Capistrano is just inland along I-5 north from Dana Point, set in roll-ing hills between the Santa Ana Mountains and the sea. It has many old adobe buildings, and the 1895 Santa Fe Railroad depot has been lovingly restored and is now an Amtrak station and restaurant. Since San Juan Capistrano is good enough for thousands of swal-lows to return to every year, you know you cannot go wrong here, or for that matter any-where in Orange County—the ultimate family vacation destination.

Mission San Juan Capistrano and Cultural Center

Two blocks west of the junction of Highway 74 and I-5 at 31882 Camino Capistrano; (949) 248-2048; www.missionsjc.com. Open every day except Good Friday, Christmas, and Easter, 8:30 a.m. to 5:00 p.m. $$

This "jewel of the missions" was founded on November 1, 1776, by Father Junípero Serra and is seventh in his famous chain of twenty-one missions along the California coast. On your self-guided walk through history, you will first enter the Serra Chapel, the oldest building still in use in California; then tour the ruins of the Great Stone Church, which was destroyed by an earthquake in 1812; and view the padres' quarters, soldiers' barracks, an Indian cemetery, and the mission kitchen. You can also view the site of an ongoing archaeological dig as well as revel in the majestic gardens. Even the crankiest toddlers seem to unwind here.

Today the mission is famous for the swallows that arrive every March 19 (St. Joseph's Day) and leave on October 23. These remarkably constant birds fly approximately 6,000 miles from Goya, Argentina, to nest and rear their young in San Juan Capistrano. As early as 1777, a record of their return was first noted in the mission archives, spawning ceremonies and celebrations each year since (not to mention the celebrated song "When the Swallows Come Back to Capistrano").

For More Information

San Juan Capistrano Chamber of Commerce. 31421 La Matanza Street, 92675; (949) 493-4700; www.sanjuanchamber.com.

the Inland Empire and Beyond

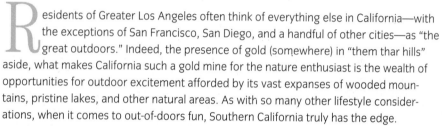

Residents of Greater Los Angeles often think of everything else in California—with the exceptions of San Francisco, San Diego, and a handful of other cities—as "the great outdoors." Indeed, the presence of gold (somewhere) in "them thar hills" aside, what makes California such a gold mine for the nature enthusiast is the wealth of opportunities for outdoor excitement afforded by its vast expanses of wooded mountains, pristine lakes, and other natural areas. As with so many other lifestyle considerations, when it comes to out-of-doors fun, Southern California truly has the edge.

Even those areas with the most striking natural beauty, however, have rich cultural heritages stretching back to the days of the Spanish explorers and Native Americans before them. A wide variety of museums—many geared toward children—sprinkle the scenic splendor of the Southern California wilds. The combination of history, festive special events, and, towering above it all, those glorious mountain peaks makes for an unforgettable family adventure.

When considering which areas to travel to or through, it helps to think like a native Southern Californian: In other words, think big! We tend to take wide-open spaces for granted, but in a state where many counties are bigger than other entire states, can you blame us? We like to drive, and we consider many areas easily within the orbit of Greater L.A. These include, among others, the sizable chunks of San Bernardino and Riverside Counties east of L.A. (a 28,000-square-mile region known as the Inland Empire); vast Kern County north of the city, with its celebrated Kern River; Tulare County, farther north, gateway to Sequoia and Kings Canyon National Parks; and the ski resort of Mammoth, at the southern end of the Sierra Nevada range. The latter areas may be more central than Southern California, but a true Californian just hops in the car, puts the top down, and goes. Getting there is easy, and with landscapes like these, easily half the fun.

It is California's Inland Empire that furnishes the archetypal images of the Golden State: acre upon acre of lush orange groves guarded by snowcapped mountains in the not-so-far-off distance. To the East Coast eye—that is, one accustomed to cities arranged on neat grids and self-contained countryside speckled with small towns—the Inland Empire can be a bit overwhelming. The valley floor is an immense patchwork of farmlands and small cities. It's sometimes hard to tell where one town ends and another begins.

THE INLAND EMPIRE AND BEYOND

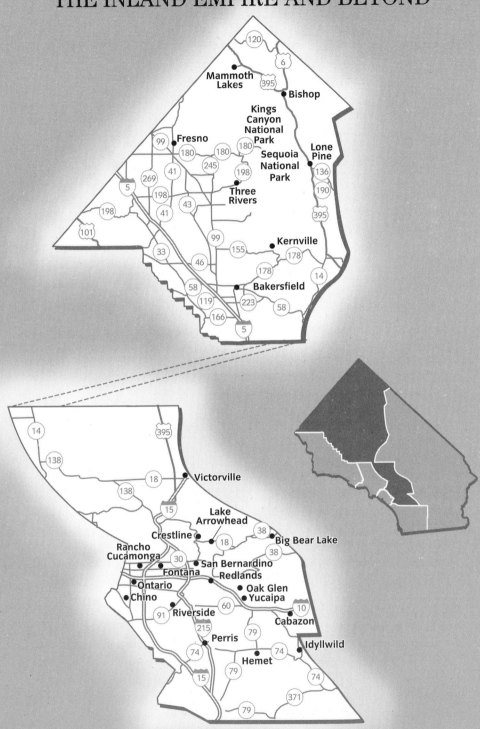

Malls, museums, and roadside fruit stands all vie for the motorist's attention. There are more than 660,000 acres of national forest. All this makes for a slightly rough-and-tumble atmosphere, but a relaxed one, too. Though still growing, the palm-studded Inland Empire is a less pressured kind of place than adjacent L.A. County. It's about as far away from stuffy as you can get—and that's very Southern California.

If the sight of citrus crops right and left is quintessential Southland, those snow-capped mountaintops house a part of the state perhaps less well-known to the visitor. Mountain vacation spots such as Lake Arrowhead and Big Bear, with its 7,000-foot-high lake, are like old-fashioned New Hampshire lakeside resorts a la California. They offer calm, cool respite from the L.A. basin and surrounding valleys and loads of outdoor activities from the simple to the simply adventurous. But to really appreciate the roominess of the Inland Empire, we recommend that you make stops along the way. Those who value the journey as well as the destination won't be disappointed, and during road trips kids need as much stretch-run-and-have-fun time as itineraries allow.

Ontario Area

If, like most people, you enter the Inland Empire via Interstate 10, heading east out of Los Angeles, you'll want to make a couple of stops in the Ontario area. With its bustling international airport, Ontario is the hub of this region within a region.

Welcome to the **Ontario International Airport (ONT),** a terrific gateway for families on the grand Southern California tour route. The airport is serviced by all the major carriers. You can start your itinerary from here without the enormity that is LAX. This state-of-the-art terminal is a major link in Southern California's air transportation network. You can easily rent a van or car from here and head for the hills, mountains, desert, and beyond.

The nearby town of **Chino,** founded in 1887 on a Spanish land grant, is a prosperous community today of more than 68,000 residents.

Graber Olive House

315 East Fourth Street, Ontario; (909) 983-1761 or (800) 996-5483; www.graberolives.com. Open Monday through Sunday 9:00 a.m. to 5:30 p.m. Free admission.

This is a fitting place to visit just in case the area's warm Mediterranean-like breezes have put thoughts of—what else?—olive oil in your mind. They've been doing wonderfully delicious things with homegrown olives at Graber House since 1894. An on-site olive processing and packing plant and a museum will enlighten kids and adults alike.

Planes of Fame Air Museum

7000 Merrill Avenue, Chino (just south of Ontario on Highway 60); (909) 597-3722; www .planesoffame.org. Open daily 9:00 a.m. to 5:00 p.m. except Thanksgiving and Christmas. $$

This museum houses a very impressive collection of more than 100 vintage World War II airplanes from around the world and military aviation memorabilia. It's a vivid reminder of the pivotal role the aviation industry has played in California's history.

Mall Break!

If you have visions of a megamall, with everything the kids could ever imagine (more than 200 shops, including Disney Store Outlet, Off 5th/Saks Fifth Avenue, plus thirty AMC Theatres, KB Toys Outlet, and Game Works), you'll be glad to know that the **Ontario Mills** (1 Mills Circle; (909) 484-8300; www.ontariomills.com), Southern California's largest entertainment and outlet mall, is open seven days a week. At the intersection of Interstate 15 and I-10, Ontario Mills has it all. It's mere minutes from the airport, thirty minutes from Disneyland, and forty minutes from downtown L.A. Start with a noisy lunch at the **Rainforest Cafe** (909-941-7979), where you'll find animated wildlife, environmental education, and a spunky menu with hamburgers, salads, and more. You'll hear the sounds of the rain forest as you dine. **Dave & Busters** (909-987-1557) is another hit here with state-of-the-art interactive games and simulators. Snackers will like the humongous food court, which is near the Virgin Megastore. Parents will love the smooth-as-silk cheesecake in more flavors than you thought possible at the **Cheesecake Factory Cafe.** Dig in!

Yanks Air Museum

7000 Merrill Avenue, Hangar A207, Box 35, Chino, 91710; (909) 597-1734; www.yanksair .com. Open: Tuesday through Friday 8:30 a.m. to 3:30 p.m., Saturday 8:30 a.m. to 2:00 p.m. Closed Monday. $$

Located just east of Planes of Fame, this museum strictly focuses exclusively on American aviation history and technology. The collection now numbers more than 120 aircraft and continues to grow. The scope of the collection covers the entire history of American aviation, from Jennies to Jets. Impressive!

Where to Stay

Doubletree Hotel Ontario Airport, 222 North Vineyard; (909) 937-0900 or (800) 222-8733; www.doubletree.com. The hotel is next to the Convention Center, boasts 484 guest rooms, two restaurants, a pool, and a spa. $$$

Ontario Airport Marriott, 2200 East Holt; (909) 975-5000 or (800) 228-9290; www .marriottontario.com. This 293-room property is within walking distance of the Ontario Convention Center and restaurants and is close to the Ontario International Airport. Twenty-four-hour **free** airport shuttle. $$

For More Information

Chino Valley Chamber of Commerce. 13150 Seventh Street, 91710; (909) 627-6177; www.chinovalleychamber.com.

Ontario Convention and Visitors Bureau. 2000 Convention Center Way, 91764; (909) 937-3000 or (800) 455-5755; www.ontariocvb.com.

Rancho Cucamonga

Rancho Cucamonga, northeast of Ontario along historic Route 66, has a name kids love to make fun of. But there's also fun to be had in the town. There's a monument here to Jack Benny (you'll have to explain to the kids who Jack Benny was), as he often mentioned Rancho Cucamonga on radio and television shows. For more civic information access the Chamber of Commerce at www.ranchochamber.org.

Where to Eat

Magic Lamp Inn, 8189 Foothill Boulevard; (909) 981-8659; www.themagiclampinn.com. If you want to get more kicks on Route 66 around the dinner hour, visit this legendary, classic 1955 restaurant with its comfortable red banquettes and the look and feel of yesteryear. The menu includes old favorites such as chicken marsala and roast prime rib of steer au jus. $$$

Sycamore Inn, 8318 Foothill Boulevard, Bear Gulch; (909) 982-1104; www.thesycamoreinn.com. This rustic inn, just across the street from the Magic Lamp, opened in 1848. The children's menu includes the Hot Dogger, Burger Master, Mr. Chicken, and the Big Cheese. Tell your kids this restaurant was in business a long time before McDonald's and Burger King—even before the California burger was invented. $$

Crestline

All right. You've taken in a bit of culture, a bit of sunshine, and hopefully a bite of something to eat from one of the myriad fast-food establishments along the interstate (**In-N-Out,** 800-786-1000 or www.in-n-out.com for locations, makes the best burgers. Try the number three; it's a bargain and includes a burger, fries, and drink). Now, why not get away from it all, or above it all, as the case may be? There are three main resorts in the mountains framing the northern tier of the Inland Empire: Crestline, Lake Arrowhead, and Big Bear. Choose according to taste: a day for a detour, two or three for a mini-vacation. On your way to or from Lake Arrowhead, you'll pass through Crestline, a smallish (population 10,000), rather funky, no-nonsense mountain village that lures passersby in for a meal or a lakeside stroll.

Lake Gregory County Regional Park
24171 Lake Drive, located off Highway 18; (909) 338-2233; www.co.san-bernardino.ca.us/parks/lake.htm.

The eighty-six-acre Lake Gregory is Crestline's centerpiece, a popular though rarely crowded spot for swimming, shore fishing, and paddle-boarding. Some scenes from Disney's most recent *Parent Trap* movie were filmed here as well. From May through

No Earplugs **Required**

If you're near Claremont, home of Claremont Colleges, and have an evening free, consider tickets for Ben Bollinger's **Candlelight Pavilion Dinner Theatre** (455 West Foothill Boulevard; www.candlelightpavilion.com), exiting from I-10.

The box office is open Tuesday and Wednesday 11:00 a.m. to 5:00 p.m., Thursday and Friday 11:00 a.m. to 7:00 p.m., and Sunday 10:00 a.m. to 6:00 p.m. Call (909) 626-1254 for performances, times, and cost of tickets.

This is a far cry from a rock concert, so let the kids know in advance. This is where musicals of yesteryear such as *Singin' in the Rain* (based on the MGM film), *The Sound of Music*, and *Ain't Misbehavin'* come alive. Dinner is served a la carte with appetizers, entrees, desserts, and a selection of kid-friendly, nonalcoholic beverages, such as the Melinda May (with coconut cream) and the Show Stopper (a frozen raspberry piña colada and cream concoction).

This is a large theater, which was once a gymnasium. The seating is spacious and comfortable, and the sight lines are excellent, even if you sit in the back at a banquette. It's a perfect way for the family to enjoy live theater and to learn about the marvelous vintage musicals, where you could really hear the words, and they meant something, too.

September, Friday night in Crestline means Lakeside Family Market Night, a festival of fun that features not only plenty of food and fresh produce but also kids' rides, crafts vendors, and entertainment.

Lake Arrowhead

Summer days find many folks at **Lake Arrowhead Village,** a hundred-year-old resort area named for the arrowhead landmark at the base of the San Bernardino Mountains. No one knows exactly how the 1,115-foot-tall, 396-foot-wide geological imprint got there, but it certainly helps those with a less-than-stellar sense of direction. Virtually every imaginable aquatic activity—swimming, waterskiing, fishing, sailing—is available on the lake, which is ringed by accommodations ranging from camping facilities to deluxe rooms. In the winter this 5,000-plus-foot elevation welcomes snow sports and recreation. A true wonderland only two hours from the beach!

Arrowhead Queen
Lake Arrowhead Village waterfront; (909) 336-6992. $$$

A great summertime way to experience the lake. The Louisiana-style paddle-wheel vessel departs hourly for fifty-minute narrated tours.

McKenzie's Waterski School

28200 Highway 189, Lake Arrowhead; at the marina; (909) 337-3814.

The longest-running school of its kind in the United States, McKenzie's offers lessons for children of all ages (summertime only).

Snow Valley Mountain Resort

P.O. Box 2337, 35100 Highway 18, Running Springs 92382; general information: (909) 867-2751, snow report: (800) 680-SNOW; www.snow-valley.com. Thirty-five ski trails served by eleven lifts. The longest run is 1.25 miles long. $$$$

The seasonal (Thanksgiving to April) Snow Valley Mountain (base elevation 6,800 feet) is located in the heart of the San Bernardino National Forest and operated under a special-use permit with the USDA Forest Service. Resort features include a multitude of food and beverage venues, complete rental operations, a ski and snowboard school, great alpine skiing, and separate snowboarding terrain.

Where to Eat

Belgian Waffle Works, 28200 Highway 189, Lake Arrowhead Village, dockside; (909) 337-5222; http://belgianwaffle.com. Open for breakfast, lunch, and dinner since 1982—they use an exclusive waffle mix that is so delicious. $

Woody's Boat House, Lake Arrowhead Village, lower level; (909) 337-2628. Dockside merchants offer another view of the lake, so spend some time exploring this corner of the village. If you are a fan of the Chris Craft boats of the 1950s, stop by for breakfast, lunch, or dinner. Woody's has a salad bar in a boat, a separate kids' menu, and fair prices. Beautifully restored Chris Craft boats serve as booths and your platform for viewing the lake. $$

Where to Stay

Arrowhead Pine Rose Cabins, 25994 Highway 189, Twin Peaks, at Grandview; (909) 337-2341 or (800) 429-PINE; www.lakearrowheadcabins.com. Individuality reigns supreme at this great base camp for sightseeing. It's centrally located between Lake Arrowhead and Lake Gregory. Seventeen cabins (one, two, and three bedrooms) and two four- to seven-bedroom lodges are scattered around five forested acres. No charge for cribs. Children welcome and stay free in same cabin as parents. $$

Lake Arrowhead Resort & Spa, 27984 Highway 189, Lake Arrowhead Village; (909) 336-1511; www.lakearrowheadresort.com. Located right on Lake Arrowhead; a $17 million renovation in 2007 boasts 162 sparkling redone guest rooms and 11 luxurious suites with all of the amenities, plus its own beach and cushy Spa of the Pines. $$$$

For More Information

Lake Arrowhead Communities Chamber of Commerce. P.O. Box 219, 92352; (909) 337-3715; www.lakearrowhead.net.

Lake Arrowhead Village. P.O. Box 640, 28200 Highway 189, Suite F-240, 92352; (909) 337-2533; www.lakearrowheadvillage.com

Big Bear Lake

If you follow Highway 18 east from Lake Arrowhead to Big Bear Lake, you'll be cruising along the Rim of the World Scenic Byway, with its spectacular vistas of thick forests and the sprawling valley below. It's a fitting entry to the 5-mile-long lake, the perennial favorite of thousands of local residents.

Big Bear is many things to many people. The area includes the city of Big Bear Lake, Fawnskin, Big Bear City, and Moonridge. Some come for the great water sports (23 miles of shoreline), others for the chance to see the stars and meteor showers during the refreshingly cool nights, and others for the hiking opportunities. Hiking trails abound in the area, including a section of the 2,600-mile Pacific Crest Trail that extends from Canada to Mexico. In winter—and often well into spring—Big Bear means top-notch skiing and snowboarding, plus sledding, tubing, and snowball fights. Elevation ranges from 6,750 to 9,000 feet, and the area is dominated by pine and oak forests and rare bald eagles.

Big Bear Discovery Center

San Bernardino National Forest, 40971 North Shore Drive (Highway 38), P.O. Box 66, Fawnskin 92333; (909) 866-3437; www.bigbeardiscoverycenter.com.

Get your family to the marvelous Big Bear Discovery Center before you make any decisions on where to go and what to do. Try one of the tours, such as the Grout Bay Canoe Tour, Mountain Mining Tour, or Woodland Trail Tour; children are welcome. The USDA Forest Service has made great strides in opening this area to tourists. There is an orientation video, a gift shop, cafe, exhibits, an amphitheater, and information on more than fifty activities, from horseback riding, hiking, and backpacking to fishing and bird-watching. Ask about the Children's Forest, a 3,400-acre site on Highway 18 between Running Springs and Big Bear Lake, where kids learn about the preservation of our magnificent wildlands.

Big Bear Queen at the Marina

500 Paine Road, Big Bear Lake; (909) 866-3218; www.bigbearmarina.com. Seasonal.

Enjoy the water up close during a ninety-minute cruise aboard a paddle wheeler. Dinner cruises available. Pontoon boats and fishing boat rentals and charters available, too.

Snow Summit

880 Summit Boulevard, P.O. Box 77, Big Bear Lake 92315; (909) 866-5766; www.snow summit.com. For Snow Summit snow reports, call (909) 866-4621 or (888) SUMMIT-1. $$$$

Here is a paradise for snow seekers, traditional skiers, snowboarders, and families with children. Take it all in from View Haus, where rustic dining will enchant you and the kids with a marvelous mountain view. If there is no natural snow, don't worry, they will make it happen for you! Snow Summit has a drop of 1,175 feet. There is a children's school and a mountaintop family park. Ample **free** parking. During the summer enjoy rides on the scenic sky chair and practice at the Bear Mountain Driving Range.

Bear Mountain Resort

43101 Goldmine Drive, Big Bear; (909) 585-2519; www.bearmountain.com. $$$$

"The Park" at Bear Mountain is the only ski resort in the world devoted almost entirely to free-style snowboarding, with 117 jumps, 57 jibs, and 2 pipes on 195 acres. Bear Mountain (sister resort of Snow Summit) boasts a vertical drop of 1,700 feet. Excellent and inexpensive ski instruction centers abound, and plenty of rental companies make downhill and cross-country skiing or snowmobiling easy for those without equipment of their own.

Pleasure Point Boat Landing

603 Landlock Landing Road (Cienega Road off Big Bear Boulevard at Metcalf Bay), Fawnskin; (909) 866-2455. Open from 6:00 a.m. daily May 1 to November 1.

Tour boat casts off daily from the Pleasure Point Marina at noon and 2:00 and 4:00 p.m. for a two-hour cruise around the scenic shoreline of Big Bear Lake. There are also canoes, pedal boats, pontoons, and eight-, ten-, and fifteen-horsepower motorboats at the landing.

Alpine Slide at Magic Mountain

800 Wild Rose Lane, Big Bear Lake; (909) 866-4626; www.alpineslidebigbear.com. Slide open daily 10:00 a.m. to 4:00 p.m. Year-round. $$

A Big Bear must. Few can resist the lure of "bobsledding" down the concrete runs. The maximum attainable speed is fast enough to thrill, but not fast enough to frighten. Actually, you control your own pace as you glide down the hillside. There are go-karts and miniature golf, too. In winter, kids can inner-tube down a mountain of snow, then be rope-towed back to the top again.

Moonridge Animal Park

43285 Goldmine Drive (across the street from Bear Mountain Ski Resort), Big Bear Lake; (909) 584-1171; www.moonridgezoo.org. Open year-round 10:00 a.m. to 5:00 p.m. $

Kids will love Big Bear's little zoo, which is home to around a hundred orphaned and injured wild creatures, from black bears, ringtail cats, wolves, and foxes to raccoons and cougars.

Where to Stay

Goldmine Resort, 42268 Moonridge Road, 0.5 mile east of Big Bear Boulevard, Big Bear Lake; (909) 866-5118; www.bigbear-goldmine-lodge.com. Open year-round and only 1 mile to Snow Summit and Bear Mountain. Under new family ownership since November 2007, lots of upgrades include new beds, carpets, and fresh decor in every lodge room, one- and two-room suites, and cabins. Vacation-home rentals also offered. Large playground, horseshoe pit, and fireplaces; family reunions and weddings welcomed. $$

Northwoods Resort, 40650 Village Drive, Big Bear Lake; reservations: (800) 866-3121; www.northwoodsresort.com. This 1930s-style, 148-room mountain lodge is great for families; there are comfortable connecting rooms, heated outdoor pool and spa with poolside food service, fitness room, and WiFi and Nintendo for those who can't quite disconnect. You are right at the village, where there are inviting shops and restaurants, all amid those enchanting whispering pines. Stillwell's Restaurant serves breakfast, lunch, and dinner in this unique, rustic mountain atmosphere. $$$

For More Information

Big Bear Chamber of Commerce. 630 Bartlett Road, Big Bear Village, PO Box 2860, Big Bear Lake 92315; (909) 866-4607; www .bigbearchamber.com.

Big Bear Lake Resort Association and Visitor Center. 630 Bartlett Road, Big Bear Village, P.O. Box 1936, Big Bear Lake 92315-1936; (909) 866-6190 or (800) 4-BIG-BEAR; www.bigbearinfo.com or www.bigbear.com.

Victorville

If you take I-15 a bit north of the San Bernardino Mountains (another section of the Route 66 Heritage Corridor), before you get too far into the Mojave Desert you'll come across the little town of Victorville. In addition to its role as a gateway to the Mojave, it has a few worthwhile stops.

California Route 66 Museum

16825 D Street (take exit D off I-15); (760) 951-0436; www.califrt66museum.org. Open Thursday through Monday 10:00 a.m. to 4:00 p.m. Free.

Kids may not appreciate the incredible array of memorabilia gathered by Route 66 fans, but this museum will make them wonder and ask questions about what travel was like before freeways. That alone is worth making the stop. From the high desert landmark called Hulaville (once an open-air museum along Route 66 on Victorville's southern fringes built by an eccentric ex-carney) to cute Route 66 fanny packs (for sale), the curiosities displayed here reveal an era of American travel left to the pages of history. Just a refresher, Route 66 debuted in 1926, connecting Chicago to L.A. (Santa Monica).

Check out the historical exhibits, contemporary gallery, research library, and loads of travel info. "Get your kicks" here, on Route 66!

Mojave Narrows Regional Park

18000 Yates Road, off Bear Valley Road; (760) 245-2226; www.co.sanbernardino.ca.us/parks/mojave.htm.

This picturesque, not-quite-yet-the-desert site spans 840 acres and overlooks the Mojave River. With an eighty-seven-unit campground (with thirty-eight full utility pads), year-round fishing, and rowboat rentals, the park is well equipped for families interested in a little communing with nature. Mojave Narrows Regional Park is home to the Huck Finn Jubilee during Father's Day weekend (http://huckfinn.com). This festival is loaded with toe-tappin' bluegrass music, a watermelon seed spittin' contest, arts and crafts booths, and a catfish derby.

For More Information

Victorville Chamber of Commerce.
14174 Green Tree Boulevard, 92329; (760)
245-6506; www.vvchamber.com.

Fontana

The city of Fontana is located at the "crossroads" of the Inland Empire at the intersection of I-10 and I-15 and Highways 66 and 30, only ten minutes away from Ontario International Airport. Metrolink rail service makes connections easy to Greater Los Angeles. Your family and the city's population of 139,100 can enjoy easy access to mountains, beaches, twelve regional parks, the desert, and the best-known attraction—the California Speedway just west of downtown. Access www.fontana.org for more information.

Auto Club Speedway

9300 Cherry Avenue; (909) 429-5000 or (800) 944-RACE; www.autoclubspeedway.com. $$$

Known as "America's Ultimate Race Place," the Auto Club Speedway (formerly California Speedway) opened in June 1997 with the Inaugural Nascar Nextel Cup Series California 500, presented by Napa. More than 90,000 fans watched Jeff Gordon win the 500-mile race. Since then the speedway has hosted hundreds of Nascar, IROC AMA Superbike, and Grand-Am Cup Series races; IndyCar Series events; CART Champ Car races; and Dayton

Huzzah!

The Renaissance Pleasure Faire (Santa Fe Dam Recreation Area, 15501 East Arrow Highway, Irwindale; 626-969-4750 or 800-52-FAIRE; www.renfair.com/socal) is indeed a pleasure. A lively re-creation of a sixteenth-century English country fair, this is the largest outdoor theatrical event of its kind. But for the conspicuous absence of fog, you'd swear you were in merry olde England. How often do you get the chance to toast the arrival of Queen Elizabeth I on her royal barge, see knights in shining armor battling one another in a royal joust, and ride on an elephant all in the same day?

Then there's the Elizabethan theater, music, and country dance on six stages, old English-style crafts, and historically accurate foodstuffs to partake of (mega-size turkey legs are a perennial favorite). You can also opt to get your palm read by a gypsy, have a fortune teller teach you all about tarot cards, or just pause to chat with a strolling, fully costumed jester. The festive atmosphere at the fair is simply contagious, an unforgettable treat for both youngsters and oldsters. The fair is open 9:00 a.m. to 6:00 p.m. on eight weekends plus Memorial Day from the beginning of April.

Indy Lights Series races. The grandstand capacity is 92,000 seats, plus there are 63 Terrace Suites overlooking the pit road and 28 luxury Skybox Suites. In addition, more than 1,800 RVs can be accommodated in the infield—a popular choice for families. The speedway is also the home of the quarter-mile NHRA-sanctioned dragstrip—California Dragway. Suffice it to say, if your family loves racing, this is where you need to be!

San Bernardino

Nestled at the base of local mountain resorts and at the crossroads of the Interstate 215 and I-10 Freeways, "San Berdoo," as it's called locally, offers pleasures of a more municipal, but certainly no less stimulating, nature. It is the gateway to the resorts of Big Bear and Lake Arrowhead. San Bernardino is home to year-round sports such as the Class "A" affiliate of Los Angeles Dodgers, the Inland Empire 66ers, and the Western Region Little League Tournament. The historic California Theater in downtown San Bernardino features Broadway plays, musicals, and cultural shows from the San Bernardino Symphony Orchestra. For a large variety of restaurants, cuisine, lodging, and shopping, visit Hospitality Lane, located right off the I-10 freeway.

Historic Site of the World's First McDonald's
1398 North "E" Street. Open daily 10:00 a.m. to 5:00 p.m.

In 1948, brothers Dick and Mac McDonald opened their original namesake restaurant on this site on the business district loop of Route 66. It sold hamburgers, cheeseburgers, fries, soft drinks, and milk shakes at low prices and became very popular with residents and tourists. Ray Kroc encountered the restaurant in 1954 when he was working as a food-mixer salesman, and proposed and managed a plan to open franchised McDonald's around the USA. The McDonald brothers eventually sold the company to Kroc in 1961 for $2.7 million. Their original building has been razed, but there is a display of early McDonald's memorabilia—an homage to the American Dream. Ironically, it is now the headquarters for the Juan Pollo fast-food chain (909-885-6324). Another fun factoid: Taco Tia, Taco Bell, Del Taco, and Der Weinerschnitzel fast-food chains also all started in San Bernardino!

Glen Helen Regional Park
2555 Glen Helen Parkway; (909) 887-7540; (909) 880-6500 for concert information; www.co .san-bernardino.ca.us/Parks/glen.htm.

The "jewel in the crown" of the area's regional parks, 1,425-acre Glen Helen comes complete with a half-acre swimming lagoon, a 350-foot water slide, and a beach. And proof positive that Southern Californians think big, the park also boasts the Glen Helen Hyundai Pavilion (909-88-MUSIC; www.hyundaipavilion.com) outdoor concert venue, the largest amphitheater in the United States (total capacity is 65,000). The adjacent Glen Helen Raceway (18585 Verdemont Ranch Road; 909-880-3090; www.glenhelen.com) features the best in motocross events.

Route 66 Rendezvous

(800) 867-8366; www.route-66.org.

If you're up for a healthy dose of nostalgic honky-tonk (more than 500,000 were in 2008), check out this four-day affair that kicks off every year in mid-September. Southern Californians have always had a special relationship with their automobiles; what wine is to the French, cars are to us—sacred objects, worthy of adulation. This is clearly in evidence as squeaky-clean Corvettes, Cobras, and Chevys limited to 1,900 pre-1974 classics, customs, hot rods, and other vehicles receive an assigned reserved parking space for the four-day event. Vehicles cruise a 36-block area of downtown San Bernardino while visitors enjoy the beautiful cars, food, vendors, sponsor displays, and live entertainment.

Drag races, an auto sound challenge, and an antique performance parts swap are also on the annual activity roster. Dozens of vendors hawk their wares, which range from antique milk caps and Elvis clocks to new stereo equipment. And to put a little honk into the tonk, celebrities come to life via ongoing Legends in Concert performances. The rendezvous, which is **free** to spectators, is sponsored and produced by the San Bernardino Convention and Visitors Bureau.

National Orange Show

NOS Events Center, 689 South E Street; (909) 888-6788; www.nationalorangeshow.com. Held from Thursday through Monday (Memorial Day weekend). Admission is free.

Here's an event you'll never find in Kansas. Started way back in 1911, the show has been getting juicier ever since. Today it features fireworks, top entertainment, a rodeo, livestock shows, art exhibits, kid-friendly rides, and, of course, a broad range of oranges and orange food products.

Where to Eat

Guadalaharry's, 280 East Hospitality Lane; (909) 889-8555. Specializing in fajitas, Guadalaharry's is also known for its fried-ice-cream dessert. $–$$

Isabella's, 201 North E Street, #101; (909) 884-2534. Tasty Italian cuisine in a relaxing atmosphere. $$

Yamazato of Japan, 289 East Hospitality Lane; (909) 889-3683. Teppanyaki chefs are very entertaining as they prepare your meal on a grill at your table. It's fun to watch them flip an egg into their hat or a shrimp into their pocket! Delicious teriyaki, tempura, and sushi dishes. $

Where to Stay

Hilton San Bernardino, 285 East Hospitality Lane; (909) 889-0133 or (800) 445-8667; www.hilton.com. Located off I-10 at the North Waterman exit. As the street name suggests, this area of San Bernardino is visitor-friendly. You'll find an extensive variety of restaurants on Hospitality Lane within walking distance of the hotel, including Guadalaharry's, Yamazato, and others. $$$$

For More Information

San Bernardino Convention and Visitors Bureau. 1955 Hunts Lane, Suite 102, San Bernardino, 92408; (909) 889-3980 or (800) 867-8366; www.sanbernardino.travel.

California Welcome Center–Inland Empire. 1955 Hunts Lane, Suite 102, San Bernardino, 92408; (909) 891-1874; www.cwcinlandempire.com.

Redlands

Quiet little Redlands, named for the color of the local soil and home of the eponymous and highly regarded university, awaits exploration just a few minutes east of San Bernardino on I-10. If you're on the way to, say, Palm Springs and have time for only one detour, make it Redlands. You'll be in excellent company, for in the latter part of the nineteenth century, Midwesterners and East Coasters of certain means began a time-honored tradition of wintering in Southern California, and one of their favorite spots was Redlands. Among the city's attractions are several mansions that bear witness to the Golden State's brief Victorian renaissance.

San Bernardino County Museum

2024 Orange Tree Lane, near the California Street exit from I-10; (909) 307-2669 or (888) BIRD-EGG; www.co.san-bernardino.ca.us/museum/. Open Tuesday through Sunday 9:00 a.m. to 5:00 p.m. $, children younger than five free.

This local landmark is easily recognized by its large geodesic dome (actually a seminar room). Here you'll find exhibits on early Californian ranch life and the Native Americans who once lived in these parts. But the real strong suits of the museum are the earth and biological science exhibits, which also happen to be among the most popular with younger children. For starters, there are more than 40,000 birds' eggs, the state's only dinosaur tracks, a dazzling collection of minerals and gemstones, and the Exploration Show. Kids are captivated by the live insect, reptile, and amphibian displays. Both kids and adults can contemplate the forces that formed the Inland Empire's beautiful mountains by keeping an eye on the always-on seismometer.

Kimberly Crest House and Gardens

1325 Prospect Drive; (909) 792-2111; www.kimberlycrest.org. Open Thursday through Sunday 1:00 to 4:00 p.m. September through July. Closed August. $

With its commanding views of the San Bernardino Valley, this six-acre estate, purchased in 1905 by J. Alfred Kimberly (of Kimberly-Clark fame) and his wife, Helen, features Louis

XVI decor on the inside and formal Italian gardens and lush orange groves on the outside. See if you can spot the great southern magnolia, for years the Kimberlys' outdoor Christmas tree. The most impressive of the city's mansions, this French château-style home is off I-10 at the Ford exit. It is California Registered Historic Landmark No. 1019.

The Frugal Frigate

9 North Sixth Street; (909) 793-0740. Open Monday through Friday 10:00 a.m. to 6:00 p.m. (Thursday until 8:00 p.m.), Saturday 10:00 a.m. to 5:00 p.m., and Sunday noon to 5:00 p.m.

A delightful source for "carefully chosen children's classics," this unique bookstore is located in historic downtown Redlands and has plenty of special events your kids will enjoy. Call for schedule.

Where to Eat

Doughlectibles and the Eating Room, 107 East Citrus Avenue; (909) 798-7321 or (909) 792-5400; www.allmarthagreen.com/doughlectibles.html. The bakery has all varieties of fresh pastries and breads. The restaurant serves breakfast and lunch. The French toast is worth the calories. Lunch choices include a great patty melt. $

The Gourmet Pizza Shoppe, 120 East State Street; (909) 792-3313; www.gourmet pizzas.com. Closed Monday. Here you'll find ninety different combinations of pizza, including peanut butter and jelly! The beverage list features sodas from all over the world, including cream sodas, root beers, black cherry sodas, and six varieties of orange soda. You won't find noisy arcade games or a TV in the dining room—instead, children's books are available for kids to read while they wait. $$

Oscar's Mexican Restaurant, 19 North Fifth Street; (909) 792-8211. Oscar's is an institution in downtown Redlands, serving great Mexican food that is sure to satisfy your appetite. They have great "lite combos," too. $

For More Information

Redlands Chamber of Commerce. 1 East Redlands Boulevard, 92373; (909) 793-2546; www.redlandschamber.org.

Riverside

If one views the Inland Empire as a vast stage, its outdoor attractions tend to steal the show. Maybe that's why so few people seem to know much about Riverside, the city built on oranges. Riverside is accessible via Highway 60 or Highway 91, both south of I-10. By 1895 more than 20,000 acres of navel orange trees had made then-sleepy Riverside into the nation's wealthiest city per capita. This distinctly Californian heritage is still evident, thanks to the presence of a handful of old California-style structures: the old City Hall (3612 Mission Inn Avenue); restored 1892 Heritage House (8193 Magnolia Avenue), the finest example of Victorian lifestyle in the West; and the city's landmark, the restored Mission Inn (3649 Mission Inn Avenue). Originally a twelve-room adobe built in 1875 (a very long time ago by Californian standards), this grand hostelry expanded along with the town.

Riverside Metropolitan Museum

3580 Mission Inn Avenue; (951) 826-5273; www.riversideca.gov/museum/. Open Monday 9:00 a.m. to 1:00 p.m., Tuesday through Friday 9:00 a.m. to 5:00 p.m., and Saturday and Sunday 11:00 a.m. to 5:00 p.m. Admission is free; donations suggested.

The area's roots are on display at this museum, with its large collection of Native American artifacts and early citrus-industry exhibits in the former 1912 Post Office.

Jurupa Mountains Cultural Center

7621 Granite Hill Drive; (951) 685-5818; www.jmcc.us. Open Saturday 8:00 a.m. to 4:30 p.m. $

If you missed the San Bernardino County Museum (see the Redlands section in this chapter) and it's Saturday, bring the kids here for an educational guided nature walk. Along with excellent fossil and crystal exhibits, the museum has a cache of moon rocks on eighty-four acres nestled in the foothills of the Jurupa Mountains, founded in 1964.

California Citrus State Historic Park

Take Riverside Freeway (Highway 91) to Van Buren Boulevard at 9400 Dufferin Avenue; look for the big orange; (951) 780-6222; www.parks.ca.gov/?page_id=649.

This California state park was built to celebrate one hundred years of citrus production in Riverside with support from Sunkist growers. Located on the 377 acres are the Varietal Grove, which has a hundred different species of citrus; an outdoor amphitheater where concerts are held on Friday evenings during summer (the last concert is the first Friday in August); and a visitor center. As you walk around the park, you will encounter interpretive displays and picnic areas.

Botanic Gardens at University of California—Riverside (UCR)

University of California at Riverside; (951) 787-4650; www.gardens.ucr.edu. Open daily from 8:00 a.m. to 5:00 p.m. Admission is free, although donations are appreciated.

These gardens are nestled in the foothills of the Box Springs Mountains in East Riverside and cover forty hilly acres. The gardens boast more than 3,500 plant species from around the world. More than 200 species of birds have been observed in the gardens. From Highway 60/I-215, exit at Martin Luther King Boulevard and turn right. Turn right again at Canyon Crest Avenue and enter the UCR campus. Follow signs to the gardens and park in Lot 13.

Rancho Jurupa Park

4600 Crestmore Road; (951) 684-7032; www.riversidecountyparks.org/park-directory/all-parks/rancho_jurupa

There are thirty-five parks in Riverside County's Regional Park and Open Spaces system. Rancho Jurupa Park is located just outside the city limits of Riverside and provides fishing, biking, hiking, and equestrian trails as well as camping. Don't forget to stop in the Luis Robidoux Nature Center on the park grounds. Only a mile (as the crow flies) from Rancho Jurupa is the Jensen-Alvarado Ranch. This was the first non-adobe building in the Riverside area. Many school groups come to learn how to make homemade ice cream and tortillas (on a potbellied stove!). The Jensen-Alvarado Ranch is located at 4307 Briggs Street in Riverside. Take Freeway 60 west from Riverside, exit at Rubidoux Boulevard, drive south to Tilton Avenue, and head west on Briggs.

Castle Amusement Park

3500 Polk Street; (951) 785-3000; www.castlepark.com. Open daily; call for hours. No admission fee; ride tickets and game tokens can be purchased inside the park.

This twenty-five-acre park has it all. It was built in 1976 to be the "Ultimate Family Entertainment Park." The three-level castle houses more than 400 state-of-the-art games. The rare Dentzel carousel (built in 1898) is one of the oldest in America and has fifty-two hand-carved, brightly painted animals and two sleighs on highly polished brass poles. Add to these four world-class, eighteen-hole, championship miniature par 4 golf courses surrounded by gorgeous palm trees. The Big Top Restaurant has everything from a salad bar to super sundaes, and Plaza Café and Snack Bar are two more kid-friendly options.

Where to Eat

Anchos Southwest Grill and Bar, 10773 Hole Street; (909) 352-0240 www.anchos.net. Delicious Mexican and Southwestern cuisine. Watch the flour tortillas being made and rotating in the warmer. $

Mario's Place, 3646 Mission Inn Avenue; (951) 684-7755. Some of the most savory Italian dishes available. The Palagi family has made Mario's Place a landmark in Riverside. $$–$$$

Where to Stay

The Mission Inn, 3649 Mission Inn Avenue; (951) 784-0300; www.missioninn.com. This full-service, beautifully restored 1902 European-style hotel encompasses an entire city block in downtown Riverside. Come stroll the halls of this great inn, which has hosted several of our nation's presidents. There are 239 elegant rooms and suites, no two alike. Five restaurants will serve you classic California cuisine. The Mission Inn Foundation/ Museum offers walking history tours (www .missioninnmuseum.com; $, children under 12 **free**). $$$$

For More Information

Greater Riverside Chambers of Commerce. 3985 University Avenue, 92501; (951) 683-7100; www.riverside-chamber.com.

Riverside Convention & Visitors Bureau. 3750 University Avenue, Suite 175, 92501; (951) 222-4700 or (888) 748-7733; www.riversidecb.com.

Perris

For a taste of the real Riverside County, you have to delve into deep Riverside—in other words, let the country roads be your guide. If you take I-215 south from Highway 60 (which runs right through Riverside), in about twenty traffic-free minutes you'll come across the town of Perris, population 36,000. The locals always say there's nothing like Perris in the springtime—a reference to the California golden poppies and other wild-flowers that carpet these parts round about April. Even if your visit doesn't happen to coincide with the annual flora show, Mother Nature won't disappoint. Rambling about the Temecula Valley, in which Perris lies at the northern head, is like entering a time warp to old California. Bring your camera.

The Perris area is well-known for the outdoor activities afforded by its laid-back coun-try setting. The early morning and late evening stillness, coupled with mild temperatures, spells paradise for aviation buffs. Hot-air-balloon, sailplane, hang glider, and even skydiv-ing outfitters (Skydive Perris, 800-SKY-DIVE; www.skydiveperris.com) abound in the area. It can be quite a spectacle simply to watch these folks in action at the private Perris Val-ley Airport (www.airnav.com/airport/L65). At ground level, campers, swimmers, boaters, fishers, hikers, and bikers will enjoy a detour to the Lake Perris State Recreation Area (LPRA), 1781 Lake Perris Drive (951-657-0676; http://www.parks.ca.gov/default.asp?page_id=24006). Visit the YA-I Heki Museum, located at LPRA, for information on Native Ameri-can history of the area.

Orange Empire Railway Museum

2201 South A Street; (951) 657-2605; www.oerm.org. Open most weekends except holi-days. Free admission, $$ for trolley and train rides.

This is the West's biggest railway museum, with electric cars, buildings, and other arti-facts. The museum covers sixty acres, so there is plenty of room for a family picnic among streetcars, trains, and municipal buses from yesteryear.

More than 150 historic train cars, locomotives, and streetcars are on display indoors and outside. Are you ready to ride the rails, kids? Each Saturday and Sunday from 11:00 a.m. to 5:00 p.m., vintage streetcars circle the museum property (it takes about seven minutes), and antique Southern Pacific train cars make a ten-minute trip to the Perris Depot and back.

Hemet

If you're heading from the Perris area to Hemet or Idyllwild (more on that next), you could take either Highway 74 east or drive along the Juan Bautista de Anza National Historic Trail. This scenic corridor, which skirts Lake Perris, dairy farms, and other quiet farmlands, follows the tracks de Anza made when he explored the region for Spain in 1775. For more information call (951) 658-3211 or visit www.hemetsanjacintochamber.com.

Highland Springs Resort
and Guest Ranch

This 900-acre ranch, at 10600 Highland Avenue in Cherry Valley, offers horse-back riding, cookouts, hayrides, and barbecues. Once a stagecoach stop for gold panners headed for the Colorado River, this rustic resort, at 3,000 feet in elevation, has been a good choice for a family vacation since 1884. It is also the home of popular Camp Highland Outdoor Science School (www.camp highland.net). Palm Springs is 30 miles east, and Idyllwild is 20 miles south. Call (951) 845-1151 or visit www.highlandspringsresort.com.

Ramona Outdoor Play

2400 Ramona Bowl Road; (951) 658-3111 or (800) 645-4465; www.ramonabowl.com. Late April/early May.

Performed by more than 400 of the town's residents, the play is adapted from the 1884 novel *Ramona,* which depicts the romantic spectacle of early California. It has been an annual event since 1923, earning it the designation as the official outdoor play of California. The play runs on weekends from 3:30 to about 6:30 p.m. Not to be missed. Other productions are performed throughout the year; for example, look for *A Christmas Carol* in December.

Diamond Valley Lake

Visitor center located next to the Western Center for Archaeology and Paleontology (www .westerncentermuseum.org), 2325 Searl Parkway, Hemet; (951) 765-2612; www.dvlake .com. Open Thursday through Sunday; 10:00 a.m. to 4:00 p.m. Free.

These 4,000 square acres of water storage and recreational land are the great attraction of the Hemet Valley. Inside the visitor center you can see the mastodon exhibit as well as other artifacts retrieved from excavations made as this lake began to fill in 1999. Diamond Valley Lake is embarking on a substantial trail system that will allow families to hike and ride through the hill surrounding the reservoir. The first set of trails are along the north hills overlooking the lake, and another circumnavigates the lake. Other amenities at the east dam area include a swimming pool and soccer and other sports fields.

Idyllwild

Take Highway 74 east out of Hemet to Highway 243, which leads to the hamlet of Idyll-wild. You will be traveling on the **Palms to Pines Scenic Highway,** and as the name indicates, you'll observe desert palm and oak trees giving way to pine and fir forests as the elevation increases. Idyllwild, which looks like a village from the Swiss Alps dropped into the heart of the **San Bernardino National Forest,** makes for one of the most enchanting detours in the Inland Empire, especially in winter. This town, at an altitude of 5,400 feet with zero days of smog, is a mile-high oasis nestled in the San Jacinto Mountains and a favorite choice for a well-balanced family vacation in Southern California. It is devoid of fast-food joints (and their comforts), but the exceptional opportunities for family recreation more than compensate. Since the town is nestled 5,400 feet up, Idyllwild nights are cool and crisp, even in the summer. Idyllwild is home to fifteen art galleries and more than thirty art events annually. Get ready to tackle the great outdoors by ordering up a savory Belgian waffle first—any time of day—at the **Idyllwild Cafe,** 26600 Highway 243 (951-659-2210), next to Idyllwild School.

Living Free Animal Sanctuary

54250 Keen Camp Road, at Mountain Center on Highway 74; (951) 659-4684; www.living-free.org. Self-guided tours on Friday through Monday 11:00 a.m. to 3:00 p.m. Other days by appointment. Guided tours on Saturday only. Admission free; donations welcome.

This is a most unusual retreat for dogs and cats, a nonprofit animal sanctuary founded by Emily Jo Beard on 180 bucolic acres. The retreat is home to a variety of dogs, plus cats who have found a new life and home in this caring environment. The emphasis is on education, and children will find the dogs "living in harmony" and the cats "contented," enjoying spacious yards, play structures, and shady trees.

Idyllwild Arts

P.O. Box 38, 92549 (52500 Temecula Road, located at the end of Tollgate Road); (951) 659-2171; www.idyllwildarts .org. $$$$

Idyllwild Arts offers a family camp in late June and early July. There are separate activities for children, teenagers, and adults, including hiking, wilderness activities, swimming, and just relaxing. Evening activities include concerts, folk dancing, and family talent night.

Where to Stay

Quiet Creek Inn, 26345 Delano Drive; (951) 659-6110 or (800) 450-6110; www.quietcreek inn.com. Deluxe cabins with fireplaces, spas, and private decks overlooking Strawberry Creek will immediately relax you and your family. Owner also offers vacation rentals. As recommended by Sunset magazine (2007). $$$$

For More Information

Idyllwild Chamber of Commerce. 54295 Village Center Drive, 92549; (951) 659-3259 or (888) 659-3259; www.idyllwildchamber .com.

Oak Glen and Yucaipa

Washington State doesn't have a monopoly on apples. Oak Glen, just north of Yucaipa, is the core of the Inland Empire's tranquil apple country, which both tourists and natives are often surprised to find. September through December means apple-picking time at the 900-acre **Los Rios Rancho,** 39611 Oak Glen Road (909-795-1005; www.losriosrancho .com), and **Parrish Pioneer Ranch,** 38561 Oak Glen Road; (909-797-1753; www.parrish ranch.com).

In the summer, you can pick raspberries instead—not a bad alternative. The New England atmosphere of Oak Glen is particularly strong in wintertime, when snow often coats the apple orchards. But any time of year, the place is simply charming. Contact the Oak Glen Apple Growers Association at www.oakglen.net or call (909) 797-2364 for the latest news on this year's crop and the annual Apple Blossom Festival.

Are you there yet? The town of Oak Glen is like a West Coast version of Sleepy Hollow, with its antiques stores and scent of fresh apple pie wafting out of the windows of little restaurants. The pace is slower up here, and residents seem to like it that way. Not

Dinosaurs, Fruit, and Shopping

As you drive along I-10, the kids will make you pull over in **Cabazon** (population 2,200) the instant they see two hulking dinosaurs stalking drivers on the left (exit at Main Street). One's an *aptosaurus* (Dinny) with a mini-museum and gift shop tucked into his belly. His friend is a not-too-friendly-looking *Tyrannosaurus rex* named Mr. Rex. Like Pee Wee Herman in *Pee Wee's Big Adventure* (if you haven't seen it, your kids probably have), you can climb up to the dinosaur's jaw to take in the view. These Jurassic monstrosities are California camp at its best. They seem to be made expressly for family vacation fun. For more information call (951) 922-8700 or visit www.cabazon dinosaurs.com. You can fill up at the **Wheel Inn** diner (50900 Seminole Drive; 951-849-7012), serving great grub 24/7 since 1964. We love this roadside classic, especially the pies!

There are other attractions in Cabazon, easily visible from I-10. The first is **Hadley's Fruit Orchards** (888-854-5655; www.hadleyfruitorchards.com), an all-natural dried fruit and produce emporium famous for its deliciously frosty date shakes. The others are **Desert Hills Premium Outlets** (48400 Seminole Road; 951-849-6641; www.premiumoutlets.com) and **Cabazon Outlets** (48750 Seminole Road, 951-922-3000; www.cabazonoutlets.com), three rambling retail complexes. If your kids have been pining for a new pair of Nikes, or you have designs on some off-price Ralph Lauren apparel or home furnishings, you've hit the jackpot. And this isn't even Las Vegas!

everything's coming up apples, though. At the **Mously Museum of Natural History,** 35308 Panorama Drive, Yucaipa (909-790-3163; www.co.sanbernardino.ca.us/museum/ branches/mousley.htm), seashells, minerals, and fossils take center stage.

Riley's Farm and Orchard

12261 South Oak Glen Road; Oak Glen; (909) 790-2364; www.rileysfarm.com. Open Monday through Saturday 10:00 a.m. to 4:00 p.m.

"Villagers and country folk" are cordially invited to "come and be one hundred years behind the times" at the Old Packing Shed Bakery and Grill and the Hawk's Head Public House for victuals like chicken pot pie and corn chowder bottles of vintage sodas. During apple season you can take the kids on a hayride that includes a farm tour, cider pressing, and hot-caramel-dipped apples. Check out their summer tours, dinner events, and "Colonial Farm Life" Adventure Trips.

Where to Eat

Parrish Pioneer Apple Ranch, 38561 Oak Glen Road, Yucaipa; (909) 797-4020; www .parrishranch.com. Home to Apple Dumplin's Restaurant. Stop in for lunch (they have a great selection of sandwiches) and hot apple pie a la mode daily from 10:00 a.m. to 6:00 p.m. Ranch shops sell plenty of food and gifts. $

Kern County

Unlike many other states, California never quite seems to end. If you thought the sweeping vistas stopped after the San Bernardino Mountains, think again. Just north of them lies Kern County, nestled between the Sierra Nevada and the coastal range. With its 8,073 square miles, Kern is the third-largest county in California and is as large as Massachusetts. It forms the southern tier of the agriculture- and oil-rich Central Valley, the one of *Grapes of Wrath* fame, acre for acre the richest in the world. No matter what time of year you happen to be driving through, you'll see boundless fields of grapes, almonds, carrots, apples, watermelons, tomatoes, and more. The fruits and vegetables grown here are shipped all over the world, but you can sample them first at any of the numerous roadside farmers' markets.

Even if you've never been to Kern County before, you or your kids may feel as though you have because of the numerous movies that have been filmed here over the years, from *Star Packer* (with John Wayne, 1934) to *Jurassic Park.* This portion of the vast, semi-arid valley is perhaps best known, though, for white-water river rafting on the Kern River. It was the river, in fact, that put the region on the map: Gold was discovered in the riverbed in 1851. There is even more to explore, but basically the area is less tourist intensive than the California that lies farther south. It is, above all, a place to appreciate the great outdoors, slow down a bit, and smell the forest.

Kernville

Have you been contemplating a **white-water river-rafting adventure** for your family? If so, you're in the right place. From its headwaters at Lake South America in the Sierra Nevada (elevation 11,800 feet), the Kern River falls more than 12,000 feet in 150 miles. That makes it one of the fastest-falling rivers in North America. But the pace of the rapids ranges from wild to mild. According to the International River Classification System, rapids ratings range from Class I—very easy, like a swimming pool with a current—all the way up to Class VI, which is virtually unrunnable. Class I and II rapids are perfectly suitable for most children; older ones who enjoy a good soaking can take on Class III. The important thing to remember is that you don't just drive up to the river and hop in with an inner tube. There are several professional rafting outfitters whose sole purpose is to orchestrate a fun, safe time for everyone who signs up.

Most of these outfitters are based in Kernville, the traditional jumping-off point for rafting trips. If you've never done this kind of thing before, ask them about one-day instruction sessions.

If you happen to be in Kernville in late February (before the rafting season kicks in), enjoy the carnival atmosphere of **Whiskey Flat Days,** when the town travels back in time to the gold-rush days. With a parade, rodeo, whisker and costume contests, and frog races, the event is designed for families in search of a little quality fun time. Call (760) 376-2629 or visit www.kernvillechamber.org/wfdfestival.htm for dates and other information.

Kernville straddles the northern end of **Lake Isabella,** built in 1953 for flood control and as a hydroelectric source and reservoir. It is Southern California's largest freshwater lake. With up to 11,000 surface-acre feet, it also happens to be a prime body of water for Jet Skiing, waterskiing, windsurfing, sailing, and fishing.

The region around the lake is surrounded by the **Sequoia National Forest;** for camping information and details about other outdoor activities, stop by the USDA Forest Service's visitor center off Highway 155, just south of the lake's main dam, at 4875 Ponderosa Road (760-379-5646; www.fs.fed.us/r5/sequoia/).

Sierra South Mountain Sports Outfitters

11300 Kernville Road; (760) 376-3745 or (800) 376-2082; www.sierrasouth.com. Prices vary.

This company offers a wide range of rafting and kayaking excursions, including a two-and-a-half-hour Lickety-Blaster run. On this eminently manageable aquatic jaunt, rafters experience Class II and III rapids. Lake kayaking is an alternative to river rafting for those traveling with kids younger than twelve, say the folks at Sierra South, because it is more relaxed and there is swimming at Lake Isabella. It's a family paddle adventure at a mellow pace. Sierra South is a permittee of Sequoia National Forest, U.S. Forest Service.

Whitewater Voyages

11252 Kernville Road; (800) 400-RAFT; www.whitewatervoyages.com. Open daily May through August. $$$$

Since 1975, offers Class I and II family trips that accommodate kids as young as age four. Whitewater's guides were stunt doubles for Meryl Streep and Kevin Bacon in the movie *The River Wild*.

Mountain and River Adventures

11113 Kernville Road; (760) 376-6553 or (800) 861-6553; www.mtnriver.com. $$$$

Offers mountain-biking and rock-climbing rambles in addition to white-water rafting trips—all under expert supervision by guides who know the lay of the land (and water) inside out. There's also a tent campground on-site.

Kern Valley Turkey Vulture Festival

Contact Kernville Chamber of Commerce; (760) 376-2629 or (800) 350-7390; http://kern .audubon.org/tvfest.htm.

Just when you think you've heard about the most unusual festival imaginable (for instance, the tobacco-spitting competition in Calico), along comes this one. Held between September 1 and October 31, depending on when the big birds decide to fly through Kern Valley, the festival offers such activities as a turkey vulture slide show, workshops on raptor rehabilitation, a bird-banding demonstration, and an official Turkey Vultures Lift-Off. There are turkey vulture T-shirts to buy and enough information to satisfy the most rabid bird-watcher (or turkey vulture buff). The festival takes place in Weldon at Audubon's Kern River Preserve.

Where to Eat and Stay

Cheryl's Diner, 11030 Kernville Road; (760) 376-6131. Open from 6:00 a.m. to 9:00 p.m. Breakfast, lunch, and dinner served at family-friendly prices. $

The River View Lodge, #2 Sirretta Street, P.O. Box 887, Kernville 93238; (760) 376-6019; www.riverviewlodge.net. This historic eleven-room inn welcomes families and pets.

You'll find refrigerators in every room and a picnic area, too. The country-style rooms with two queen-size beds are ideal for families. $$

For More Information

Kernville Chamber of Commerce. 11447 Kernville Road, P.O. Box 397, 93238-0397; (760) 376-2629; www.kernvillechamber.org.

Bakersfield

There are several attractions in and around the pleasant city of Bakersfield, Kern's county seat.

Buck Owens' Crystal Palace

2800 Buck Owens Boulevard; (661) 869-BUCK; (661) 328-7500 for dinner reservations. Call (661) 328-7560 or (808) 855-5005 for show reservations; www.buckowens.com. Daily free tours are available. Dinners Tuesday through Saturday and brunch on Sunday. Closed Monday except for special concerts/events.

Opened in 1996, this all-in-one restaurant, museum, and theater is a must-see! Even if the kids are unaware that Buck Owens starred in *Hee Haw*, they'll love the smashingly sensational decor. You'll be amazed by what's above the 50-foot-long bar: the car Elvis never drove, a vintage 1970s Pontiac land yacht, studded with silver dollars! It's mounted at a tilt so you can check out its luxurious interior. Buck Owens passed away in March 2006, but his friends still perform country favorites evenings, matinees, and weekends. State-of-the-art sound, lighting, and giant screens throughout make this a visual marvel. And we haven't even mentioned the 35-foot mural showing Buck's rise from the cotton fields to Carnegie Hall to entertaining presidents at the White House. Country music has found a honky tonk home in Bakersfield.

Kern County Museum and Lori Brock Children's Discovery Center

3801 Chester Avenue; (661) 852-5000; www.kcmuseum.org. Open Monday through Friday 8:00 a.m. to 5:00 p.m. and Saturday 10:00 a.m. to 5:00 p.m. $

This museum provides more than a glimpse into the history of Bakersfield and its environs. Kids have room to roam here, for it's a sixteen-acre walk-through site with more than sixty historic and refurbished structures, ranging from the Havilah Courthouse and Jail (1866) and the Calloway Ranch Blacksmith Shop (circa 1880) to an 1898 Southern Pacific locomotive. The Spanish Mission–style main museum building houses permanent

Vroom **Vroom**

If you and your kids are feeling the need to see some speed, feel the roar, and taste the dust, Kern County is renowned for its racetracks. Here's where the action is!

Auto Club Famoso Raceway, 33559 Famoso Road, McFarland; (661) 399-2210; www.famosoraceway.com. Quarter-mile drag strip featuring the Good Guys Nostalgia March Meet, the NHRA FM series in April, and the NHRA CHRR IX in October.

Willow Springs International Motorsports Park, 3500 Seventy-fifth Street, West, Rosamond; (661) 256-2471; www.willowspringsraceway.com. Races held every weekend; five circuits available. Car, motorcycle, go-kart driving, and racing schools.

Buttonwillow Raceway Park, 24551 Lerdo Highway, Buttonwillow; (661) 764-5333; www.buttonwillowraceway.com. Three-mile road-racing track. Indy cars, sports cars, motorcycles, and go-karts go here.

and changing exhibitions that chronicle Kern County's history, natural history, and culture. The Lori Brock Children's Discovery Center, since 1976, has provided hands-on displays and activities for kids on the premises. The newly refurbished Kid City is a self-guided tour that features the basics of any town—a library, a bank, a doctor's office, a restaurant, a park, a theater, an ambulance, and fire department among others so kids can explore career options.

California Living Museum (CALM)

Just north of Bakersfield, 14000 Alfred Harrell Highway; (661) 872-2256; www.calmzoo.org. Open daily 9:00 a.m. to 5:00 p.m.; closed major holidays. $

Whereas the Kern County Museum focuses on the human history of the area, the natural environment occupies center stage here. This is an ideally situated spot for a family-oriented wildlife experience. The thirteen acres house a botanical garden, petting zoo, and natural history museum. The animal exhibits assemble fauna native to California: coyotes, desert tortoises, shorebirds, and birds of prey, including hawks, raptors, owls, and eagles. The Mammal Round exhibit features mountain lions, raccoons, foxes, and bobcats—yes, all native to the Golden State! The Living Museum merits at least a ninety-minute visit.

Tule Elk State Reserve

Twenty-seven miles west of Bakersfield, 4 miles west of Interstate 5, and off the Stockdale Highway, south of Buttonwillow; (661) 764-6881 or (661) 248-6692; www.parks.ca .gov/?page_id=584. Open daily 8:00 a.m. to sunset. $$

For a slightly wilder look at the wild kingdom, head to this 953-acre site. Tule elks were once as common in California as the antelope of South Africa are today, but they are now a rare species. The State Division of Beaches and Parks keeps a herd of about thirty adult elk at the park, which is equipped with a shaded picnic and viewing area. With the sweeping grassland forming a backdrop, gawking at the elks' regal antlers (which only the males have) is rather like taking a mini-safari. The best times to view the elk are in summer and fall.

Fort Tejon State Historic Park

I-5, 36 miles south of Bakersfield. Exit off I-5, 70 miles northwest of Los Angeles at the top of Grapevine Canyon; (661) 248-6692; www.forttejon.org. Living-history programs held the first Sunday of each month; Civil War reenactments, third Sunday, April through October. $

The fort is well worth a few hours' stop, especially for a realistic perspective of the 1850s to 1860s.

Where to Eat

Dewar's Candy and Ice Cream Parlor, 1120 Eye Street; (661) 322-0933; www.dewars candy.com. Savor sweet confections and ice cream from the Dewar's family recipes, originating in 1909. $

Where to Stay

Red Lion Hotel Bakersfield, 2400 Camino Del Rio Court; (661) 327-0681; reservations: (800) RED-LION; www.bakersfieldredlion .com. There are 165 rooms and suites, some with Jacuzzis. Prime location at junction of

Culinary Surprise

Bakersfield has an unexpected culinary surprise: numerous Basque restaurants. One of the largest Basque communities outside the Pyrenees is in Kern County, and any chance to sample this special cuisine should not be missed. A highlight of the meal is the scrumptious Basque salsa, made of chopped tomatoes, yellow and jalapeño chiles, garlic, onion, and salt. Here are some great places to experience Basque for you and your family. (Family-style service is also very popular with this cuisine . . . *Ongi etorri!*)

Benji's French Basque Restaurant, 4001 Rosedale Highway; (661) 328-0400; www.geocities.com/benjisbasque/

Chalet Basque, 200 Oak Street; (661) 327-2915; www.chalet basque.net/

Pyrenees Cafe, 601 Sumner Street; (661) 323-0053

Wool Growers, 620 East Nineteenth Street; (661) 327-9584; www.woolgrowers.net

Noriega Hotel, 525 Sumner Street; (661) 322-8419. One seating at noon and one seating at 7:00 p.m. Our favorite family-style dining spot. Make sure you know how to get there, as first-timers have some trouble. Hungry diners sit at long tables (you may not know who'll be next to you), sharing up to seven courses of hearty Basque food. No set menu. We've tried soup, salad, chicken, ribs, fresh-cut french fries—all excellent. The ambience is, well, plain, but the service is efficient and the fare is robust. Only the most ravenous will have room for dessert.

Freeway 99 and Highway 58 (Rosedale High- way exit) for all your family's Kern County adventures. Smokin' Joe's Beach Bar & Wood- fired Cuisine restaurant on-site $$$

For More Information

Greater Bakersfield Chamber of Com- merce. 1725 Eye Street, P.O. Box 1947, 93303; (661) 327-4421; www.bakersfield chamber.org.

Greater Bakersfield Convention and Visitors Bureau. 515 Truxton Avenue, 93301; (661) 325-5051 or (866) 425-7353; www.bakersfieldcvb.org

Kern County Board of Trade and Tour- ist Information Center. Mailing address: P.O. Bin 1312, Bakersfield 93302; street address: 2101 Oak Street, Bakersfield; (661) 861-2367 or (800) 500-KERN; www.visitkern .com.

Home on the Ranch

If your kids spot some elk, they may be disappointed to learn that no, they can't ride or even pet them. However, they can pet and ride horses to their hearts' content at **Rankin Ranch,** minutes north of Bakersfield in Walker's Basin. To get there, take I-5 north to the Lamont–Lake Isabelle exit. The ranch is 38 miles from the exit, past the town of Caliente. Members of the Rankin family have been ranching at their Quarter Circle U since 1863, and they've got the western way of life down pat. This is a working, 31,000-acre cattle and guest ranch where kids and adults can help out with farm chores and horseback ride at their leisure. Fourteen cozy cabins with no room phones or TV. Family-style meals, horseback riding, swimming, and hiking. Seasonal supervised children's program is first-rate. Call for current rates (which include riding, lodging, and three meals a day) and other information at (661) 867-2511, or visit www.rankinranch.com.

Tulare County

Encompassing 4,863 square miles (slightly larger than Connecticut) in the San Joaquin Valley, Tulare County is nestled between the Sierra Nevada to the east and the Coastal Mountain Range to the west. Tulare County's extensively cultivated and very fertile valley floor is the second-leading producer of agricultural commodities in the United States. The rest of the county is composed of foothills, timbered slopes, and high mountains ranging in elevations from 270 feet to 14,495 feet (the top of Mt. Whitney, the highest point in the continental United States). There are more than 110 mountain peaks in eastern Tulare County, which furnish a backdrop of scenic wonder. Tulare County is home to Sequoia National Park as well as Inyo and Sequoia National Forests—offering an amazing array of dining, lodging, camping, winter sports of all kinds, fishing, boating, backpacking, hunting, hiking, and waterskiing options that attract thousands of visitors annually.

Sequoia National Park and
Kings Canyon National Park

Office of the Superintendent, 47050 Generals Highway, Three Rivers; general visitor infor-mation: (559) 565-3341; www.nps.gov/seki. The two main entrances, Ash Mountain on Highway 198 and Big Stump on Highway 180, are open daily year-round. Certain areas of the park are open part of the year: The Mineral King area is open late May through October 31 in Sequoia National Park, and the Cedar Grove area in Kings Canyon is open mid-April through mid-November. Crystal Cave, some campgrounds, and several side roads close for the winter. The main park road, the Generals Highway, may close between Lodgepole and Grant Grove during and after storms for plowing. The highest visitation is in July and August. It can be difficult to find a campsite at popular campgrounds on

summer Saturdays. Driving times: To Sequoia Park Ash Mountain entrance from Highway 99 at Visalia, take Highway 198 east for approximately one hour. To Kings Canyon Park Big Stump entrance from Highway 99 at Fresno, take Highway 180 east approximately one and a quarter hours. Admission per vehicle: $20 for a seven-day pass, $30 for annual vehicle pass. Note: Gasoline is not sold within park boundaries, but it is available at locations near the park boundaries. Be sure to fill up in one of the towns near the park entrances or at one of three locations in the national forest that border parts of the park.

Tulare County is best known as the home of these parks. Even though it's part of Fresno County, Kings Canyon shares its east-west boundary with Sequoia, and the two parks are generally referred to together. If the wooded retreats of Big Bear and Lake Arrowhead in the Inland Empire are imbued with an "escape from the city" atmosphere, up here you'll really feel a zillion miles away from it all. This is nature at its most unbridled, God's country with a very capital G. With more than 800 miles of marked hiking trails and 1,200-plus campsites and other lodging options, it's no wonder Sequoia and Kings Canyon are a California family favorite for camping and nature trips.

The biggest attractions are trees. Autumn in New England may be prime leaf-peeping time, but the trees of the central Sierra Nevada are marvels to behold any time of year. This is mainly due to their gargantuan size. Of the thirty-seven largest sequoia trees in the world, twenty giants roost here in Sequoia and Kings Canyon. You'll find the most stupendous grove of sequoias in the Giant Forest, longtime home of the General Sherman Tree. Weighing in at 2.7 million pounds, the 275-foot-tall tree is the largest living thing in the world. At more than 2,300 years, it's also one of the oldest. Each year the venerable Sherman grows enough wood for another 60-foot-tall tree. Imagine the tree-house possibilities! For an easy, rewarding hike the whole family will enjoy, try the 2-mile, two-hour Congress Trail, which begins at the Sherman and circles around the grove.

Kings Canyon is where the General Grant Tree, the earth's third-largest, has its roots. It's also known as the "Nation's Christmas Tree." Annual Noel celebrations are held beneath its considerable and magnificent canopy. Walk along the easy 0.3-mile-long trail, marked with informative signposts, to learn more about trees and the peoples who lived here.

Conservationist John Muir called Kings Canyon a rival to Yosemite, and it's not hard to see why. The depths of the canyon at Cedar Grove, where the Kings River gushes between sheer granite walls, bottom out at 8,000 feet. Both Sequoia and Kings Canyon offer incomparable vistas, hiking trails, camping, and other natural wonders, including more than a hundred caves.

There are several excellent visitor centers throughout the parks that offer free information, weather updates, naturalist programs, slide shows, maps, and services. **Grant Grove Visitor Center** in Kings Canyon (559-565-4307) is open daily. **Lodgepole Visitor Center** in Sequoia (559-565-4436) is open daily in summer and on weekends only in winter. **Cedar Grove Visitor Center** (559-565-3793; 30 miles east of Kings Canyon park entrance) is open daily during the summer only.

The **Giant Forest Museum** in Sequoia (559-565-4480) is open daily and should not be missed. It is housed in a historic log building in the Giant Forest sequoia grove at 6,500 feet elevation, 16 miles from the Ash Mountain entrance on Highway 198. Wonderful

The Biggest Trees in the World

Giant sequoias (*Sequoiadendron giganteum*) grow only on the western slopes of the Sierra Nevada in central California. The groves are scattered across a narrow 260-mile belt, no more than about 15 miles wide at any point in elevations mainly between 5,000 and 7,500 feet. Closely related are the coastal redwoods (*Sequoia sempervirens*) found along the Northern California coast. Giant sequoias are slightly shorter than the coastal redwoods, but they are more massive, and they're considered the largest tree in the world in terms of volume. The largest sequoia and the most massive living organism on the planet is the **General Sherman Tree** in Sequoia National Park.

interactive exhibits tell the story of the sequoias of Giant Forest, and what we have learned about how to protect them.

Activities vary according to season, but no matter the time of year, the best way to get into the park is to get out of the car. "Don't leave until you have seen it," advised 1920s park superintendent Col. John R. White, "and this you cannot do from an automobile." In summer, rangers lead walks and talks in the foothills, the sequoia groves, and the high country. Take a tour of the exquisite Crystal Cave. There are rivers to enjoy—carefully—and pack stations offer horseback riding.

Come winter, cross-country skis or snowshoes can be rented to explore the sequoia groves beyond the roads, and there are ranger-guided snowshoe walks. Wolverton is a wonderful free-terrain snow-play area (sometimes even in April). If you prefer warmer activities, trails in the foothills are usually snow-free, and by February they are graced with wildflowers. Check bulletin boards and visitor centers to find what activities are being offered.

Where to Eat and Stay

Cedar Grove Lodge (operated by Sequoia–Kings Canyon Park Services Company); (559) 335-5500; www.sequoia-kingscanyon.com. Open late April through October. Twenty-one motel rooms in Cedar Grove Village, deep in the canyon of Kings Canyon Park. Restaurant, market, and gift shop also in building. $$

Grant Grove Village (operated by Sequoia–Kings Canyon Park Services Company); (559) 335-5500 or (866) JON-MUIR; www.sequoia-kingscanyon.com. Open all year. Here you will find the two-story John Muir Lodge, thirty modern hotel rooms with forest views, and

more than forty rustic tent and housekeeping cabins, all in the Grant Grove area of Kings Canyon Park, only a half-mile stroll to a sequoia grove. Casual dining on American fare (breakfast, lunch, and dinner daily) at Grant Grove Village Restaurant, next to the visitor center; market/general store; gift shop; and post office. $$$

Montecito–Sequoia Lodge (privately owned by founder Dr. Virginia Barnes and family since 1946; in January 2007, acquired and now operated by the Dally family); (559) 565-3388 or (800) 843-8677; www.mslodge

Sequoia and Kings Canyon
Junior Ranger Program

Kids of any age can participate in this program. Kids ages five through eight earn the Jay Award. Those ages nine through twelve work for the Raven Award, and kids ages thirteen through one hundred and three can earn the Senior Patch. To get started, purchase a Junior Ranger booklet at any visitor center. Follow the instructions and have fun!

.com. Open year-round. Located on its own Lake Homavalo in Sequoia National Forest, adjacent to Sequoia and Kings Canyon National Parks. This rustic property functions as a weekly family vacation camp in summer and a cross-country ski center in the winter. Thirty-six basic lodge rooms with private baths and thirteen cabins with nearby bathhouses. Reasonable rates vary according to season and include all meals, which are served buffet style in the lodge. On-site summer and children's activities include canoeing, sailing, waterskiing, swimming, horseback riding, tennis, archery, trampoline, riflery, fencing, nature, stream fishing, arts and crafts instruction, theme nights, dances, sing-along campfires, variety shows, water carnivals, fort building, junior gymnastics, and pony rides. In 2006, Montecito Sequoia Lodge was rated one of the best family camp resorts in the country by *Good Morning, America*. $$$

Wuksachi Village & Lodge (operated by Delaware North Park Services, in Sequoia National Park, 4 miles from the Giant Forest and 23 miles from Sequoia Park entrance); (559) 253-2199 or (888) 252-5757; www .VisitSequoia.com. Open all year. Opened in 1999, the striking log lodge forms the center of the village and houses the full-service dining room (breakfast, lunch, and dinner daily), cocktail lounge, gift shop, and conference rooms, where naturalist-led programs are held (**free** and not to be missed). There are 102 modern rooms housed in three separate log buildings up on the hillside (ask for the Sequoia building for the best views of Mt. Silliman and Silver Peak). The eighteen large family suites have sofa sleepers in alcove sitting areas—ideal for your clan. Reserve early, especially in summer and on weekends. $$$

Mammoth Lakes Area

The Mammoth Lakes area is California's answer to the Alps. Southern Californians have been known to schlep their ski equipment to locales as far off as Chile and Chamonix, but most will agree that some of the best skiing anywhere is found 300 miles north of Los Angeles at **Mammoth Mountain Ski Area** in the heart of the Eastern Sierra Nevada. The statistics bespeak world-class thrills: an 11,053-foot summit, a 7,953-foot base, 30 lifts, 150 trails, and 3,500 acres of skiable terrain. The ski season often extends as late as July. Don't let the fact that the U.S. Ski Team trains at Mammoth each spring deter you from coming: Fully 30 percent of the ski runs are rated for beginners. Plus, Mammoth boasts one of the finest ski schools in the country, with family lessons and a children's ski school offered regularly.

Throughout the Mammoth Lakes region, not only will your family groove on skiing and snowboarding but also at cross-country ski centers, on snowmobile rentals, sledding, tobogganing, outdoor ice skating, and snowshoeing. Summer means even more activities to keep the family fit. In the summer, enjoy mountain biking, hiking, jazz and art festivals, swimming, picnicking, fishing, boating, hot springs, and canoeing, kayaking, or riding your Jet Skis and Wave Runners at Lakes Topaz, Klondike, Grant, Diaz, Walker, and Crowley. Or check out national monuments—visit Devils Postpile, formed more than 100,000 years ago, or Rainbow Falls, where the San Joaquin River drops more than 100 feet. How about a horseback ride—most of the major canyons in the Eastern Sierra have pack stations, offering anywhere from one-hour to full-day or multiday trips. Your family will discover endless choices for accommodations (condos, chalets, hotels, cabins, inns), for dining (from fast food to continental cuisine), and for shopping (from trinkets to fine art), and a shuttle route connects all the fun year-round!

Mammoth is one of the best choices for a family vacation—summer or winter.

Inyo National Forest

Headquarters, 351 Pacu Lane, Suite 200, Bishop; (760) 873-2400; www.fs.fed.us/r5/inyo/index.shtml.

The name "Inyo" comes from a Native American word meaning "dwelling place of the great spirit." The Inyo National Forest was named after Inyo County, in which much of the forest resides. Here you'll find more than two million acres of clean air, crystal-blue skies, mountain lakes and streams, challenging trails, high mountain peaks, and beautiful views. The Inyo National Forest is home to many natural wonders, including Mt. Whitney, Mono Lake, Mammoth Lakes Basin, and the Ancient Bristlecone Pine Forest, as well as seven congressionally designated wildernesses, comprising more than 650,000 acres of land. Recreational opportunities include camping, picnicking, hiking, backpacking, equestrian use, and off-highway vehicle use. One hundred-plus miles of trails are groomed for multiple-purpose winter use (snowmobiling, skiing, and hiking), and approximately 45 miles of trails are groomed for cross-country skiing.

Mammoth Mountain Ski Area

1 Minaret Road, Mammoth Lakes; snowphone: (760) 934-6166 or (888) SNOWRPT; general information: (760) 934-0745 or (800) MAMMOTH; www.mammothmountain.com. Open year-round. $$$$

Mammoth Mountain is the leading four-season mountain resort in Southern California, encompassing four day lodges, ten sports shops, twelve rental/repair shops, one on-hill snack bar, four food courts/cafeterias, a ski and snowboard school, a race department, lockers, hotel and condominium accommodations, five restaurants, seven bars, child-care area, and game room. Rates for lodging, dining, and attractions are available in a wide range to fit any budget or taste.

Mammoth Kids Ski Schools

Info: www.mammothmountain.com or call (800) MAMMOTH.

Mammoth has three learning centers where instructors specialize in working with kids: Woollywood at Main Lodge, Canyon Kids at Canyon Lodge, and Eagle Lodge Ski and Snowboard School. Mammoth Kids programs feature instruction, child care, and combination packages. The school is divided into Mammoth Explorers (ages four to six and seven to twelve), the Big Kahuna Snowboard Club (seven to twelve), children's private lessons (four to twelve), the Custom Kid's Camp (seven to twelve), and a three-day ski/snowboard camp. Helmets are required for ages four through twelve.

Wonderland Park

Info: www.mammothmountain.com or call (800) MAMMOTH.

Family Fun Terrain Park at Canyon Lodge has undergone a $250,000 renovation in 2007. The park has been relocated from under Schoolyard Express to under Chair 7, on runs Hansel and Gretel, to decrease through-traffic and provide an additional fifteen acres of park terrain focused on freestyle development that includes box tops that sit on the snow, short rail slides, banked turns, rollers, and jumps.

Red's Meadow Pack Stations

P.O. Box 395, Mammoth Lakes 93546; (760) 934-2345 or (800) 292-7758; www.redsmeadow .com. $$

If you're in the market for a modern A-frame cabin, these newer but rustic cabins are furnished with butane heating, running water, large bathrooms with showers, gas ranges, and refrigerators. There are also motel units, a grocery store, and cafe—both open 7:00 a.m. to 7:00 p.m. daily. From Red's Meadow there are various group riding and hiking trail trips to such places as the John Muir Wilderness, Bishop to Bodie (camping along the old stagecoach route via saddle horse, mule, and wagon), and other off-the-beaten-path tours your family will long remember. These tours begin in late May and end about the first of October. If you're into more comfort, reserve a condominium in Mammoth for the family and take the shuttle bus into Red's Meadow.

Paul Schat's Bakkery

3305 Main Street, Mammoth; (760) 934-6055. Open daily 6:00 a.m. to 6:00 p.m. $

If the name sounds familiar, you're right. Father Erick has a "bakkery" in Bishop. From delectable caramel-encrusted pecan rolls to scintillating sweet rolls with sweet sliced apples, and fresh baked breads, this place, near the outlets in Mammoth, is an absolute must. Drop by for breakfast or lunch in the adjoining Cafe Vermeer, where you can order sandwiches on the freshest bread on the planet. $$

Manzanar National Historic Site

During World War II, Manzanar Relocation Center, just off U.S. Highway 395, 12 miles north of Lone Pine, was one of ten camps where Japanese-American citizens and Japanese aliens were interned. Located at the foot of the imposing Sierra Nevada in eastern California's Owens Valley, Manzanar has been identified as the best preserved of these camps. A twenty-minute film shows at the Interpretive Center between 9:00 a.m. and 4:30 p.m. daily. Open all year during daylight hours with **free** admission.

There is a 3.2-mile-long self-guided auto tour of the camp, with a tour description and map available at the camp entrance. A walking tour of the Manzanar Camp takes one to two hours. A self-guiding walking-tour booklet is available at the Interagency Visitor Center in Lone Pine and at the Eastern California Museum in Independence. For more information call (760) 878-2194 or visit www.nps.gov/manz/.

Tamarack Lodge & Resort and Cross-Country Ski Center
Located 2 miles from the town of Mammoth in the Mammoth Lakes Basin on Twin Lakes Road; (800) 237-6879; www.tamaracklodge.com. $$$$

A great bet for families, with its 19 miles of groomed trails that weave through pine forests (open November through April). The resort has been welcoming guests since 1924—with cabins and lodge rooms from rustic to deluxe; and serving hearty lunch and dinner meals at the Lakefront Restaurant. Boat and canoe rentals are available summertime at the lodge. You can fish from Tamarack's front yard in Twin Lakes (April through October); or hike around one of the many trails in the nearby Lakes Basin.

Mammoth Dog Teams
(760) 934-6270 or (800) MAMMOTH; www.mammothdogteams.com. $$$$

Tours (on an honest-to-goodness dogsled) mush off from the Main Lodge at Mammoth Mountain Inn. Rides in the winter, kennel tours in the off-season. Call in advance.

For More Information

Mammoth Lakes Visitor Bureau. 2520 Main Street, Box 48, Mammoth Lakes, 93546; (760) 934-2712 or (888) GO-MAMMOTH (888-466-2666); www.visitmammoth.com.

Mono County Tourism & Film Commission. P.O. Box 603, Mammoth Lakes, 93546; (760) 924-1700 or (800) 845-7922; www.monocounty.org.

Lone Pine

How can you not stop in Lone Pine, in southern Inyo County, once you realize you can explore one of the earth's oldest geological formations by car? Among others, these phantasmagoric formations resemble a bullfrog, a polar bear, Hannibal the Cannibal, and an owl. Hundreds of rock sculptures can be imagined in these bizarre hills, and you can drive the route in about half an hour.

You're on historical turf here; this is where Republic Pictures filmed dozens of spaghetti Westerns during the 1940s and '50s. Chase scenes from these cowboy flicks, with such stars as Hopalong Cassidy, were immortalized in this stunning landscape. Scenes for *Maverick* (starring Mel Gibson) were shot here. If you see *The Shadow* with Alec Baldwin, you'll recognize the Alabama hills backdrop. Many stars return for the mid-October **Annual Lone Pine Film Festival.** Spend a few hours or a few days here, within view of the majestic Mt. Whitney, at 14,494 feet high, the tallest mountain in the continental United States, 13 miles west of town on Whitney Portal Road. The summit is 11 miles up by strenuous trail from the end of the road; permits are required year-round (760-873-2483). Before or after your ascent, enjoy the California charisma and satisfy your hunger at the **Totem Café,** 131 South Main Street, or at the **Mount Whitney Restaurant,** 227 South Main Street.

Where to Stay

Best Western Frontier Motel, 1008 Main Street at US 395, 0.5 mile south of Lone Pine; (760) 876-5571, (800) 528-1234; www .bestwestern.com. Rates include continental breakfast at this simple, clean, seventy-three-room property. Beautiful mountain views from the lawn. $$

For More Information

Lone Pine Chamber of Commerce. 126 South Main Street, 93545; (760) 876-4444 or (877) 253-8981; www.lonepinechamber.org.

Bishop

Chances are quite good you'll pass through the town of Bishop on your way to or out of the Mammoth Lakes area. You'll see why Bishop calls itself the Mule Capital of the World if you arrive during Memorial Day weekend's annual **Mule Days** (www.Muledays.org), when the streets are abuzz with mule and chariot races, jumping events, and myriad other equine-related activities. Approximately 40,000 mule lovers gather for what the *Guinness Book of World Records* called (in 1994) the world's longest-running nonmotorized parade. Call (760) 872-4263 for more information.

September in Bishop is a special event in itself thanks to the **Millpond Traditional Music Festival** (760-873-8014 or 800-874-0669; www.inyo.org) that takes place at

Millpond County Park, sponsored by Inyo County and the Inyo Council for the Arts. Featured are top performers of bluegrass, folk, and country music. Families will find this musical weekend ideal for picnics and outdoor adventures.

Laws Railroad Museum and Historical Site

A bit north of Bishop; (760) 873-5950; www.lawsmuseum.org. **Free;** donations welcome.

This eleven-acre indoor/outdoor museum harks back to the rough-and-tumble pioneer days in the Owens Valley. Kids can climb into the cab of locomotive 9 to ring the bell, and explore the compartment cars of the 1883 Slim Princess narrow-gauge train, which, says the sign, BEGAN NOWHAR, ENDED NOWHAR, AN' STOPPED ALL NIGHT TO THINK IT OVER. The museum is on the National Register of Historic Places. Check out the bell rack, featuring antique bells from Bishop-area schools; the Original Laws School, refurbished with local artifacts; and a country store with old-time school items and supplies on display.

Erick Schat's Bakkery

763 North Main Street; (760) 873-7156; www.erickschatsbakery.com.

This is a local institution. Home since 1907 of the original "sheepherder bread," a hearty country loaf, Schat's also has delicious sweet rolls and scrumptious sandwiches. You'll leave well fortified and ready to tackle another stretch of scenic California.

For More Information

Bishop Area Chamber of Commerce and Visitors Bureau. 690 North Main Street, 93514; (760) 873-8504 or (888) 395-3952; www.bishopvisitor.com. Request a copy of the *Vacation Planner*.

the Deserts

The California deserts conjure up different images for different people. To some they suggest glittering resort cities, brilliant skies, mid-century architectural marvels, and the verdant greens of impressive Palm Springs golf courses. To others they raise thoughts of a barren, even desolate, landscape of boulders, sand, and cacti lining the freeway from Los Angeles to Las Vegas. To yet others they inspire thoughts of pioneer history, rustic ghost towns, and abandoned gold mines. The advent of tribal Indian casinos has changed tourism throughout Southern California, with five major gaming establishments luring throngs to the desert. It is important to note that Indian casinos do not allow any guests under the age of twenty-one, so they will not be listed in this guidebook. Yet, vast opportunities for family fun endure under the desert sun! Whatever desert-related pictures may come to mind, however, one fact is indisputable: The desert is big. It is immense—stretching from the Mojave Desert and ultra-arid Death Valley National Park in the north to the Colorado Desert area that reaches south to the border of Mexico.

Although the region is strikingly—or starkly—beautiful, much of it is what some might call wasteland or others environmentally pristine. Either way, a good portion is off-limits to nonmilitary personnel. These two attributes certainly make it simpler for families who want to catch the desert's highlights but lack the time (or inclination) to explore every gully or gulch. As a matter of fact, vast tracts of the desert have no highways, and if something akin to a "road" exists, it can be rock-strewn, meandering, signless, and dusty, leading you and your clan (best-case scenario) to an old ghost town or some other remnant of long-gone Wild West days, or (worst-case scenario) to nowhere, nowhere at all.

If you are willing to take a modest chance, to be marginally adventuresome in checking out a few of the desert's endless nooks and crannies, you'll find that here, too, the Golden State is indeed a land of contrasts.

As its name suggests, Death Valley—at 282 feet below sea level, the lowest land surface in the Western Hemisphere—is about as dry as a place can get. In sharp contrast, much of Palm Springs and other resort communities of the Coachella Valley, some 150 miles to the south of Death Valley, are as verdant and lush as a tropical oasis—primarily because of irrigation, but partly because of cool mountain streams that have flowed into

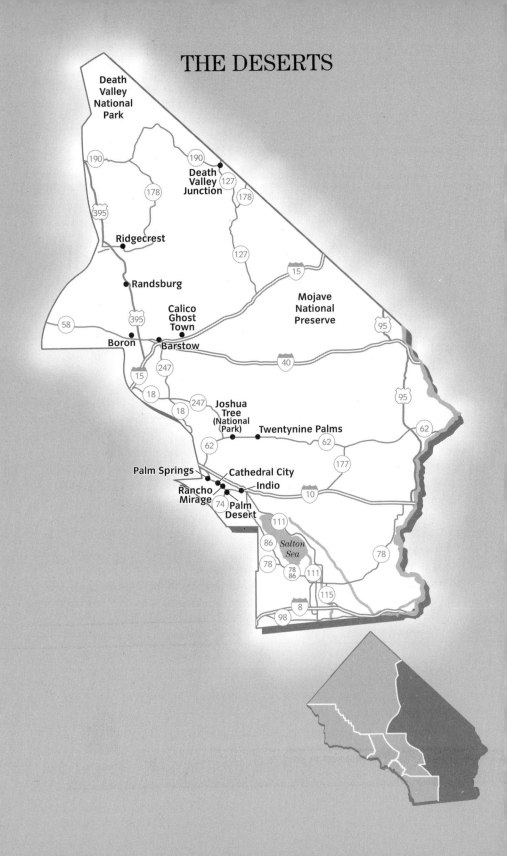

THE DESERTS

Death Valley National Park

190

190

Death Valley Junction

127

178

178

395

Ridgecrest

127

15

Randsburg

Mojave National Preserve

58

395

Calico Ghost Town

95

Boron

Barstow

15

247

40

95

18

247

18

Joshua Tree (National Park)

62

Twentynine Palms

62

62

177

Palm Springs

Cathedral City

Indio

62

Rancho Mirage

74

Palm Desert

10

111

86

Salton Sea

78

78

78
86

111

78

115

98

8

the area for centuries. Even in summer, when 110-plus-degree temperatures expose the desert's true personality, it's still a great time to visit. During the summer months, many Palm Springs–area hotels reduce their rates 50 to 70 percent. And throughout the desert, summer seems to go by a little slower than elsewhere in California. Of course, the sun certainly shines brighter. It's almost as if nature is telling you to enjoy the offerings of the desert at a pace that suits you—and reminding you to bring along the sunscreen!

Palm Springs

Approximately 100 miles east of Los Angeles on Interstate 10 lies the **Coachella Valley,** home to the desert resort communities of Palm Springs, Rancho Mirage, Cathedral City, Palm Desert, Indio, Indian Wells, Desert Hot Springs, and La Quinta. The other high-desert destinations are Yucca Valley, Morongo, Twentynine Palms, and Joshua Tree. Seen from an airplane window or hot-air balloon, these cities appear as rather artificial patches of green against a flat, arid landscape framed by mountain ridges.

If you drive into the valley from L.A., however, the first things you'll notice are rows and rows of windmills protruding sentrylike from the hillsides. These are actually working wind turbines that generate electricity for nearly 100,000 homes.

Other desert areas may be more scenic (read: more barren), but the Coachella Valley (local population 408,624, which swells to 800,000 during the peak season from January through April) has the monopoly on recreational attractions and leisure opportunities. Just consider a few valley stats: 600 tennis courts, 16,200 hotel rooms in 130 hotels, and 111 golf courses, meaning more than one golf course per square mile in the desert resort area. Add to these numbers 40,000 swimming pools, probably a zillion hot tubs (or spas), and 350 days of fun in the sunshine to the recipe, and it's a no-brainer why three and a half million people visit the area every year. But the valley never seems crowded, even during the peak season, because things are so spread out. To see how vast the desert really is, ride the Palm Springs Aerial Tramway for a "natural high."

World-famous as "America's Premier Desert Resort," Palm Springs has ranked high on everybody's Coachella Valley must-visit list since the 1930s, when the small town (current population 43,800) was a favorite playground for California's unofficial royalty—movie stars. Gone but not forgotten are Frank Sinatra and Liberace, who once had estates here. Barry Manilow, Carol Channing, Jack Jones, Suzanne Somers, Keely Smith, and Dick Van Patten still call the desert home for at least part of the year. It doesn't take a rocket scientist to understand the valley's appeal. Average winter temperatures in the mid-seventies are enough to turn even Los Angelinos green (as in putting green) with envy. And the restaurants and resorts are truly world-class.

The *Desert Entertainer* (760-776-5181; www.desertentertainer.com) is published weekly, **free** of charge; you can pick it up on news racks all over town. It's a useful source for desert happenings. Listings include such items as local hikes, museums, various valley attractions, a daily calendar, and information on family-oriented events.

Elite Land Tours

540 South Vella Road; (760) 318-1200 or (800) 514-4866; www.elitelandtours.com. $$$$

All tours conducted in fully air-conditioned, best-in-class all-terrain vehicles—the Hummer H2—accommodating up to five passengers plus professional guide. Includes resort pickup (door-to-door service), admissions, gourmet snacks, and assorted refreshments. Gourmet picnic lunch optional. Tour destinations include visits to the San Andreas Fault; Covington Flats, to see the world's largest Joshua tree; Mojave and Colorado/Sonora Desert trails; a Night Vision experience; the Salton Sea or the Spirit of the Indian Canyons; a wind farm; or experience the "P" Tour, featuring a visit to Pioneertown (where more than 200 western films were made), Pipes Canyon, and Indian petroglyphs. Featured on the Travel Channel and in *Condé Nast Traveler*. A one-of-a-kind experience.

Moorten Botanical Gardens

1701 South Palm Canyon Drive, corner of East Palm Canyon; (760) 327-6555; www.palm springs.com/moorten/index.html. Open 9:00 a.m. to 4:30 p.m.; closed Wednesday. Self-guided tours. $

Kids will learn about the diversity of desert flora at the world's first "cactarium," where 3,000 varieties of cacti flourish in a natural setting. Established in 1938, this unusual botanical garden bristles with 3,000-plus cacti in all shapes and sizes. Ask the kids to look for colorful desert flowers because there's "always something in bloom."

Palm Springs International Film Festival

1700 East Tahquitz Canyon Way, Suite 3; (760) 322-2930; www.psfilmfest.org.

Held annually since 1989, this film festival has become a mecca for buyers seeking films for distribution. Films screened here include comedy, romance, experimental, animation, period pieces, suspense, and thrillers. You're sure to find a few family flicks among the offerings. The 2008 festival screened over 200 films, with an impressive representation

Jet Set Travel for Toddlers

The next time you see a "sherpa" dad carrying tons of toddler gear, you know he hasn't heard about "Sit 'n' Stroll." An ingenious five-in-one stroller that has revolutionized travel for toddlers has won the approval of the FAA and gratitude of countless parents. Simply, take a full-function stroller, a car seat, and a dining booster seat, add the "simple push of a lever," and voila! Parents have consolidated their toddler's needs thanks to one convenient contraption. Hats off to Lilly Gold, who designed Sit 'n' Stroll over twenty years ago when she got tired of carrying so much toddler gear on and off planes. Instead of complaining, she invented this stellar stroller! The Sit 'n' Stroll is suitable for newborns to children up to 40 pounds. Info: www.lillygold.com.

of family films such as the inspirational *Red Like the Sun* (Italian) about a young hearing-impaired boy who became a famous sound engineer. Plan ahead for family-friendly films by ordering tickets in advance.

Palm Canyon Theatre

538 North Palm Canyon Drive at corner of Alejo (in Frances Stevens Park); (760) 323-5123 (box office); www.palmcanyontheatre.org. Box office hours Tuesday through Saturday 10:00 a.m. to 5:00 p.m. Closed June through August, but a special five-week children's camp is offered then. $$

This Palm Springs theater group, celebrating its twelfth season in 2008, is located in a former elementary school auditorium. Strictly family-type plays such as *My Fair Lady* and *Annie Get Your Gun* make this an ideal choice for a family matinee. This is an Equity Theatre and there is ample **free** parking and refreshments between acts.

Celebrity Tours

4751 East Palm Canyon Drive, in the Rimrock Shopping Center; (760) 770-2700 (reservations required); www.celebrity-tours.com. Tour A is a narrated one-hour drive including up to forty movie stars' homes. Tour B lasts two and a half hours and adds the Walter Annenberg Estate, country clubs, and the Eisenhower Medical Center. All tours are made in air-conditioned coaches. Pickups at Palm Springs hotels and the tour office. $$; from May through September children under fourteen are free with a paid adult.

If you've been wondering how to find Elvis's honeymoon hideaway or the place where Liberace entertained, book your family on an air-conditioned coach for a guided tour of the Las Palmas district (also known as the movie colony) and other areas where history was made. Well-rehearsed guides tell all, and you won't want to miss a word of their entertaining narrative. This is far better than a self-guided tour through the quiet neighborhoods of walled vines and winding streets—and it's the only way to get the lowdown on how Hollywood established itself in the desert.

Sunny Daze Cafe, next door to Celebrity Tours, is good for a refreshing nibble before or after your tour.

Golf Courses

If in L.A., the celebrities are all on the beach in Malibu; in Palm Springs, they're probably on the golf course. Although many clubs are private, there are several beautiful courses open to the public. Remember, a licensed driver is required for any golf cart, and only two people per cart. Greens fees are substantially reduced at most desert courses in the summer.

Tahquitz Creek Golf Academy. 1885 Golf Club Drive; (760) 328-1005; www.tahquitzgolfresort.com. Junior and adult clinics can be arranged. $$

Desert Dunes Golf Club. 19300 Palm Drive, Desert Hot Springs; (760) 251-5368; www.desertdunesgolf.com. Designed by world-renowned golf course architect Robert Trent Jones Jr. Ages sixteen and under receive discount rates. $$$$

Practice Makes **Perfect**

If you have a budding Tiger Woods in the family or just want to practice your shots, visit the **College Golf Center** at the College of the Desert, 73–450 Fred Waring Drive (760-341-0994), open 7:00 a.m. to between 7:00 and 9:00 p.m. A bucket of 105 balls is $9.

Cimarron Golf Club. 67–603 Thirtieth Avenue, Cathedral City; (760) 770-6060; www.cimarrongolf.com. Golfers of all ages will find the thirty-six holes at this club sheer paradise. There is a short (Pebble) and a long (Boulder) course. Inquire about golf clinics and other events. Tee times can be booked up to 120 days in advance. Children under fifteen are eligible for discount rates. $$$$

The Golf Resort at Indian Wells. 44–400 Indian Wells Lane; (760) 346-GOLF; www.indianwellsgolfresort.com. Two Ted Robinson–designed championship courses. Home of the LG Skins Game and the only thirty-six-hole facility in California with both courses ranked in the Top 20 "Best Courses You Can Play" in California by *Golfweek Magazine*. $$$$

Desert Willow Golf Resort. 38–995 Desert Willow Drive, Palm Desert; (760) 346-0015 or (800) 320-3323; www.desertwillow.com. There is an excellent junior golf program, "Fairway Kids," offered year-round. Inquire about spring break and summer golf camps, too. $$$$

Tommy Jacob's Bel Air Greens. 1001 South El Cielo; (760) 322-6062 Family-style golf during the season (January through April). Eighteen short holes on a beautiful course for adults and kids (they call it a putt-putt course). This is an all par 3 layout. The nine-hole Executive Course is ideal for juniors and adults. Children age seventeen and younger pay $7.50 for nine holes of golf. $$

Tahquitz Creek Palm Springs. 1885 Golf Club Drive; (760) 328-1005 or (800) 743-2211; www.tahquitzcreek.com. Here is the place to enjoy resort golf "without paying for the rest of the resort." The club has two Arnold Palmer–managed courses, Resort and Legend, both rated four-star by *Golf Digest* magazine. All-inclusive golf packages feature breakfast, lunch, greens fees, cart, and more. $$$

Best of the Best Tours

15831 La Vida Drive; (760) 320-4600 or (760) 320-1365 for reservations; www.bestofthebest tours.com. Open daily, prices and times subject to change. $$$$

These are awesome adventures in spacious, open-air vehicles you'll long remember. All tours depart from the lobby of the Spa Hotel and Casino in Palm Springs at 100 North Indian Canyon. The expedition starts at Whitewater Hill (elevation 2,500 feet) and makes its way through the Cahuilla Canyons of Snow Creek and Chino. Then it's on to the legendary Movie Colony, once a second home to Hollywood stars, including Elvis Presley and Jack Benny. There is a thirty-minute trek into Andreas Canyon and a drive into Palm

Canyon. Before leaving the Indian Canyons, you'll visit an authentic trading post. It's filled with Native American souvenirs, maps, dream catchers, cassettes, and exquisite handmade turquoise jewelry. The variety of merchandise crammed into this shop is overwhelming! There is limited parking and a small menu for cold drinks. The most popular tour, the Bonanza, which lasts from three and a half to four hours, visits the windmills, canyons, and celebrity homes.

Indian Canyons

Toll-gate entrance, south end of Palm Canyon Drive; (760) 325-3400 or (800) 790-3398; www .tahquitzcanyon.com. Open fall and winter 8:00 a.m. to 5:00 p.m., spring and summer 8:00 a.m. to 6:00 p.m. Admission fee to enter canyon, plus additional fees for guided tours. Be sure to call for specific times/tours since prices and hours are subject to change. $$–$$$

Revenues from the Canyons help fill the Agua Caliente tribe's coffers, but this cluster of oases is a priceless natural jewel that you really don't want to miss. With some of the thickest concentrations of palm trees in the world, thanks to the cool mountain streams that flow through them, the site provides a refreshing refuge from the heat of the desert. There are actually four separate canyons, comprising 32,000 acres: Tahquitz, Palm, Murray, and Andreas. All have trails for walking or hiking. The unusual rock formations in Andreas Canyon are the repository of ancient Cahuilla rock art. Note that the Tahquitz Canyon entrance is at 500 West Mesquite Road; guided hikes of 2 miles round-trip and two and a half hours' duration leave the Visitor Center there at 8:00 and 10:00 a.m., noon, and 2:00 p.m., and self-guided hikes may be taken between 7:30 a.m. and 3:30 p.m. The Tahquitz Canyon Trail leads to Tahquitz Falls and back. From the Visitor Center to the falls, you will be gaining 350 feet in elevation. The trail is steep and rocky with many rock steps as high as 12 to 15 inches to climb. This canyon has very little shade, no restroom facilities, and no water fountains. Call (760) 416-7044 for details. Note that the entrance for Palm, Murray, and Andreas Canyons is at 38520 South Palm Canyon Drive. Call (760) 323-6018 for more details.

Agua Caliente Cultural Museum

219 South Palm Canyon Drive; (760) 778-1079; www.accmuseum.org. Open Labor Day through Memorial Day, Wednesday through Saturday 10:00 a.m. to 5:00 p.m. and Sunday

Agua Caliente Indians

The first people to fall under Palm Springs's spell were ancestors of the Agua Caliente band of Cahuilla (Kaw'-we-ah) Indians, who developed communities in the palm canyons at the foot of the San Jacinto Mountains. These canyons, along with other chunks of the Coachella Valley, were deeded in trust to the Indians in 1876. The Cahuillas control 42 percent of the valley, making them the wealthiest tribe in North America. Visit www.aguacaliente.org for more information.

noon to 5:00 p.m. Summer hours Friday, Saturday, and Sunday 10:00 a.m. to 4:00 p.m.
Free.

Artifacts and historical photos from the early Cahuilla era that preserve the native spirit of the desert, permanent collections on local history, changing exhibits (example, Cahuilla basketry), plus two shops with jewelry, clothing, music, and assorted Indian arts and crafts from tribes nationwide.

Smoketree Stables (ages 7 and up)

2500 Toledo Avenue; (760) 327-1372; www.smoketreestables.com. Ages seven and older can ride his or her own horse, led by a guide. Open year-round except July and August, 8:00 a.m. to 4:00 p.m. (when days are longer, hours to 6:00 p.m.). $$$$

In the same location for more than fifty years, the stables are next door to Fess Parker's former home (for the young 'uns, he played Davy Crockett). It's Coachella Valley horseback riding at its best.

Palm Springs Aerial Tramway

Entrance on the north edge of town, at the end of Tramway Road, off Highway 111; (760) 325-1449 or (888) 515-TRAM; www.pstramway.com. Tram rides depart on the half hour, starting at 10:00 a.m. Monday through Friday, 8:00 a.m. weekends and holidays. Last ride off at 9:45 p.m. There are two rotating tramcars with breath-stopping views. Schedules

Powwows

While you're in the desert, check with the *Palm Springs' Life Desert Guide* (**free** and available at most hotels and restaurants) to see if there are any powwows scheduled during your visit. The entire family will find these colorful events a living-history lesson. Adding to the pageantry are the dozens of artisans selling Native American jewelry and arts and crafts. And of course, Indian fry bread is readily available.

The **Morongo Band of Indians** holds an annual powwow adjacent to the Casino Morongo that features gourd dancing, drum contests, exhibitions, and ceremonies that showcase Native American traditions. The costumes, with feathers and fabulous beading, are a sight to behold. Bird songs, a means of aesthetic expression among the Cahuilla people, are preserved and sung at this powwow.

There are other Native American events organized by the **Twentynine Palms Band of Mission Indians,** such as an intertribal powwow.

For more information on powwows, check the *Palm Springs Visitors Guide*, the official publication of Palm Springs Bureau of Tourism (760-778-8415 or 800-347-7746; www.palm-springs.org).

subject to change without notice. Please call ahead for times and weather conditions. No advance reservations. Children three and under ride free. $$$$

If you'd like to know where all those mountain streams come from, take a ride on the spectacular tramway, a thrilling and manageable adventure for the whole family. Two suspended cable cars whisk you from the parched desert floor up nearly 6,000 feet up Chino Canyon to the top of 10,800-foot Mt. San Jacinto (Yah'-sin-toh) in a mere fifteen minutes. Up here, there's not a palm tree in sight: This is pine tree country, some forty degrees cooler than the valley below. Really! What a relief in the summer!

At the Mountain Station, Peaks Restaurant offers fine contemporary California cuisine (760-325-4537 for information and reservations) and The Pines Café, a cafeteria-style restaurant, offers a variety of menu selections. A special Ride 'n' Dinner combination ticket is a great value at The Pines Café. The Lookout Lounge is a full cocktail bar offering a variety of alcoholic beverages and appetizers and is located on the same level as the restaurants, all managed now by Aramark.

From here, there are breathtaking views of the sprawling valley floor and, off to the left, the unmistakable imprint of the San Andreas Fault. The station is at 8,516 feet and also has a fun gift shop, museum, and hiking/cross-country skiing trails leading out into the backcountry.

Mount San Jacinto Wilderness State Park

(951) 659-2607; www.parks.ca.gov/?page_id=636

Behind you at the top of the tramway is the 13,000-acre park, with 54 miles of hiking trails. If it's winter, chances are you'll be able to cross-country ski, too. The Adventure Center, open November 15 through April 15, rents equipment for adults and kids. So you can build a snowman and, back in Palm Springs, take a swim on the same day.

Desert Adventures (ages 6 and up)

(760) 324-JEEP or (888) 440-JEEP; www.red-jeep.com. All two-hour tours leave from the office. Meet at 67–555 East Palm Canyon Drive, Suite E-106. Tours operate year-round. $$$$

Desert Adventures runs a Mystery Canyon tour, which lasts four and a half hours, covering the area where *Land of the Lost* was filmed. For families, the San Andreas Fault Adventure called "Earthquake" is the most popular, hands down (must be at least four years old to participate). For a decidedly more twenty-first-century adventure, and a perfect way for families to explore the desert, consider hopping aboard a red, seven-passenger, four-wheel-drive jeep for one of the tour offerings. The Lost Legends of the Wild West Adventure, Indian Cultural Adventures, and Mystery Canyon jeep adventures are among the tour options. Mary, the owner, says the tours are perfect "for ages six to one hundred and six." Ask about the Night Watch Stargazing Tour.

The Smoke Tree **Ranch**

It's "home on the ranch" Palm Springs style at the historic Smoke Tree Ranch. Best defined as friendly, casual, and understated, this is one of the most perfect family vacation choices in the Coachella Valley. Enjoying a history as old as Palm Springs, this approximately 400-acre ranch, home to eighty-five "colonists" (the residents, actually), is the desert's best-kept secret. Twenty acres are devoted to fifty-five comfortable ranch cottages. Activities abound, including tennis at first-rate facilities, hiking, birding, nature trails, swimming pool, hot tub, fitness center, three-hole practice golf course, and, best of all, organized activities for kids at Camp Kawea. Adding to the vintage ambience is an old-fashioned playground.

Ranch guests savor cookouts in the nearby Indian Canyons, marshmallow roasts, cowboy crooners (remember those soothing sounds?), scavenger hunts, and even bonfires. Breakfast rides and cookouts are on the calendar of events, too. The bountiful buffets will keep the family energized, and that's what is needed to explore this pristine desert paradise. The Indian Canyons location reveals a peaceful sanctuary the entire family will find refreshing, reflective of a time when fast food and freeways were not part of our lives. Some more surprises are here: Check out Disney Hall for a collection of Disney memorabilia, since Walt Disney was one of the original colonists.

Rates start at $396 per cottage double occupancy (Full American Plan—all meals, lodging, and gratuities). Children ages five through eleven are $39 each in same cottage as parents. No charge for children younger than age five. Be sure to ask about multiroom cottages and family units. Outstanding venue for family groups and reunions. For additional information and reservations: 1850 Smoke Tree Lane; (800) 787-3922; www.smoketreeranch.com.

Dollsville Dolls & Bearsville Bears

296 North Palm Canyon; (760) 325-2241, (800) CAL-DOLL, or (800) CAL-BEAR; www.dollsville .com.

This charming shop is full of teddy bears and an astounding variety of Barbie collectibles. There are literally hundreds of dolls and bears to peruse. As much a museum as a shop, it will impress parents and kids of all ages.

The Fabulous Palm Springs Follies (ages 6 and up)

At the Plaza Theatre, 128 South Palm Canyon Drive; (760) 327-0225; www.psfollies.com. Evening and matinee performances beginning in November and running through May. $$$$

A Palm Springs original since 1991, this three-hour revue has a cast all older than fifty years of age, and they kick up a storm. Kids of all ages will get a kick out of "The Follies

Palm Canyon Drive & Walk of Stars

For many families, the most enjoyable aspect of Palm Springs is taking a stroll on palm tree–lined Palm Canyon Drive, the historic center of the city. This celebrated stretch of pavement is flanked by a seemingly endless array of cafes, restaurants, boutiques, and theaters (www.palmcanyondrive.org).

While you're strolling along Palm Canyon, notice more than 300 celebrity stars on the sidewalks. They include such notables as Elvis Presley, Frank Sinatra, Sophia Loren, Elizabeth Taylor, Carol Connors (remember the song "Gonna Fly Now" from *Rocky*?), Monty Hall (of *Let's Make a Deal* fame), and Pamela Price, coauthor of this book (at the corner of Palm Canyon Drive and Tahquitz)! There seems no end to the Palm Canyon "star placing" ceremonies throughout the year. We've often encountered a ceremony going on in front of one of the stores. Of course, passersby are welcome to watch the festivities. It ain't Hollywood Boulevard, but it's still a kick (www.palmspringswalkofstars.com).

Man, Riff Markowitz"as he shuffles through jokes like a deck of cards. This colorful, always humorous vaudeville-style program gives kids a feel for what showbiz used to be all about, despite a few harmlessly off-color jokes now and then. Stars change with the season. Vintage performers will ring a bell with anyone fifty-plus for sure, such as The Four Aces (hint: they sang "Love is a Many Splendored Thing" and "Three Coins in the Fountain"). It's a far cry from Madonna, but a fine way to share a moment of intergenerational nostalgia with the kids.

Villagefest

**Palm Canyon Drive, between Baristo and Amado Roads; (760) 320-3781; www.villagefest
.org. Open every Thursday 6:00 to 10:00 p.m. except major holidays. Free.**

This street fair transforms Palm Springs's main thoroughfare into a lively bazaar with street entertainers, live bands, food booths, 150 arts and crafts vendors, a farmers' market, and pony rides. This is your chance to buy anything from a quilted comforter that doubles as a pillow to scrumptious fudge. If you need to park, go early. Villagefest operates rain or shine.

Palm Springs Art Museum

**101 Museum Drive; (760) 322-4800; www.psmuseum.org. Open October through May.
Closed Monday and major holidays. Tuesday, Wednesday, Friday, Saturday, and Sunday
10:00 a.m. to 5:00 p.m.; Thursday noon to 8:00 p.m. Free public admission every Thursday from 4:00 to 8:00 p.m. during downtown Villagefest. $$; youths under seventeen
free at all times.**

The Palm Springs Art Museum was founded as a one-room facility in 1938 and has grown to the current 125,000-square-foot museum that has become the center of the desert's

Consignment **Shopping**

Palm Springs is a veritable paradise for consignment-shop fans. Take the kids by the hand when perusing the infinite displays of other people's treasures. Items range from rocking horses to Roy Rogers tin lunch boxes. (Kids, ask your parents if they have any in the attic. They go for at least ten times more than what your parents paid way back when!) A retro place to start your Palm Springs consignment shopping tour of the 1950s through 1970s is **Modern Way,** at 745 North Palm Canyon Drive (760-320-5455); proceed to **Panache,** at 968 North Palm Canyon Drive (760-416-9001); and then hit **Revivals,** one of the best thrift shops in the desert, with six locations including 611 North Palm Canyon Drive #22 (760-318-1892) and 611 South Palm Canyon Drive (760-318-6491). **Ruddy's General Store at the Village Green Heritage Center,** 221 South Palm Canyon Drive (760-327-2156), re-creates a general store—including exhibits of unused merchandise seldom seen in any Wal-Mart that will fascinate kids and bring back memories for parents and grandparents. Call it quaint or delightful, it's a tribute to Jim Ruddy, a Depression-era liquidator who donated this treasure trove—an authentic display that today's shoppers will find nostalgic. Fan out from there! And don't rush. This takes time! Ample free parking in the area.

artistic community. What began as a museum about the desert has evolved into an oasis for the arts with modern and contemporary American works of all genres. You will enjoy the free family programming on the fourth Thursday of each month from 6:00 to 7:30 p.m. featuring hands-on activities inspired by the museum's current exhibitions. For example, the recent Picasso to Moore sculpture exhibit was used to inspire children to create their own free-form sculptures. Adjacent to the Desert Museum is the Annenberg Theater (760-325-4490), which has weekend concerts, especially during the October-through-April peak season. The Toor Gallery Café serves sandwiches, salads, and desserts. Hours are 11:00 a.m. to 3:00 p.m. daily.

Palm Springs Air Museum

745 North Gene Autry Trail; (760) 778-6262; www.palmspringsairmuseum.org. Open year-round 10:00 a.m. to 5:00 p.m. $$, children under six free.

Visit the Air Museum for a close-up look at propeller-driven aircraft from an era your kids will know only from old movies, documentaries, and (perhaps) their history books. Vintage planes, many colorful and perfectly restored, recall the World War II era. The planes are on display to educate the public about aviation's role in winning the big war. Many guides are wartime vets whose knowledge will amaze you and the kids. The second floor has flight simulators (arrange to use them in advance) and a library. The gift shop carries a treasure trove of aviation gifts, books, and jewelry.

Lucky you if you're in the desert in July, because the Air Museum celebrates Cool Kids Month! with flying model airplane contests and other hands-on activities.

Knott's Soak City Water Park

1500 South Gene Autry Trail; (760) 327-0499; www.soakcityusa.com. Open daily mid-March through Labor Day and weekends only through September. Call for specific hours and promotions. Life vests provided free**. $$$$**

Museums and movie stars aside, here's why kids flock to Palm Springs. The park is an immaculately clean twenty-one-acre fantasy playground where cool water reigns supreme. There is amusement for kids of all ages, from Kahuna's Beach House and the tranquil Sunset River inner-tube ride to more than eighteen other water slides ranging from simple to simply outrageous. The Sea Snake slide is a case in point. Those who dare coast in inner tubes along a 54-inch-wide, 450-foot-long slide that at certain points takes riders through total darkness and down a 50-foot drop—yikes! Plus there is stand-up surfing and body boarding. The three-man inner-tube ride is fast and furious!

The most surprising attraction—and arguably the most fun—is California's largest wave-action pool (800,000 gallons), a broad expanse of water that starts out calm but churns away every fifteen minutes to be a sort of Malibu-in-the-desert. Actually, giant fans create the artificial tide, but it feels like the genuine article. Another favorite is Pacific Spin, a four-person raft ride that blasts down a 132-foot-long tunnel, and then drops into another 75-foot, six-story tunnel.

Where to Eat

Grill A Burger, 166 North Palm Canyon Drive; (760) 327-8175. Call for seasonal hours. Say it fast, and it sounds like "gorilla burger"! Kids love the giant-size "stuffed" version at this compact diner-style burger joint in the heart of downtown. The french fries are soaked in ice water before frying and are considered some of the best in the desert. The handmade shakes get folks shook up, but the one with a fresh banana is something special. Burgers come in nineteen varieties, including some for vegetarians. There is a small patio, counter service, and four tables if you are lucky enough to find one empty at this popular joint. (Another location is at 73-091 Country Club Drive in nearby Palm Desert.) $

Bus Around!

The SunBus will take you to most of the attractions we've tried and tested, from the Art Museum to the movies, malls, and more. Rides cost $1 (transfers 25 cents); $3 for a day pass for unlimited rides. Call SunLine Transit for free personalized trip planning and information at (760) 343-3451 or (800) 347-8628 or visit www.sunline.org.

Manhattan in the Desert, 2665 East Palm Canyon; (760) 322-DELI. Open Sunday through Thursday 7:00 a.m. to 9:00 p.m. and Friday and Saturday until 10:00 p.m. **Free** parking. This deli restaurant has as much panache as a Paris bistro. The upbeat, albeit noisy ambience is pure deli-lightful, and there is something on the twelve-page menu for everyone, including light eaters. There are marvelous soups, from cold borscht to sweet and sour cabbage, and a terrific home-style chicken soup (with choice of rice, noodles, or matzo ball). Try Super Combo Number 12—brisket, pastrami, and Jack cheese served on an onion roll with lettuce and tomato. The "Just for Kids" menu (age ten and under) features a $5.95 lunch special with a choice of tuna, egg salad, or grilled cheese sandwich or hamburger, hot dog, or chicken strips; french fries or applesauce; milk or fountain drink; and a yummy sprinkle cookie. With fair prices and friendly service, this Manhattan-style deli is worth a visit. $

Ruby's Diner, 155A South Palm Canyon Drive; (760) 416-0138; www.rubys.com. One of a chain (also in Rancho Mirage). Breakfast, lunch, and dinner daily with very reasonable prices and fast service. Re-creates the diner era of the 1950s with deluxe malts, shakes, blue-ribbon burgers, fries, and breakfast served until 11:30 a.m. Dee-lish! $

Tyler's, 149 South Indian Canyon Drive; (760) 325-2990. Open Monday through Saturday 11:00 a.m. to 4:00 p.m. Lunch only. This tiny hamburger haven was once a bus station and then an A & W root beer stand. It reopened as Tyler's, serving, as far as this coauthor is concerned, the best hamburgers in town. The half-pound burger is $5.50 and worth every cent. Kids will like the sliders, three mini hamburgers that can be decorated with hot sauce, pickles, grilled onions, and ketchup. The menu is small, but the essentials are there, from chilidogs and egg salad sandwiches to homemade potato salad and coleslaw. Before noon every bar stool along the counter is taken with serious foodies. The root beer floats ($2.50) are divine, and the fresh lemonade ($1.50) is like Grandma used to make.

During winter, Diana, the proprietor, prepares soups you dream about, from red pepper to fresh mushroom. On Friday, ask for the clam chowder. There is a small patio in the back, but it's advisable to arrive early because this landmark beacon of comfort food, par excellence, fills up fast. You might try the take-out service if there is a long wait. And be sure to tell Diana, a whirlwind, that Pam sent you. $

Where to Stay

Holiday Inn Palm Springs, 1800 East Palm Canyon Drive; (760) 323-1711 or (800) 245-6907; www.holidayinn.com. At last, a comfortable, affordable family-friendly hotel has opened its doors downtown. The 229-room (plus 20 suites with living room) 100 percent nonsmoking property welcomes kids and canines! At Billy D's kids dine, compliments of the hotel from the Pit Stop PS menu with AM/PM items; all are **free** for registered guests twelve and under (limit four kids per family). More benefits include outdoor pool, whirlpool, **free** parking, and **free** shuttles to the airport. $$$

Casa Cody, A Country Bed & Breakfast Inn, 175 South Cahuilla Road; (760) 320-9346 or (800) 231-2639; www.casacody.com. Historic and charming, this twenty-three-room inn reflects all that made this desert destination resort a living legend. Founded in the 1920s by Harriet Cody, cousin of Buffalo Bill, accommodations are in early California–style adobe bungalows framed by bougainvillea and citrus-filled courtyards. The 1910 adobe, recently restored, was the getaway of Lawrence Tibbett, the bon vivant Metropolitan baritone turned movie star, and his good friend Charlie Chaplin. Children and pets always welcome here. $$$$

Desert Hotel Reservations, (800) 896-7334; www.deserthotelreservations.com. Local agency in business since 1988, providing personal service. One of the largest sources of hotel accommodations in the Palm Springs area. You pay no fee and get the rooms and rates you want. Highly recommended. $$$$

For More Information

Palm Springs Bureau of Tourism. 777 North Palm Canyon Drive, Suite 201, Palm Springs 92262; (760) 778-8415; www.palm-springs.org. Open Monday through Friday 8:30 a.m. to 5:00 p.m. Publishes the *Palm Springs Visitors Guide,* which highlights the wide variety of dining, attractions, shopping, art galleries, events, and lodging establishments in the city. This guide is updated twice a year to reflect the latest information for many of the listed establishments.

Palm Springs Chamber of Commerce. 190 West Amado Road, Palm Springs 92262; (760) 325-1577; www.pschamber.org.

Cathedral City

Cathedral City is one of seven distinct Coachella Valley communities that you will pass on Highway 111 heading east out of Palm Springs. You'll know you've arrived when you see a complex of colorful yellow structures, all loosely connected. There is a small but marvelous mini-park where the most amazing mosaic fountain attracts kids of all ages. Once a sleepy, nondescript community on the way to somewhere else, Cathedral City has grown rapidly every season and now offers many reasons to stop and spend a day. There is a new shopping arcade and a growing population of 52,000-plus people.

Big League Dreams Sports Park

33–770 Date Palm Drive; (760) 324-1133 or (760) 324-5600; www.bigleaguedreams.com.

Ever imagined visiting Yankee Stadium, Fenway Park, and Wrigley Field all in one day? It's possible at this thirty-acre park. Sports enthusiasts will go for the batting cage stations and the sand volleyball courts. This is the nation's first amateur-sports facility of its kind and merits at least a two-hour visit. There's a "Tot Lot" for the younger set.

Desert IMAX Theater

68–510 East Palm Canyon Drive at Cathedral Canyon Boulevard; (760) 324-7333; www.desertimax.com. Free parking at the Cathedral City Civic Center.

The big news in Cathedral City is the big screen—and we mean big. It's 50 by 70 feet—that's six stories high! Kids love "Learning at the Edge of Your Seat" here. Showtimes are subject to change, so call ahead. Adjacent to the theater are several new eateries including Big Mama's Soul Food, Trilussa, Mad French Woman, and Cold Stone Creamery.

Boomer's Family Fun Center

67–700 East Palm Canyon Drive; (760) 770-7522. Open 365 days a year; Monday through Thursday 3:00 p.m. to 9:00 p.m. (extended hours during the summer and on holidays),

Friday 3:00 to 11:00 p.m., Saturday 10:00 a.m. to midnight, and Sunday 10:00 a.m. to 9:00 p.m. Admission free, but inside fun is pay-as-you-play, with varying ticket prices for combinations. $$$

For some decidedly nonprofessional-level golf action, take the tykes to the home of three fun eighteen-hole miniature golf courses. There are also bumper boats, go-karts, batting cages, a 10,000-square-foot games pavilion, 200 video and sports games, and a rock wall.

Where to Eat

El Gallito Mexican Restaurant, 68820 Grove Street; (760) 328-7794. A desert classic near the City Hall complex owned and operated by Petra Cantu. The homemade cuisine includes chicken or beef tacos or taquitos, authentic rice, beans, and fresh guacamole, with family-friendly service for lunch and dinner. Call for days/hours of operation. $

Rancho Mirage

Known as the "Realm of the Desert Big Horn," the city of Rancho Mirage seems larger than 25 square miles. Its population of 17,000 does not include the "snowbirds" (seasonal residents) who flock here to participate in and enjoy the high-profile charitable events that dominate the January-to-May social-season calendar. Rancho Mirage's main attraction is golf, and the city is home to many private country-club communities, such as Tamarisk, Mission Hills, Thunderbird, and Morningside. Don't be discouraged—many of these emerald green courses are open to the public or have reciprocal agreements with hotels.

Children's Discovery Museum of the Desert

71–701 Gerald Ford Drive; (760) 321-0602; www.cdmod.org. Open Tuesday through Saturday 10:00 a.m. to 5:00 p.m. and Sunday noon to 5:00 p.m. Call for seasonal changes. $$

This 8,000-square-foot facility with more than fifty hands-on exhibits encourages kids to touch, explore, and discover. Youngsters can paint a Volkswagen Beetle, dig for Cahuilla Indian treasures, or make a pretend pizza in the Pizza Place. An ideal museum for children and parents who enjoy experiencing hands-on activities. Upstairs there are trunks and suitcases, and costumes and hats for kids to dress up in—this is a good photo opportunity!

City of Rancho Mirage Public Library

71-100 Highway 111; (760) 341-7323; www.ranchomiragelibrary.org. Open Monday through Saturday 9:00 a.m. to 6:00 p.m. (November through April open Sunday noon to 4:00 p.m.). Free.

This popular library reaches out to visitors with a marvelous calendar of programs and events such as concerts and a recent sky-watching program featuring a lecture and the total lunar eclipse. There is an excellent children's library with storytelling hours, a cafe, changing exhibits, a used-book shop, and an extensive DVD collection with many choices for family viewing.

The River at Rancho Mirage

71–800 Highway 111, corner of Bob Hope Drive; (760) 341-2711; www.theriveratrancho mirage.com.

It's the desert, but there's water everywhere at this outdoor mall. Fascinating shops and pushcarts loaded with everything from designer togs for dogs to funky accessories will keep kids busy before and after breakfast, lunch, or dinner and a flick. For the best family dining in this 200,000-square-foot complex, check out the Cheesecake Factory, Baja Fresh, Babe's Barbecue, Yard House, and Ben & Jerry's.

Where to Stay

Westin Mission Hills Resort & Spa, 71–777 Dinah Shore Drive, at the corner of Dinah Shore and Bob Hope Drive; (760) 328-5955 or (800) 544-0287; www.westin.com. The Cactus Kids Club program designed for children ages four to twelve offers a good mix of arts, crafts, nature walks, games, and swimming. Hours are daily 8:00 a.m. to noon and 1:00 to 5:00 p.m. There are rental bikes and, in all guest rooms, a Sony Playstation. Kids love the 60-foot, S-curved water slide, basketball, softball, and bicycle rentals. Then there are two golf courses and tennis courts. Inquire about special packages. $$$$

For More Information

Palm Springs Desert Resorts Convention and Visitors Authority. 70–100 Highway 111, Rancho Mirage 92270; (760) 770-9000 or (800) 41-RELAX; www.giveinto thedesert.com. Open Monday through Friday 8:30 a.m. to 5:00 p.m. Ask for an updated vacation planner. The bureau has the latest information on all eight desert resort communities: Palm Springs, Cathedral City, Rancho Mirage, Palm Desert, La Quinta, Indian Wells, Indio, and Desert Hot Springs.

Palm Desert

In recent years Palm Desert, "where the sun shines a little brighter," has been something of a boomtown with a growing population of 50,000-plus, with shopping and dining opportunities to rival—some would say surpass—those of Palm Springs. The city of Palm Desert helps make the Coachella Valley the "golf capital of the world," not only on account of the many courses it boasts but also because golf carts are legal transportation on several city streets. There's even a **Golf Cart Parade** every November, in which a hundred carts decorated as floats parade along El Paseo, the "Rodeo Drive of the Desert."

Palm Desert is home to one of the most interesting street fairs in Southern California. Look for the **College of the Desert Street Fair,** 435 Monterey Avenue in Palm

Desert—there's plenty of **free** parking. Kids will love wandering through the farmers' market and checking out the endless vendors selling original art, jewelry, T-shirts, designer eyeglass frames, and faux designer purses. You name it . . . it's for sale here somewhere. Open Saturday and Sunday year-round. Don't miss it! And now, we will go from simple to "simply elegant" shopping, from the street fair to El Paseo.

The undisputed style center of the desert is El Paseo, a 7-block drive between Highway 74 and Portola Avenue.

While strolling on El Paseo, stop at the **Daily Grill,** 73–061 El Paseo (on the corner; 760-779-9911; www.dailygrill.com), which is open Monday through Saturday 11:00 a.m. to 10:00 p.m. and Sunday 10:00 a.m. (for brunch) to 10:00 p.m. There's something for everyone, from a delicious Cobb salad to a hearty serving of meat loaf and mashed potatoes. The children's menu has the usual—hamburgers, grilled cheese, and chicken fingers. Wash it down with a giant glass of fresh lemonade. At the **Gardens on El Paseo** (between San Pablo and Larkspur), sample a taste of the Caribbean at **Tommy Bahamas,** 73595 El Paseo (upstairs; 760-836-0188). The conch fritters are truly a taste from the islands. Downstairs is a boutique with shirts in wild designs—chic but expensive. More families are inviting Rover to join in their vacations.

Living Desert Zoo and Gardens

47–900 Portola Avenue; (760) 346-5694; www.livingdesert.org. Open daily year-round. Call for seasonal hours. $$

This is a must-see for families, we insist! Giraffes in the desert? That's just the tip of the sand dune at this extraordinary attraction. New is the butterfly house, which has an added cost of $2 admission for adults. During December "Wild Lights," the entire preserve is lit up with holiday orbs and illuminated exhibits. Plan to spend at least three hours here and do include a visit to the cactus garden and the gift shop, of course! This 1,200-acre preserve lets parents and kids have a close-up look at everything from a desert cactus

Path of the **Big Horn**

Kids, be on the lookout for a posse of creatively decorated bighorn sheep wandering around the Coachella Valley. This is actually a public art project exhibiting more than one hundred painted, life-size sculptures of these legendary sheep—all placed in locations around the desert for public viewing. Celebrities (Cher, Chevy Chase, Phyllis Diller, and Stephanie Powers) decorated many of these sheep sculptures. This is an ongoing project to learn about taking responsibility for the environment.

Santa Rosa and San Jacinto Mountains National Monument

Be sure to visit the **Santa Rosa Mountains National Scenic Area Visitor Center,** 51–500 Highway 74 (3.25 miles south on Highway 111 at the base of the mountain); www.blm.gov/ca/st/en/fo/palmsprings/santarosa.html. The **Friends of the Desert Mountains Bookstore** at the visitor center (760-862-9084) stocks hiking and nature guides, giving you a fuller picture of what to expect in this rugged corner of Southern California. This area is under the stewardship of the Bureau of Land Management (760-862-9984). Open Friday through Monday 9:00 a.m. to 4:00 p.m. (except federal holidays). Walk along the Ed Hastey Interpretive Garden Trail and try the interactive exhibits dealing with natural and cultural resources of the Coachella Valley and surrounding mountain before you embark on exploring this area.

to a bobcat. Common desert inhabitants roam freely in addition to the world's smallest fox, bighorn sheep, gazelles, tortoises, and zebras. Although much of the desert fauna is nocturnal (cooler temperatures bring out the animals), you will surely encounter some of it, especially if you take a hike on one of the several trails on the premises. The family will enjoy the live animal shows daily in the outdoor Tennity Amphitheater. Some favorites: the Critter Close-Up, a daily event that permits kids to see small desert animals, and Gecko Gulch Play Land. At the Village Watutu, kids can get up close with camels, hyenas, birds, and a petting kraal. Stop for a cool drink at the Thorn Tree Grill to soak in this experience.

McCallum Theatre

73000 Fred Waring Drive; (760) 340-ARTS; www.mccallumtheatre.com.

For the culturally inclined, the popular McCallum features theatrical, dance, classical, and celebrity events such as the Moiseyev Dance Company—the masters of agility and grace; the one and only Peking Acrobats; and the rousing Rancho Mirage Family Circus.

Sky Watcher Star Gazing Tours (ages 5 and up)

73-091 Country Club Drive, Suite A 42; (760) 831-0231; www.sky-watcher.com. $$$$

If the kids insist upon staying up late at night, consider Sky Watcher Tours as the solution. A sky guide leads a tour of the heavens using high-powered telescopes and sky binoculars. It's mythology mixed with astronomy and a stellar story kids will enjoy.

Where to Eat and Stay

Keedy's Fountain & Grill, 73–633 Highway 111, Palm Desert; (760) 346-6492. Serving breakfast and lunch daily, Keedy's is an authentic blast from the past featuring fluffy pancakes, yummy patty melts, creamy milk shakes, and frothy ice cream sodas. This classic cafe and its burgers haven't changed an iota since Bob Keedy established the joint in 1957. When he threatened to close the place in 1987 and retire, locals Bob and Patty Downs stepped in and bought it, and everything stayed the same, right down to the Formica on the counter. $

Desert Springs, A JW Marriott Resort & Spa, 74855 Country Club Drive, Palm Desert; (760) 341-2211 or (800) 331-3112; www.desert springsresort.com. Among the many lodging options available in the Palm Desert area, this one stands above the rest. As you enter this immense resort, you will be surrounded by the sounds of water flowing and birds calling. Your preferred mode of transport? Gondolas, Venetian style. While some find this a bit Disneyland-esque, people still flock here for the dramatic ambience of this mega-resort fresh from a $30 million makeover in 2007. The newly renovated eight-story atrium lobby serves as a gateway to 884 luxurious guest rooms, thirty-six holes of Ted Robinson championship golf, twenty multi-surface tennis courts, seventeen retail shops, five award-winning restaurants, a 30,000-square-foot European Health Spa, fitness center and gym, and waterways entwining nine resort swimming and whirlpools. This sprawling resort is home to the Kid's Klub, where kids can spend quality time pursuing their own recreational activities while Mom and Dad are on the golf course or in the spa. Designed for ages four to twelve (kids younger than age four require a babysitter, available through the concierge), the program generally operates seven days a week and features arts and crafts, putt-putt golf, boat rides, animal tours, lunch, and movie screenings. $$$$

La Quinta Resort & Club, 49499 Eisenhower Drive, La Quinta; (760) 564-4111 or (800) 598-3828; www.laquintaresort.com. Located adjacent to Rancho Mirage in the city of La Quinta, this property is a legendary hideaway, renowned since 1926 for its charm and serenity; featuring ninety holes of some of the country's best golf, including the famous Stadium Golf Course at PGA West and the picturesque Mountain Course; plus Spa La Quinta with a variety of unique indoor and outdoor treatments including open-air Celestial Showers, Sacred Stone Massage, and more. La Quinta is the longtime gold-standard ideal place for families, with something for everyone. Children will like Camp La Quinta from 9:00 a.m. to 3:00 p.m. seven days a week. Programs include nature walks, arts and crafts, and miniature golf. Evening programs are from 6:00 to 10:00 p.m. Friday and Saturday only. Children four and older are welcome; those younger than four must be accompanied by a babysitter. Up to two children stay free in a casita with parents. Call for current pricing and schedules. $$$$

Hyatt Grand Champions Resort, Villas & Spa, 44-600 Indian Wells Lane, Indian Wells; (760) 341-1000; www.grandchampionshyatt .com. Offering your choice from 428 spacious guest rooms, with views from private balconies; twenty-six penthouse suites with garden, mountain, golf, or pool views; and forty-three one- and two-bedroom villas with backyard, spas, and butler service that are perfect for families. This lavish resort boasts seven swimming pools, including a 60-foot spiral water slide and a toddler-size wadding pool. You'll appreciate the private cabanas complete with TV and bottled water. The Oasis Pool Bar & Roadrunner Café gets our family vote. One of the best reasons to stay here? Camp Hyatt is open 9:00 a.m. to 4:00 p.m. daily and Friday and Saturday evenings from 6:00 to 10:00 p.m. for kids whose parents appreciate supervised care with an educational touch, such as tours of nearby flora and fauna. Why don't we adults head for the award-winning Agua Serena Salon, Day Spa & Medical Skin Spa? This is one complete experience. $$$$

Renaissance Esmeralda Resort and Spa, 44400 Indian Wells Lane, Indian Wells; (760) 773-4444 or (800) 228-9290; www .renaissanceesmeralda.com. At the Esmeralda, there is all a family could ask for, including a "sand" beach, three swimming pools, lots of space to spread out, and family-friendly rates. Up to five guests are allowed in each spacious room. Here is the place to kick back and relax. Dad can try the links, and Mom can indulge in the stunning Spa Esmeralda. $$$$

For More Information

Palm Desert Visitor Information Center. 72–567 Highway 111, 92260; (760) 568-1441 or (800) 873-2428; www.palm-desert.org.

Indian Wells Chamber of Commerce. 74-980 Highway 111, Suite 101, Indian Wells, 92210; (760) 346-7095; www.indianwells.com and www.indianwells.com.

La Quinta Chamber of Commerce. www .laquintachamberofcommerce.com.

Indio

The first city in the Coachella Valley, Indio—also known as the Date Capital of the Desert—was founded in 1930 and currently has a population exceeding 77,000. Fully 95 percent of the dates grown in the United States are cultivated in and around Indio.

This is truly the "city of festivals," beginning with the National Date Festival, which was founded here more than sixty years ago. Indio looks rather plain until you drive by the fairgrounds and glimpse the exotic entrance, which comes alive each February for the National Date Festival. The multicolored plaster domes, reminiscent of a scene from *Arabian Nights,* are sure to make your kids wonder if they have just seen Disneyland. But there's more on this stretch of highway! Every December, the **Indio International Tamale Festival** is an absolute must for those who take the art of the tamale seriously. From sweet to spicy, every type of tamale to tantalize taste buds is available over the weekend. Recently, the Food Network ranked the Indio International Tamale Festival (www.tamalefestival.net) in the top 10 "All-American Food Festivals" in the nation!

Riverside County Fair and National Date Festival

Riverside County Fairground, 46–350 Arabia Street; (800) 811-FAIR; www.datefest.org. $$

For ten days each February, Indio celebrates its principal crop—the tasty, versatile date. The festival is held in conjunction with the annual Riverside County Fair. The festive ambience attracts families for rides, food, games, local entertainment, and camel rides. Don't miss the Arabian Nights Musical Pageant each evening. This fair celebrated its sixty-second year in 2008, making it one of the oldest in California. Competitions abound such as a livestock auction and a fashion show for sheep and their owners. Coauthor Pamela Price judged this "Lads and Lassies" show, where proud owners paraded their favorite sheep, often wearing matching outfits! You never know what you will find here.

Empire Polo Club and Equestrian Park

81–800 Avenue 51 (at Monroe); (760) 342-2762. Open Monday through Friday 9:00 a.m. to 5:00 p.m. For a polo schedule call (760) 342-2223 or visit www.empirepoloevents.org.

Indio is paradise for polo lovers. If you want to see polo in action, plan to have breakfast or lunch at the Empire Polo Club's Tack Room Tavern. This former horse shelter turned restaurant is open seven days a week from 7:00 a.m. to 9:00 p.m. Off the beaten path at Avenue 51 and Monroe, the setting is peaceful and very different from the weekend crowds and traffic. There is a great children's menu with burgers, hot dogs, and mac and cheese.

The park covers 175 acres of landscaped grounds, including five world-class polo fields, a picturesque rose garden, and the tropical Medjhool Lake (named for the delectable dates that grow on the Indio date farms). The **Coachella Valley Music Festival** calls this place home. In 2008, on the last weekend of April, Prince performed along with dozens of other top entertainers (www.coachella.com).

Oasis Date Gardens

59–111 Highway 111, Thermal; (760) 399-5665; www.oasisdategardens.com. Open 9:00 a.m. to 5:30 p.m. daily. $

This is a 250-acre working date farm, where you can take a guided tour of the groves, have a picnic in a palm garden, or simply partake of the offerings at the Country Store. There are always **free** samples available (ask for a **free** date shake). If you like dried fruits and nuts, this is the place to stock up.

The Salton Sea—**Nature's Accident**

If you're heading south from Indio, explore the 35-mile-long Salton Sea (760-564-4888; www.saltonsea.ca.gov), the largest body of water entirely in California and saltier than the ocean. It was formed by accident between 1905–07 when the Colorado River floodwaters filled the Salton Sink, once an ancient seabed. The sea's surface is 228 feet below sea level and is a popular area for anglers and hunters. Families should visit the **Salton Sea National Wildlife Refuge and Imperial Wildlife Area** (760-393-3052), where there are viewing stations for "bird's-eye" views of what else but countless birds! Seeing the annual migrations of various birds is an experience children will find fascinating and educational, a dynamic duo. According to the U.S. Fish and Wildlife Service, they can identify 295 species here. In the **Salton Sea State Recreation Area,** boating and saltwater fishing are the order of the day. Several campsites and nature trails are located around the "sea" shores. Call (800) 444-7274 for camping reservations.

For More Information

Indio Chamber of Commerce. 82921
Indio Boulevard, 92201; (760) 347-0676 or
(800) 44-INDIO; www.indiochamber.org.

Joshua Tree National Park

Joshua Tree National Park, 74485 National Park Drive (park headquarters), Twentynine Palms, 92277-3597; visitor information line: (760) 367-5500; www.nps.gov/jotr. Open year-round. Each season adds its personality to the desert's character. Three entrances to the park—Oasis Visitor Center, open all year 8:00 a.m. to 5:00 p.m.; Cottonwood Visitor Center, open all year 8:00 a.m. to 4:00 p.m.; and Black Rock Nature Center, open October through May, Saturday through Thursday 8:00 a.m. to 4:00 p.m. and Friday noon to 8:00 p.m. There is a $15 fee per car entering the park that allows unlimited entry and exits for seven days. For $30, the Joshua Tree National Park Annual Pass admits the pass signee and accompanying passengers entering in a single, non-commercial vehicle and is valid for twelve months from the month of purchase.

Joshua Tree National Park lies 140 miles east of Los Angeles and less than an hour north of Palm Springs. You can approach it from the west via I-10 and Highway 62 (Twentynine Palms Highway). The north entrances to the park are located at Joshua Tree Village and the city of Twentynine Palms. The south entrance at Cottonwood Spring, which lies 25 miles east of Indio, can be approached from the east or west, also via I-10. Motels, stores, restaurants, and auto services are located in the nearby towns of Yucca Valley, Joshua Tree Village, and Twentynine Palms.

Visitor centers and wayside exhibits, providing opportunities to acquaint you with park resources, are located along main roads leading into and through the park. Park rangers are here to help you have an enjoyable, safe visit. Detailed information on weather, road conditions, backcountry use, campgrounds, and regulations may be

Gublers Orchids

If anyone in the family is fascinated by orchids, by all means stop by **Gublers Orchids,** 2200 Belfield Boulevard, Landers (760-364-2282; www.gublers.com). You'll find it "off the map" when traveling on Highway 62 toward Joshua Tree National Park. This state-of-the-art orchid farm is in the middle of nowhere, it seems. However, once you see the gorgeous display of orchids, marvel at the climate-controlled greenhouses and the solar greenhouses, and peruse the bromeliads, ferns, and yes, even carnivorous plants, you'll be glad you went out of your way. **Free** tours Monday through Saturday 10:00 a.m. to 3:30 p.m. Closed Sunday and major holidays.

The **Integratron**

The Integratron, 2477 Belfield Boulevard, Landers (760-364-3126; www
.integratron.com), is a white-domed structure, 38 feet tall, 55 feet in diameter,
deemed an "acoustically perfect tabernacle" and energy machine sited on a
powerful geomagnetic vortex in the magical Mojave Desert. The Integratron is
the creation of George Van Tassel and is based on the design of Moses's Tabernacle, the writings of Nikola Tesla, and telepathic directions from extrater-
restrials. This one-of-a-kind nonmetallic structure was originally designed by
Van Tassel as a rejuvenation and time machine. Today, it is the only all-wood,
acoustically perfect sound chamber in the United States. The Integratron is
available for docent-led tours by appointment only, Tuesday through Sunday
10:00 a.m. to 7:00 p.m. For groups of four or more, the cost is $15 per person
(and/or a minimum fee of $60 applies). The tour describes the structure's
UFO connection, unique rejuvenative properties, unusual architecture, and
its original intent as an electrostatic generator. It's a *Close Encounters of the
Third Kind* experience for your family for sure.

obtained at visitor centers and entrance stations. Walks, hikes, and campfire talks are conducted chiefly in the spring and fall; information is posted on campground bulletin boards,
at ranger stations, and at visitor centers. Ranger-conducted activities can increase your
enjoyment and understanding of the park.

There are nine campgrounds with tables, fireplaces, and toilets. You must bring your
own water and firewood. Several picnic areas for day use are available. Ask about the
Junior Ranger Program.

In addition to the pass information listed above, there is also an Interagency Annual
Pass for $80, which is valid for one full year from the month of purchase; this pass
replaces the National Park Pass and Golden Eagle Passport. It provides access to Federal
recreation sites, including National Park Service, U.S. Fish and Wildlife, Bureau of Land
Management, Bureau of Reclamation, and U.S. Forest Service. The pass can be purchased
in person at any Federal recreational fee area, including Joshua Tree National Park. You
may also call (888) ASK USGS, ext. 1, or go online at http://store.usgs.gov/pass.

Even if your kids have never been to Joshua Tree National Park before, they will probably recognize the short, bristly, and oddly contorted trees that thrive here from the cover
of the popular U2 album *The Joshua Tree.* It was actually Mormon settlers who named the
trees. They thought their thick branches, which protrude toward the sky, resembled the
biblical Joshua praying.

Less than an hour's drive north of the Coachella Valley, and worth at least a half-day
detour, Joshua Tree is where the southern Colorado Desert (elevation less than 3,000
feet) meets the vast expanse of the Mojave (high desert). The park, formerly a national
monument, covers 794,000 acres and in some places affords unobstructed views of more

than 50 miles. The highlight for many kids will be scrambling about the lower portions of giant quartz-monzonite boulders and monoliths in the Mojave Desert portion of the park. Be sure to check out the inspiring Junior Ranger program here.

Try to schedule your visit to Joshua Tree around a sunset. The photographic opportunities here are unparalleled, especially when the shadows dance on the colossal rock formations and the cholla cacti and Jóshuas seem to glow in the fading sunlight. The whole place has the feel of a rather eerie lunar landscape, a boundless place in which to take time out and wonder. It's not a geographical experience anyone in your family will soon forget.

Insider tip: A stellar new attraction is Sky's The Limit Observatory & Nature Center on Utah Trail at the main entrance to Joshua Tree National Park (760-327-0030; www.skysthe limit29.org). The ideal destination for families who search the sky! This center is dedicated to providing hands-on learning opportunities about astronomy and environmental science. There is a telescope builder's workshop and weather station among other interactive displays that explore the magnificent Mojave Desert.

General Patton Memorial Museum

#2 Chiriaco Road, Chiriaco Summit; (760) 227-3483; www.generalpattonmuseum.com. Open daily 9:30 a.m. to 4:30 p.m. $, children younger than eleven admitted free when accompanied by an adult. Military are free if in uniform.

Thirty miles east of Indio and 70 miles from the Arizona state line on I-10 is a museum not to be missed. Exit at Chiriaco Summit and look for the American flag. You are at what was once the entrance to Camp Young, the famous Desert Training Center. This

Music in Joshua Tree

The California high desert is known for nurturing budding talent—such as groundbreaker Gram Parsons, folk-rock guru Donovan, and English blues legend Eric Burdon. Irish rockers U2 found inspiration here in the 1980s (remember their hit album *The Joshua Tree*?).

The privately owned Joshua Tree Lake Campground (located 9 miles from the park entrance) is soul central for the **Joshua Tree Music Festival** in May and the **Joshua Tree Roots Music Festival** in October. On-site are two performance stages featuring world music, funk, soul, jazz, and blues, plus a world market, tasty food village, and kidzville—eco-education with Joshua Tree Tortoise Rescue, stargazing, arts and crafts, open mike, storytelling, face painting, juggling, playground, volleyball, bubbles, puppets, and nature walks and talks. Families are encouraged to camp for the entire three-day event. There are hot showers, tent sites, picnic tables, barbecue pits, a lake for fishing, and ample parking. For current information visit www.joshuatreemusic festival.com or call (877) 327-6265.

Magical Mystery **Tour**

En route to Joshua Tree National Park, if you've exited from I-10 to Highway 62, you'll be on a stretch of highway that takes you through some fascinating scenery and worthwhile places to stop. This is a two- to three-hour trip in itself, especially if you stop for lunch and visit a few museums and art galleries along the route.

The high desert sweeps the vast area straddling San Bernardino and Riverside Counties. You know you've arrived when the temperature dips about ten degrees from that of the stunning sun-dappled mountains of the ritzier side of I-10, that being Palm Springs. Families head for the high desert when they want to explore a portion of the 800,000-acre Joshua Tree National Park.

Along the way, you'll pass Morongo Valley and Yucca Valley prior to arriving at Joshua Tree. The Yucca Valley lies at the gateway to the Mojave Desert's Morongo Basin.

At the Community Center Complex, 57116 Twentynine Palms Highway (760-369-7212; www.yuccavalley.org), you'll find the **Hi-Desert Nature Museum** (open Tuesday through Sunday 10:00 a.m. to 5:00 p.m.; free; www.hidesertnaturemuseum.org). This is a family-oriented facility related to the high desert's unique natural and historical environments. The museum shop has nature theme gifts and children's science gifts. Kids can interact with resident snakes and insects or spend some time on arts and crafts.

Twentynine Palms is home to the Marine Corps Air Ground Combat Center. While this immense military base, rivaling the size of the state of Rhode Island, is not open to the public, it is the site on occasion of military events on the parade ground, such as the Battle Color Ceremony presented by the Marine Corps.

While in the area, make it a point to stop at **Pappy & Harriet's Palace** (760-365-5956; www.pappyandharriets.com) on Pioneertown Road ("eatin', drinkin', and sleepin' in an old western town," says their ad), established in 1972 and now owned by Linda Krantz and Robyn Celia. They serve up great food and entertainment Thursday through Sunday 11:00 a.m. to 2:00 a.m. This is a far cry from any chain restaurant, and the kids' menu features hamburgers and quesadillas. The ambience is authentic: Old West, rustic, and noisy. Local characters looking like vintage cowboys are often sitting around. There's so much going on here with dinners and western entertainment that a monthly schedule is published.

Pioneertown (www.pioneertown.com), 4 miles out of the Yucca Valley, was founded by Gene Autry, Roy Rogers, and Dick Curtis in 1946 and was used as a filming location. The kids may not remember the film *Gunfight at the OK Corral*, but a few parents and grandparents might. This was filmed here along with many other stories of the Old West. This area is truly a time warp, but it's the real McCoy.

Several hiking trails start here, such as the 2-mile Water Canyon Trail and the Pipes Canyon Trail, where you can see the original "pipes," or springs, that attracted the first settlers.

To stay in the western mood, check into the **Pioneertown Motel,** 5040 Curtis Road (888-365-4879; www.PioneertownMotel.com).

As you enter the town of Twentynine Palms along the **Twentynine Palms Highway** (it's the alternative route to Arizona, the Colorado River, and Las Vegas, by the way), look for the magnificent historical murals painted on the sides of eleven buildings throughout the town. They depict Indians, miners, homesteaders, and ranchers. One mural kids might find interesting is found on the south wall at 6308 Adobe Road, *Jack Cones the Flying Constable.*

Bet you never thought there was so much to see and do along the way. Like an experienced travel writer once said, "Value the journey as well as the destination."

is the site chosen by Maj. Gen. George Patton Jr. in March 1942 as a training center for desert warfare. Nearly one million American servicepeople trained here. Patton commanded the camps for four months, departing in August 1942 to lead Operation Torch, the allied assault on German-held North Africa. The camp closed on April 30, 1944. The museum has an excellent twenty-six-minute video, plus exhibits. Many of the artifacts were donated by servicepeople. There are armored tanks on display, along with memorials and a small outdoor chapel. The newest addition is the West Coast Vietnam Veteran's Wall engraved with the names of servicepeople who served during the Vietnam War (1959–1975).

Next to the General Patton Memorial Museum is the **Chiriaco Summit Travel Center** (760-227-3227), owned by the Chiriaco family. There is a U.S. Post Office here and a service station, as well as a Fosters Freeze fast food. Enjoy the gift shop with antiques. Plus, there's a selection of fresh fruits, nuts, and desert dates.

The General Patton Museum was established through the tireless efforts of Margit Chiriaco Rusche and the Bureau of Land Management. Margit recalls seeing the tanks from her front yard as a five-year-old, when the Desert Training Center was in full swing. Be sure to have breakfast, lunch, or dinner at the charming coffee shop, where comfortable booths have looked out on the desert since 1933. Margit bakes the best chocolate cake, slathered with chocolate frosting and walnuts, for miles! On the menu is the DTC (Desert Training Center) burger, made with Spam (kids, ask your grandparents about that!). There are also corn dogs with chips and many sandwiches kids will enjoy. The Traveler's Special breakfast includes two each of pancakes, eggs, and sausage patties or bacon. It's worth driving out to Chiriaco Summit for this breakfast bargain! On the weekend, enjoy the *carne asada* and on Wednesday don't miss Grandma Ruth's pot roast—a family recipe. Kids may find this corner of the desert an oddity but many folks of the "Greatest Generation" think of it as treasured landmark

Twentynine Palms

Located between Interstate 15 and I-10 on Highway 62, 57 miles east of Palm Springs and incorporated in 1987, the city of Twentynine Palms encompasses 58 square miles (larger than the city of San Francisco) and has grown from a population of 11,000 to more than 28,000 today. Twentynine Palms hosts the headquarters offices of Joshua Tree National Park as well as the **Marine Corps Air Ground Combat Center** (www.29palms.usmc.mil). Since the 1950s, the Combat Center has grown from a few buildings, a glider runway, and about 120 Marines to more than 19,000 Marines, sailors, family members, and civilian workers, the largest and fastest-growing base in the Marine Corps.

Twentynine Palms has pristine air, beautiful natural surroundings, and a small-town family lifestyle your family will enjoy visiting. Highlights include Oasis of Murals (www.oasisofmurals.com) and the Old Schoolhouse Museum. The most-well-known special event is the annual celebration **Pioneer Days,** held during the month of October, with the excitement of outhouse races, a carnival, a parade, dances, contests, chili cook-offs, and lots more fun stuff. Dig out your Stetson, your boots, and your bandana and come on along!

Where to Eat and Stay

Ricochet, 62705 Twentynine Palms Highway, Joshua Tree; (760) 366-1898; www.richochetjoshuatree.com. A shop with good snacks for the drive to and through Joshua Tree. When owner Tanja Pslueger isn't busy baking buttermilk bran muffins for hikers and bikers, she's stocking the shelves with organically inspired nibbles such as Whales Tails tortilla chips.

Best Western Yucca Valley Hotel & Suites, 56525 Twentynine Palms Highway (Highway 62), Yucca Valley; (760) 365-3555; www.bestwestern.com. This ninety-five-room property has thirty-three suites and features a complimentary hot breakfast for the family, including biscuits and gravy. There are several units with kitchenettes as well. Heated outdoor pool and hot tub. Only 9 miles from Joshua Tree National Park.

Oasis of Eden Inn and Suites, 56377 Twentynine Palms Highway, Yucca Valley, Eden; (800) 606-6686; www.oasisofeden.com. If you've had a dream about spending a night in a Grecian, Roman, safari, or Oriental suite, make a reservation at the one and only Oasis of Eden Inn and Suites, where high desert hospitality means a full or studio kitchenette with adjoining rooms (perfect for a family), deluxe complimentary continental breakfast, and a marvelous heated whirlpool, surrounded by a colorful, hand-painted mural. There are thirty-eight units total; fourteen are themed. This is a one-of-a-kind hideaway with a personality. $$$

Spin and Margie's Desert Hideaway, Joshua Tree, off Highway 62, and ten minutes from Joshua Tree National Park; (760) 366-9124; www.deserthideaway.com. This adorable little property has a fun Southwest feel. With only four suites with kitchens, there is definitely a "get away from the hustle and bustle of city life" feeling here. There are videos in the rooms for the children when they are through discovering the desert for the day. $$$

29 Palms Inn, 73950 Inn Avenue, Twentynine Palms; (760) 367-3505; www.29palmsinn .com. Founded in 1928, this is another high desert discovery. Its cozy restaurant serves lunch and dinner. Yes, you are slightly off the beaten path, but the high desert air is invigorating, and kids will find the spacious grounds perfect for exploring. Guests spending the night enjoy a complimentary continental breakfast. Brunch is served on Sunday from 9:00 a.m. to 2:00 p.m. Desert cottages are roomy and ideal for a family; the decor is authentic with vintage furnishings. You may want to linger an extra day. $$$

For More Information

California Welcome Center–Yucca Valley. 56711 Twentynine Palms Highway (Highway 62), Yucca Valley, 92284; (760) 365-5464; www.visitcwc.com/destinations/yuccavalley/. Located 22 miles off I-10 on Highway 62. Open daily for complete area information, lodging referrals, and public Internet access.

Yucca Valley Chamber of Commerce. 56300 Twentynine Palms Highway, Suite D, Yucca Valley, 92284; (619) 365-6223; www .yuccavalley.org.

Joshua Tree Chamber of Commerce. 61325 Twentynine Palms Highway #F, P.O. Box 600, 92252; (760) 366-3723; www.joshua treechamber.org.

Twentynine Palms Chamber of Commerce. 73660 Civic Center, Suite C & D, Twentynine Palms, 92277; (760) 367-3445; www.29chamber.com.

Mojave National Preserve

The Mojave National Preserve is open-year round. The preserve is easily reached via I-15 or Interstate 40 east of Barstow and west of Needles, California, and Las Vegas, Nevada. Six freeway exits provide visitor access. Road conditions vary from paved, two-lane highways to rugged four-wheel-drive roads; see a map for major routes. Maps showing all dirt roads are available at park information centers. **Hole-in-the-Wall Ranger Station** (760-928-2572) is open on Friday, Saturday, and Sunday from 9:00 a.m. to 4:00 p.m. The Office of the Superintendent, Mojave National Preserve, is located at 222 East Main Street, Suite 202, Barstow (headquarters 760-255-8800; www.nps.gov/moja/).

Many visitors to Southern California are surprised to learn how extensive the state's desert lands really are. Some of the most prominent natural features in the preserve are the **Kelso Dunes,** situated in the southern section. Rising to 600 feet, the dunes are the third highest in the United States. Shifting sands on the steep side of the dunes create a unique rumbling sound that has given these mobile mounds the alias "the singing dunes." The dunes are ringed by high mountain ranges, and the overall effect is one of a great, stark beauty. A red-tailed hawk soaring above may be the only reminder that this is Southern California.

Kelso Depot Visitor Center

From I-15, exit at Baker, California. Kelso is 35 miles south of Baker. From I-40, exit on Kelbaker Road. Kelso is 22 miles north of I-40 on Kelbaker Road. (760) 252-6108; www.nps .gov/moja/planyourvisit/visitorcenters.htm. Open every day except Christmas, 9:00 a.m. to 5:00 p.m. Free.

The renovated Kelso Depot is now the primary visitor center for Mojave National Preserve. Most of the former dormitory rooms contain exhibits describing various aspects of the surrounding desert, from tortoises to sand dunes to desert mining and ranching. A twelve-minute film is shown in the theater. A gallery in the basement features rotating fine-art collections by local artists, focusing on the cultural history and natural splendors of Mojave.

Providence Mountains State Recreation Area

P.O. Box 1, Essex 92332; (760) 928-2586; www.parks.ca.gov. In the northern portion of the preserve.

Some three dozen ancient volcanic cinder cones are scattered throughout the area. Bighorn sheep are often sighted near the visitor center, which is close by the limestone Mitchell Caverns. The intrepid actor Val Kilmer found the Mitchell Caverns "a trip" in the vintage film *The Doors*. Ranger-led tours reveal the inside info on these stunning, illuminated wonders of nature. Tours are at 10:00 a.m., 1:30 p.m., and 3:00 p.m. for ninety minutes on Saturday and Sunday; Monday through Friday there is one tour daily at 1:30 p.m. The Mitchell Caverns are remote, yet they attract families year-round who want to explore some of the indescribable geographic wonders, off the beaten path in Southern California.

For More Information

Barstow Area Chamber of Commerce and Visitors Bureau. 681 North First Avenue, P.O. Box 698, Barstow, 92311; (760) 256-8617 or (888) 4-BARSTOW; www.barstow chamber.com.

California Welcome Center at Tanger Outlets. California has eleven official welcome centers placed strategically throughout the state. The Barstow center is located at 2796 Tanger Way, Suite 106 (760-253-4782). Located off I-15; exit Lenwood Road and follow the "traveling bear" signs to the Tanger Outlet Center. California welcome centers provide information on all twelve regions. Other welcome centers are located in Rohnert Park, Pier 39 in San Francisco, Carlsbad, Santa Ana, and the Shasta-Cascade region, to name a few. Visit www.visitcwc.com for locations of all the welcome centers.

Barstow Area

The western portions of the Mojave, though as desolate as the lands to the east, offer a very different kind of experience. Barstow, once a railroad crossroads and transportation center, lies halfway between L.A. and Las Vegas at the junctions of I-15 and I-40. Right in the center of the Mojave, it's the traditional base from which to explore Calico Ghost Town, Rainbow Basin, and Mitchell Caverns.

Bun Boy

1890 West Main Street, Barstow; (760) 256-8082. Open at 6:00 a.m. and close at 10:00 p.m. daily. $–$$

One of the main attractions in Barstow itself is stopping for lunch at a more-than-fastfood-but-less-than-a-restaurant kind of eatery, where all Southern Californians seem to have had a burger at some point in their lives. It's the kind of place you might imagine Jack Kerouac pulling into for a quick bite before waxing beatific about the experience. Nevertheless, families will enjoy giant-size servings of homemade peach, strawberry, and apple pie and the twenty-ounce t-bone steaks for under $15.

Rainbow Basin and Owl Canyon

Once you've filled your gas tank (and your tummy tank), it's time to leave civilization behind again. You won't miss the sounds of the city one bit as you head north on Fort Irwin Road, out of Barstow, and enter the realm of Rainbow Basin (www.blm.gov/ca/barstow), a national natural landmark, where the colors of the rainbow decorate gorge walls housing an inestimable quantity of fossilized remains that are ten to thirty million years old.

And may the force be with you as you drive through the rock-strewn, otherworldly landscape of Owl Canyon, where the movie *Star Wars* was filmed. If your kids don't know R2D2 from C3PO, this would be the place to fill them in.

The Bureau of Land Management (BLM) field office in Barstow (760-252-6091) administers Owl Canyon; general location: 8 miles north of downtown Barstow, off Irwin Road. The canyon is open year-round and **free,** although there is a $6 fee for primitive camping sites. Activities to enjoy include bird-watching, camping, hiking or backpacking, picnicking, rock hounding or gold panning, scenic driving, and wildlife and wildflower viewing.

Calico Ghost Town

Located minutes off I-15, east of Barstow, 36600 Ghost Town Road, Yermo; (760) 254-2122 or (800) TO-CALICO; www.calicotown.com. Open daily 8:00 a.m. to dusk (shops, playhouse, and railroad hours 9:00 a.m. to 5:00 p.m.). Closed Christmas Day. Campgrounds, cabins, and bunkhouse open 24/7. $$

A not-to-be-missed item on your Mojave Desert itinerary, the ghost town—the most celebrated of many such once-booming settlements that pepper the Mojave—contains remnants of the flourishing mining culture of more than a century ago. In the town's heyday in the 1880s, some 4,000 people called this dusty outpost home. Before you begin to feel too sorry for them, remember they made fortunes from silver mines that yielded $65 million worth of rich ore. One interesting nugget of information: The town was prosperous enough to keep twenty-two saloons in business.

In 1896 the price of silver plummeted, as did the town's fortunes. In the bat of an eyelash, Calico went from boom to bust. The Town of Calico is State Historic Landmark #782, and survived in the early 1900s because of borax mining within the District. This was the last place in California that the picturesque "twenty-mule teams" were used. Today the restored mining town lives on after a fashion as part of the San Bernardino County Regional Park. A stop in Calico is about as close to time travel as you'll ever get. Some of the town's original buildings, such as Lil's Saloon, Lucy Lane's House, and the General Store, have been restored so well that western-theme movies continue to be filmed here.

But Calico is more than atmospheric building facades. You can actually enter Lil's or the Top of Hill Cafe and Ice Cream Parlor for some modern-day refreshment. There are twenty-three shops along Main Street—the only street—a favorite being the 1880s-style candy store. You and the kids also might hop aboard a narrow-gauge train for a ride to the silver mine areas north of town.

At Maggie's Mine, the very adventurous can get an inside look at the miner's workplace, the 30-mile network of tunnels and mine shafts beneath Calico, by taking a self-guided tour. Maybe you'll even spot a wedge of silver. This is one ghost town that is very much alive.

Festivals in Calico take place throughout the year. Check to see when historical reenactments are scheduled, such as President Lincoln inspecting General Grant's troops. It's better than watching a DVD.

Peggy Sue's
I-15 at Ghost Town Road exit, Yermo, 8 miles east of Barstow; (760) 254-3370. Open daily for breakfast, lunch, and dinner. $$

Soda fountain, ice-cream parlor, pizza parlor, burgers, steaks, homemade chili and soups, old-fashioned candy, 1950s music, a 1950s-style dime store, TV and movie memorabilia, curios, and souvenir shop. Extensive children's menu. The kids will appreciate the game arcade, plus a park featuring cool lagoons and sparkling waterfalls surrounded by shady weeping willow trees.

Boron

Located between Barstow and Mojave, Boron was founded in 1927 when Pacific Coast Borax (now U.S. Borax) discovered one of the richest deposits of borax ore here. In recent decades, Boron has served as the main runway approach for Edwards Air Force Base (the famous site of space shuttle landings and supersonic flight). During the first weekend of October, Boron celebrates its rich mining and aerospace history with the annual Twenty Mule Team Days. For more information call the Boron Chamber of Commerce at (760) 762-5810 or visit www.boronchamber.org.

Twenty Mule Team Museum

26962 Twenty Mule Team Road; (760) 762-5810; www.20muleteammuseum.org. Open daily 10:00 a.m. to 4:00 p.m. Kids welcome. **Free.**

If you find yourselves on Highway 58 at the junction of U.S. Highway 395 ("Four Corners") and think you're in the middle of nowhere, think again. Another 6 miles and you're here. Your kids may not remember the TV series *Death Valley Days* or the product Borax (it used to make our wash sparkle), but here's a good way to refresh your memory. The museum, located in a renovated house from the old Baker Mine campsite, depicts borax mining and early life in Boron. There are plans to add an air and space museum here, so look for an F4D airplane that was retired here. There's also a train station that was brought in from Kramer.

The Borax Visitor Center

14486 Borax Road, off Highway 58 at the Borax Road exit; www.borax.com. Open daily from 9:00 a.m. to 5:00 p.m., excluding major holidays and weather permitting.

Everyone who finds his or her way to this center gets a sample of "TV rock." After watching the seventeen-minute video on the worldwide uses of Borax, the kids will understand why there really is a treasure in "them thar hills." And it's Borax!

Ridgecrest

While Barstow is the crossroads of the Mojave Desert as a whole, little Ridgecrest, a town of some 30,000 about 70 miles to the northwest, is the best base camp for branching out to explore the natural wonders and attractions of Mojave's northwestern portions.

Ridgecrest is the hub high desert community for visiting the natural attractions of **Mt. Whitney** and **Death Valley,** a two-hour drive away. For further information contact the Ridgecrest Area Convention and Visitors Bureau (100 West California Avenue; 760-375-8282 or 800-847-4830; www.visitdeserts.com) or Ridgecrest Chamber of Commerce (128-B California Avenue; 760-375-8331; www.ridgecrestchamber.com).

You've seen Ridgecrest in dozens of movies, television shows, and videos. More than 500 television commercials have been filmed here since 1990. Think back to *Star Trek V*, *Flight of the Intruder, ET,* and *Dinosaur,* which was filmed on location at the Trona Pinnacles. Jawbone Canyon has seen the likes of *Wayne's World II, Desert Blue,* and *Woman Undone.* And Olancha Sand Dunes hosted *Star Trek V.* Cuddleback Dry Lake Bed was the set for scenes in the movies *Hidalgo* and *I Iolcs.*

Head east out of Ridgecrest on Highway 178 and take in the panorama of the **Panamint Mountains,** which frame Death Valley. About 20 miles up the road, the **Trona Pinnacles** pierce the clear desert sky. The pinnacles, more than 500 in number, are composed of tufa (a porous rock formed as a deposit from springs and streams) and reach heights of 150 feet.

Maturango Museum

100 East Las Flores Avenue, at China Lake Boulevard; (760) 375-6900; www.maturango.org. Open 10:00 a.m. to 5:00 p.m. daily. $; free admission to visitor centers.

The museum was established in 1962 to tell the story of the northern Mojave Desert. There are exhibits showcasing animals, birds, paleontology, and Native American displays. The hands-on Discovery Area appeals to children of all ages. The museum is also home to the Death Valley Tourist Center and the Northern Mojave Visitor Center.

Ridgecrest Regional Wild Horse and Burro Corrals

(760) 384-5765 or (866) 4-MUSTANGS; www.blm.gov/ca/ridgecrest/whb.html. Open Monday through Friday 7:00 a.m. to 4:00 p.m. Closed in July. $$

Three miles east of Ridgecrest, off Highway 178, a right turn just as the road reaches the top side of the rise brings you to the Bureau of Land Management's Wild Horse and Burro Corrals. This is where the animals are held, fed, and prepared for adoptions locally and throughout the country.

U.S. Naval Museum of Armament and Technology at China Lake

East end of Blandy Road in the old Officer's Club building; (760) 939-3530; www.china lakemuseum.org. Open Monday through Saturday 10:00 a.m. to 4:00 p.m. Guest passes allowing entrance to NAWS China Lake are available for visiting the museum. Contact the museum to arrange them.

China Lake has been a research, development, and test site since 1943 and covers more than a million acres in Southern California's Mojave Desert. The museum focus is on technical advances in the defense industry made at China Lake. Soon to come: the refurbishment of an FA-18 Hornet aircraft, the first of twenty prototypes manufactured for China Lake in the late 1970s. Kids can see missiles, free-fall weapons, and a variety of other intimidating weapons of war such as a Tomahawk submarine, a Shrike, and a Maverick. More benign is the Lunar Soft Landing Vehicle. Kids should find the actual Sidewinder missile to be especially awesome.

On quite a different note, the Naval Air Weapons Station (NAWS) China Lake houses the largest cache of ancient Native American rock art in North America. Little Petroglyph Canyon, the only site open for public tours, is about 1.2 miles long, with walls 20 to 40 feet high. Elevation is about 5,000 feet. The road to the site is steep and mostly paved, with only the last 7 miles being dirt. The canyon floor is a sand and rocky wash bottom. Visitors have to negotiate over and around a variety of rocks and boulders to enter the canyon. From there, the walk is moderate.

The round-trip from the NAWS main gate is about 90 miles. To arrange for a tour, call the Corporate Communications/Public Affairs Office (PAO) at least two months in advance at (760) 939-1683. The PAO representative will explain how to coordinate your tour and how to get assistance in securing NAWS-approved guides, mandated post–9/11. Questions regarding the petroglyphs may be directed to NAVAIR, Naval Air Warfare Center Weapons Division, Code 750000D, 1 Administration Circle, China Lake, 93555-6100; www.nawcwd.navy.mil/.

Where to Eat and Stay

Texas Cattle Company, 1429 North Chinalake Boulevard, Ridgecrest; (760) 446-6602; www.texascattlecompany.com. This family-oriented restaurant has an extended children's menu. Try the grilled cheese for sure, pardners. Closed Sunday. $$

The Heritage Inn & Suites, 1050 North Norma Street; (760) 446-6543 or (800) 843-0693; www.heritageinnsuites.com. The hotel offers 126 comfortable guest rooms and 44 suites and features complimentary American breakfast for guests. Film crews stay here often, as do many military personnel from nearby China Lake Naval Air Weapons Center. $$$

Randsburg Area

Twenty-two miles south of Ridgecrest, off US 395, is the home of the living ghost town of **Randsburg** (population 77). While certainly not as well known as Calico Ghost Town, Randsburg shared much the same fate as its desert neighbor. Today, visitors can stop for a snack, browse among antiques stores, and take a peek at the bullet slug still lodged in one of the local bars. When you turn off US 395 at the sign to Randsburg, the first building you will see is the old jail to your left. Park your car and browse among the vintage structures. This area is desolate but photogenic and has been used as a location for movies and television productions.

Desert Tortoise Natural Area

South of Randsburg, off Highways 14 and 58, near California City; (760) 384-5400; www.ca .blm.gov/ridgecrest. Free.

You've come this far, so don't miss the Desert Tortoise Natural Area (DTNA), just southwest of Randsburg. This 40-square-mile chunk of land has been reserved for the protection and preservation of the largest known population of the shy desert tortoise, an endangered species. There is an information kiosk and self-guided interpretative trails. If you want to see this desert reptile (California's official reptile) at its most active, make your visit in April or September. The preserve boasts a rich flora and fauna representative of the intricate Mojave Desert ecosystem. In 1980 the Bureau of Land Management, U.S. Department of Interior, recognized the significance of the DTNA by designating it an "Area of Critical Environmental Concern" and as a "Research Natural Area." For additional information, visit www.tortoise-tracks.org/dtna.html.

Red Rock Canyon State Park

Red Rock Canyon State Park Headquarters. The park is 25 miles northeast of Mojave on Highway 14, near Cantil. Go west ¼ mile on Abbott Drive. Signage indicating the turnoff is clearly visible on Highway 14. The park is 120 miles north of Los Angeles, via I-5 and Highway 14. (661) 942-0662; www.parks.ca.gov/?page_id=631. Open year-round. The visitor center is open Friday through Sunday; hours vary. Guided nature hikes are offered on Saturday and Sunday at 9:00 a.m. during the spring and fall, as well as campfire programs on Saturday at 7:00 p.m.; (661) 320-4001.

This beautiful, scenic wonder of California was established as a state park in 1968, located where the southernmost tip of the Sierra Nevada converges with the El Paso Range. After wet winters, the park's floral displays are amazing. Wildlife includes roadrunners, hawks, lizards, mice, and squirrels. The colorful rock formations in the park served as landmarks during the early 1870s for twenty-mule-team freight wagons slogging through the desert.

Just south of Red Rock Canyon State Park, stop by the Jawbone Canyon Visitor's Center on Highway 14, site of the annual Moose Anderson Days spring festival. For more information contact Friends of Jawbone Canyon, P.O. Box 1902, Cantil 93519; (760) 373-1146; www.jawbone.org. Open daily.

Red Rock Canyon State Park is a favorite site for filmmakers, and the beginning scene of *Jurassic Park* was filmed here. There is a self-guided nature trail offering a good introduction to indigenous plants, animals, and awe-inspiring vistas. If you'd like to see more breathtaking desert-scapes, cross over to Highway 14, which skirts red-, pink-, orange-, and white-colored canyons that seem to change color as the light shifts.

Death Valley

It's awesome to imagine that twenty-seven acres of "empty" California desert make up what we now know as Death Valley. The region is one of 265 areas worldwide recognized and preserved by the Man and the Biosphere organization. This one, the **Mojave and Colorado Desert Biosphere Reserve,** is the ideal place to share with your children the importance of environmental protection. Before you enter the dazzling desolation of Death Valley, consider making a stop in **Darwin Falls,** a little bit off Highway 178 before the valley. The whole family can manage the half-mile hike to the oasis of lower Darwin Falls. The upper falls aren't far behind. Your memories of green will serve you well as you head into Death Valley, the lowest point in the United States at 282 feet below sea level and reportedly the hottest place on earth. Average summertime highs are 115 degrees, and with scarcely a tree in sight, there isn't much shade to cool off in. If you happen to come here between June and September, remember to take it easy and drink water frequently—dehydration is dangerous and can happen faster than you think.

But don't let the heat deter you from visiting. Or the intimidating name, for that matter. With a rich mining heritage dating from 1849 and modern tourist facilities, Death

Junior Ranger Program

Children ages six and older will get the most out of visiting Death Valley National Park if they ask for the Death Valley workbook at the park's visitor center front desk. There are special credit activities on projects kids can delve into while exploring the park. Upon the completion of the listed activities, all age-appropriate kids are presented with a Valley Junior Ranger Badge, and the park staff may undertake, time permitting, a small ceremony. Check out all the details online here: www.nps.gov/learn/juniorranger.htm.

Death Valley Fun Facts

(courtesy of Furnace Creek Inn and Ranch Resort)

• The hottest recorded temperature in Death Valley was 134 degrees (Fahrenheit) in 1913.

• The average rainfall in Death Valley is 1.8 inches per year.

• Death Valley was named a national monument on February 11, 1933, by President Herbert Hoover.

• Death Valley became a national park on October 31, 1994, by an act of Congress.

• The average humidity in Death Valley ranges from zero to 5 percent.

• Death Valley has more than 900 species of plants, 6 types of fish, 5 amphibians, 36 reptiles, and 51 mammals native to the region.

• There are 346 species of birds that migrate through or reside in Death Valley.

• *Death Valley Days* ran as a radio show from 1930 to 1944 and as a television series from 1952 to 1968.

Valley can actually be a very lively place. Geological wonders have, however, always been at center stage. You can see the famous ones in a day or so, but savor the barren beauty slowly. Death Valley has more than 1,000 species of plants and more than 50 are endemic (kids, look that word up) and found nowhere else in the world—wouldn't that make an impressive report for your next science assignment?

Artist's Palette Drive is a famous byway that winds through pastel-colored hills laced with minerals. Early morning is the best time to take photographs from **Zabriskie Point,** which overlooks ancient lakebeds. By contrast, **Golden Canyon** is at its best in the afternoon. In between, you could investigate the bizarre salt formations of the **Devil's Golf Course** and get an elevated perspective from 5,474 feet up at **Dante's View,** where the Panamint Mountains and snowcapped Mt. Whitney will be visible.

Death Valley National Park

The hottest, driest, lowest place in the Western Hemisphere. Open year-round. Office of the Superintendent, P.O. Box 579, Death Valley 92328; (760) 786-3200; www.nps.gov/deva/. Furnace Creek Visitor Center and Borax Museum, open year-round 8:00 a.m. to 6:00 p.m.; Stovepipe Wells Ranger Station, open all year, seasonal hours.

Highway 190, the Badwater Road, the Scotty's Castle Road, and paved roads to Dante's View and Wildrose provide access to the major scenic viewpoints and historic points of interest within the park. More than 350 miles of unpaved and four-wheel-drive roads provide access to wilderness hiking, camping, and historical sites. All vehicles must be licensed and "street legal." Admission fees are by permit, $20 per car for seven days. Death Valley Annual Pass for $40 per passholder/vehicle.

Amargosa Opera House and Hotel (ages 5 and up)

(760) 852-4441; www.amargosaoperahouse.com. Doors open 7:45 p.m.; show starts 8:15 p.m. Saturday only. $$

Plan your trip so that you can visit this site in the ghost town of Death Valley Junction, near the junction of Highways 127 and 190. Performances star Marta Becket, who plays all of the characters. Murals depict gypsies, revelers, clerics, and Spanish royalty. Eccentric, yes, but charmingly unusual. The fourteen-room hotel is a rustic, historic hoot. No phones or TV mar this quirky outpost.

Scotty's Castle

(760) 786-2392; www.nps.gov/deva/Scottys/Scottys_main.htm. Guided, living-history tours of Scotty's Castle main house interior are conducted daily year-round. The first tour begins at 9:00 a.m., and the last begins at 5:00 p.m. Castle grounds close at 6:00 p.m. Tours last approximately fifty minutes and are given at least once every hour. Limited to nineteen people per tour, the guided tour is the only way to get inside the main house. Tour tickets are sold on a first-come, first-served basis. $$

Located in the northern part of the valley in an area known as Grapevine Canyon, this Spanish Moorish–style mansion was the creation of Walter Scott (and some of his desert friends), who built his home in the 1920s at the cost of $200 million. The building took ten years to complete, but you can see it inside and out in considerably less time. Save your visit here for the second day of your Death Valley tour. Near the castle is the Ubehebe Crater and the Sahara-scale sand dunes.

Where to Eat and Stay

Furnace Creek Inn and Ranch Resort, Highway 190, Box 1; (760) 786-2345; www .furnacecreekresort.com. This privately owned property operated by Xanterra is actually one resort with two hotels: the AAA 4-diamond rated luxurious, historic 1927 sixty-six-room **Furnace Creek Inn** (open only mid-October to mid-May) and the more family-friendly 224-room **Furnace Creek Ranch,** circa 1933, open year-round. Choose the ranch for you and the kids and the inn for a couple's private romantic getaway. Wandering around the western-theme ranch grounds, you'll feel like you've been transported back to the 1800s but with all the twenty-first-century amenities: air-conditioning, TV, telephones, a spring-fed swimming pool, tennis courts, and a children's playground. Ride a horse (except in summer season, when it's too darn hot to trot), take a hike, or challenge your kids to a game of horseshoes. Visit the eighteen-hole Furnace Creek Golf Course, the world's lowest golf course at 214 feet below sea level. Visit the general store for a quick snack and some great gifts. Check out the antique stagecoaches, mining tools, and the steam locomotive at the Borax Museum. For year-round casual, American-style dining ($$), choose from the Wrangler Steakhouse and Buffet, the 49'er Cafe, and the Corkscrew Saloon. It's been said about Death Valley, "You can travel greater distances but no place will take you further away." $$$–$$$$

San Diego County

What does summer vacation mean to your family? How about one with plenty of outdoor recreation—boating, hiking, biking, picnicking, swimming, golfing, baseball, surfing, or sunbathing on miles of beach? Does it include excursions to great parks full of wildlife and sea life, exciting museums with hands-on displays of fun things from outer space to automobiles, old sights with new twists, all surrounded by the Pacific Ocean, mountains, and desert and capped by a clear blue sky with mega-sunshine? The year-round answer is San Diego County, Southern California's endless summer vacation destination, encompassing metropolitan San Diego, the coastal areas of North County including Oceanside, and to the east, the mountains and desert of the Back Country, featuring Julian and Anza-Borrego.

San Diego County's location at the extreme southwest corner of the contiguous United States helps explain not only its temperate climate (an average year-round temperature of seventy degrees) but also its friendly spirit. In this geographically varied, 4,269-square-mile region, you can head west out to sea, south into Mexico, east into forested mountains that receive more rain and snow than Seattle and deserts that are hotter and drier than Phoenix, and north into 70 miles of sandy, palm-lined beaches that rival Florida. You will find country kitchens and apple farms, cosmopolitan bistros and burger joints, craft shops and giant retail malls, high-rises and bungalows, dirt roads and ten-lane freeways—inhabited by 3.2 million culturally and ethnically diverse people. Their sheer numbers make San Diego America's seventh most populous area and the Golden State's second-biggest metropolis, after Los Angeles—who all pulled together in October 2007 to help those affected by Mother Nature's fiery outbursts in the region. (Rest assured, all is well now.)

Kudos! San Diego's LEGOLAND California was named "Best Children's Park" in the world by *Amusement Today* magazine, the fourth year it has won this Golden Ticket Award from this international trade publication. In March 2006, San Diego was chosen by *Bicycling* magazine as "the best bicycling city with one million population" followed by Chicago and New York. *Family Fun* magazine continues to rank the area as "one of the coolest in the southwest."

SAN DIEGO COUNTY

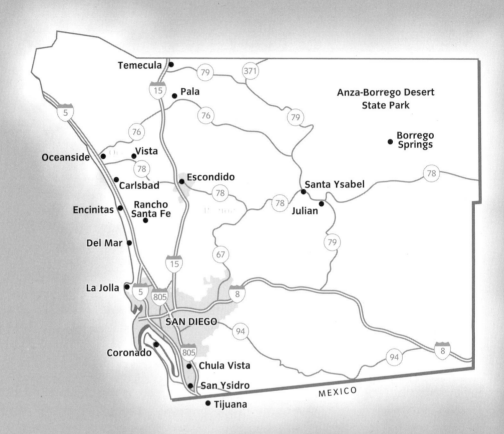

Temecula

79 371

15 Pala

76 79

Anza-Borrego Desert
State Park

5

76

Vista

Oceanside

78

Borrego
Springs

Carlsbad

Escondido

78

Santa Ysabel

78

78

Rancho
Santa Fe

Encinitas

Julian

Del Mar

67

79

15

78

La Jolla

5 805

8

SAN DIEGO

94

Coronado

805

Chula Vista

94

8

San Ysidro

Tijuana

MEXICO

Metropolitan San Diego

Touring the greater San Diego area is best accomplished by automobile. Your choices of activities and attractions are incredibly diverse. Many families start in the Mission Bay area at SeaWorld and are entertained by the penguins, sharks, and killer whales. Or you might begin at the world-famous San Diego Zoo with its exotic and rare species of animals and plants. Or the San Diego Wild Animal Park may beckon, where the animals roam free and really wild. Balboa Park's museums, art galleries, and theaters provide you with some fantastic cultural attractions. If outdoor recreation is your family's favorite, there are hundreds of beaches, parks, sailing, and fishing options. We like to begin at the beginning by visiting the Old Town State Historic Park and Presidio district, then touring the first California missions, downtown's restored Gaslamp Quarter, or Point Loma's Cabrillo National Monument, which commemorates the first European to set sight on San Diego Bay. But no matter how you divide and conquer it, you will find incredibly fun things to see, do, and taste throughout metropolitan San Diego.

Cabrillo National Monument

1800 Cabrillo Memorial Drive, Highway 209, off Interstate 5; (619) 557-5450. Open 9:00 a.m. to 5:15 p.m. daily, possibly extended in summer. $$

Cruising the Pacific Coast north of Mexico in 1542, explorer Juan Rodriguez Cabrillo first landed at Point Loma, a 400-foot-high peninsula separating San Diego Bay from the ocean. He claimed it (and everything else in sight) for Spain. Today you can marvel at the same view Cabrillo had of the southernmost tip of this narrow finger of land. On Point Loma's plateaulike surface are two military reservations, a cemetery, and informative attractions for young and old alike. You can get your bearings at the visitor center, tour the monument's small museum, and take in a **free** film or a ranger-sponsored program in the auditorium. Then let the kids climb Old Point Loma Lighthouse, with its breathtaking panorama of the city meeting the sea. This is a superb spot for winter whale-watching.

Old Town San Diego State Historic Park and Presidio Park

Located in a 6-block area bounded by Wallace, Juan, Twiggs, and Congress Streets, sandwiched between I-5 and Interstate 8; (619) 220-5422. Open daily 10:00 a.m. to 5:00 p.m. Free admission. Free guided walking tours depart the Robinson–Rose House daily at 2:00 p.m. All buildings are closed New Year's Day, Thanksgiving, and Christmas.

In 1769, a mere 167 years after Cabrillo arrived, Gaspar de Portolá established the first Presidio Royal (military fort) while Father Junípero Serra founded the first in a string of twenty-one California missions. Since both the fort and the mission were built in San Diego, they earned the city the moniker "birthplace of California." This is, of course, California-ish hyperbole, because for centuries before de Portolá or Serra, Native Americans—quite successfully, in fact—had prospered from the area's fertile lands and bountiful seas.

The fort and mission were located originally in what today is called Old Town. The cluster of adobe buildings at the base of Presidio Hill has swollen over time into a fascinating complex of historic landmarks, museums, art galleries, shops, and ethnic restaurants. These include the Black Hawk Smith & Stable, the Colorado House/Wells Fargo Museum, the Courthouse, the Johnson House, La Casa de Estudillo, the Machado-Stewart Adobe, the Mason Street School, the Plaza, the Robinson–Rose House, the San Diego Union Newspaper Museum, Seeley Stables, and the Whaley House. Our best advice is just to go, park, walk, and enjoy this family-friendly district.

Junípero Serra Museum

2727 Presidio Drive, in Presidio Park; (619) 297-3258; www.sandiegohistory.org. Open Tuesday through Saturday 10:00 a.m. to 4:30 p.m. and Sunday noon to 4:30 p.m.; closed major holidays. $$

This museum stands above the sites of the eighteenth-century presidio and Father Junípero Serra's first mission in Alta, California. It's a great place to learn about San Diego's early Spanish and Mexican periods. Exhibits include artifacts from archaeological excavations at the site.

Who Was **Alonzo Horton?**

For some years after California won statehood in 1850, San Diego remained a relatively quiet community with a Spanish and Mexican flavor. That changed dramatically when Alonzo E. Horton arrived in town from San Francisco in 1867. Buying up some 960 acres of waterfront land, he began the process of developing what was to become today's downtown area. The **Gaslamp Quarter,** bounded by Broadway, Fourth, and Sixth Streets and Harbor Drive, is the historic 16-block quarter where Horton made his first land purchase and where his legacy lives on. A twenty-year restoration and cleanup campaign to return the Gaslamp Quarter to its gay 1890s splendor has paid off: The area sparkles with period streetlamps, old-time trolley stops, and, of more recent vintage, trendy restaurants, hotels, offices, artists' studios, and nightspots. For complete information, including walking tours and audiotapes, contact the **Gaslamp Quarter/Historical Society Museum,** 410 Island Avenue; (619) 233-4692; www.gaslampquarter.org; Open Monday through Friday 10:00 a.m. to 2:00 p.m., Saturday 10:00 a.m. to 4:00 p.m., and Sunday noon to 4:00 p.m. Ask about the new Children's Historical Walking Tour and the Virtual Learning Center. Or contact the **Gaslamp Quarter Association;** 614 Fifth Avenue, Suite E; (619) 233-5227; www.gaslamp.org.

Mission Basilica San Diego de Alcala

10818 San Diego Mission Road (east on I-8, exit Mission Gorge Road north to Twain Avenue, then drive west to San Diego Mission Road); (619) 281-8449; www.missionsandiego .com. Open 9:00 a.m. to 4:45 p.m. daily except Thanksgiving and Christmas. $

Father Serra's first mission, relocated east to its current location in 1774, was burned down by Indians the following year. Rebuilt in 1781, the fully restored mission remains an active parish. Behind the chapel is a small museum containing robes, relics, and original records in Serra's own handwriting. "California's first church" is a National Historic Landmark, California Historic Landmark #242, and honored with a City of San Diego Historic Designation #113.

Horton Plaza

Between Broadway, First, and Fourth Avenues and G Street, downtown; (800) 214-7467; www.westfield.com/hortonplaza/. Open Monday through Saturday 10:00 a.m. to 9:00 p.m. and Sunday 11:00 a.m. to 7:00 p.m. Hours adjusted seasonally and during holiday periods. Three hours of free parking with any purchase.

Named after Alonzo Horton but opened in 1985, this five-story, lavishly decorated and landscaped open-air mall houses more than 150 shops and restaurants, fourteen movie theaters, and two live performance stages. Parking is available at an adjacent garage. Kids will love the festive atmosphere and food courts. The ARTSTIX booth at Westfield Horton Plaza near the corner of Third and Broadway sells half-price day-of-show tickets to many local music, dance, and theater events. Some shows also are sold in advance. Visit or call the ARTSTIX hotline at (619) 497-5000.

Old Town Trolley Tours/Historic Tours of America

(619) 298-8687; www.historictours.com/sandiego/. Every thirty minutes, daily, beginning at 9:00 a.m. $$$$

Two-hour narrated tours of most of the key San Diego sites are available on propane-powered vehicles. You can exit and reboard anytime during the day at any of the ten fun stops (such as Balboa Park, Horton Plaza, Gaslamp Quarter, Seaport Village, Embarcadero, Old Town, and Coronado) along the route. This is a wonderful way for the entire family to become acquainted with the city without the hassles of driving and parking your own car. Also available is **San Diego SEALs Harbor Tour**'s "Boat on Wheels," a hydra-amphibious land and sea tour, plus the "Ghosts and Gravestones" tour. All highly recommended.

San Diego Trolley System and the Transit Store

102 Broadway, near Horton Plaza; (619) 233-3004 or (619) 685-4900; www.transit.511sd .com. Runs daily 5:00 a.m. to 1:00 a.m. every fifteen minutes. One-way fares start at $1.25; day-tripper passes (unlimited use of all types of public transit) are $5.00 per day.

An electric trolley run by the Metropolitan Transit System is a superb, car-free way to travel around San Diego. The North-South Blue Line runs from downtown San Diego to the Mexican border at San Ysidro; the East-West Orange Line runs along the bay and includes

San Diego **Art & Soul**

This is an unprecedented cooperative partnership formed between the San Diego Convention and Visitors Bureau, the City of San Diego Commission for Arts and Culture, and hundreds of organizations and businesses to promote the rich cultural diversity of the area. For an updated daily list of events; links to hundreds of art, music, and cultural Web sites; and a free color brochure, visit www.sandiegoartandsoul.com or call (619) 533-3050.

Seaport Village, the Gaslamp Quarter, downtown, and El Cajon. The Green Line runs from Old Town to El Cajon and Santee as well.

Firehouse Museum

1572 Columbia Street; (619) 232-3473; http://thesdfirehousemuseum.org. Open Thursday through Sunday 10:00 a.m. to 4:00 p.m.; closed major holidays. $, firefighters admitted free.

Admire antique fire equipment and helmets from around the world in San Diego's oldest firehouse.

Museum of Contemporary Art–San Diego

1001 Kettner Boulevard at Broadway; (619) 234-1001; www.mcasd.org. Open Thursday through Tuesday 11:00 a.m. to 5:00 p.m. $; ages 25 and under free every day and free museum admission Thursday evenings from 5:00 to 7:00 p.m. Free public tours are available every Thursday at 6:00 p.m. and weekends at 2:00 p.m.

In the spectacular thirty-four-story America Plaza, this museum features four galleries on two levels with permanent and changing exhibits of modern paintings, sculpture, and designs. The all-glass exterior gives dramatic views of the San Diego Trolley Station, AMTRAK Depot, and the skyline. Call for current exhibitions.

San Diego Aircraft Carrier Museum/USS *Midway*

Navy Pier, 910 North Harbor Drive; (619) 544-9600; www.midway.org. Open daily 10:00 a.m. to 5:00 p.m. except on holidays. $$–$$$, children younger than six and active-duty servicepeople in uniform free.

Opened in June 2004, the museum is located aboard the USS *Midway*, permanently docked at Navy Pier in San Diego Bay. Marvel at a floating "city at sea" and share in an

odyssey that began in 1945 when the USS *Midway* was commissioned as the largest ship in the world. Audio guide provided. More than thirty-five exhibits and displays. You have access to the mess deck, berthing spaces, hangar deck, and flight deck. The museum includes flight simulators, a gift shop, and a cafe and is constantly adding new programs. An outstanding experience.

San Diego Children's Museum/ Museo de los Ninos de San Diego (ages 2–12)

200 West Island Avenue on the corner of Front Street (just a block from the convention center); (619) 233-8792; www.sdchildrensmuseum.org. $$

"The Muse" re-opened in May 2008 in a brand-new 50,000-square-foot three-story building—more than doubling previous public space. The new museum has multiple galleries for hands-on experimentation, two meeting/birthday party rooms, a 250-seat theater, and an indoor/outdoor cafe. Call for current schedules and fees.

Maritime Museum of San Diego

1492 North Harbor Drive; (619) 234-9153; www.sdmaritime.org. Open daily 9:00 a.m. to 8:00 p.m. $$

The museum will really get your family in a seafaring mood. You can explore three ships: the square-rigged *Star of India,* launched in 1863 and the oldest merchant vessel afloat; the ferry boat *Berkeley,* circa 1898; and the *Medea,* a steam-powered luxury yacht built in 1904.

Seaport Village

West Harbor Drive and Kettner Boulevard; (619) 235-4014; www.seaportvillage.com. Open daily 10:00 a.m. to 9:00 p.m.

Encompassing fourteen acres, this village looks like a transplanted New England fishing town, complete with a carousel, lighthouse, and clock tower along with almost one hundred shops, theme eateries, and restaurants. The Loof Carousel, circa 1890, is worth a whirl. You could easily spend most of the day here wandering the waterfront and enjoying a harbor cruise.

Balboa Park

Just northeast of the downtown business district; (619) 239-0512 for general information; www.balboapark.org.

In 1868 some farsighted city leaders set aside 1,200 acres of barren pueblo land for a city park. Now that land contains the world-famous San Diego Zoo and fifteen museums (the largest concentration outside the Smithsonian in Washington, D.C.). The best way to see the rest of Balboa Park's attractions is on foot. Park at the Plaza de Panama lot (by Laurel Street near the Cabrillo Bridge crossing) or take the **free** tram from the Inspiration Point parking lot (the tram has eleven stops through the park). Admittance to the park grounds is **free,** but admission prices to attractions vary by institution. Memberships are also available for purchase from the museums and performing arts organizations, offering an opportunity for visitors to support these San Diego cultural treasures on an annual basis.

San Diego Zoo

In Balboa Park. From I-5 take Pershing Drive exits and follow the signs; (619) 234-3153; www.sandiegozoo.org. Opens at 9:00 a.m. every day; closing hours vary by season, so be sure to call ahead. $$$

Let the zoo be your San Diego headquarters for at least two days of family adventure. The Spanish colonial buildings here were built originally along El Prado (the Promenade) for the 1915 Panama-California Exposition. Part of the exposition was a modest menagerie, which a certain Dr. Harry Wegeforth took over, expanded, and turned into what is now one of the world's rarest collections. The zoo's size is formidable: more than 4,000 animals, more than 900 species, and 100-plus magnificently landscaped acres with 6,500 exotic plants. The zoo has the largest population of giant pandas in the United States and is one of only four facilities in the nation to house critically endangered giant pandas. Its family of giant pandas includes male panda Gao Gao; female panda Bai Yun; a young male Mei Shen, born in August 2003; and female cubs Su Lin, born in August 2005, and Zhen Zhen, born in August 2007.

Animals are "on display" outdoors year-round. Viewing is enhanced by many exhibition areas that do not have bars. Areas include Gorilla Tropics (with incredibly humanlike

Passport to Balboa Park Is a Great Value

There are so many incredible things to see and do in Balboa Park, it would probably take you a week to do it all! The **Passport to Balboa Park** is designed with that in mind. Experience up to thirteen Balboa Park museums for $39 (a $95 value). This Passport to Balboa is valid for seven days. Also available is the Zoo/Passport Combo for adults for only $65, a value of more than $125, and $36 for children three to twelve, which is a value of more than $63. This combo passport includes entrance to the museums as well as 1-Day Deluxe San Diego Zoo Admission. Obtain yours at any of the museums or the Balboa Park Visitor Center House of Hospitality at 1549 El Prado. Call (619) 239-0512 for more information or www.sandiego.gov/park-and-recreation/parks/balboa/pass.shtml.

In August 2006, the Balboa Park Visitors Center began renting one-hour audio listening tours that highlight the park's history, architecture, and horticultural offerings. The children's version features narrations by actors voicing two Balboa Park historic figures—George Marston, a local civic leader instrumental in the park's founding, and Kate Sessions, often called the mother of Balboa Park for her horticultural contributions. Check these out for an iPod alternative listening experience!

Other Things to See and Do
in Balboa Park

Museums, galleries, and gardens are not the only things going on in Balboa Park for your family. The forty-eight-passenger **Miniature Railroad** will take you and yours into a bygone era. The **Carousel** will set you spinning. The **Starlight Bowl,** where the San Diego Civic Light Opera Association presents delightful musicals, is a sure hit, so call (619) 544-7827 for current schedules. The **Spreckels Organ Pavilion** has **free** concerts on weekends. The pavilion houses the world's biggest outdoor pipe organ; call (619) 235-1100 for program information. The San Diego Junior Theatre presents year-round, family-friendly productions at the Casa del Prado Theatre (www.juniortheatre.com). The **Morley Field Sports Complex,** in the northeastern section of the park, can satisfy just about every recreational need your family can dream of (no matter how complex), with a tennis club, two golf courses, a swimming pool, a kiddie pool, some bocce courts, a fitness center, a playground, an archery range, a couple of baseball diamonds, assorted picnic areas, two recreation centers, and a zippy eighteen-hole Frisbee golf course.

primates), the Tiger River section, a tropical rain habitat, the Sun Bear Forest, a Southeast Asian jungle, a Hippo Beach (with underwater viewing to see how graceful a swimmer this huge land mammal can be), and the largest koala exhibit outside of Australia. (Get ready for new stuffed teddy bear requests after this particular show!)

The Children's Zoo is user-friendly, with more chances for your kids to pet animals than you can wave a carrot at, plus an incubator for baby chicks and an animal nursery. The Skyfari tram is a great way to see the zoo by air. Our recommendation for "doing the zoo" is the Deluxe Tour, which includes admission to the big zoo, a forty-five-minute double-decker bus tour (marvelous view), the Children's Zoo, and a Skyfari aerial tramway ride.

Reuben H. Fleet Space Theatre and Science Museum

In Balboa Park, 1875 El Prado; (619) 238-1233; www.rhfleet.org. Open daily 9:30 a.m.; closing times vary. $$

This awe-inspiring facility features a planetarium, hands-on exhibits, and the incredible OMNIMAX, which features new IMAX films. From birds to the Wright brothers to jets, you and the kids will thrill to the history and magical science of flight. For ages infant to six years, Kid City (a permanent exhibition) has conveyer belts and cranes to air chutes and grocery stores for youth to work, create, play, and learn as they experience the wonders of the everyday working world. Throughout it, tips and strategies are offered on parent-child interaction to encourage children's learning. Don't miss this!

San Diego by the Sea

The **Embarcadero,** located at the west end of Broadway, is the thoroughfare forming the heart of downtown San Diego's waterfront action. It's home to the **Broadway Pier,** with berths for cruise ships and freighters, a debarkation platform, U.S. Customs offices, and a cool observation deck. Definitely plan on taking the kids on one of the San Diego Bay excursion cruises to view all the action around Harbor Island, Shelter Island, Point Loma, and Coronado Island. Dinner cruises and whale-watching trips also depart here. Here are some options.

The Original San Diego Harbor Excursions. 1050 North Harbor Drive; (619) 234-4111 or (800) 442-7847; www.sdhe.com. $$$. In operation since 1915. Dinner cruises also available. Scheduled departures vary seasonally. Generally they are daily between 10:00 a.m. and 5:30 p.m. Sights you will enjoy include the Navy fleet and the stunning Coronado Bay Bridge.

Orion Sailing Charters. 1380 Harbor Island Drive; (619) 574-7504; www.orion sailing.com. $$$. Guided sailing and whale-watching cruises.

San Diego–Coronado Ferry. 1050 North Harbor Drive; (619) 234-4111 or (800) 44-CRUISE (27847). Operates daily beginning at 9:00 a.m.; last trip 9:00 p.m. (later on Friday and Saturday). $. Every hour on the hour departs from San Diego's Broadway Pier and takes you to Coronado Landing Marketplace. Reservations not necessary. This is a super way to do Coronado for the day!

Hornblower Cruises and Events–San Diego. 1066 North Harbor Drive; (619) 686-8715; www.hornblower .com. $$$$. Reservations required for one- or two-hour cruises, brunch, and dinner/dancing excursions aboard these deluxe vessels.

San Diego Hall of Champions Sports Museum

In Balboa Park; (619) 234-2544; www.sdhoc.com. Open daily 10:00 a.m. to 4:30 p.m.; closed major holidays. $

Offers a fascinating peek into local sports history via photographs, memorabilia, videotapes, and audiotapes. You can call play-by-play action for San Diego Padres' Tony Gwynn and hall-of-fame star Ted Williams in the state-of-the-art media center, follow the evolution of the surfboard or soar with local skateboard legend Tony Hawk.

San Diego Air & Space Museum

In Balboa Park, 2001 Pan American Plaza; (619) 234-8291; www.aerospacemuseum.org. Open daily 10:00 a.m. to 4:00 p.m.; closed major holidays. $$; admission is free to all on fourth Tuesday of every month.

Check out the replica of Lindbergh's *Spirit of St. Louis* and an A-12 Blackbird. The hall of fame honors heroes of aviation and space flight including a up-close and personal view of NASA's Apollo 9 Command Module.

San Diego Model Railroad Museum

In Balboa Park in the Casa de Balboa Building; (619) 696-0199; www.sdmodelrailroadm .com. Open Tuesday through Friday and some holidays 11:00 a.m. to 4:00 p.m., Saturday and Sunday 11:00 a.m. to 5:00 p.m. $; admission is free to all on first Tuesday of the month.

Four scale-model railroad layouts detail the geography and development of the railroad industry in Southern California. Your kids will love the hands-on model railroad.

San Diego Museum of Art

In the center of Balboa Park; (619) 232-7931; www.sdmart.org. Open Tuesday through Sunday 10:00 a.m. to 4:30 p.m.; closed major holidays. $$

The lovely facility has a permanent collection of Italian Renaissance works, Spanish baroque Old Masters, and American, Asian, and Native American art and culture.

San Diego Museum of Photographic Art

1649 El Prado, in Balboa Park; (619) 239-5262; www.mopa.org. Open daily 10:00 a.m. to 5:00 p.m. $$; admission is free on second Tuesday of every month.

Devoted exclusively to the photographic arts. Year-round changing exhibitions display everything from fine-art photography to images from around the world.

San Diego Museum of Man

In Balboa Park, the group of buildings around the California Quadrangle; 1350 El Prado; (619) 239-2001; www.museumofman.org. Open daily 10:00 a.m. to 4:30 p.m.; closed major holidays. $$; admission is free on third Tuesday of the month.

These multifaceted exhibit halls explore the origins of humankind and feature the cultures of American Indians, ancient Egypt, Mexico, and Latin America. Special features on folk art, textiles, and early man.

San Diego Natural History Museum

East end of Balboa Park; (619) 232-3821; www.sdnhm.org. Open daily 9:30 a.m. to 5:30 p.m.; hours may be extended seasonally. $$; admission is free on first Tuesday of the month.

Houses both permanent and changing exhibits and displays detailing the plants, animals, and geology of San Diego County as well as Baja California. Be sure to call for current displays.

Diversity Dining

From ethnic takeout to historic hangouts to oceanfront glimmer, San Diego chefs use the region's freshest ingredients to create hearty and intriguing dishes. The county's estimated 6,400 restaurants offer everything from new taste sensations to traditional favorites and are attracting some of the nation's top culinary talents. You can sample the tastes of Thailand one evening and Mexico the next, and snack on such local favorites as fish tacos and smoothies in between. Best bet? Ask your hotel's front desk for nearby favorite dining spots or contact the San Diego Convention and Visitors Bureau (www.sandiego.org) for its list of restaurant members (more than 300 choices). Just a couple of our spots to consider: **Corvette Diner** in Hillcrest district near Balboa Park for meat loaf sandwiches and milk shakes (619-542-1476); the **Filippi's Pizza Grotto** downtown in Little Italy (family owned since 1950; 619-232-5094); and **Old Town Mexican Café** for the fresh tortillas and combo plates (619-297-4330).

Timken Museum of Art

1500 El Prado, in Balboa Park; (619) 239-5548; www.timkenmuseum.org. Open Tuesday through Saturday 10:00 a.m. to 4:30 p.m. and Sunday 1:30 to 4:30 p.m.; closed major holidays. Always free admission and tours.

This charming gallery contains Old Masters, eighteenth- and nineteenth-century American paintings, and Russian icons.

Botanical and Floral Gardens, Botanical Building

In Balboa Park; (619) 235-1100. Gardens are open year-round. Building is open 10:00 a.m. to 4:00 p.m. daily except Thursday. Free.

Revitalize yourself and give the kids some fresh air by heading into Balboa Park's magnificent display of botanical wonders. Included are more than 7,600 trees, 67 kinds of palms, and 2,200 rosebushes, plus desert cacti, lilies, ferns, orchids, bamboo, and other oxygen-rich flora. Tour the building (an old Santa Fe railroad station) for explanations of what you've just encountered.

Qualcomm Stadium

9449 Friars Road, in Mission Valley; (619) 641-3100; www.sandiego.gov/qualcomm.

Home to the National Football League's San Diego Chargers (619-280-2121 for schedules; www.chargers.com) and the San Diego State University Aztecs (619-283-SDSU; www .goaztecs.cstv.com).

This venue was the site of the Super Bowl in 1998 and 2003, and it hosts many other events and concerts during the year, including Poinsettia Bowl and Pacific Life Holiday Bowl. It is owned by the city of San Diego and has a seating capacity of 70,561.

PETCO Ballpark

Located downtown, within walking distance to hotels, shopping, and the waterfront; (888) MY-PADRES; www.padres.com.

Major League Baseball's San Diego Padres inaugurated the PETCO Ballpark in spring 2004. The 46,000-seat facility has spacious concourses, garden terraces, and state-of-the-art services and amenities. Ask about the new ninety-minute "Behind the Scenes" tour when the Padres are away. Call (619) 795-5011 for times, days, and fees. Reservations required.

Mission Bay Park

2688 East Mission Bay Drive, just minutes west from Mission Valley; (619) 276-8200 (phone for visitor center). Open 9:00 a.m. to dusk daily. Free.

The park is on a former mudflat transformed into a 4,600-acre aquatic playground by creative dredging, filling, and landscaping. You can easily worship outdoor recreation at its finest here: swimming, power boating, fishing, sailing, volleyball, softball, horseshoes, bicycling, roller-skating, kite flying, Frisbee tossing, and jogging—framed by 27 miles of beaches on Mission Bay and 17 miles of Pacific Ocean frontage. Spread throughout Mission Bay are great resort hotels and campgrounds. The Bahia Belle is an old-time stern-wheeler that plies the bay between the Bahia and Catamaran Hotels most evenings during the summer and weekends in the winter.

SeaWorld San Diego

1720 South Shores Road, on Mission Bay; (619) 226-3901 or (800) SEA-WORLD; www.seaworld .com. Open daily 10:00 a.m., earlier in the summer; closing hours change daily and seasonally. Be sure to call for current times. Parking is $10 per car. $$$$

For kids, this is probably the number one reason to visit San Diego. Opened in 1964, this celebrated 189-acre marine amusement park features trained killer whales, ponderous sea lions, playful otters, and lovable dolphins. You can take in five different shows and more than twenty educational exhibits, including the Penguin and Shark Encounters, containing the world's largest collection of these species. Don't miss Journey to Atlantis, a wet and wild thrill ride with a 60-foot plunge into a lake, and check out a 130,000-gallon Commerson's dolphin habitat. Also Caribbean Realm, just south of Dolphin Stadium, which includes the Calypso Bay Smokehouse restaurant and Pineapple Pete's Island Eats plus two retail stores—Splish Splash, a children's water gear and clothing store, and Caribbean Breeze gifts.

How about Forbidden Reef, an underwater cave with eels and bat rays, and the not-to-be-missed whale and dolphin Petting Pool? Of course, you've got to see Baby Shamu, only the sixth killer whale to be born in a zoo in a fantastic performance alongside other killer whales (www.shamu.com). Spring 2006 welcomed the debut of "Believe," a brand-new Shamu whale show in a greatly expanded and enhanced performance pool. You and the kids will scream with laughter at the crazy antics of Clyde and Seamore, the infamous sea lion duo. Try out the family adventure land, Shamu's Happy Harbor, where you get to crawl, climb, jump, and definitely get wet in a dozen or so play areas. In May 2008, a new two-acre Sesame Street-themed interactive play area opened with three kid-friendly rides:

SeaWorld **Special Programs**

For some unforgettable experiences, check out these special programs. You can share a meal with an orca family in Dine with Shamu—a scrumptious all-you-can-eat buffet with SeaWorld's biggest star. You will eat at a reserved table alongside the killer-whale habitat in an area restricted to trainers and animal-care specialists. Buffet breakfast or dinner includes a special just-for-kids menu.

For an amazing hour, take a public behind-the-scenes tour that brings you to areas you will not find on the SeaWorld map. Many of the tours are interactive, and each is a unique aquatic adventure. Offered daily, this one-hour tour gives you a glimpse at animal care, training, and rehabilitation. Group size is limited to twenty-five plus the educator/guide so you really get the "insider's view."

The Public Animal Spotlight Tour is a two-hour interactive tour with a chance to touch and feed bottlenose dolphins, feed moray eels and sea turtles, and touch sharks. This tour is offered Wednesday through Sunday year-round for an additional fee that is well worth the time and money.

Other specialized tours include Saving-a-Species Tour, Wild Arctic Experience, and Penguin Experience. Private tours can also be arranged as well as Trainer for a Day, sleepovers, and group day-camper programs. All are highly recommended as wonderful ways to enhance your family's up-close nature experience.

Elmo's Flying Fish, Abby's Sea Star Spin, and Oscar's Rocking Eel along with the musical production *Big Bird's Beach Party* at Pets Playhouse stadium, and the new movie *Sesame Street Presents Lights, Camera, Imagination! in 4-D* starring Elmo, Bert and Ernie, Cookie Monster, and Big Bird will showcase at the park's Mission Bay Theater.

Shipwreck Reef Cafe will handle any castaway's appetite (the best dining among twenty or so food options). The Sky Tower and the Bayside Skyride ($3 each or $5 for both) are great ways to see the park.

Belmont Park/Giant Dipper

3146 Mission Boulevard, Mission Bay; (619) 491-2988; www.giantdipper.com. Open every day, but hours vary with the season. Free admission to amusement park, but you pay as you go for your choice of rides and games.

Fun, fun, and more fun. Take a ride on the Giant Dipper, a completely restored and rowdy 2,600-foot-long wooden roller coaster, first put into service in 1925 (current cost is $5). Then take another dip in the Plunge, the world's largest indoor swimming pool. Pirate's Cove is an indoor playground designed for children ages two to twelve, accompanied by parents. The arcades and Virtual Reality Zone will send everyone for another loop.

Where to Stay

Omni Hotel San Diego, 675 L Street; (619) 231-6664; www.omnihotels.com. Opened in March 2004, this thirty-two-story luxury hotel with 511 rooms and suites is connected via sky bridge to the fab PETCO Ballpark, home of Major League Baseball's San Diego Padres. With an excellent location in the heart of the historic Gaslamp Quarter and across the street from the convention center, the hotel is a superb headquarters for enjoying the city's top sites and attractions, only minutes away. The San Diego Trolley stops in front, and the train station is 6 blocks away, so staying car-free is an option, too. (Moreover, the hotel is only eight minutes/4 miles from San Diego International Airport.) All accommodations have a choice of views of San Diego Bay, PETCO Ballpark, or the city; they are very attractively furnished with outstanding twenty-first-century amenities (and windows that open, unique for a high-rise, so you can catch the fresh ocean breezes). For dining, the hotel offers McCormick & Schmick's Restaurant, which serves forty varieties of fresh seafood, pastas, and salads in a casually elegant atmosphere; open for breakfast, lunch, and dinner. Morsel's espresso bar and gift shop has an assortment of delicious desserts and treats. The Terrace Grill offers great barbecue and poolside beverage service with a view of the bay. Be sure to ask about ballpark packages and other family discount specials—you will score a lodging home run for sure at this property. $$$$

Sommerset Suites Hotel, 606 West Washington Street (just west of Highway 163, near Balboa Park and San Diego Zoo); (619) 692-5200 or (800) 962-9665; www.sommersetsuites.com. Eighty one-bedroom suites with fully equipped kitchens. Complimentary continental breakfast and evening refreshments. Outdoor pool, spa, barbecue area. Very family-friendly environment; call for special rates and packages. $$$

Town & Country Resort Hotel, 500 Hotel Circle North, in Mission Valley; (619) 291-7131 or (800) 77-ATLAS; www.towncountry.corn. This thirty-two-acre resort has 1,000 newly redone rooms and suites of every motif and configuration to suit your family's particular needs. There are four swimming pools and spas, nine restaurants and lounges, an eighteen-hole golf course, tennis courts, and a shopping village. Best of all, kids stay **free,** and there are innumerable package plans that include tickets to nearby SeaWorld and the zoo. A venerable choice for your San Diego headquarters. $$$

For More Information

San Diego Convention and Visitors Bureau. 401 B Street, Suite 1400, 92101-4237; (619) 232-3101; www.sandiego.org.

Hotel Circle Drive and Mission Valley

Mission Valley is a suburban area of metro San Diego that is bisected by Interstates 8 (east-west) and 805 (north-south). **Fashion Valley Center** and **Mission Valley Center** are megamalls in this district that can provide you and your family with plenty of dining and entertainment options. They are conveniently located next to a big concentration of accommodations at Hotel Circle Drive, where you will find an abundant selection of family-friendly properties, such as the Comfort Inn & Suites at Hotel Circle (619-881-6800) and Doubletree Club Hotel (619-291-8790).

San Diego International Visitor Information Center. 10401/3 West Broadway, on the Embarcadero, corner of Harbor Drive and West Broadway; (619) 236-1212. Open 8:30 a.m. to 5:00 p.m. Monday through Saturday year-round. In the summer, open on Sunday from 11:00 a.m. to 5:00 p.m. Experienced, multilingual staff members are super helpful to all visitors, especially foreign travelers.

Chula Vista

Located in the southern tip of San Diego County, the suburb of Chula Vista, with a population of more than 201,000, offers an interesting variety of visitor attractions, all less than twenty minutes from downtown and twenty minutes to the Mexican border.

ARCO/U.S. Olympic Training Center

Eight miles east of I-805 at Telegraph Canyon Road and Wuente Road, 2800 Olympic Parkway; (619) 656-1500; www.usolympicteam.com. Free hourly tours are available daily from 10:00 a.m. to 3:00 p.m.; holidays excluded, varies seasonally.

This is the nation's first warm-weather, year-round, multisport Olympic training complex, which complements the U.S. Olympic Committee's other training centers at Colorado Springs, Colorado, and Lake Placid, New York. The 150-acre training site includes a fifty-lane archery range and support building; a six-bay boathouse and a 2,000-meter course for canoeing, kayaking, and rowing; a cycling course and support building; a synthetic surface field hockey pitch and support building; four regulation grass fields and support buildings for soccer; a four-court complex and support building for tennis; a 400-meter track and support building; and a separate, dedicated five-acre throwing area for field events. In the Copley Visitors Center, a short film captures the dedication and emotion involved with the Olympic movement. After the film, you'll be taken on a narrated tour of the 150-acre campus. Inspiring!

Knott's Soak City U.S.A.—San Diego

2052 Entertainment Center (next to the Coors Amphitheater); (619) 661-7373; www.knotts .com/soakcity/sd. Open daily Memorial through Labor Day; Saturday and Sunday only during May, September, and October. Hours of operation vary; be sure to call ahead on your preferred day to splash. $$$$

Thirty-two waterlogged acres packed with twenty-two of the most intense water rides imaginable and appointed with a 1950s San Diego surf theme. Body slides, tube slides, wave pools, beaches, and a kiddie play zone will supply your youth with a water wonderland filled with surprises. Food and snacks available on the premises.

Len Moore Skatepark Chula Vista (ages 6 and up)

1301 Oleander Avenue; east of I-805, between Telegraph Canyon and Orange Avenue; (619) 421-4011, ext. 12; www.cvskatepark.com.

This two-acre facility features a 55,000-square-foot concrete skatepark, 10,000-square-foot wood skatepark, lighting for night skating, fully stocked skate shop, shaded bleachers, and a snack bar. Open daily; hours vary by season. Call for session times.

For More Information

Chula Vista Chamber of Commerce. 233 Fourth Avenue, 91910; (619) 420-6603; www.chulavistachamber.org.

Chula Vista Convention and Visitors Bureau. 233 Fourth Avenue, 91910; (619) 426-2882. Open Monday through Friday 9:00 a.m. to 5:00 p.m. Visitor Information Center at 750 E Street, at the Bayfront Trolley Station off I-5; (619) 425-4444; www.chulavistaconvis.com. Friendly and knowledgeable bilingual staff is available to assist you at the visitor center seven days a week.

Coronado

Coronado (translated as Crown City) lies between San Diego Bay and the Pacific. Coronado Beach is recognized annually by the Travel Channel as the best family beach in North America. A vast expanse of white sand greets families toting umbrellas, sand toys, beach towels, and picnic coolers for an all-day stay. Recreational activities abound with paddleball, sandcastle building, kite flying, and volleyball. Many people call Coronado an "island," but it is actually a peninsula connected to the mainland on the south by a long, narrow sandbar, the Silver Strand that boasts a year-round population of 24,000. You will want to enter this picturesque city by way of the dramatic San Diego–Coronado Bay Bridge. This 2-mile expanse of graceful splendor dates from 1969. The Ferry Landing Marketplace has plenty of shopping and dining options to handle your family's needs if you come over by ferry (another pretty option, especially if you just plan on spending the day).

Bikes & Beyond

1201 First Street at the Coronado Ferry Landing; (619) 435-7180; www.hollandsbicycles.com. Rates vary; call for current hours and schedules.

Your family's source for rental bicycles, skates, and surreys in Coronado. A super way to explore Crown City. Another source is Bikes & Beyond's sibling, Holland's Bicycles, at 977 Orange Avenue (619-435-3153).

Where to Stay

Hotel Del Coronado, 1500 Orange Avenue; (619) 435-6611 or (800) 468-3533; www.hoteldel.com. "The Del," as the hotel is known here, has attracted the rich and famous, including thirteen U.S. presidents, since its opening in 1888. The turrets, tall cupolas, hand-carved wooden pillars, and Victorian filigrees of this stunning, magnificently restored 691-room National Historic Landmark resort have served as the backdrop for many movies and films. So much history has unfolded within the Del's walls that a cassette walking tour has been made available. For example, at its opening more than a century ago, it was the largest structure outside New York City to be electrically lighted, and the installation was supervised by Thomas Edison himself!

Today the Del offers a wide variety of accommodations to suit any family's taste and pays close attention to the needs of children. Tent City Kids' Camp allows children ages four to twelve to meet new friends, develop new skills, participate in beach fun, create crafts, and more. (For specific info and fees, call 619-522-8815.) Coast Club Teen Lounge is The Del's hot spot dedicated strictly to those ages twelve to seventeen. It features video games, pool, food and drinks, music, TVs, computers to check e-mail and send e-Postcards to friends back home, and the chance for teens to meet other people their own age. (Open during the summer and December holiday season.) The Del also offers teenagers tours and lessons in kayaking, surfing, and biking. For those stressed-out teens and the ones who love them, the Spa at The Del offers the Teen Spa Sampler and the Teen Break Package.

Food and beverage options abound and children's menus flourish. Choose from the formal main dining room, two restaurants, and a twenty-four-hour deli. The Del's beach provides great swimming and sunbathing, plus rental boats, windsurfers, and paddleboats. Just watch out for some of the smaller, original rooms, and you'll be in grand shape at this venerable place. World-renowned and definitely worth a visit! $$$$

Loews Coronado Bay Resort, 4000 Coronado Bay Road; (619) 424-4000 or (800) 815-6397; www.loewshotels.com. Located on a private, fifteen-acre peninsula named Crown Island, surrounded by water and astonishing views of the downtown San Diego skyline and marina. Five guest-room towers feature 438 very deluxe guest rooms with minibars and fax machines. There are three outdoor pools, whirlpools, and decks; five tennis courts; an exercise club; and a private eighty-slip marina with rentals galore—sailboats, paddleboats, Wave Runners, Jet Skis, and beach equipment.

Most important for your family is the award-winning program called the Commodore Kids Club, offering supervised educational and entertaining options for ages four to twelve provided by fully licensed caregivers. Offered seven days a week, activities change daily and include nature walks, sand-castle building, face painting, arts and crafts, and G-rated video screenings. Full-day, half-day, and evening programs are available. Families with more than one child get to send the second child at half price. Call for current rates.

Kids also enjoy the game room with pinball, video, and Ping-Pong. This program is a real winner. A new "Teen Education Package" called "My Super Suite Vacation" includes private surfing lessons on INT surfboards that are custom-designed for each teen to take home; two spa treatments in the resort's Teen Sea Spa Room, and a two-night stay in an executive suite for the family with teens enjoying a connecting double guest room of their own. We think your family will enjoy this resort enormously. Be sure to call for special holiday programs and value packages that combine SeaWorld and other attractions' tickets, too. A very helpful staff is ready and waiting for your family. Like the slogan says, "Loews Loves Kids," and it shows! $$$$

For More Information

Coronado Visitors Center. 1100 Orange Avenue, 92118; (619) 437-8788 or (800) 622-8300; www.coronado.ca.us or www.coronado visitorcenter.com.

La Jolla

Heading up the coast along Pacific Coast Highway 1 from Mission Bay and Pacific Beach will lead you directly into the tony suburb of La Jolla (say la-hoy-ya; it's Spanish for "the jewel"). This truly precious area is home of the University of California–San Diego (UCSD) and the distinguished Salk Institute for Biomedical Research. There is also some fabulous real estate along the beaches, coves, and caves, and trendy shopping and dining along downtown's Prospect Avenue, the Rodeo Drive of San Diego.

Birch Aquarium at Scripps Institution of Oceanography

2300 Expedition Way, off La Jolla Village Drive, on the campus of UCSD, overlooking La Jolla and the Pacific; (858) 534-3474; www.aquarium.ucsd.edu. Open daily 9:00 a.m. to 5:00 p.m. except Thanksgiving and Christmas. $$

These facilities are among the most prestigious world leaders in research and instruction. Inside the aquarium you can see more than 3,000 fish in thirty tanks, including a two-story, 70,000-gallon kelp forest with species from the waters of the West Coast, Mexico's

Go San Diego Card

There is so much to see and do in greater San Diego, you and your family may start feeling overwhelmed and wonder how to afford all the great attractions. Not to worry! Check out the Go San Diego Card—for one low price, you can get unlimited sightseeing with **free** general admission to more than forty-five area attractions; save more than $500 at shops and restaurants, plus get **free** gifts at certain places; and, to make it really simple, a full-color pocket guide-book to the city, with which you can plan your itinerary—all included in one low price. Visit the attractions at your own pace, without the hassle of buying separate tickets and paying separate admission fees. Here's how easy it is: First, purchase the Go San Diego Card in one-, two-, three-, five-, or seven-day increments. It is valid for that day and the number of consecutive calendar days that you have purchased. Second, go to a participating attraction, restau-rant, or shop. Third, present your Go San Diego Card at the ticket office/desk, and you'll be granted general admission or get the stated discount. The card becomes active the first time you use it.

You can buy a Go San Diego Card directly on its Web site, www.gosan diegocard.com, or if you're in San Diego, at a variety of outlets—most conve-niently at the International Visitor's Information Center, 1040 1/3 West Broad-way, at Harbor Drive (619-236-1212). This is an outstanding value and a highly recommended way for you and your family to save considerable time and money in greater San Diego.

Sea of Cortez, and the South Pacific. There is also a human-made interpretive tide pool. The innovative and interactive museum introduces the world's largest oceanographic exhibition, Exploring the Blue Planet. The bookshop has educational souvenirs and books for all ages on the science of the seas. This attraction strikes an educational counterpoint to the frenetic action of SeaWorld.

Museum of Contemporary Art, La Jolla

700 Prospect Street; (858) 454-3541; www.mcasd.org. Open 11:00 a.m. to 5:00 p.m. daily except Wednesday. Hours change seasonally. $$

Children can enjoy the outdoor sculpture garden and food court. Everyone will view outstanding examples of minimalist, conceptual, and California art in a beautiful setting.

For More Information

La Jolla Visitor Center. 7966 Herschel Avenue, Suite A, 92037; (619) 236-1212; www .lajollabythesea.com.

North County— Coastal Communities

Just north of La Jolla along the ocean, be sure to take the drive up Pacific Coast Highway 1/U.S. Highway 101 for a relaxing trip through some classic Southern California beach communities, inhabiting what the locals call North County. The charming seaside hamlets of **Solana Beach, Cardiff-by-the-Sea, Encinitas, Del Mar,** and **Leucadia** have miles of sandy beaches with rocky coves, cliffs above, and lots of friendly folks waiting to welcome you at the small shops, restaurants, and inns in these charming enclaves.

Torrey Pines State Beach and Reserve

12500 North Torrey Pines Road, San Diego; (858) 755-2063; http://www.torreypine.org/. Open daily 9:00 a.m. to dusk. $

This 2,000-acre beach/reserve stretches between La Jolla and Del Mar. Enjoy one of just two places in the world where the Torrey pine tree grows (the other is Santa Rosa Island, near Santa Barbara). A visitor center has interpretive displays, and there are miles of great hiking and nature trails. The beach below is a favorite for swimmers; the cliffs above are a popular take-off spot for hang gliders.

Del Mar Fairgrounds & Race Track

2260 Jimmy Durante Boulevard, Del Mar; (858) 755-1141; www.sdfair.com. $$

This is where "the turf meets the surf" with two attractions. The San Diego County Fair runs here June 15 through July 4. Then thoroughbreds are off and running July through September. The combined facility is a gorgeous, 350-acre historic site overlooking the Pacific. More than a hundred events are held here each year. Call for this year's schedule. At the Del Mar Thoroughbred Club (858-755-1141 or 858-793-5533; www.dmtc.com), races held July through September, dark Tuesday. Ages seventeen and younger are **free** but must be accompanied by a parent. Camp Del Mar (www.campdelmar.com) is open every race day for children ages five through twelve. Supervised recreational activities while parents are at the club.

Quail Botanical Gardens

230 Quail Gardens Drive, just east of I-5, Encinitas; (760) 436-3036; www.qbgardens.com. Open daily 9:00 a.m. to 5:00 p.m.; closed major holidays. $$; first Tuesday of every month is free.

The gardens contain one of the world's most diverse plant collections, including California natives, exotic tropicals, palms, and bamboo. This site was formerly owned by avid plant collector and naturalist Ruth Baird Larabee, who donated her thirty-acre estate to the public in 1957. The gardens are open for self-guided tours as well as a super chance to see the namesake resident quails in a natural bird refuge. When it opened to the public in 2003, the Seeds of Wonder became the West Coast's first interactive children's garden. It includes living topiaries and a grassy "rolling hill"—grass stains complimentary—as well as an exotic Baby Dinosaur Forest and sculpture and interactive nature-play areas. The garden hosts periodic special events, such as the "Fairy Festival" held in August 2008.

For More Information

Del Mar Regional Chamber of Commerce. 1104 Camino del Mar, 92014; (858) 755-4844; www.delmarchamber.org.

Encinitas Chamber of Commerce and Visitors Center. 859 Second Street; entrance on the corner of H and Second, 92024; (760) 753-6041 or (800) 953-6041; www.encinitaschamber.com.

Rancho Santa Fe

If you've had it with hype and just want to reeee-laaaax, the postcard-perfect Spanish colonial–style village of Rancho Santa Fe is known for its quiet, peaceful setting. Go 6 miles inland, amid magnificently fragrant eucalyptus trees. They were planted by the Santa Fe Railroad in hopes they would make great railroad ties—but the wood was too soft to even hold a spike! Today these trees provide a magnificent backdrop for the family-welcoming upscale village.

Hot-Air **Ballooning**

North County is famous for its hot-air balloon rides. Several companies offer sunrise and sunset flights that feature scenic views of the coastline, rolling hills, and reservoir-dotted valleys. Most companies fly year-round, weather permitting. Rides depart early in the morning or just before dusk and last about an hour. All pilots are FAA certified. Fares start around $135, but package and family plans are offered. Not advised for children age eight or younger. Companies offering rides include A Skysurfer Balloon Company (858-481-6800), California Dreamin' Balloon Adventures (800-373-3359), and Sky's the Limit (760-602-5060). Call for current prices and schedules.

Where to Eat and Stay

Inn at Rancho Santa Fe, 5951 Linea Del Cielo; (858) 756-1131 or (800) THE-INN-1; www.theinnatrsf.com. This is a classic family-owned and family-friendly inn. On the twenty-two manicured acres there are twenty-three cottages with eighty-nine individually styled accommodations, including many family suites—all set against a magnificent backdrop of eucalyptus trees and lush gardens. The entire clan can enjoy tennis, croquet on the front lawn, or a swim in the heated outdoor pool. The spa and the gym have your basic workout gear, and you can dine in the coffee shop, main dining room, or poolside. $$$$

Carlsbad

The picturesque beach community of Carlsbad (named for the famous Karlsbad spa in Europe) is home to many coves and the Batiquitos Lagoon, as well as golf resorts, bistros, inns, and antiques emporiums. LEGOLAND California, a must-do family experience, opened here in 1999 and put this city on the family fun map.

LEGOLAND California (ages 2 to 12 recommended)
1 Legoland Drive (just off I-5; exit Cannon Road or Palomar Airport Road and follow signs); (760) 918-LEGO or (877) LEGOLAND; www.legoland.com. Open daily; hours vary seasonally, call for times. $$$$

Since opening in 1999 to well-deserved and continued acclaim (Best Children's Park in the World award, *Amusement Today* magazine; one of the best theme parks in the world, Forbes.com), this 128-acre theme park features more than fifty interactive attractions and rides that are "kid powered," where kids push, pull, steer, pedal, squirt, climb, or build their way through a myriad of activities. In March 2008 a forgotten city, Land of Adventures, with four new rides and attractions debuted including Lost Kingdom Adventure, the park's first dark ride; Beetle Bouncers; Pharaoh's Revenge play area filled with catapulting foam balls; and Cargo Ace. Summer 2008 welcomed **Sea Life LEGOLAND®California,** a two-story, 36,000-square-foot aquarium featuring play zones, fun facts, quiz trails, and marine exhibits designed to educate children about life under the sea. In March 2007 Miniland welcomed **Miniland Las Vegas,** built out of more than two-million bricks. **Pirate Shores,** the park's largest expansion, opened in June 2006 with four water-based attractions: Splash Battle, Treasure Falls, Swabbies Deck, and the Soak-N-Sail giant play structures. Other activities and attractions to enjoy include Block of Fame (a gallery of famous busts made of LEGOs), Coastersaurus (a Jurassic-themed roller coaster), Dig Those Dinos (an interactive archaeological site), Fun Town Fire Academy (families can test their teamwork), LEGO TECHNIC Coaster, BIONICLE Blaster, Captain Cranky's Challenge, and Knights' Tournament. Be sure to schedule a day to really enjoy LEGOLAND at your young-sters' pace.

Biplane Rides and Aerial Dogfights/Barnstorming Adventures, Ltd.

6743 Montia Court; (760) 438-7680 or (800) SKY-LOOP; www.barnstorming.com. Open year-round during daylight hours. Call for prevailing winds, schedules, and fees. $$$$

Open-air flights in vintage cockpit biplanes and mock aerial combat in military-style air-craft could make for an unforgettable family adventure. All pilots are FAA certified, and safety comes first, followed by fun! Since 1994, this family-owned business based at Palomar Airport has been committed to preserving and sharing aviation history. Named one of the "101 Top Things to Do" by the Travel Channel. Tell "Tailspin Tom" and "Cash Register Kate" we sent you.

Flower Fields at Carlsbad Ranch

East of I-5 at Palomar Airport Road and Paseo del Norte; (760) 431-0352; www.theflower fields.com. Open March through May generally, during daylight hours. $$

The only commercial ranunculus (buttercups) field in the world that is open to the public. Wear comfortable walking shoes as you and the kids traipse through more than fifty acres of gently sloping hillside covered with a floral rainbow.

Where to Eat

Tip Top Meats & Deli, 6118 Paseo Del Norte, just off I-5 at Palomar Airport Road; (760) 438-2620. Open daily 6:00 a.m. to 8:00 p.m. Don't be fooled by the name—this local favorite offers the best value meals for miles around. A full breakfast starts at $4.49 (one egg, home-fried potatoes, toast, and ham, bacon, or sausage); burgers are $3.49; din-ners start at $5.98 (prime rib roast, potatoes, cabbage, sauerkraut, soup or salad, and roll is only $9.98). Just enter through the market and proceed to the deli area, where you'll place your order. Pick a seat in the dining room and wait for your number to be called—and dig in to a tip-top meal! Say hi to owner "Big John" Haedrich for us. $

Where to Stay

Four Seasons Resort Aviara, North San Diego, 7100 Four Seasons Point; Carlsbad; (760) 603-6800; www.fourseasons.com/ aviara. Located on a plateau overlooking the

Batiquitos Lagoon, a wildlife sanctuary, and the Pacific Ocean, this opulent 331-unit property opened in August 1997 and is rated five diamonds by AAA. The adjacent Aviara Golf Club, designed by Arnold Palmer, opened in 1991 and is ranked in the top ten nationally by golf magazines. Your family can take part in three- or four-day golf academies to see if you've got a Tiger Woods in the making!

Part of a 1,000-acre master planned community, the resort will remain more than 50 percent open space. In the Spanish colonial–style main hotel, standard guest rooms are large (average 540 square feet) and feature five-star amenities.

The best feature for families is undoubtedly the **free** Four Seasons' Kids for All Seasons program for ages four to twelve available year-round (summer daily, call for schedule rest of year). Upon check-in, kids receive a personal invitation to visit the center and take part in kite flying, swimming and beach games, lagoon nature trail exploration, table games, and other supervised activities. The main pool area is very family-friendly with its adjacent kiddie pool now since the addition of a separate "quiet pool" and whirlpool. Your kids will receive a welcome cookie-and-milk turn-down treat on their first night as well as children's menus in all the restaurants. Cribs, strollers, high chairs, and playpens are all complimentary, along with a selection of toys to check out. The California Bistro serves three meals daily and should be your choice for the family. The new Beach Butler service includes complimentary transportation to the beach (a five-minute trip) with all the necessary amenities: chairs, umbrella, towels, and blankets. $$$$

Grand Pacific Palisades Resort & Hotel, 5805 Armada Drive (exit Palomar Airport Road east from I-5); (760) 827-3200; www.grandpacificpalisades.com. Across the street from LEGOLAND, overlooking the Carlsbad Flower Fields and the Pacific Ocean, this should be your family's headquarters for affordable fun in North County. You can leave your car in the hotel parking lot and walk across the street to the side entrance to LEGOLAND. Return during the day for naps and lunch breaks—an ideal way to plan your stay. The contemporary Mediterranean architecture of the hotel encloses ninety spacious hotel rooms and 161 fully equipped vacation villas with full kitchens. A full-service restaurant, room service, two inviting outdoor heated pools and whirlpools, concierge services, a social activity director, a game room, and a fitness center—all staffed with friendly, helpful people—make this a grand place! $$$

For More Information

Carlsbad Convention and Visitors Bureau. 400 Carlsbad Village Drive, 92008; (760) 434-6093 or (800) 227-5722; www.visitcarlsbad.com.

Oceanside

Bustling Oceanside, at the mouth of the San Luis Rey Valley, is home base to the U.S. Marine Corps' Camp Pendleton (approximately 125,000 acres—the largest of all USMC amphibious training bases—www.pendleton.usmc.mil) and the ever-popular Municipal Pier—California's longest, which planks in at a whopping 1,942 feet. Check out the great fishing, seafood restaurants, and ice-cream shop located on this wooden wonder.

California Surf Museum

223 North Coast Highway; (760) 721-6876; www.surfmuseum.org. Open daily from noon to 4:00 p.m. (unless the surf is awesome!). Call for special events and seasonal operating hours. **Free** admission; donations appreciated, dudes.

Everything you wanted to know about surfing—for the novice to learn and for the experienced to enjoy. A real kicked-back gem since 1986.

Helgren's Sportfishing Center

315 Harbor Drive South; (760) 722-2133; www.helgrensportfishing.com. Open year-round; call for times and fees. $$$$

Take your choice of charter fishing vessels—half-day, full-day, and overnight trip options—as well as whale-watching cruises between December and February.

Mission San Luis Rey

4050 Mission Avenue, 4 miles east of town on Highway 76; (760) 757-3651; www.sanluisrey .org. Open Monday through Saturday 10:00 a.m. to 4:30 p.m. and Sunday noon to 4:30 p.m. $

This "king of the missions" is number eighteen in the famous chain of twenty-one California churches begun by Franciscan Father Junípero Serra. It's also the largest and has wooden double-dome construction. The museum houses exhibits relating to the colorful history of the area and includes artifacts from Native American, Spanish Mission, Mexican Secularization, and American Military periods. Picnicking facilities are available on the attractive grounds.

Where to Eat

101 Cafe, 631 South Coast Highway; (619) 722-5220; www.101cafe.net. Open daily from 6:30 a.m. to midnight. Established in 1928, this family diner serves up traditional American-style home-cooked meals. The hamburgers are the best, and the milk shakes a dream. There are historic photos all over the walls. Old-fashioned cash only (but an ATM is available on-site). $

Where to Stay

Oceanside Marina Suites, 2008 Harbor Drive North; (760) 722-1561 or (800) 252-2033; www.omihotel.com. Secluded at the tip of Oceanside's bustling harbor, the inn offers sixty-four one- and two-bedroom units with kitchens. Wonderful water views; many units have fireplaces and balconies. A pool, spa, and barbecue area are other highlights. This perfect family waterfront stopover is close to many North County attractions. $$

For More Information

Oceanside Chamber Tourism Information Center. 928 North Coast Highway, 92054; (760) 721-1101 or (800) 350-7873; www.oceansidechamber.com.

California Welcome Center Oceanside. 928 North Coast Highway, 92054; (760) 721-1101; www.visitcwc.com/destinations/oceanside/.

Escondido and Vicinity

Inland from the Pacific, the north-south I-5 and Interstate 15 run several miles apart, embracing gently rolling hillsides, forests, and streams that will make you pinch yourself and wonder, "Are we still in California?" In the center of it all is the city of Escondido. Other scenic communities scattered through inland North County include Fallbrook, San Marcos, Poway, Rancho Bernardo, La Costa, Vista, and Valley Center.

Heritage Walk and Escondido's Historical Society Museum

321 North Broadway in Grape Day Park, Escondido; (760) 743-8207; www.escondidohistorical society.org. Open Thursday through Saturday 1:00 to 4:00 p.m. **Free.**

Includes a Victorian house, Indian *metate* (grinding stones), a circa 1888 Santa Fe Railroad depot, Wagonworks Shop, and the Bandy Blacksmith Shop.

California Center for the Arts, Escondido

340 North Escondido Boulevard, Escondido; (760) 839-4138 or (800) 988-4253; www.art center.org. Call for current programs, schedules, and fees. $; children eleven and under **free.**

This center, located on a twelve-acre campus, has an art museum, a 1,500-seat concert hall, and art education programs for young people in a world-class facility. Also here is the Escondido Children's Museum (760-233-7755; www.escondidochildrensmuseum.org). The 4,500-square-foot space houses Wildlife Tree House, Bubble Tower, and River in the Garden exhibits. Varying hours/call for schedule.

Iceoplex

555 North Tulip, Escondido; (760) 489-5550; www.iceoplexescondido.com. Open daily at 8:30 a.m.; closing times vary. $$

This is a massive facility that boasts two Olympic-size ice-skating rinks, a fitness center, a spa, an Olympic lap pool, a Jacuzzi, a sauna, and a training room. You can chill out here after all your fun in the sun!

San Diego Wild Animal Park

15500 San Pasqual Valley Road, located 5 miles east of I-15 on Highway 78, just outside Escondido; (760) 747-8702 or (760) 234-6541; www.wildanimalpark.com. Open daily beginning at 9:00 a.m. Closing times vary by season. $$$$

On 2,100 acres of prime sanctuary land, and without a doubt the showpiece of North County, the park was designed originally as a breeding facility for the San Diego Zoo (its sister facility). You and your family will want to spend a full day here to see more than 3,000 wild animals roaming freely in settings that resemble their native habitats. The Journey into Africa Tour, aboard an open-air tram inspired by the legendary safari trains of Africa, replaces the historic Wgasa Bush Line Railway monorail tour after more than thirty years in service and brings you eye-level with white rhinoceros, Cape buffalo, Roosevelt's gazelles, and African crowned cranes. The *African Express* runs on eco-friendly biodiesel as it traverses the perimeter of the park's three expansive African field enclosures: Lion Camp, Heart of Africa, and Nairobi Village.

You will see large herds of antelopes, gazelles, deer, rhinos, and exotic sheep and goats. Flocks of flamingos, pelicans, cranes, geese, ducks, herons, ostriches, vultures, and storks live in the big enclosures as well. Even the single-species exhibits—herds of African and Asian elephants, families of gorillas and chimpanzees—are large and natural, such as a one-acre lion habitat. There is also DINOS, a life-size robotic dinosaur display and the bird show "Frequent Flyers."

The seventeen-acre Nairobi Village holds most of the visitor facilities, including restaurants, gift shops, and picnic areas. Plan to attend the wild animal show and elephant demonstrations held here. And make some new friends in the petting kraal.

The Kilimanjaro Hiking Trail is a 1.75-mile walking safari where you can see rhinos, tigers, elephants, cheetahs, and giraffes up close and personal. Special Photo Caravan Safari Tours take you right into the middle of the habitats in a large, open-air truck for an additional fee. We cannot recommend this activity highly enough. The chance to pet a rhino or feed a giraffe as it bends over your head is a thrill of a lifetime. Other special experience options include the Cheetah Run Safari, Sleepovers, VIP Tours, Cats & Carnivores Tour, Savanna Safari, and the Vets Center Tour We really were impressed and amazed here. Do not miss this!

Kit Carson Park/Queen Califia's Magical Circle

3333 Bear Valley Parkway, Escondido; (760) 839-4691; www.queencalifia.org or www.ci .escondido.ca.us/glance/parks/kitcarson/. Open from sunrise to sunset daily. Free.

The park was named after Christopher "Kit" Carson, the famous scout who guided Capt. John C. Fremont over the Sierra Nevada during an exploration expedition. This large regional day-use park features 100 developed acres and 185 undeveloped acres, beautiful walking/hiking trails, ball fields, lighted tennis courts, soccer fields, 3,000-seat outdoor amphitheater, three ponds, tot lot/playground, shaded picnic areas with tables/barbecues, Sports Center complex with pro shop, 20,000-square-foot skate park, two full-size roller hockey arenas, and one full-size and one mini soccer arena.

Opened in October 2003, Queen Califia's Magical Circle in the Iris Sankey Arboretum is the only American sculpture garden created by the renowned French-American artist Niki de Saint Phalle. The garden's outside diameter measures 120 feet and is encircled by an undulating wall across which slither large, playful serpents decorated in colorfully patterned mosaics. The Snake Wall has one entrance into the garden—a mazelike passageway whose walls and floor are also decorated in bold patterns of black, white, and mirrored tiles. The garden takes its name from the legendary black Amazon queen, Califia, who was believed to rule a terrestrial island paradise of gold and riches. Be sure to include a visit to this amazing, unique structure to indulge your family's magical senses.

The Wave Waterpark

161 Recreation Drive off Broadway, Vista, 7 miles inland on Highway 78; (760) 940-WAVE; www.thewavewaterpark.com. Open May through September, 10:30 a.m. to 5:30 p.m. $$$

The state-of-the-art wave maker is called Flow Rider, and your family's dudes can body surf all day long and never have to wait for that perfect wave—because they're all perfect! Four wild water slides, an underwater playground, an Olympic-size pool, and a picnic area make this inland water spot a great experience. It's a great value, too.

San Pasqual Battlefield State Historic Park and Museum

15808 San Pasqual Valley Road, Escondido; (760) 737-2201; www.parks.ca.gov/?page_id=655. Open Friday through Sunday 10:00 a.m. to 5:00 p.m. Free.

On October 21, 2007, the Witch Creek Fire burned through the area. The museum building survived the fire, but there was significant damage to the park infrastructure, including utilities, fencing, and footbridge. It reopened in summer 2008. The museum honors those who participated in the 1846 San Pasqual Battle during the Mexican-American War. See videos and exhibits regarding that historic time.

Antique Gas and Steam Engine Museum

2040 North Santa Fe Avenue, Vista; (760) 941-1791 or (800) 5-TRACTOR; www.agsem.com. Open daily from 10:00 a.m. to 4:00 p.m. $; children five and under free.

Weekend threshing bees in June and October are really fun! Our kids were impressed with the blacksmith. Catch a bit of history at the museum. Forty acres of turn-of-the-last-century farming equipment, all maintained in working order. Kids can see actual corn, wheat, and oat crops harvested from the field and into the kitchen—what a concept!

Where to Eat

Bates Nut Farm, 15954 Woods Valley Road, 3 miles east of Valley Center; (760) 749-3333; www.batesnutfarm.biz. Open daily 9:00 a.m. to 5:00 p.m. This is a family favorite because of its free petting zoo, shady picnic grounds, fresh produce, and terrifically tasty array of fruits, nuts, and candy. There are arts and crafts fairs each April and November; pumpkins predominate in October, and fir trees in December. $

Where to Stay

Welk Resort, Museum, and Dinner Theatre, 8860 Lawrence Welk Drive, 7 miles north of Escondido off I-15; (760) 749-3000 or (800) 932-9355; www.welksandiego.com. This 1,000-acre hideaway has 146 one- and two-bedroom suites (all with kitchenettes or full kitchens), on-site golf course, tennis, five swimming pools, spa, new Canyon Grille Restaurant, and Boulder Springs Water Park & Club House. Museum (**free** admission) opens daily at 10:00 a.m.; closing times vary. Dinner-theater performances offer musical variety for the whole family. Call for times, programs, and ticket prices. Not just for Grandma and Grandpa, with their memories of the legendary band leader, it's a great place for that multigenerational reunion. (But the suites are on three floors with no elevators, so if you don't want the extra steps, be sure to ask for the ground floor!) $$$$

For More Information

San Diego North Convention and Visitors Bureau. 360 North Escondido Boulevard, Escondido 92025-1899; (760) 745-4741 or (800) 848-3336; www.sandiegonorth.com.

Temecula Valley

The town of Temecula was founded in 1882 and served as an important stop on the Butterfield Stagecoach Route between San Bernardino and San Diego. The name Temecula means "sun shining through the sea mist," in Luiseno tribal lore. Today it is a fast-growing community nestled between San Diego and Riverside Counties with some award-winning vineyards, more than a dozen wineries, horse ranches, seven golf courses, harvest festivals, and antiques shops.

Old Town Temecula

Front Street between Moreno Road and Third Street. Open daily, hours vary. Old Town Visitor Center is located at 28464 Old Town Front Street; www.oldtowntemecula.com.

Get a walking-tour map and visit the Welty Building, jail, First National Bank, and G. Machado's store. Many of these historic buildings are antiques malls now, sure to delight shoppers. But there's no predicting how long they will grab your kids' attention (before they start acting like the proverbial bull in a china shop). Probably a half hour will do it.

Mission San Antonio de Pala Asistencia

Pala Mission Road, north of Highway 76, Pala; (760) 742-1600. Open Tuesday through Sunday 10:00 a.m. to 3:00 p.m. $

A branch of the Mission San Luis Rey, it was built in 1816 as part of an inland chain of missions that provided assistance to the main ones. The chapel, gardens, and mineral room have all been restored. Very quaint, with a still-active parish.

Where to Eat and Stay

Pala Mesa Resort, 2001 Old Highway 395, off I-15, Fallbrook; (760) 728-5881 or (800) 722-4700; www.palamesa.com. This newly renovated enclave on 270 acres is ideal for families, with its 133 connecting rooms, views of rolling hills, eighteen-hole golf course, and irresistible family-size swimming pool. You'll find plenty of outdoor recreation, including horseshoes, croquet, volleyball, tennis, badminton, a whirlpool, and a spa. AquaTerra restaurant is open 6:00 a.m. to 2:00 p.m. and 5:30 to 10:00 p.m. and has a nice golf-course view. The early California decor will make you appreciate the reasonably priced children's menu even more. $$$$

Temecula Creek Inn, 44501 Rainbow Canyon Road, Temecula; (909) 694-1000 or (800) 962-7335; www.temeculacreek inn.com. Opened in 1969 and beautifully enhanced in 2008, with 130 deluxe rooms and suites overlooking lush grounds that feature Native American art. Golf is king and queen here, with twenty-seven holes (rated four stars by *Golf Digest*); plus tennis, swimming pools, fitness studio, Temet Grill. Excellent packages for families. $$$$

Warner Springs Ranch, 31652 Highway 79, Box 10, Warner Springs; (760) 782-4200; www.warnersprings.com. With 25,000 acres nestled in the foothills of Palomar Mountain, Warner Springs Ranch offers plenty of room to roam. Stay in one of the 240 cozy bungalows (most with fireplaces); no phones or TVs. Miles of scenic walking, horseback riding, and hiking trails. Three pools (one is heated with hot spring water), eighteen-hole championship golf course, basic health spa, plus a private airport and glider school. High marks for the equestrian program, which is very kid-friendly (kids eight and older on trail rides; ages six and older for riding lessons in the arena; pony rides/animal-care sessions for really young children). The ranch offers a variety of stuff designed specifically for kids: arts and crafts, nature walks, movie nights, a game room, and more. There are no streetlights, so bring a flashlight here! Outstanding activities schedule means your kids will never say they're bored! $$$$

For More Information

Temecula Valley Chamber of Commerce. 26790 Ynez Court, Temecula 92591; (951) 676-5090 or (866) 676-5090; www .temeculacvb.com or www.temecula.org.

The Mountains (Back Country)

Don't miss the eastern portion of San Diego County, affectionately known by locals as the Back Country. Bisected by three main roads—Highways 76, 78, and 79—the Back Country offers mountain peaks rising more than 6,000 feet, dazzling foliage in fall, snowfalls in winter (and sometimes even in April!), and desert flora year-round. This land of contrasts has fabulous hiking, biking, camping, and fishing options for your active times and plenty of bucolic beauty for your off-tour hours.

Palomar Mountain Observatory and State Park

From Oceanside, off Highway 76 (about 11 miles inland on County Road S6); (760) 742-2119; www.astro.caltech.edu/palomarnew. Open daily 9:00 a.m. to 4:00 p.m. Free. **Self-guided tours.**

For a grand perspective, ascend Mount Palomar (elevation 6,140 feet) to the observatory. Inside this striking white-domed structure, you'll find one of the world's largest scientific instruments—the 200-inch Hale Telescope You and the kids can watch its inner workings and see a video at the museum nearby describing all the functions of this scientific wonder. Along with the observatory, enjoy the completely uncrowded state park (760-742-3462 for general information or www.parks.ca.gov/default.asp?page_id=637), with wildlife, fishing, camping, and hiking trails. Coniferous forests cover much of the 1,862 acres, in contrast to the dry lowlands surrounding the mountain.

For More Information

San Diego East Visitors Bureau. Viejas Outlet Shopping Center, 5005 Willows Road, Suite 208, Alpine 91901; (619) 445-0180 or (800) 463-0668; www.visitsandiegoeast.com.

Julian and Vicinity

For a piece of living history, continue toward the interior of North County along Highway 78, and you'll arrive at Julian. In the hills only 60 miles inland from Oceanside, Julian lies in the heart of the Cleveland National Forest. Beautiful downtown Julian looks much as it did a century ago. It was founded in 1870 by settlers Drew Bailey and his cousin Mike Julian, hence the name. A gold strike yielding nearly $5 million made the town of Julian famous back in the 1870s. When the gold rush ended, apples became the cash crop of choice. Now Julian is famous for hillside acres of apple orchards (Julian is known as Southern California's apple capital) and beautiful fields of spring wildflowers. The 2-block-long Main Street and surrounding area has everything you'll want within easy walking distance. Yes, you are still in Southern California—just an early-1900s version!

Seeing Julian in Slow Motion

Our favorite way to see Julian is by way of Country Carriages (760-765-1471), located right downtown on Main Street. To get your bearings on the area, begin with a ride on a horse-drawn carriage, all hitched up and ready to go. A thirty-minute clop-clop trip around town costs $30 per couple with two children—worth it for the history lesson alone. After your buggy ride, stay in the old-fashioned mood with an ice-cream treat at Ye Olde Soda Fountain/ Miner's Diner (760-765-3753) at the Julian Drug Store. Kids of all ages love the chance to sit on the old-fashioned stools and see how such classics as an egg cream or black cow are made by hand (and you can grab breakfast and lunch here, too).

Eagle Mining Company

North end of C Street, downtown; (760) 765-0036. Open daily 10:00 a.m. to 3:00 p.m., weather permitting. $$

Guided tours through this old gold mine will show you how those shiny, precious flakes were extracted from Mother Earth. A fascinating journey into the mountainside for the entire family.

Cuyamaca Rancho State Park

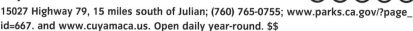

15027 Highway 79, 15 miles south of Julian; (760) 765-0755; www.parks.ca.gov/?page_id=667. and www.cuyamaca.us. Open daily year-round. $$

Twenty-six thousand acres of beautiful terrain include pine, oak, and cedar trees; meadows; lakes; streams; and the Green Valley waterfall. Explore via 100 miles of trails for mountain biking, hiking, and horseback riding. You can see more than a hundred species of birds in the area, or perhaps even a mule deer or coyote. Lake Cuyamaca, operated by the Helix Water District, is 2 miles north of Paso Picacho campground and offers boating and fishing. Interpretive programs are offered during the summer season. The park has a visitor center, gift shop, and a museum depicting the gold rush days at the Stonewall Mine during its 1886–91 peak. We love just going for a simple picnic.

Mission Santa Ysabel Asistencia

23013 Highway 79, Santa Ysabel; (760) 765-0810. Open daily 7:00 a.m. to dusk. Free.

You can take a self-guided tour of this charming satellite mission built in 1818. There is also an Indian burial ground and museum. It's a pleasant stopover on your way to Julian.

Where to Eat

Dudley's Bakery and Snack Bar, on Highway 78 in downtown Santa Ysabel; (760) 765-0488; www.dudleysbakery.com. Open Wednesday through Sunday; hours vary seasonally. Here you will find an incredible selection of seventeen famous breads, plus cookies, pies, and yummy pastries since 1963. This is a great place to have breakfast or lunch with your family and pick up treats for later. Don't miss this place. It's usually jammed, so you won't be able to! $

The Julian Grille, 2224 Main Street; (760) 765-0173. Housed in a homey cottage, the restaurant serves lunch daily and dinner Tuesday through Saturday. The menu features steaks, pasta, and seafood your family will savor. $$

Where to Stay

Pine Hills Lodge, 2960 La Posada Way, Julian; (760) 765-1100; www.pinehillslodge .com. A variety of rustic and very nicely refurbished accommodations are offered in sixteen lodge and cabin units at reasonable rates. Brunch is served every Sunday on the 5 Cedars Deck, and The Pub is open for libations on the weekends. It's a simple place for your backcountry family retreat. $$

For More Information

Julian Chamber of Commerce. 2129 Main Street, 92036; (760) 765-1857; www.julianca .com.

Borrego Springs

This peaceful resort community is located inside the Anza-Borrego Desert State Park and has a wide variety of lodging, camping, dining, golf, and recreation options. The community hosts a Grapefruit Festival in April. The Borrego Days Festival in October includes a parade and an arts and crafts fair to welcome back snowbirds for the warm winter season. We think the best time to visit the area is during the spring, when desert wildflowers are in magnificent bloom.

Anza-Borrego Desert State Park

Approximately two hours east of downtown San Diego, just west of County Road S22 and surrounding the quaint town of Borrego Springs. The visitor center is located at 200 Palm Canyon Drive; (760) 767-4205 for general information or (760) 767-4684 for recorded wildflower information; www.parks.ca.gov/?page_id=638. Open daily October through May 9:00 a.m. to 5:00 p.m.; rest of year open only on Saturday and Sunday. Camping fees vary, and reservations are strongly suggested. $

This is the biggest state park in California, with 600,000 acres of wildly rugged mountains (highest elevation 6,000 feet) and desert (elevation 40 feet), along with flora, fauna, and fossils dating back 540 million years. You will see mesquite, yucca, and smoke trees; cacti; and thousands of native plants and flowers, as well as the chance to see roadrunner, golden eagles, kit foxes, mule deer, and bighorn sheep as well as iguanas, chuckwallas, and the red diamond rattlesnake.

Start your visit at the magnificent 7,000-square-foot visitor center, built into the hillside, with exhibits, maps, natural history books, a twenty-minute video presentation, and volunteers who are eager to help your family plan your desert experience. There are nature walks, campfire programs, fossil programs, and guided hikes to choose from.

The park is geared for off-road travel and exploration. The most dramatic and popular attraction is the spring wildflowers. Our favorite hikes include the Borrego Palm Canyon Nature Trail, a gentle 3-mile round-trip, as well as the Pygmy Trail, a 1-mile round-trip that leads to fifty short palm trees. Among the park's many other points of interest: the Box Canyon Historical Monument, Coyote Canyon, the Culp Valley Overlook, the

Crossing the Border into Mexico at Tijuana

Fifteen miles south of downtown San Diego is the border town of San Ysidro, California, the U.S. gateway to Tijuana, Baja California, and the rest of Mexico. San Ysidro, with its largely Hispanic population, provides services to American travelers bound for Baja as well as Mexican nationals leaving and entering California. This highly commercialized sector has signs in both English and Spanish. San Ysidro Boulevard leads directly to the border crossing. It's filled with Mexican-style stores, eateries, auto insurance dealers, pawn shops, and money-exchange houses. (Even though the U.S. dollar is widely accepted in Tijuana, you will need pesos farther into Mexico.) Keep in mind that Tijuana is the world's busiest port of entry, with more than 37 million border crossings each year. The city itself is bursting with more than 2.5 million people in a semi-developed country with rapidly changing economics and politics.

You can cross the border on foot (we recommend you leave your car in one of the secured parking lots) or by car (not recommended for day trips since you need to purchase Mexican auto insurance). The San Diego Trolley (Blue Line) from downtown provides the easiest access since it terminates at the San Ysidro border crossing. The cost is only $3 each way (phone 619-234-1060 for schedules). I-5 and I-15 also terminate at the border, along with many of the amenities we take for granted.

Tijuana is a duty-free zone, which makes the city very popular for bargain shoppers seeking hand-crafted jewelry, pottery, and leather products. U.S. residents may return home with up to $800 worth of merchandise, including one liter of alcoholic beverages, 100 cigars, and 200 cigarettes (providing the person is at least twenty-one). Some merchandise, particularly fruits and vegetables, is not allowed into the United States. Tijuana's diverse shopping, dining, and entertainment options are not necessarily geared for everyone in your family, but the city does offer a sampling of cultural diversity and exposure to a bustling Mexican border town. For specific identification requirements (proof of citizenship, passports, driver's licenses, insurance), please call the U.S. Department of State at (888) 407-4747 or visit www.travel.state.gov.

Elephant Tree Discovery Trail, the Mason Valley Cactus Garden, and the Vallecita Stage-coach Station.

San Diego County, with its rich Spanish and Mexican heritage and American spirit, is a world-class destination with an ideal climate, fantastic natural wonders, and enough excitement to create a wonderfully satisfying family adventure. Adios!

Where to Eat and Stay

Borrego Ranch Resort & Spa, 3845 Yaqui Pass Road, Borrego Springs; (760) 767-5323 or (800) 824-1884; www.borregoranch.com. Any of the nineteen two- or three-bedroom casitas (homes) will have you and your family feeling totally relaxed within hours at this forty-two-acre resort. Each bedroom has its own bath (such an advantage), and some casitas even have a private pool; or choose from one of the forty-four newly revitalized deluxe poolside rooms, each with a service bar, sitting area with fireplace, marble bath, and private patio or balcony. This historic desert resort started in 1937 and is renowned as a haven of rest and tranquility. It is rated four stars by Mobil and four diamonds by AAA. You can't go wrong choosing from any of the seventy-seven accommodations, especially in the summer value season. On the property, you'll find an eighteen-hole Tom Fazio Signature Golf course, five heated pools, whirlpools, and six lighted tennis courts. The restaurant serves all three meals daily, surrounded by beautiful views and early

California decor. It's a great family-destination getaway. $$$$

For More Information

Borrego Springs Chamber of Commerce and Visitors Bureau. 786 Palm Canyon Drive, P.O. Box 420, Borrego Springs 92004; (760) 767-5555 or (800) 559-5524; www.borregosprings.org.

Tijuana (Baja California, Mexico) Tourism Bureau. P.O. Box 434523, San Diego 92143-4523; (888) 775-2417 or (800) 025-0888; www.seetijuana.com. You can call the office in Mexico direct by dialing 011-52-66/84-05-37.

Tijuana Convention & Visitors Bureau. Main Office: Avenida Paseo de los Heroes 9365-201; (664) 684-0537; www.tijuanaonline.org. Operates visitor information centers with English-speaking personnel at: Pedestrian Border Crossing, right across the bridge (664-607-3097) and Av. Revolución between Third and Fourth Streets (664-685-2210).

Annual Events

The Central Coast

The Central Coast covers a lot of wonderful territory, but your Southern California family fun has only just begun! These events are subject to change without notice. Please call ahead.

JANUARY

Winter Bird Festival—Morro Bay
(805) 772-4467 or (800) 231-0592
Guided tours of estuary and surrounding areas; plentiful bird-watching. **Free.**

FEBRUARY

Whale Celebration—Ventura
(805) 644-0169
Celebrate the annual gray whale migration with music and entertainment, environmental booths, and touch tanks in Ventura Harbor Village. **Free.**

International Film Festival—Santa Barbara
(805) 963-0023
Premieres and screenings of independent U.S. and international films; gala opening, celebrity awards, panels, and seminars by film professionals. Admission fees vary.

Celebration of the Whales—Oxnard
(805) 385-7545 or (800) 269-6273
Weekend celebration highlights gray whale migration; full-day trips, arts and crafts, and photo exhibit. **Free.**

MARCH

Taste of Solvang—Solvang
(805) 688-6144 or (800) 458-6765

This annual food and wine festival features a dessert reception showcase, walking smorgasbords, wine tasting room walking tour, and entertainment. Fees vary.

APRIL

Ventura County Food and Wine Festival—Oxnard
(805) 985-4852

Waterfront festival featuring fine foods from local restaurants accompanied by musical entertainment. Fees vary.

I Madonnari Italian Street Painting Festival—San Luis Obispo
(805) 781-2777

Event features sidewalk and street pastel creations. **Free.**

Children's Day in the Plaza—San Luis Obispo
(805) 781-2777

More than forty booths featuring spin art, water toys, face painting, and a petting zoo; singers, dancers, clowns, and jugglers. **Free.**

Presidio Day—Santa Barbara
(805) 966-1279

Celebration of early California arts, crafts, and music at historic 1782 Presidio Park. **Free.**

MAY

Garden Festival—San Luis Obispo
(805) 781-2777

Floral displays and sale at judges' show with speakers, exhibits, demonstrations, children's activities, music, and commercial and gardening booths. **Free.**

Annual California Strawberry Festival—Oxnard
(805) 385-7578

Strawberry foods, contests, music, and arts and crafts.

I Madonnari Street Painting Festival—Santa Barbara
(805) 569-3873

More than 200 local artists and children create chalk paintings in front of the Old Mission, Italian market and entertainment. **Free.**

JUNE

Summer Solstice Celebration—Santa Barbara
(805) 965-3396

See complete description in Central Coast chapter. **Free.**

Seafest—Ventura
(805) 644-0169

Celebrate the beginning of summer with entertainment booths, environmental instruction, a chowder cook-off, and a children's harbor land and show.

Elks Rodeo and Parade—Santa Maria
(805) 922-6006

Calf roping, bull riding, bronco riding, steer wrestling, and barrel racing.

JULY

Fireworks by the Sea—Oxnard
(805) 385-7545 or (800) 269-6273

Family-oriented daytime activities (arts and crafts, entertainment, and more), concluding with a fireworks display over the water. **Free.**

Fourth of July Celebration—Ventura
(800) 333-2989

Parade, street fair with 8 blocks of arts and crafts, food, and entertainment; fireworks in the evening. **Free.**

Santa Barbara County Fair—Santa Maria
(805) 925-8824

Country fair includes carnival, produce, livestock, and western music.

AUGUST

Olde Towne Fair—Lompoc
(805) 736-4567 or (800) 240-0999

Celebrate Lompoc's century-plus history with children's events, live music and entertainment, and an arts and crafts fair. **Free.**

California Mid-State Fair—Paso Robles
(805) 239-0655 or (800) 909-FAIR

The Central Coast fair includes five stages of entertainment featuring top names daily, PRCA rodeo, Destruction Derby, animal exhibits, arts and crafts, a working farm, wine tasting, pig races, and nightly dancing. Admission fees vary.

Annual Salsa Festival—Oxnard
(805) 483-4542

Salsa-making contest, 5K run, arts and crafts, dancing, music, and a carnival for children. **Free.**

Old Spanish Days (Fiesta)—Santa Barbara
(805) 962-8101

See complete description in Central Coast chapter. Free.

Ventura County Fair—Ventura
(805) 648-3376 or (800) 333-2989

Traditional county fair features top-name entertainment, exhibits, livestock, motor sports, rodeo, food, and fireworks. Admission fees vary.

SEPTEMBER

Taste of the Town—Santa Barbara
(805) 892-5556

More than eighty local restaurants and wineries provide tastes of their best fare in the beautiful Riveria Research Park overlooking the city. Always held the first Sunday after Labor Day as a benefit for the local branch of the Arthritis Foundation. Ticket prices vary.

Simi Valley Days—Simi Valley
(805) 581-4280

Fair features a carnival, hoedown, barn dance, horse show, parade, 5K and 10K runs, food, and entertainment. Admission fees vary.

Danish Days—Solvang
(805) 688-6636 or (800) 468-6765

Annual celebration of Solvang's rich Danish heritage features Danish folk dancing, music, food, parade, and entertainment. Free.

California Beach Festival—Ventura
(805) 654-7830 or (800) 333-2989

Three stages of entertainment, food, a surfing contest, and beach volleyball. Free.

OCTOBER

California Avocado Festival—Carpinteria
(805) 684-0038

Annual avocado celebration includes food, arts and crafts, music, and a flower show. Free.

Lemon Festival—Goleta
(805) 967-4618

Family event featuring a lemon pie–eating contest, food, arts and crafts show, children's activities, farmers' market, and entertainment. Free.

NOVEMBER

Holiday Walk and Light the Downtown—Paso Robles
(805) 238-4103

Lighted trees, candlelight caroling, farmers' market, and Santa and Mrs. Claus. Free.

DECEMBER

Julefest—Solvang
(805) 688-6144

Monthlong Danish Village celebration features thousands of twinkling lights, carolers around town, tree lighting ceremony, parade, Santa Lucia Pageant and Nativity Pageant, open houses, and concerts. **Free.**

Holiday Parade—San Luis Obispo
(805) 541-0286

Holiday celebration includes floats, marching bands, youth organizations, and Santa Claus. **Free.**

Ventura Harbor Parade of Lights—Ventura
(805) 644-0169 or (800) 333-2989

Colorful parade of decorated lighted boats on Ventura Harbor. **Free.**

Christmas Lite Parade—Paso Robles
(805) 238-4101

Christmas parade includes youth organization, merchant floats, bands, and Santa Claus. **Free.**

Holiday Boat Parade of Lights—Oxnard
(805) 389-9495 or (800) 269-6273

Lighted boat parade in the Channel Islands Harbor, holiday activities, and entertainment. **Free.**

Greater Los Angeles

The following list of Greater Los Angeles–area events is subject to change without notice. Please always call ahead to verify.

JANUARY

Tournament of Roses Parade—Pasadena
(626) 449-4100

World-class parade of flowers features music and fantasy. The annual Rose Bowl collegiate football game follows.

Dr. Martin Luther King Day Parade and Festival—Long Beach
(562) 570-6816

Parade, entertainment, and celebrations. **Free.**

Martin Luther King Jr. Celebration—Santa Monica
(310) 434-4209

Interfaith celebrations with music, dramatic readings, and inspirational messages. **Free.**

FEBRUARY

Golden Dragon Parade—Los Angeles
(213) 617-0396

Chinese New Year parade. Colorful floats, multicultural performances, arts and crafts.
Free.

APRIL

***Los Angeles Times* Festival of Books—Los Angeles**
(213) 237-5000; www.latimes.com

More than 800 exhibitors and 600 authors, speakers, and celebrity presentations, plus a giant children's area, all take over the UCLA campus for the weekend. For the love of reading, don't miss this! **Free.**

Toyota Grand Prix—Long Beach
(562) 436-3645 or (800) 4LB-STAY

International field of world-class drivers and high-performance racecars negotiate the tight turns of the city in heated wheel-to-wheel competition.

Pasadena Spring Art Show—Pasadena
(626) 795-9311

Fine arts and crafts, children's amusement area, international food court. **Free.**

MAY

Cinco de Mayo—Los Angeles
(213) 485-6855

Celebrate Mexico's 1862 victory over French forces in Pueblo, Mexico, with popular and traditional music, cultural presentations, dancing, and ethnic cuisine. **Free.**

Old Pasadena Summer Fest—Pasadena
(626) 797-6803

Festival includes Taste of Pasadena, arts and crafts, children's activities, jazz festival, and entertainment. **Free.**

JUNE

San Fernando Valley Fair—Burbank
(818) 557-1600

Live entertainment, rodeo, agricultural education, competitive exhibits, a carnival, arts and crafts, and an international food court.

Theater and Arts Festival—North Hollywood
(818) 508-5115 or (818) 508-5156

More than fifteen theaters host two days of live theater and entertainment, arts and crafts, food booths, and a children's court. **Free.**

JULY

Fireworks Extravaganza—Long Beach
(562) 435-3511

Features strolling entertainment and fireworks display. **Free.**

Celebration on the Colorado Street Bridge—Pasadena
(626) 441-6333

Festival features bands, local restaurants, classic autos and motorcycles, art exhibits, and performance groups.

Art Festival—Malibu
(310) 456-9025

Live music, food fair, orchid display and sale, pancake breakfast, and more than 200 artists on hand with exhibits. **Free.**

San Fernando Fiesta—San Fernando
(818) 898-1200

San Fernando's largest family event, including food, games, carnival rides, top-name Latin entertainment, and a consumer trade show. **Free.**

Fourth of July Celebration—Avalon
(310) 510-1520

Golf cart parade, dinner, and fireworks over Avalon Bay.

Lotus Festival—Los Angeles
(213) 485-8745

Experience a variety of Asian cultures, entertainment, art exhibits, ethnic cuisine, and children's activities.

Celebrate America—Santa Monica
(310) 452-9209

Celebrate July Fourth Santa Monica style with music, booths, and spectacular fireworks. **Free.**

AUGUST

Catalina Ski Race—Long Beach
(714) 994-4572

World's largest water-ski race involving 110 boats pulling skiers from Long Beach's Belmont Pier to Catalina.

Taste of San Pedro—San Pedro
(310) 832-7272

San Pedro restaurants present their signature entrees. Arts and crafts and a vintage car show are other highlights.

African Marketplace and Cultural Faire—Los Angeles
(323) 734-1164

More than 2,000 performing artists, 300 vendors and exhibitors, 15 cultural and ethnic festivals, 7 stages of live performers, an international food court, and a children's village.

SEPTEMBER

Catalina Festival of the Arts—Avalon
(310) 510-2700

Exhibits include mixed media, photography, crafts, and sculpture. **Free.**

Los Angeles County Fair—Pomona
(909) 623-3111

California's sensational county fair you can't miss! It takes at least a full day to visit the flower and garden exposition, midway, and various entertainments. Kids can participate in educational activities.

Greek Festival—Arcadia
(626) 499-6943

Authentic Greek festival with food, pastries, folk dances, music, dance lessons, and children's games.

OCTOBER

Catalina Jazz Festival—Avalon
(818) 347-5299; www.jazztrax.com

Contemporary-jazz musicians and instrumentalists perform in the renowned Catalina Casino ballroom.

Scandinavian Festival—Santa Monica
(626) 795-9311

Daylong smorgasbord celebrates the riches of Denmark, Finland, Iceland, Norway, and Sweden with food, music, imports, costumes, arts, crafts, and a raffle.

Oktoberfest—Pasadena
(626) 795-9311

Music, dancing, German food, games, and a pumpkin patch. **Free.**

Sabor De Mexico Lindo Festival—Huntington Park
(323) 585-1155; www.hpchamber1.com

Cultural celebration that pays tribute to the heritage of Mexico, through music, dancing, food, displays, and arts and crafts. The festival brings together more than 125 food, arts and crafts, and commercial exhibitors, plus concerts, live entertainment, two amusement and carnival areas, and a petting zoo. Three days and nights. **Free.**

NOVEMBER

Doo Dah Parade—Pasadena
(626) 795-9311

Eccentric parade features unique performing groups and artist teams; includes wacky costumes and cars. **Free.**

DECEMBER

Main Street Merchants Holiday Festival—Santa Monica
(310) 395-3648

Sand sledding, face painting, and loads of holiday festivities kids will enjoy. **Free.**

Christmas Parade—Whittier
(562) 696-2662

Bands, floats, horses, and Santa. **Free.**

Holiday Open House—Avalon
(310) 510-2414

Each year the Catalina Island Museum hosts open house at the Inn at Mount Ada, formerly the Wrigley Mansion. The mansion is exquisitely decorated for Christmas. The event culminates with a raffle of an all-expense paid stay at the inn to benefit the Catalina Island Museum. **Free.**

The Hollywood Christmas Parade
(323) 469-2337

This festive parade features celebrities, marching bands, classic cars, and, last but not least, Santa Claus!

The Glory of Christmas at the Crystal Cathedral—Garden Grove
(714) 544-5697

A blending of Christmas carols, live animals, flying angels, and special effects brings the nativity to life in this highly orchestrated stage show.

Orange County

The following list of Orange County events is subject to change without notice. Please call ahead to confirm.

FEBRUARY

Festival of Whales—Dana Point
(800) 290-DANA

Coastal whale-watching cruises and arts/crafts exhibition. **Free.**

MARCH

Swallows Day—San Juan Capistrano
(949) 248-2048

This fiesta celebrates the annual return of the swallows to Capistrano, featuring pageantry, entertainment, and food.

APRIL

Glory of Easter—Garden Grove
(714) 971-4069

This annual Easter play features special events, live animals, and a cast of more than 200 in the dramatic presentation of the last seven days of Christ on earth.

MAY

Strawberry Festival—Garden Grove
(714) 638-0981

Festival features strawberry dishes, including strawberry shortcake, pie, and tarts, entertainment, beauty contests, arts, crafts, and rides. **Free.**

JULY

Sawdust Art Festival—Laguna Beach
(949) 494-3030

Laguna Beach becomes a magical village created by artists. The two-month (July and August) festival includes handcrafted treasures, entertainment, jugglers, and storytellers, and jazz, country, rock, and contemporary musicians. Become an artist yourself by attending one of the many hands-on workshops.

Fourth of July Celebration—Huntington Beach
(714) 536-5496

Red, white, and blue bash with a 5K run, parade, and fireworks. **Free.**

Festival of Arts and Pageant of the Masters—Laguna Beach
(949) 494-1145 or (800) 487-3378

Colorful exhibit of fine, strictly original creations by 160 South Coast artists; includes the world-famous Pageant of the Masters "living pictures" performances.

Orange County Fair—Costa Mesa
(949) 708-1543

This rural fair in an urban setting offers livestock, a carnival, a rodeo, commercial wares, themed attractions, and fiber arts.

AUGUST

U.S. Open of Surfing—Huntington Beach
(714) 366-4584

Watch the best surfers in the world compete for a large sum. **Free.**

SEPTEMBER

Taste of Newport Beach—Newport Beach
(949) 729-4400

Savor the cuisine of more than thirty Newport Beach restaurants; entertainment.

OCTOBER

Oktoberfest—Huntington Beach
(714) 895-8020

Old-world village features German food, drink, and oompah bands. **Free.**

NOVEMBER

Sawdust Art Festival Winter Fantasy—Laguna Beach
(949) 494-3030

Unique holiday arts and crafts festival features 150 artists and craftspeople from around the country, with artist demonstrations, hands-on workshops, children's art activities, continuous entertainment, Santa Claus, and a snow playground. Continues through December.

DECEMBER

Glory of Christmas—Garden Grove
(949) 544-5679

Live Nativity scene includes animals, flying angels, holiday music, and pageantry.

Christmas Boat Parade—Newport Beach
(949) 729-4400, (949) 729-4417, or (800) 94-COAST
More than 200 illuminated and decorated boats cruise the harbor. **Free.**

Christmas at the Mission—San Juan Capistrano
(949) 248-2048

Holiday celebration includes music, entertainment, and refreshments. **Free.**

The Inland Empire and Beyond

The following list of events in the Inland Empire is subject to change. Please always call ahead.

FEBRUARY

Whiskey Flats Days—Kernville
(760) 376-2629 or (800) 350-7393

Parade, carnival, rodeo, gunfighters, various contests, frog jumping, arts and crafts, a petting zoo, and much to eat. **Free.**

MARCH

Redlands Bicycle Classic—Redlands
(909) 798-0865

Thousands of cyclists from around the world compete. **Free.**

Winterfest—Mammoth Lakes
(760) 934-6643 or (800) 367-6572

Winter celebration with cross-country ski races, snowmobile competition, and fun rides for the kids.

APRIL–MAY

Ramona Pageant—Hemet
(909) 658-3111 or (800) 645-4465

Unique outdoor pageant portrays the lives of the Southern California mission-period Indians and Hispanics. Play adapted from Helen Hunt Jackson's 1884 novel *Ramona*.

Indian Powwow—Kernville
(760) 376-2696 or (800) 350-7393

A celebration of American heritage, dancers, drumming, Native American foods, arts and crafts. **Free.**

Orange Blossom Festival—Riverside
(951) 715-3400

This citrus celebration takes place in downtown Riverside. Besides three entertainment stages, citrus cooking demonstrations, and arts and crafts booths, the festival has a children's grove and a living-history village.

MAY

May Trout Classic—Big Bear Lake
(909) 585-6260 or (800) 4-BIG-BEAR

Fishing competition.

Spring Aire Arts and Crafts Faire—Big Bear Lake
(909) 585-3000

Show features hundreds of handcrafted items. Vendors, raffles, and loads of antiques.

JUNE

Huck Finn's Jubilee—Victorville
(760) 245-2226

River celebration and campout relives the life and times of Huckleberry Finn. Raft building, parade, big-top circus, hot-air balloon rides, music, crafts, and more. **Free.**

JULY

All Nations Powwow—Big Bear
(909) 584-9394 or (800) BIG-BEAR

American Indians from across the United States participate in traditional dancing and crafts.

Fourth of July Festivities—Mammoth Lakes
(760) 924-2360 or (800) 367-6572

Fireworks (of course!), a parade, a pancake breakfast, an arts and crafts show, a chili cook-off, a quilt show, and a horseshoe tournament.

July 4 Fireworks Over the Lake—Big Bear
(909) 866-2112 or (800) BIGBEAR

Barbecue, entertainment, and spectacular fireworks.

Jazz Jubilee—Mammoth Lakes
(760) 934-2478

World-class jazz bands perform outdoors.

Sierra Summer Festival—Mammoth Lakes
(760) 934-3342 or (800) 367-6572

Music festival spotlights master's classes, plus chamber, pop, and folk music.

AUGUST

Labor Day Arts and Crafts Festival—Mammoth Lakes
(760) 873-7242

More than seventy arts and crafts booths in an outdoor setting, along with entertainment, kids' activities, and lots of food.

SEPTEMBER

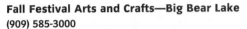

Apple Harvest—Oak Glen
(909) 797-6833

Southern California's top apple-growing region is the site for this event, with apple picking, a candy factory, hayrides, arts and crafts on display, an art show, and (yum!) barbecues. **Free.**

Eastern Sierra Tri-County Fair and Wild West Rodeo—Bishop
(760) 873-3588

Old-fashioned country-fair fun, with exhibits, a carnival, pig races, pony rides, a petting zoo, horse shows, and a PRCA rodeo.

Fall Festival Arts and Crafts—Big Bear Lake
(909) 585-3000

Hundreds of handcrafted items on display.

Kern County Fair—Bakersfield
(805) 833-4900

Family entertainment par excellence, a livestock show, a carnival, agricultural and floricultural exhibits, plus an auction.

OCTOBER

Calico Days Festival—Calico
(760) 254-2122 or (800) TO-CALICO

Go back in time to Calico's glory years with a Wild West parade, a gunfight, stunts, burro races, rock pulling, and games circa the 1880s.

Desert Empire Fair—Ridgecrest
(760) 375-8000

Five-day event with 4-H competition, arts and crafts, entertainment, a rodeo, a demolition derby, and a livestock auction.

Oktoberfest—Big Bear Lake
(909) 866-4607

Music, singing, dancing, contests, arts and crafts, food, and games in a mountain setting. Wunderbar!

Wild West Daze Rodeo—Kernville
(760) 378-3157

Wild horse races, bull riding, saddle broncoing, bareback riding, steer decorating, barrel racing, and mutton busting.

NOVEMBER

Gem and Mineral Society Show—Ridgecrest
(760) 377-5192

Dozens of gem and mineral exhibits, plus field trips. Educational.

Harvest Fair—San Bernardino
(909) 384-5426

Re-creation of an 1881 Old West town, with a country/bluegrass show, crafts, and a unique car show.

DECEMBER

Children's Christmas Parade—Victorville
(760) 245-6506

More than 150 holiday-theme floats, bands, novelty vehicles, and marching by equestrian units. **Free.**

Christmas Parade—Lone Pine
(760) 876-4444

Old-fashioned Christmas parade with (you guessed it) Santa Claus.

Festival of Lights—Riverside
(909) 683-7100 or (909) 683-2670

Holiday lighting of the historic Mission Inn and surrounding downtown locations. Entertainment and specialty booths. **Free.**

The Deserts

The following list of events is subject to change without notice. Please always call ahead to verify.

JANUARY

Palm Springs International Film Festival—Palm Springs
(760) 322-2930

More than 200 international films with a special awards gala honoring industry greats.

FEBRUARY

South West Arts Festival—Indio
(760) 347-0676 or (800) 44-INDIO

Marketplace for contemporary and traditional Southwestern art; 150 acclaimed artists showcase fine and craft art.

Riverside County Fair and National Date Festival—Indio
(760) 863-8247 or (800) 811-FAIR

The festival features exhibits of dates and produce; fine arts; floriculture; gems and minerals; a livestock show; and pig, camel, and ostrich races. See more in Deserts chapter.

MARCH

La Quinta Arts Festival—La Quinta
(760) 564-1244

Takes place at Center for the Arts (south of Highway 111). Stunning art creations from more than 270 juried artists. Families will enjoy the Children's Art Garden; with activities for ages seven through twelve (must be accompanied by an adult). It all takes place thirty minutes from downtown Palm Springs in a dramatic desert setting at the base of the Santa Rosa Mountains, as it has annually since 1982. Live entertainment and tastes of Coachella Valley's great restaurants.

MAY

Grubstake Days—Yucca Valley
(760) 365-6323

Parade, carnival events, dancing, demolition derby, games, food, hometown crafts booths, children's activities, PRCA rodeo; takes place Memorial Day weekend. **Free.**

SEPTEMBER

Rodeo Stampede—Barstow
(760) 252-3093

PRCA rodeo.

OCTOBER

Mardi Gras Parade—Barstow
(760) 256-8657

Halloween parade includes floats, bands, horses, clowns, costumed children, plus contingents from the military, fire, and sheriff's departments.

DECEMBER

Festival of Lights Parade—Palm Springs
(760) 778-8415 or (800) 927-7256

Illuminated bands, floats, and automobiles make this one of the area's top holiday events.

Tamale Festival—Indio

See listing in Deserts chapter.

Joshua Tree National Park Festival—Twentynine Palms
(760) 367-5522

Exhibits and sales by more than twenty artists.

San Diego County

The following list of events is subject to change without notice. Please call in advance to confirm dates and times.

MARCH

Shamrock Festival—San Diego
(619) 233-4692

St. Patrick's Day block party in San Diego's Gaslamp District with live music, Irish entertainment, food, and face painting. **Free.**

APRIL

Santa Fe Market—San Diego
(619) 299-6055

Festival of southwest American Indian arts and crafts, including guest artists and cultural demonstrations. **Free.**

Encinitas Street Fair—Encinitas
(760) 943-1950

More than 300 vendors, children's rides, face painting, clowns, arts and crafts. **Free.**

MAY

Fiesta Cinco De Mayo—San Diego
(619) 299-6055

Mexican celebration in Old Town includes nonstop entertainment and food booths. **Free.**

Carlsbad Village Faire—Carlsbad
(760) 434-8887

One-day street fair features 800 booths; arts, crafts, antiques, international foods, and live entertainment.

JULY

San Diego County Fair—Del Mar
(858) 792-4262

Annual county fair featuring world-class entertainment, rides, exhibits, livestock, and food.

Fourth of July Parade and Celebration—Coronado
(800) 622-8300

Includes fireworks and demonstrations by the U.S. Navy. **Free.**

An Old-Fashioned Fourth of July—San Diego
(619) 220-5423

Activities include hayrides, music, entertainers, dancing, sack races, and pie-eating contests. **Free.**

Fourth of July Freedom Days—Oceanside
(760) 722-1534

Parade, street fair, festivities, fireworks, and music at the outdoor beach amphitheater. **Free.**

AUGUST

Latin American Festival—San Diego
(619) 299-6055

Latin American crafts, artists, demonstrations, entertainment, and food booths. **Free.**

SEPTEMBER

Fall Fiesta—Old Town San Diego
(619) 220-5422

Celebrating the Hispanic heritage of Alta California with foods, crafts, music, and dance. **Free.**

Harbor Days—Oceanside
(760) 721-1101

Celebrate a festival of crafts and events at the beautiful Oceanside Marina and Harbor. **Free.**

OCTOBER

Oktoberfest—Carlsbad
(760) 434-6093 or (800) 227-5722

Patriotic, traditional German music; children's games and lots of German food.

NOVEMBER

Community Tree Lighting—Julian
(760) 765-1857

Old-fashioned Christmas tree lighting, costumed carolers, living Nativity pageant, and horse-drawn carriage rides. **Free.**

Festival of Lights—San Diego
(619) 299-6055

Celebration includes dances from around the world and dramatic Nativity scene lighting. **Free.**

DECEMBER

Holiday of Lights—Del Mar
(858) 755-7161

Holiday light display featuring more than 200 themed entries, including Santa's elves, Twelve Days of Christmas, and a magical forest. **Free.**

Holiday in the Park—San Diego
(619) 220-5422

Candlelight tours of museums and historic homes featuring period decorations and entertainment.

Mission Christmas Faire—Oceanside
(760) 721-1101

More than 200 booths, amusement rides for children, and entertainment. **Free.**

Harbor Parade of Lights—Oceanside
(760) 721-1101

Lighted boat parade through the Oceanside harbor. **Free.**

Index

A

Adventure City, 91
Agua Caliente Cultural Museum, 155–56
Alpine Slide at Magic Mountain, 121
Amargosa Opera House and Hotel, 186
American Girl Place Los Angeles, 66
Anaheim/Orange County Visitor and
    Convention Bureau, 96
Anaheim Resort area, 87–96
Angel Stadium of Anaheim, 89–90
Annual Lone Pine Film Festival, 147
Antique Gas and Steam Engine
    Museum, 214
Anza-Borrego Desert State Park, 219–21
ARCO/U.S. Olympic Training Center, 202
Arrowhead Queen, 118
Arroyo Grande, 14
Artist's Palette Drive, 185
Atascadero, 6–8
Atascadero Chamber of Commerce, 8
Auto Club Speedway, 123–24
Autry National Center, 59
Avalon, 82

B

Back Country (the Mountains), 217
Bakersfield, 136–40
Balboa Park, 193–94
Balboa Pavilion, 106
Ballard, 20
Barstow area, 179–80
Barstow Area Chamber of Commerce and
    Visitors Bureau, 178
Bear Mountain Resort, 121
Bel Air, 68
Belmont Park/Giant Dipper, 200
Belmont Shore, 78
Bergamot Station Arts Center, 75–76
Best of the Best Tours, 154–55
Beverly Center, 68

Beverly Hills, 67–68
Beverly Hills Chamber of Commerce, 68
Beverly Hills Conference and Visitors
    Bureau, 68
Big Bear Chamber of Commerce, 122
Big Bear Discovery Center, 120
Big Bear Lake, 120–22
Big Bear Lake Resort Association and
    Visitor Center, 122
Big Bear Queen at the Marina, 122
Big League Dreams Sports Park, 163
Bikes & Beyond, 203
Biplane Rides and Aerial Dogfights/
    Barnstorming Adventures, Ltd., 209
Birch Aquarium at Scripps Institution of
    Oceanography, 205–6
Bishop, 147–48
Bishop Area Chamber of Commerce and
    Visitors Bureau, 148
B.J.'s ATV Rentals, 12
Bolsa Chica Ecological Reserve and
    Interpretive Center, 105
Boomer's Family Fun Center, 163–64
Borax Visitor Center, 181
Boron, 180–81
Borrego Springs, 219–21
Borrego Springs Chamber of Commerce
    and Visitors Bureau, 221
Botanic Gardens at University of
    California—Riverside (UCR), 128
Botanical and Floral Gardens, 198
Bowers Museum of Cultural Art and
    Kidseum, 100–101
Buck Owens' Crystal Palace, 136–37
Buellton, 19
Buellton Visitors Bureau and Chamber of
    Commerce, 23
Buena Park, 96–99
Buena Park Convention and Visitors
    Office, 99
Bun Boy, 179

Burbank, 70
Burbank Chamber of Commerce, 70

C

Cabrillo Marine Aquarium, 81
Cabrillo National Monument, 189
Cachuma Lake Recreation Area, 22–23
Calico Ghost Town, 179–80
California African American Museum, 49
California Avocado Festival, 33
California Center for the Arts,
    Escondido, 212
California Citrus State Historic Park, 128
California Living Museum (CALM), 138
California Oil Museum of Santa Paula, 38
California Polytechnic State University, 11
California Route 66 Museum, 122
California Science Center, The, & IMAX
    Theater, 49
California Surf Museum, 211
California Welcome Center at Tanger
    Outlets, 178
California Welcome Center–Inland
    Empire, 126
California Welcome Center Oceanside, 212
California Welcome Center Oxnard, 41
California Welcome Center Pismo
    Beach, 13
California Welcome Center–
    Santa Ana, 102
California Welcome Center–Yucca
    Valley, 177
Cambria, 4–5
Cambria Chamber of Commerce, 5
Capitol Records, 57
Cardiff-by-the-Sea, 206
Carlsbad, 208–10
Carlsbad Convention and Visitors
    Bureau, 210
Carnegie Art Museum, 39
Carnegie Cultural Arts Center, 39–40
Carpinteria, 33
Carpinteria Valley Chamber of
    Commerce, 33
Carpinteria Valley Historical Society and
    Museum, 33

Castle Amusement Park, 129
Catalina Adventure Tours, 83
Catalina Casino, 82
Catalina Island Visitors Bureau and
    Chamber of Commerce, 83–84
Cathedral City, 163–64
Cathedral of Our Lady of the Angels, 48
CEC/Seabee Museum, 41
Cedar Grove Visitor Center, 141
Celebrity homes tours, 56, 153
Celebrity Tours, 153
Centennial Heritage Museum, 101
Centennial Plaza, 39–40
Channel Islands Harbor & Visitor
    Center, 40
Charles Paddock Zoo, 7
Chase Palm Park & Carousel, 28
Children's Discovery Museum of the
    Desert, 164
Children's Museum at La Habra, 91
Children's Museum at the Paso Robles
    Volunteer Firehouse, 7
Chinatown, 46, 50
Chino, 115
Chino Valley Chamber of
    Commerce, 116
Chiriaco Summit Travel Center, 175
Chula Vista, 202–3
Chula Vista Chamber of Commerce, 203
Chula Vista Convention and Visitors
    Bureau, 203
City of Rancho Mirage Public Library,
    164–65
Coachella Valley, 151
College of the Desert Street Fair,
    165–66
Coronado, 203–4
Coronado Visitors Center, 204
Costa Mesa, 102–3
Costa Mesa Conference and Visitor
    Bureau, 103
County History Center and Museum, 10
Covarrubias Adobe, 26
Crestline, 117–18
Crystal Cathedral of the Reformed Church
    in America, 91–92
Cuyamaca Rancho State Park, 218

D

Daily Grill, 166
Dana Point, 110–11
Dana Point Chamber of Commerce and
    Visitors Center, 111
Dana Point Harbor Information
    Service, 110
Dante's View, 185
Darwin Falls, 184
Davey's Locker Sportfishing, 106
Death Valley, 181, 184–86
Death Valley National Park, 185–86
Del Mar, 206
Del Mar Regional Chamber of
    Commerce, 207
Del Mar Fairgrounds & Race Track, 206–7
Desert Adventures, 157
Desert IMAX Theater, 163
Desert Tortoise Natural Area, 183
Devil's Golf Course, 185
Diamond Valley Lake, 131
Discovery Science Center, 101–2
Disneyland Park, 87–88
Disney's California Adventure Park,
    88–89
Doc Burnstein's Ice Cream Lab, 14
Dollsville Dolls & Bearsville Bears, 158
Dromo 1, 100

E

Eagle Mining Company, 218
1892 Heritage House, 127
El Capitan Theatre, 55
Elite Land Tours, 152
El Paseo, 166
El Presidio de Santa Barbara State Historic
    Park, 26
El Pueblo de Los Angeles Historic
    Monument/Olvera Street, 50, 51
Elverhoj Museum of History and Art, 20
Empire Polo Club and Equestrian Park, 170
Encinitas, 206
Encinitas Chamber of Commerce and
    Visitors Center, 207
Erick Schat's Bakkery, 148
Escondido, 212–15

Escondido Historical Society Museum, 212
Exposition Park Area, 49

F

Fabulous Palm Springs Follies, The, 158–59
Farmers' Market, San Luis Obispo, 11
Farmers Market, Westside, 65–66
Ferry Landing Marketplace, 203
Festival of Arts and Pageant of the
    Masters, 109
Fillmore, 38
Fillmore Chamber of Commerce, 38
Fillmore & Western Railway, 38
Firehouse Museum, 192
Fisherman's Village, 74
Flower Fields at Carlsbad Ranch, 209
Fontana, 123–24
Fort Tejon State Historic Park, 138
Frugal Frigate, The, 127

G

Gardens on El Paseo, 166
General Patton Memorial Museum, 173,
    174–75
Getty Villa, 77
Giant Forest Museum, 141–42
Glacial Gardens Skating Arena, 90
Glen Helen Regional Park, 124
Golden Canyon, 185
Goleta Valley Chamber of Commerce, 32
Golf Cart Parade, 165
golf courses, The Deserts, 153–54
Graber Olive House, 115
Grand Central Market, 47–48
Grant Grove Visitor Center, 141
Great American Melodrama and Vaudeville
    Theatre, 12–13
Greater Bakersfield Chamber of
    Commerce, 139
Greater Bakersfield Convention and
    Visitors Bureau, 139
Greater Riverside Chambers of
    Commerce, 129
Griffith Park, 58–59
Grove, The, 66

Guadelupe-Nipomo Dunes Preserve, 16
Gull Wings Children's Museum, 39
Gum Alley, 10

H

Hans Christian Andersen Museum, 20
Hearst San Simeon State Historical
    Monument, 3–4
Helgren's Sportfishing Center, 211
Hemet, 130–32
Heritage Square, 39
Heritage Valley Tourism Bureau, 38
Heritage Walk, Escondido, 212
Historic Site of the World's First
    McDonald's, 124
Hole-in-the-Wall Ranger Station, 177
Hollywood, 54–58
Hollywood & Highland Entertainment
    Complex, 54
Hollywood Bowl and Hollywood Bowl
    Museum, 57
Hollywood celebrity tours, 56
Hollywood Chamber of Commerce, 58
Hollywood Guinness World Records
    Museum, 56
Hollywood Toys and Costumes, 57
Hollywood Visitor Information Center, 58
Hollywood Wax Museum, 56
Hollywood's Rock Walk of Fame, 57
Honda Center (formerly Arrowhead
    Pond), 90
Hornblower Cruises and Events, 107
Horton Plaza, 191
hot-air ballooning, 208
Huntington Beach, 104–6
Huntington Beach Conference and Visitors
    Bureau, 106
Huntington Beach Surfing Walk of
    Fame, 104
Huntington Library, Art Collections and
    Botanical Gardens, 72

I

Iceoplex, 212
Idyllwild, 131–32

Idyllwild Arts, 132
Idyllwild Chamber of Commerce, 132
Indian Canyons, 155
Indian Wells Chamber of Commerce, 169
Indio, 169–71
Indio Chamber of Commerce, 171
Indio International Tamale Festival, 169
Inland Empire, 113, 115
In-N-Out, 117
International Surfing Museum, 104
Inyo National Forest, 144
Irvine, 102–3
Irvine Chamber of Commerce Visitors
    Bureau, 103
Irvine Spectrum Center, 102
Island Packers Company, 34

J

John Wayne/Orange County Airport, 100
Joshua Tree Chamber of Commerce, 177
Joshua Tree National Park, 171–76
Juan Bautista de Anza National Historic
    Trail, 130
Julian, 217–19
Julian Chamber of Commerce, 219
Junipero Serra Museum, 190
Jurupa Mountains Cultural Center, 128

K

Karpeles Manuscript Library Museum,
    26–27
Kelso Depot Visitor Center, 178
Kelso Dunes, 177
Kern County, 134
Kern County Board of Trade and Tourist
    Information Center, 139
Kern County Museum and Lori Brock
    Children's Discovery Center, 137–38
Kern Valley Turkey Vulture Festival, 136
Kernville, 135–36
Kernville Chamber of Commerce, 136
Kidspace Children's Museum, 72
Kids World, 27
Kimberly Crest House and Gardens, 126–27
Kings Canyon National Park, 140–42

Kit Carson Park/Queen Califia's Magical Circle, 213–14
Knott's Berry Farm, 97
Knott's Soak City U.S.A.–Orange County, 97
Knott's Soak City U.S.A.–San Diego, 202
Knott's Soak City Water Park, 161
Kodak Theatre, 54–55

L

Laguna Beach, 109–10
Laguna Beach Visitors and Conference Bureau, 110
La Jolla, 205–6
La Jolla Visitor Center, 206
Lake Arrowhead, 118–19
Lake Arrowhead Communities Chamber of Commerce, 119
Lake Arrowhead Village, 118, 119
Lake Atascadero Park, 7
Lake Casitas Recreation Area, 37
Lake Gregory County Regional Park, 117–18
Lake Isabella, 135
Lake Nacimiento, 5–6
Lake Nacimiento Resort, 6
Lake Perris State Recreation Area, 130
La Purisima Mission State Historic Park, 18
La Quinta Chamber of Commerce, 169
Laws Railroad Museum and Historical Site, 148
LEGOLAND California, 208–9
Len Moore Skatepark Chula Vista, 202–3
Leucadia, 206
Libbey Park, 36
Little Tokyo, 50
Living Desert Zoo and Gardens, 166–67
Living Free Animal Sanctuary, 132
Lodgepole Visitor Center, 141
Lompoc Flower Fields, 18
Lompoc Valley, 18–19
Lompoc Valley Chamber of Commerce and Visitors Bureau, 19
Lone Pine, 147
Lone Pine Chamber of Commerce, 147
Lone Pine Film Festival, 147

Long Beach, 78–80
Long Beach Aquarium of the Pacific, 78–79
Long Beach Area Convention and Visitor's Bureau, 79
Lopez Lake Recreational Area, 14
Los Alamos, 19
Los Angeles, Coastal, 73–74
Los Angeles County Museum of Art, 65
Los Angeles, Downtown, 46–53
Los Angeles Maritime Museum, 81
Los Angeles Memorial Coliseum and Sports Arena, 50
Los Angeles Times, 46
Los Angeles Zoo, 58
Los Olivos, 20
Los Olivos Business Organization, 23
Los Rios Rancho, 133

M

Magicopolis, 76
Malibu, 77–78
Malibu Beach, 77
Malibu Chamber of Commerce, 78
Malibu Creek State Park, 69
Malibu Pier, 77
Mammoth Dog Teams, 146
Mammoth Kids Ski Schools, 145
Mammoth Lakes area, 143–46
Mammoth Lakes Visitor Bureau, 146
Mammoth Lakes Visitor Center/Ranger Station, 146
Mammoth Mountain Ski Area, 143, 144
Mann's Chinese Theatre, 55
Marina del Rey, 74–75
Marina del Rey Convention and Visitors Bureau, 75
Marine Corps Air Ground Combat Center, 176
Maritime Museum of San Diego, 193
Maturango Museum, 182
McCallum Theatre, 167
McKenzie's Waterski School, 119
Medieval Times Dinner and Tournament, 98
Melrose Avenue, 63
Millpond Traditional Music Festival, 147–48

Mission Basilica San Diego de Alcala, 191
Mission Bay Park, 199
Mission Inn, 127
Mission San Antonio de Pala
    Asistencia, 215
Mission San Juan Capistrano and Cultural
    Center, 112
Mission San Luis Obispo de Tolosa, 10
Mission San Luis Rey, 211
Mission Santa Barbara, 24
Mission Santa Ines, 20–21
Mission Santa Ysabel Asistencia, 218
Mojave and Colorado Desert Biosphere
    Reserve, 184–85
Mojave Narrows Regional Park, 122
Mojave National Preserve, 177–78
Montana de Oro State Park, 9
Moonridge Animal Park, 121
Moonstone Beach, 5
Moorten Botanical Garden, 152
Morro Bay, 8–9
Morro Bay Visitors Center and Chamber of
    Commerce, 9
Morro Bay State Park, 9
Mother's Beach, 74
MotionZ Laser Tag, 16
Mountain and River Adventures, 136
Mountains, The (Back Country), 217
Mount San Jacinto Wilderness
    State Park, 157
Mously Museum of Natural History, 134
Mt. Whitney, 181
Mule Days, 147
Mulholland Drive, 69
Murphy Classic Auto Museum, 40
Muscle Beach, 74
Museo de los Ninos de San Diego, 193
Museum of Contemporary Art, La Jolla, 206
Museum of Contemporary Art, Los
    Angeles, 48
Museum of Contemporary Art–
    San Diego, 192
Museum of Latin American Art, 78
Museum of Natural History, Morro Bay, 9
Museum of Neon Art, 48
Museum of Tolerance, 66
Museum Row, 65

Music Center, 47
Mustang Water Slides, 14
MUZEO, 91

N

National Date Festival, 169
National Orange Show, 125
Natural History Museum of L.A. County, 49
NBC TV Studios, 70
Newport Beach area, 106–9
Newport Beach Conference and Visitors
    Bureau, 109
Newport Harbor Nautical Museum,
    The, 107
Newport Sports Museum, 107
Nixon Presidential Library and Museum,
    92–93
Nojoqui Falls County Park, 21
North County, 206–7
North Hollywood, 59–62

O

Oak Glen, 133–34
Oasis Date Gardens, 170
Oceanfront Walk, 74
Ocean Institute, 110
Oceano Dunes State Vehicular Recreation
    Area, 12
Oceanside, 211–12
Oceanside Chamber Tourism Information
    Center, 212
Ojai, 36–38
Ojai Center for the Arts, 36
Ojai Valley Chamber of Commerce, 38
Ojai Valley Museum, 37
Old Town San Diego State Historic Park
    and Presidio Park, 189–90
Old Town Temecula, 215
Old Town Trolley Tours/Historic Tours of
    America, 191
Ontario, 115–16
Ontario Convention and Visitors
    Bureau, 116
Ontario International Airport, 115
Orange, 99–100

Orange (City of) Chamber of Commerce, 100
Orange County Fair and Event Center, 103
Orange County Performing Arts
   Center, 103
Orange Empire Railway Museum, 130
Ostrich Land, 22
Outdoor Santa Barbara Visitor Center, 33
Owl Canyon, 179
Oxnard, 39–41
Oxnard Convention & Visitors Bureau, 41

P

Pacific Conservatory of the Performing
   Arts, 21
Pacific Park, 75
Page Museum at the La Brea Tar Pits, 65
Paley Center for Media, 68
Palisades Park, 75
Palm Canyon Theatre, 153
Palm Desert, 165–69
Palm Desert Visitor Information
   Center, 169
Palm Springs, 151–63
Palm Springs Aerial Tramway, 156–57
Palm Springs Air Museum, 160–61
Palm Springs Art Museum, 159–60
Palm Springs Bureau of Tourism, 163
Palm Springs Chamber of
   Commerce, 163
Palm Springs Bureau of Tourism, 163
Palm Springs Chamber of Commerce, 163
Palm Springs Desert Resorts Convention
   and Visitors Authority, 165
Palm Springs International Film
   Festival, 152–63
Palms to Pines Scenic Highway, 131
Palomar Mountain Observatory and State
   Park, 217
Panamint Mountains, 181
Paramount Ranch, 69
Parks-Janeway Carriage House, 22
Parrish Pioneer Ranch, 133
Pasadena, 72–73
Pasadena Convention and Visitors
   Bureau, 73
Paso Robles, 6–8

Paso Robles Chamber of Commerce and
   Visitors and Conference Bureau, 8
Paso Robles Event Center/California
   Mid-State Fair, 6
Paul Schat's Bakkery, 145
Pavilion Paddy Cruises, 106
Peggy Sue's, 180
Perris, 130
PETCO Ballpark, 199
Petersen Automotive Museum, 65
Pioneer Days, 176
Pioneer Museum, 7
Pirate's Dinner Adventure, 98–99
Pismo Beach area, 12–13
Pismo Beach Chamber of Commerce and
   Conference & Visitors Bureau, 13
Planes of Fame Air Museum, 115
Pleasure Point Boat Landing, 121
Port Hueneme, 41
Port of Los Angeles, 81
Port San Luis, 12
Providence Mountains State Recreation
   Area, 178

Q

Quail Botanical Gardens, 207
Qualcomm Stadium, 198
Queen Califia's Magical Circle,
   213–14
Queen Mary, 79
Quicksilver Miniature Horse Ranch, 21

R

Raging Waters, 73
Rainbow Basin, 179
Ramona Outdoor Play, 131
Rancho Cucamonga, 117
Rancho Jurupa Park, 128–29
Rancho Mirage, 164–65
Rancho Santa Fe, 207–8
Randsburg area, 183–84
Ravine Waterpark, 7
Redlands, 126–27
Redlands Chamber of Commerce, 127
Redondo Beach, 84

Redondo Beach Chamber of Commerce and Visitors Bureau, 84
Red Rock Canyon State Park, 183–84
Red's Meadow Pack Stations, 145
Reuben H. Fleet Space Theatre and Science Museum, 195
Ridgecrest, 181–83
Ridgecrest Area Convention and Visitor's Bureau, 181
Ridgecrest Chamber of Commerce, 181
Ridgecrest Regional Wild Horse and Burro Corrals, 182
Riley's Farm and Orchard, 134
Rim of the World Scenic Byway, 120
Ripley's Believe It or Not! Museum, 97–98
Ripley's Believe It or Not! Odditorium, 56
River at Rancho Mirage, The, 165
Riverside, 127–29
Riverside Convention & Visitors Bureau, 129
Riverside County Fair and National Date Festival, 169
Riverside Metropolitan Museum, 128
Rodeo Drive, 67
Ronald Reagan Presidential Library & Museum and Air Force One Pavilion, 42
Rose Bowl Stadium, 72
Route 66 Rendezvous, 125

S

Salton Sea, 170
Salton Sea State Recreation Area, 170
Salton Sea National Wildlife Refuge and Imperial Wildlife Area, 170
Samuel French, Inc. Bookstore, 57
San Bernardino, 124–26
San Bernardino Convention and Visitors Bureau, 126
San Bernardino County Museum, 126
San Bernardino National Forest, 131
San Diego, 189–202
San Diego Air & Space Museum, 197
San Diego Aircraft Carrier Museum/USS Midway, 192–93
San Diego Children's Museum, 193
San Diego Convention and Visitors Bureau, 201

San Diego East Visitors Bureau, 217
San Diego Hall of Champions Sports Museum, 196
San Diego International Visitor Information Center, 202
San Diego Model Railroad Museum, 197
San Diego Museum of Art, 197
San Diego Museum of Man, 197
San Diego Museum of Photographic Art, 197
San Diego Natural History Museum, 197
San Diego North Convention and Visitors Bureau, 215
San Diego Trolley System, 191–92
San Diego Wild Animal Park, 213
San Diego Zoo, 194–95
San Fernando Valley, 69
San Juan Capistrano, 111–12
San Juan Capistrano Chamber of Commerce, 112
San Luis Obispo, 10–11
San Luis Obispo Chamber of Commerce, 3
San Luis Obispo Children's Museum, 10
San Luis Obispo County, 1, 3
San Luis Obispo County Visitors and Conference Bureau, 3
San Pasqual Battlefield State Historic Park and Museum, 214
San Pedro Peninsula Chamber of Commerce, 81
San Pedro—Port of Los Angeles, 80–81
San Simeon, 3–4
San Simeon Chamber of Commerce, 4
Santa Ana, 100–102
Santa Ana Chamber of Commerce, 102
Santa Ana Zoo at Prentice Park, The, 101
Santa Anita Park, 72–73
Santa Barbara, 24–32
Santa Barbara Botanic Garden, 26
Santa Barbara Region Chamber of Commerce Visitor Center, 33
Santa Barbara Conference & Visitors Bureau and Film Commission, 33
Santa Barbara County, 14–15
Santa Barbara County Courthouse, 27–28
Santa Barbara Historical Museum, 26
Santa Barbara Museum of Art, 26

Santa Barbara Museum of Natural History and Planetarium, 24
Santa Barbara Zoological Gardens, 28
Santa Catalina Island, 82–84
Santa Catalina Island Company, 84
Santa Catalina Island Company's Discovery Tours, 82–83
Santa Clarita Valley, 71
Santa Clarita Valley Tourism Office, 71
Santa Maria, 15–17
Santa Maria Museum of Flight, 16–17
Santa Maria Speedway, 17
Santa Maria Valley Chamber of Commerce and Visitor & Convention Bureau, 17
Santa Maria Valley Discovery Museum, 16
Santa Monica, 75–77
Santa Monica Convention and Visitors Bureau, 77
Santa Monica Mountains National Recreation Area, 69
Santa Monica Museum of Art, 76
Santa Monica Pier and Pacific Park, 75
Santa Paula, 38
Santa Paula Airport, 38
Santa Paula Chamber of Commerce, 38
Santa Ynez, 20
Santa Ynez Valley, 19–24
Santa Ynez Valley Historical Museum, 22
Santa Ynez Valley Visitors Association, 24
Sawdust Art Festival Winter Fantasy, The, 109–10
Scotty's Castle, 186
Seaport Village, 193
SeaWorld San Diego, 199–200
Sequoia National Forest, 135
Sequoia National Park, 140–42
Sherman Library and Gardens, 108
Shipley Nature Center at Huntington Central Park, 105
Sierra South Mountain Sports Outfitters, 135
Simi Valley, 41–42
Six Flags Hurricane Harbor, 71
Six Flags Magic Mountain—The Xtreme Park, 71
Skirball Cultural Center and Museum, The, 67

Sky Watcher Star Gazing Tours, 167
Smoketree Stables, 156
Snow Summit, 120
Snow Valley Mountain Resort, 119
Solana Beach, 206
Solvang, 20
Solvang Chamber of Commerce, 24
Solvang Conference & Visitors Bureau, 24
South Coast Plaza: The Ultimate Shopping Resort, 103
South Coast Railroad Museum, 30
SS *Lane Victory,* 81
Stagecoach Inn Museum, 43
Sub/Sea Tours and Kayaks, 8
Summerland, 33
Sunset Boulevard, 62
Sunset Plaza, 62
Sunset Strip, 62

T

Tamarack Lodge & Resort and Cross-Country Ski Center, 146
Temecula Valley, 215–16
Temecula Valley Chamber of Commerce, 216
Third Street Promenade, 76
Thousand Oaks, 42–43
Thousand Oaks Civic Arts Plaza, 43
Tijuana Convention & Visitors Bureau, 221
Tijuana Tourism Bureau, 221
Timken Museum of Art, 198
Tommy Bahamas, 166
Torrey Pines State Beach and Reserve, 206
Tournament of Roses Parade, 72
Transit Store, The, 191–92
Travel Town, 59
Trinity Christian City International, 103
Trona Pinnacles, 181
Tulare County, 140–43
Tule Elk State Reserve, 138
Twenty Mule Team Museum, 181
Twentynine Palms, 176–77
Twentynine Palms Chamber of Commerce, 177
Two Rodeo, 67

U

Universal City, 59–62
Universal CityWalk Hollywood, 61
Universal Studios Hollywood, 59, 61, 62
University of California at Santa Barbara
  (UCSB), 30
U.S. Naval Museum of Armament and
  Technology at China Lake, 182

V

Valleys, The, 69–70
Vandenberg Air Force Base, 18
Venice Beach, 74–75
Ventura, 34–36
Ventura Boulevard, 69–70
Ventura Convention and Visitors Bureau, 35
Ventura County, 34
Ventura County Maritime Museum, 40
Ventura Harbor Village, 34
Victorville, 122–23
Victorville Chamber of Commerce, 123
Villagefest, 159

W

Walk of Fame, 55
Waller County Park, 17

Warner Bros. Studio VIP Tour, 70
Watson's Drugs and Soda
  Fountain, 100
Wave Waterpark, The, 214
Wells Fargo History Center, 48
West Hollywood, 62–63
West Hollywood Marketing and Visitors
  Bureau, 63
Westlake Village, 42–43
Westside, 63–67
Whiskey Flat Days, 135
Whitewater Voyages, 135–36
Wild Rivers Waterpark, 102–3
Windhaven Glider Rides, 21
Wonderland Park, 145
World Cruise Center, 80

Y

Yanks Air Museum, 116
YMCA Skateboard Park, 17
Yucaipa, 133–34
Yucca Valley Chamber of
  Commerce, 177

Z

Zabriskie Point, 185

About the Authors

Coauthors Laura Kath and Pamela Price have more than fifty years combined travel and life experience in sunny Southern California. Pamela resides in Palm Springs when she is not globe-trotting and writing/broadcasting about her adventures. She is the author of *100 Best Spas of the World* (The Globe Pequot Press) and consults with her children and grandson for the hottest trends in family travel. Laura is the author of sixteen nonfiction books and president of Mariah Marketing, her Santa Barbara County–based consulting business. She is a member of the International Food, Wine & Travel Writers Association and the Society of Incentive Travel Executives. She credits her active nieces and nephews for keeping her in the latest know. This dynamic duo blend the best of real-life family travel experience with the most up-to-the-minute tourism and visitor information—making this book a must-read.